E-BUSINESS

STRATEGY
TEXT AND CASES

PAUL PHILLIPS

E-BUSINESS

STRATEGY
TEXT AND CASES

The **McGraw·Hill** *Companies*

London   Boston   Burr Ridge, IL   Dubuque, IA   Madison, WI   New York   San Francisco
St. Louis   Bangkok   Bogotá   Caracas   Kuala Lumpur   Lisbon   Madrid   Mexico City
Milan   Montreal   New Delhi   Santiago   Seoul   Singapore   Sydney   Taipei   Toronto

E-Business Strategy: Text and Cases
Paul Phillips
ISBN 0077098374

Published by McGraw-Hill Education
Shoppenhangers Road
Maidenhead
Berkshire
SL6 2QL
Telephone: 44 (0) 1628 502 500
Fax: 44 (0) 1628 770 224
Website: www.mcgraw-hill.co.uk

British Library Cataloguing in Publication Data
A catalogue record for this book is available from the British Library

Library of Congress Cataloguing in Publication Data
The Library of Congress data for this book has been applied for from the Library of Congress

Acquisitions Editor: Julian Partridge
Senior Development Editor: Caroline Howell
Editorial Assistant: Deborah Newcombe
Senior Marketing Manager: Petra Skytte
Production Editor: Eleanor Hayes
New Media Developer: Douglas Greenwood

Text design by InPerspective Ltd
Cover design by Senate Design Ltd
Printed and bound in the UK by Bell and Bain Ltd, Glasgow

ISBN 0077098374

The McGraw-Hill Companies

BRIEF TABLE OF
CONTENTS

DETAILED TABLE OF
CONTENTS

CHAPTER 5: E-BUSINESS MODELS

CHAPTER 6: E-ORGANIZATIONAL DIMENSIONS

CHAPTER 9: ONLINE RESOURCES AND THEIR DEPLOYMENT

CHAPTER 10: VIRTUAL MARKETSPACE

PREFACE

AIMS

Despite the emergence of e-business strategy as a taught subject in colleges, polytechnics and universities throughout the world, this phenomenon has not been the subject of detailed academic research in the UK. I have written this book for a number of academic, student and practitioner audiences who seek to gain a comprehensive introduction to the topic of e-business strategy. The primary aim of this textbook is to provide an extensive critical reference to e-business strategy from a multidisciplinary academic and practitioner perspective.

This book covers a number of vital areas, which tend to be omitted from current e-business textbooks. *E-business Strategy: Text and Cases* provides an in-depth critique of areas such as: risk management; e-business models; e-organizational dimensions; financial appraisal of e-business organizations; online resources and their deployments and e-business strategy: lessons learned. Lecturers, students and practitioners are therefore provided with an academic framework for understanding the complex topic of e-business strategy. The book seeks to combine intellectual rigour and accessibility with practical examples. To enhance the teaching and learning process, the book contains a wide array of case studies and illustrative examples to complement the learning objectives of each chapter.

TARGET MARKET

By adopting a reflective picture of e-business strategy, prior to, during and after the dot.com crash, I have aimed to contextualize and clarify the major e-business issues. The book then goes on to describe, discuss and illustrate the strategic considerations/issues and their operational application and impact. *E-business Strategy: Text and Cases* provides academics, students and practitioners who have specific responsibilities in strategic planning, marketing and IT with a breadth of strategy exploration relating to new business models. In addition, the book places e-business strategy in context and integrates it into the mainstream business arena.

This book is primarily targeted at satisfying the emerging e-business/e-commerce higher education market at the undergraduate, diploma and postgraduate level. At the undergraduate level, second-year and third-year students studying business and/or IT courses with emphasis on e-commerce, e-business or e-marketing will find this book of greatest benefit. In addition, students who are taking business studies courses that contain discrete modules of e-business will find this book to be a good one-stop resource. At the taught MBA/MSc postgraduate level, particularly where there is a non-specialist information technology and strategic emphasis, its academic style should assist readers in understanding the core theoretical themes in the strategy, management, marketing and finance literatures that underpin the e-business strategy phenomenon. The extensive literature reviews, together with practical examples, provide the undergraduate and postgraduate student with a solid platform and ideas for e-business/e-commerce-related dissertation topics, which in my experience present problems for supervisors and students alike.

This academic feel should also be welcomed by postgraduate research students at the MSc, MPhil, DBA and PhD levels. The wide array of academic research cited will assist researchers who are looking to develop the academic literature in the areas of: e-business strategy; e-business risk management; e-business models; and the interaction of e-business and finance. They will find this book a useful resource throughout their studies.

CONTENT

E-Business Strategy: Text and Cases provides students with an academic insight into e-business models and strategies. Examining key considerations in e-business strategy, from external environmental drivers to internal organizational issues, the text offers a solid conceptual foundation that enables students to understand this rapidly changing field. Up-to-date and current, the book assesses the impact of the dot.com crash and looks into the future of e-business, illustrating emerging ideas with well-chosen contemporary examples, articles and cases featuring a variety of e-business operations and organizations.

Key features include:

- *Coverage of critical e-business issues.* The text offers a holistic assessment of the determining factors in the successful set-up and running of e-commerce ventures. It also analyses the legal and technical environment, e-business models and operational issues such as risk management, resource planning and organizational effectiveness. The book also includes chapters on the financial appraisal of e-businesses and how to conduct research online.
- *Focus on UK and European e-business.* Whilst acknowledging the globalization of e-commerce across international boundaries, the text offers a fresh European perspective on e-business models and strategies with specific reference to examples in the context of European business environments.
- *A strong collection of international case studies, mini-cases and articles.* Case illustrations encourage students to apply their knowledge to current business examples and to develop their skills of analysis. Drawn from authoritative sources such as *The Economist*, *The Guardian* and *BusinessWeek*, the cases examine both multinational brands and small business models.
- *Enriched with examples, key terms and questions.* To assist the student, each chapter features learning objectives, thought-provoking illustrative examples, and key terms boxes to define important technical and business terminology. Review questions, assessment questions and group assignments can be used in class discussion or private study to test students' comprehension.
- *The Online Learning Centre* website at www.mcgraw-hill.co.uk/textbooks/phillips provides supplementary teaching resources for lecturers and further materials for students of e-business.

E-Business Strategy: Text and Cases consists of twelve chapters and this section provides an overview of each chapter.

The first chapter sets the scene for the book and provides a comprehensive introduction with some useful explanations of technical terms. I find that it is useful for students to appreciate the origins of the Internet and consider what will happen in the future. It is also useful for the student to understand that the Internet and e-commerce are not the same and both have advantages and disadvantages. Nevertheless, the statistics cited in Chapter 1 suggest that there still remains a strong underlying commitment to e-commerce. Interestingly, etforecasts (www.etforecasts.com) reports that, at the year end of 2001, countries such as Sweden (546.31), Iceland (546.10), Canada (544.54), Denmark (540.32) and Norway (532.01) had more users per 1000 people than the USA (520.52).

As organizations rushed towards transforming their businesses, many discovered that transforming their business was not straightforward. Chapter 2 seeks to go back to basics and consider in depth how the Internet is changing business. Conceptually, some industries appear ideally suited to e-business because of their intangible and information nature. However, e-business is a complex fusion of strategic planning processes, enterprise applications and organizational structure, which if incorrectly aligned can destroy shareholder value. E-business mandates rethinking and repositioning and changes the nature of the communication and interaction between almost all parties involved in the value chain. Readers of this book should bear in mind that e-business is not merely an IT problem, but it incorporates the entire organization. This chapter considers processes in three areas:

- relationships between organizations and their suppliers
- relationships between organizations and their customers
- relationships within the organization

I believe that one of the salient lessons learned from e-business failures is that management adopted a too narrow perspective of risk management. Going back to my earlier days as a computer information auditor, I feel that the Internet has now presented us with newer and much more complex challenges. Therefore, risk-management techniques developed for the mainframe and PC environments at the end of the 1980s are inappropriate in today's myriad of business forces. Chapter 3, therefore, takes the view that risk management is an important managerial concern for financial, non-financial and e-business organizations. Moreover, the demise of the first wave of dot.coms was hardly surprising, given that venture capitalists were frequently prepared to invest in businesses that had no strategy, no special competence or even no customers.

It is anticipated that a good e-business strategy will provide a variety of benefits to organizations such as: improving the time to market; interaction with a broader base of profitable customers and suppliers; and enhancing revenue with effective cost control. To achieve these benefits and to help develop and evaluate the business proposition thoroughly, the concept of strategic planning effectiveness is proffered as an approach in Chapter 4. To assist students to appreciate the European dimension of e-business, 27 European dot.coms, as listed by the Leaders Index in October 2000, were analysed for the period 2000 to 2001. The European dot.coms were drawn from the UK, Germany, France, Italy, Holland, Sweden and Norway. The fortunes of these organizations have been mixed, with some successes and failures.

One of the buzz words in the early days of the Internet was 'business model'. A plethora of e-business models have been proposed and are reviewed in Chapter 5. This chapter seeks to deal with business models in a way that most other texts miss and provides students and academics alike with an extensive reference to academic studies. On a more practical note, looking back with hindsight, organizations were looking for the best 'business model'. It was felt that 'being online' was a sure route to instant riches; unfortunately many investors, entrepreneurs and executives got their fingers burned. However, in retrospect, it is obvious that even a good e-business model will fail if it does not cope with organization and industry dynamics. As eloquently put by Magretta (2002), a business model is not the same thing as strategy, even though many people use the terms synonymously. It must be borne in mind that business models describe, as a system, how the pieces of a business fit together. They ignore two important dimensions. Competition is one dimension, which is usually faced sooner or later. The other dimension ignored by business models is organizational dynamics and this is the focus of Chapter 6.

The Internet offers ample opportunities, yet the promise is often difficult to realize. While much has been written about the disintermediation of value chains, little has been written about the impacts on traditional organizational structures. Success depends upon the ability to align, link and manage all critical business elements. According to Geisler (2001), there is still a paucity of systematic studies of the e-phenomenon and even fewer that explore the role that structural and process variables play in the design of e-commerce organizations. This book takes the view that the organization itself is the final piece in the e-business model jigsaw. The structure and culture of the organization may need reshaping as the firm migrates from traditional to e-business form. While, an e-business infrastructure can quite significantly enhance internal communication between different functional areas such as marketing, finance and human resources with IT as the enabling process, it is pointless trying to integrate across organizational boundaries if there are ineffective internal processes and systems. According to Neilson, Pasternack and Viscio (2000), the e-business organization is no longer a single corporate entity, but rather an extended network consisting of a streamlined global core, market-focused business units and shared support services. The seven e-organizational dimensions proposed by Neilson, Pasternack and Viscio (2000), which view the e-business organization as an extended network consisting of a streamlined global core, market-focused business units and shared support services, provide a good foundation for getting to grips with the challenge.

If organizations want to exploit online opportunities, then it is imperative that they use the Internet as a marketing tool. The Internet should be viewed as an enabler by organizations of all sizes and not solely as an alternative to other distribution channels. In Chapter 7, Wilson and Abell (2002) present five types of strategies for using the Internet as a marketing tool. They can be categorized as business enhancement (communication, market research and brand building) and revenue enhancement (e-commerce and e-organization). The promotion of e-business ventures has led to a variety of approaches. For example, in the early days of the Internet organizations piled money into advertising the website, as a way of obtaining Web traffic. At the height of the bull market, valuations were based on the number of visitors drawn to a website. Dot.coms were purchased at significant sums of cash without any revenue.

The topic of e-business valuation is often skipped over in other textbooks and Chapter 8 provides a unique insight at the height of the bull market into this topic. The example of Excite@Home, when it purchased BlueMountain.com for $780m in 1999 without revenues or profits, is shown to illustrate the business valuations at the height of the bull market. The business case for Excite@Home, when it purchased BlueMountain.com, was apparently the acquisition of the 9.2 million monthly visitors to the site and therefore the 'value' lay in prospects for the future. For the two-year period ending September 2000, which covers the period of the bull Internet stock market, Lastminute.com and QXL ricardo are used to illustrate the different approaches to valuation. There was obviously the need to refine the approach to valuing e-business organization, and I believe that psychological factors should not be ignored. The editorial of the *Journal of Psychology & Financial Market* (2000) – the old psychology behind 'new metrics' – suggests that what we have experienced in recent years is not just a financial phenomenon, but a psychological one.

While the Internet provides a medium to perform online researching for investing, the abundance of available information presents problems of where to look. Chapter 9 seeks to address this problem by providing the reader with some tips on how to perform systematic searches on the Internet. Unfortunately, the Internet is not indexed like a library and, with more than three billion documents, quickly finding specific information is a priority for users – at home, school, college and work. If users are familiar with meta-search engines and subject directories, and can incorporate Boolean logic into their search strategies, they can attain their objectives more quickly. However, it must be borne in mind that the invisible Web (sometimes called Deep Web) is 400 to 500 times larger than the World Wide Web. This chapter can be used by students, researchers and practitioners as an academic support and as a guide for practitioners. I have used this chapter as a stand-alone short course for time-pressed students and executives who are unable to visit the 'bricks-and-mortar' of a university library.

Chapter 10 cements many of the concepts discussed earlier by assessing the phenomenon of the virtual marketspace, which is here to stay. This is evidenced by the fact that analysts project that by 2005 the number of worldwide Internet users will double to 1.12bn with increasing numbers of Internet users using wireless devices such as Web-enabled cell phones and PDAs to go online. As organizations migrate towards e-business, the concept of virtual organizations becomes important if managers want to enhance the efficiency and effectiveness of systems (Khalil and Wang, 2002). Concepts such as virtual teams and trust can be used to enhance the co-operation among physically dispersed members. The ability to interact globally has been cited as one of the benefits of the Internet.

Chapter 11 contains appropriate examples to introduce readers to the complexity of cyber rules and challenges. Data flowing through the Internet are now far more vulnerable to intrusion, theft and sabotage than in the traditional business environment. Rappa (2002) has postulated that there are two major issues relating to how the Internet itself, a technologically complex global communication network, can be managed so that it can continue to grow. First, the multitude of organizations that are associated with the Internet Society complicates governance. The second issue is who should be responsible for rule governance. Problems relating to online violations, crime, fraud and deceitful acts have been highlighted by Baker (2002). Additional areas that remain unresolved and highlighted by Shinohara (2001) include: contract validity and digital certification; taxes and custom duties; intellectual property rights; business model patents; and Internet domain names.

E-business Strategy: Text and Cases concludes by suggesting that e-business is alive and well with some sectors and organizations generating greater benefits than expected. The concept of e-business is becoming more commonplace, with successful organizations focusing on e-business solutions. However, whether the focus is on IT-based systems or the e-organization and/or the markets that they serve, there still remains a paucity of empirical evidence of what constitutes best practice across different industrial markets. Some successful start-ups such as: www.e-bookers.com; www.lastminute.com; www.sportingbet.com;

www.datingdirect.com; and www.friendsreunited.co.uk, together with scenarios, are used to evoke discussions amongst students and practitioners in seminars to conclude the student and practitioner experience.

MODULE PLANNER FOR *E-BUSINESS STRATEGY: TEXT AND CASES*

The book is particularly suitable for undergraduate/master-level degree-type courses that require a solid conceptual foundation combined with real-world examples. Its content and readability make it ideally suited to a 10–12 week modular course, or alternatively, this text-book can assist academics who wish to set up a lecture/seminar around the contents of the book. A unique feature of this European text is the fact that main and mini cases are used to illustrate the key themes of each chapter. The depth and quality of case material focuses on companies that most readers will have had experience with or will have heard of. The questions that can be used for discussion, assessment and group assignment are pitched at varying levels to enable all lecturers and students to derive some benefit. SMEs, which tend to be overlooked in other e-business texts, are also covered.

Module planner outline

Session	Topics	Cases
1	The Internet as a business driver	*Main* The future of e-business – *Business Week*, May 2002 *Mini* The next Web – *Business Week*, March 2002 The mobile Internet – *The Economist*, October 2001
2	The impact of the Internet on business relationships	*Main* Creating an effective customer relationship strategy in a digital world – *CRM Project*, August 2001 *Mini* Danzas AEI named top logistics e-business company – *InternetWeek*, June 2000 UK struggles to see benefits of e-business – *E-business Report*, April 2001
3	E-business risk management	*Main* Risk management in the Internet Age – *Accounting & Finance*, 2000 *Mini* Where did it go wrong for Clickmango.com – *Computing*, August 2000 Clickmango shuts up shop – Uk.internet.com, September 2000
4	Strategic planning for e-business organizations	*Main* Bloody, but unbowed – *Business Week*, March 2001

Session	Topics	Cases
		Mini E-banks still a niche – META Group, May 2001 Ten handy hints how to be an e-manager – *The Economist*, November 2000
5	E-business models	*Main* E-strategy brief: Siemens – Electronic glue – *The Economist*, May 2001 *Mini* E-strategy brief: Seven-Eleven – over the counter e-commerce – *The Economist*, May 2001 Changing the face of enterprise resource planning – *Infotech*, June 2001
6	E-organizational dimensions	*Main* eBay – *Business Week*, December 2001 *Mini* Creative Industries Mapping Document, 2001 Online education – *The Economist*, June 2002
7	Leveraging the Web for marketing	*Main* Tesco – *Business Week*, October 2001 *Mini* Amazon – *BusinessWeek*, August 2001 *The Wall Street Journal* – February 2002
8	Financial appraisals of e-business organizations	*Main* The future of e-business – *Business Week*, May 2002 *Mini* Ebookers – *MediaGuardian*, March 2001 7 lessons learned from the dot.com fallout – internetnews.com
9	Online resources and their deployment	*Main* Freshness issue and complexities with Web search engines – *Information Today* *Mini* Are best buys really unbiased? – *The Guardian*, January 2001 Indexing Deep Web content, promotionbase.com
10	Virtual marketspace	*Main* The real-time economy – *The Economist*, 2002 *Mini* What going virtual means for the hotel industry – hotelbenchmark.com, May 2002 Hilton Hotels Corporation, June 2001

Session	Topics	Cases
11	Cyber rules and challenges	*Main* The Internet's new borders – *The Economist*, August 2001 *Mini* Napster– *The Guardian*, June 2001 Internet security and Internet fraud, Confederation of British Industry, August 2001
12	E-business strategy: lessons learned	*Main* MBA programmes refine e-business courses – *The Guardian*, September 2001 *Mini* E-management older wiser webbier – *The Economist*, June 2001 Tale of a bubble – BusinessWeek, June 2002

REFERENCES

Baker, R.C. (2002) Crime, fraud and deceit on the Internet: Is there hyperreality in cyberspace?, *Critical Perspectives on Accounting*, vol. 13, no. 1, pp. 1–15.

Geisler, E. (2001) Organising for e-business: the implementation of management principles in electronic commerce, *Portland International Conference on the Management of Engineering and Technology*, Portland, Oregon, 29–2 August.

Journal of Psychology & Financial Market (2000). Editorial: The old psychology behind the 'new metrics', vol. 1, no. 3/4, pp. 888–960.

Khalil, O. and S. Wang (2002) Information technology enabled meta-management for virtual organisations, *International Journal of Production Economics*, vol. 75, pp. 127–134.

Margretta, J. (2002) Why business models matter, *Harvard Business Review*, May, pp. 127–134.

Neilson, G.L., B.A. Pasternack and A.J. Viscio (2000) Up the (E)organization! A seven-dimensional model for the centerless enterprise, *Strategy and Business*, Booz Allen & Hamilton, First Quarter.

Rappa, M. (2002) Managing the Digital Enterprise http://digitalenterprise.org/governance/gov.html.

Shinohara, T. (2001) *Cyber Rules: The Rules Governing E-commerce and the Challenges Facing Japan*, Nomura Research Institute, Papers No. 22.

Wilson, S.G. and I. Abel (2002) So you want to get involved in e-commerce, *Industrial Marketing Management*, vol. 31, pp. 85–94.

GUIDED TOUR

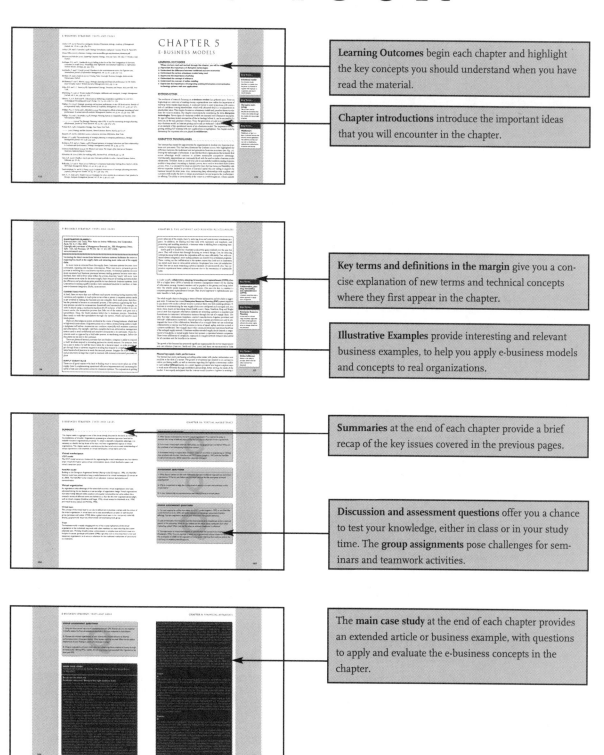

Learning Outcomes begin each chapter and highlight the key concepts you should understand when you have read the material.

Chapter introductions introduce the important ideas that you will encounter in the chapter.

Key terms and definitions in the margin give you a concise explanation of new terms and technical concepts where they first appear in the chapter.

Illustrative Examples provide interesting and relevant business examples, to help you apply e-business models and concepts to real organizations.

Summaries at the end of each chapter provide a brief recap of the key issues covered in the previous pages.

Discussion and assessment questions offer you a chance to test your knowledge, either in class or in your study time. The **group assignments** pose challenges for seminars and teamwork activities.

The **main case study** at the end of each chapter provides an extended article or business example, with questions to apply and evaluate the e-business concepts in the chapter.

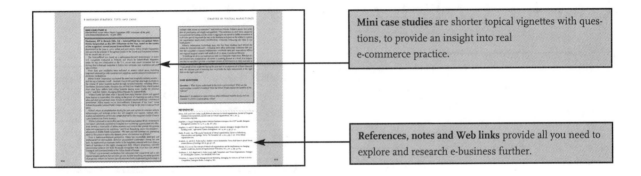

Mini case studies are shorter topical vignettes with questions, to provide an insight into real e-commerce practice.

References, notes and Web links provide all you need to explore and research e-business further.

TEACHING AND LEARNING RESOURCES

ONLINE LEARNING CENTRE

A range of teaching and learning resources has been created to accompany this new book and provide up-to-date and current learning materials. The following student and lecturer resources can be found at the Online Learning Centre website, at:

> www.mcgraw-hill.co.uk/textbooks/phillips

LECTURER RESOURCES

A range of lecturer materials has been designed to help instructors who are delivering modules in e-business, e-commerce or related areas.

■ Approximately 100 PowerPoint slides of bullet-point lecture material for presentations
■ Lecturer manual with suggested lecture plans and seminar/tutorial activities
■ Annotated Web links for further research online

To gain access to the password protected resources, contact your McGraw-Hill representative, or visit the website above for more information.

STUDENT RESOURCES

Students studying modules in e-business can also access a range of extra material to help them with their course assignments and to support preparation for examinations and tests. Go to the Online Learning Centre to find:

■ Approximately 120 self-testing Multiple Choice Questions, provided as a quick test of concepts for each chapter
■ A glossary of key terms for useful revision and recap
■ Annotated Web links to e-business sources and relevant organizations

ACKNOWLEDGEMENTS

This book could not have been completed without the collaboration between author and publisher. The author would like to thank the outstanding work of the editorial team at McGraw-Hill, especially: Julian Partridge, Acquisition Editor; Caroline Howell, Senior Development Editor; Nicola Wimpory, Editorial Assistant and Eleanor Hayes, Production Editor.

The author is also grateful to his colleagues at the University of Surrey who were happy to discuss ideas for the book. In particular, he would like to thank Alastair Day, of Systematic Finance plc, for his contribution as co-author of Chapter 8.

Many of the author's undergraduate and postgraduate students deserve thanks. They provided him with the opportunity to share his knowledge and for him to learn from them. He would like to especially thank two postgraduate students: Thomas Fjeld, who assisted with the section on online banking, and George Stasinopoulos, who assisted with the section on online retailing.

The author also wishes to thank his mother, Joyce, who provided him with the insatiable appetite for knowledge, and his wife, Cleopatra, who helped develop ideas for this book and provided continuous support and encouragement. Finally, thanks to the author's two children, Michael and Dionne, who understood his absence while he was occupied in his study trying to complete this writing project.

The author and publishers would also like to thank the reviewers who contributed to the development of the book through their suggestions and advice:

Al Bhimani, London School of Economics and Political Science, University of London
Richard Blundel, Oxford Brookes University
Debbie Gilliland, Staffordshire University
Lisa Harris, Brunel University
Robert Harris, University of Wolverhampton
Ulf Hoglind, Orebro University
Richard Hollywood, Manchester City College
Martyn Kendrick, De Montfort University
Beverly Leeds, University of Central Lancashire
Ritchie Macefield, University of Staffordshire
Ronan McIvor, University of Ulster
George Panagiotou, London Guildhall University
Bruce Partridge, University of Hull
Ifan Shepherd, University of Middlesex
Stephen Tagg, University of Strathclyde
Rana Tassabehji, University of Bradford
Paul Tregenza, London Guildhall University
Teemu Ylikoski , University of Helsinki

LIST OF
PERMISSIONS

The author and publishers would also like to thank the following organizations, publications and individuals for permission to reproduce material within the text:

Business Week p. 21, p. 27, p. 109, p. 120, p. 194, p. 222, p. 227, p. 356
The Economist p. 28, p. 129, p. 163, p. 167, p. 201, p. 308, p. 333, p. 354
Montgomery Research p. 36, p. 53
Logistics.com p. 40
Danzas AEI Intercontinental p. 58
Institute of Logistics and Transport, p. 60
Computing, p. 87
Joe Saxton, Future Foundation, p. 110
Financial Times, p. 159
Scottish Enterprise, p. 190
Documentum, p. 214
Opportunity Wales, p. 216
Steve Mathieson, p. 286
SitePoint, p. 289
American Lawyer Media Inc, p. 325
The Guardian, p. 335, p. 348, p. 352
Confederation of British Industry, p. 336
The National Underwriter Company, p. 350

DEDICATION

This book is dedicated to Cleopatra, Michael and Dionne.

CHAPTER 1
THE INTERNET AS A BUSINESS DRIVER

LEARNING OUTCOMES

When you have read and worked through this chapter, you will be able to:

- Understand the origins the Internet and World Wide Web
- Outline the benefits and problems of the Internet and World Wide Web
- Identify the unique features of e-commerce and e-business
- Appreciate the growing influence of mobile Internet
- Appreciate the current Internet penetration rates around the world
- Appreciate the importance of understanding Internet consumers
- Appreciate the major trends that will impact the Internet

This chapter describes the evolution of the **Internet** and **World Wide Web**. The much heralded Internet euphoria during the period 1998 to spring 2000 is revisited. The pros and cons of the Internet and the World Wide Web (WWW) are then discussed with emphasis on reasons for the stock-market crash in April 2000. The unique features of **e-commerce** and **e-business** are analysed. The growth of the mobile Internet is compared with the fixed Internet and a variety of Internet user statistics are used to illustrate current and future growth. The importance of understanding Internet consumers is briefly considered and the chapter concludes by identifying salient trends that will impact the Internet.

INTRODUCTION

The impact of the Internet on the commercial landscape is on par with the Industrial Revolution that took place during the mid 18th Century. The Industrial Revolution transformed the business landscape, as agriculture backed by commerce was no longer the preferred way of generating wealth. Instead machinery driven by steam power was able to increase productivity way beyond previous levels. Since the Industrial Revolution, businesses have been able to use the same basic model to compete in the marketplace. Two hundred and fifty years later it is perhaps a case of déjà vu as the business landscape is now being transformed by the Internet. For example, instead of solely concentrating on carving out a section of the industry value chain and providing a value-added product/service combination in a particular niche, the impact of e-business demands that this model change (Deise, Nowikow, King, and Wright, 2000). Instead of tangible assets being the predominant drivers of economic wealth, intangible assets driven by the velocity of e-business has become the preferred way of conducting business.

The term, 'surfing the Internet', is not heard as frequently as it once was for good reason (Rich, 2000). Users of all ages online are now searching for specific answers to specific questions. The awe-inspiring nature of the World Wide Web has given way to a realization that it is an information tool. Users have a clear purpose whether they use the Internet for communication, finding information or for shopping. This illustrates the importance of fully understanding the Web and its potential for each organisation (Briones, 1999). On

Key Term...

Internet
The Internet is a global physical network of computers that is decentralized in design. Each Internet computer, called a host, is independent. Users can choose which Internet services to use and which local services to make available to the global Internet community

Key Term...

World Wide Web
A popular method that supports specially formatted documents through web browsers. The documents are formatted in a script called HTML (HyperText Markup Language)/XML (Extensible Markup Language) that supports links to other documents, as well as graphics, audio, and video files

Key Term...

E-commerce
Relates to the buying and selling of goods and services online and concentrates on external relationships

Key Term...

E-business
E-business encompasses e-commerce but goes far beyond it to include the application of information technologies for internal business processes as well for the activities in which a company engages during commercial activity. These activities can include functional activities such as finance, marketing, human resources management and operations

the Internet, electronic groups structured around consumer interests have grown rapidly. To be effective in this new environment, e-business strategists must consider the strategic implications of their key customer segments. Compared to database-driven relationship marketing, marketers seeking success with consumers in virtual communities should consider that they are more active and discerning and are less accessible to one-to-one processes (Kozinets, 1999).

The 'death of the distance' has redefined rules of competition and the Internet's influence will continue to grow exponentially into the foreseeable future as users communicate globally and purchase products and services online (Cairncross, 1998). During the last decade of Internet activity, there has been a steady evolution of organizational structures designed to support and facilitate an ever-increasing community working collaboratively on Internet issues.

The period from October 1998 to April 2000 was the euphoric stage of the Internet bubble. The NASDAQ composite index fell by more than 65 per cent from its peak and a considerable amount of money was lost. The question on everyone lips became 'how do you make money on the Internet?' The answers proffered by the experts included 'creating new communities', 'enhancing website stickiness', focusing on 'business-to-business' (**B2B**) rather than 'business-to-consumer' (**B2C**) and a multitude of others. Several highly prominent Internet firms collapsed including boo.com and Webvan.com. The major problem was that the business model used up more cash than it generated and advertising revenue was insufficient to keep most sites running, as there was no standard way to charge for things on the Internet. Interestingly, the dot.com cycle once again showed how individuals with specialist knowledge, who are able to keep ahead of the game, can make money in the short run.

What started as the creation of a small band of dedicated researchers has grown to become a commercial tool with billions of pounds of annual investment. The following sections will provide a brief historical reflection of the Internet and WWW phenomenon.

WHAT IS THE INTERNET?

The Internet Society is a good starting point for a review of the Internet as it has a useful website (www.isoc.org), which contains several articles documenting the developments of the Internet.

Although no single individual can claim sole credit for the Internet, as the inaugural head of computer research at the United States Department of Defence's Advanced Research Projects Agency (ARPA), in 1962 J.R. Licklider was influential in the raising the profile of the networking concept. Licklider has been acknowledged as the first person to record a description of the social interactions that could be enabled through a network. He envisioned a globally interconnected set of computers through which users could quickly access data and programs remotely. Four decades later this concept remains the driving force of the Internet.

Kleinrock (1964) made another significant step along the path towards computer networking, by highlighting the benefits of communicating using packets rather than circuits. The ability of computers to communicate was the next significant achievement. The first wide-area computer network was built by Thomas Merrill and Lawrence

---

Key Term...

B2B

Business transactions between an organization and other organizations

---

Key Term...

B2C

Business transactions between an organization and consumers

CHAPTER 1: THE INTERNET AS A BUSINESS DRIVER

Roberts. A TX-2 computer in Massachusetts, USA was connected to a Q-32 in California with a low-speed dial-up telephone line. The result of this experiment was the realization that time-shared computers could work well together, running programs and retrieving data as necessary on the remote machine. Roberts (1967), making further progress, developed the computer network concept and published his work entitled 'Plan for the ARPANET' computer network. In 1972 Kahn organized a successful demonstration of the ARPANET at the International Computer Communication Conference (ICCC). This was the first public exhibition of this new network technology. In the same year, electronic mail was also introduced. Motivated by the need for easy co-ordinating mechanisms, Ray Tomlinson at BBN wrote basic **email** messages. He also expanded its usefulness by writing the first email utility program to list, selectively read, file, forward and respond to messages.

The Internet has been based on the idea that there would be a multitude of independent networks of varying design. ARPANET has been the genesis of today's Internet with its pioneering packet switching network, which later included packet satellite networks, ground-based packet radio networks and other networks. The Internet currently embodies a key underlying technical idea, namely that of open-architecture networking, introduced by Kahn in 1972. Kahn developed a new version of the protocol, which could fulfil the needs of an open-architecture network environment. This protocol eventually became known as the Transmission Control Protocol/**Internet Protocol (**TCP/**IP)**. A major initial motivation for both the ARPANET and the Internet was resource sharing – for example, allowing users on the packet radio networks to access the time-sharing systems attached to the ARPANET. Connecting the two together was far more economical than duplicating these very expensive computers. With the protocols in place, it became possible for developers to formulate much of the Internet and develop Internet services.

A key to the rapid growth of the Internet has been the free and open access to the basic documents, especially the specifications of the protocols. The initial Internet traffic was created by four applications; email, listservs, file transfer protocol and **Telnet**. The beginnings of the ARPANET and the Internet in the university research community promoted the academic tradition of open publication of ideas and results. Email has been a significant factor in all areas of the Internet, and particularly in the development of protocol specifications, technical standards and Internet engineering. Subject-based email discussion groups, which distribute postings through electronic mailing lists called **listservs**, enable users to share common interests and keep abreast of current issues. Using **file transfer protocol (FTP)**, users, who initially were scientists, were able to send or retrieve large files to and from a remote computer. Given proper permission, it is now possible to copy a file from a computer in Hong Kong to one in New York at very fast speeds. The ability for users to log in to a remote host (Telnet) gives the user the opportunity to be on one computer system and perform work on another, which may be across the street or thousands of miles away. Where the quality of modems is limited to only a single connection, Telnet provides a connection that is error-free and nearly always faster than the latest conventional modems.

As a consequence of the above events, by the mid 1980s the Internet was already well established as a technology supporting a broad community of researchers and developers, and was beginning to be used by other communities for daily computer communications. Electronic mail was being used broadly across several communities, often with different systems, but interconnection between different mail systems was demonstrating the utility of broad-based electronic communications between people.

Key Term...

Email
Short for electronic mail, which enables users to send messages over communications networks. Emails are now extensively used as they are fast, flexible, and reliable

Key Term...

Internet protocol (IP)
This specifies the format of packets, also called datagrams. Most networks combine IP with a higher-level protocol called Transmission Control Protocol (TCP), which establishes a virtual connection between applications

Key Term...

Telnet
The Internet protocol that allows users of one host to log into a remote host, so that they are seen as local users of that host

Key Term...

Listservs
An automatic mailing list server that sends messages via email to all individuals on a specific list

Key Term...

File transfer protocol (FTP)
The standard protocol used on the Internet for moving files across the Internet

3

On 24 October 1995, the Federal Networking Council unanimously passed a resolution defining the term Internet. This definition was developed in consultation with members of the Internet and intellectual property rights communities. The resolution being:

> 'The Federal Networking Council (FNC) agrees that the following language reflects our definition of the term "Internet". "Internet" refers to the global information system that – (i) is logically linked together by a globally unique address space based on the Internet Protocol (IP) or its subsequent extensions/follow-ons; (ii) is able to support communications using the Transmission Control Protocol/Internet Protocol (TCP/IP) suite or its subsequent extensions/follow-ons, and/or other IP-compatible protocols; and (iii) provides, uses or makes accessible, either publicly or privately, high level services layered on the communications and related infrastructure described herein.'

WHAT IS THE WORLD WIDE WEB?

The terms World Wide Web and Internet are often used synonymously, but are actually two different things. The Internet is the physical interconnected network of thousands of networks and millions of computers developed over the last four decades. The World Wide Web is one of the Internet's most popular services and began in 1990, when a collection of European researchers at Conseil Européen pour la Recherche Nucléaire (CERN) proposed that knowledge could be shared by linking documents contextually. Tim Berners-Lee, a scientist at CERN, came up with the idea of the World Wide Web and developed a language, which has become known as HyperText Markup Language (**HTML**). By using HTML, users are able to create an interlinked, sometimes interactive, process where documents can be retrieved from the Internet and then linked to other documents.

In 1993, Marc Andreessen of the National Centre for Supercomputing Applications (NCSA), who later co-founded Netscape, developed the first web browser with a graphical interface. HTML informs the web browser how to display graphics and has enabled non-technical users to use the Web without having to type in exact net addresses or enter data via a series of menus. HTML quickly became one of the building blocks of websites and informs browsers how data should be laid out cosmetically on screen. However, since the mid 1990s the World Wide Web Consortium or W3C (www3.com) has developed Extensible Markup Language (**XML**) that goes beyond telling systems how information should be rendered, by specifying exactly what kind of information it is. This will have a profound impact on the way data are exchanged on the Internet, as XML allows a system to recognize a string of numbers and text, such as an invoice or a set of computer-aided design images as elements in a parts catalogue. Users are able to separate content from presentation, which makes it easier to select and/or reformat the data. XML is considered highly extensible because developers can tailor the language to their unique data interchange needs.

XML is likely to become the preferred way for automating data exchange between business systems, both internal and external to the company. For example, if a customer orders a DVD player from a website and the company retailing the DVD is using XML, the order interacts with the inventory database to ensure the DVD player is in stock and communicates with the customer database to get shipping and billing information. XML can enable the third-party supplier's logistics system to make arrangements for delivery. In addition, XML can be used for a broad range of applications such as customer relationship management,

Key Term...

HTML

Short for **H**yper**T**ext **M**arkup **L**anguage, the original coding scheme used for documents on the World Wide Web. HTML defines the structure and layout of a Web document by using a variety of tags and attributes. For example, the correct structure for an HTML document starts with <HTML><HEAD>(enter here what document is about)</HEAD><BODY> and ends with </BODY></HTML>

Key Term...

XML

The acronym XML is short for e**X**tensible **M**arkup **L**anguage, which was created by the W3C. It allows users to produce enhanced documents, because XML provides users with the opportunity to create their own customized tags, enabling the definition, transmission, validation and interpretation of data between applications and between organizations where the ability of XML to help put all the data in a similar format means that users do not have to worry about cumbersome conversions.

BENEFITS OF THE INTERNET AND THE WORLD WIDE WEB

It is possible to assess the product suitability of the Internet by identifying the value of information content within it. The information intensity of the value-chain activities and linkages provides a guide as to those firms that can benefit the most in the short turn. The information intensity matrix created by Porter and Millar (1985) can be applied to Internet firms. The matrix has as its X-axis a measure of the information content of the product service. For example this is very low in the construction industry, but is very high for media firms. The Y-axis measures the quantity and cost of information exchanges, which must happen in order to execute a transaction. The two-by-two matrix is illustrated in Fig. 1.1 and can be used to determine the business importance of information systems (IS) since every activity in the value chain has an information processing component as well as a physical component. Information systems are strategically important in the top right-hand corner of the matrix. By identifying the location of a product on the matrix, advice can be given as to the benefits to be derived from the Internet.

Organisations cannot escape the breakthrough of the Internet. E-business has radically altered the way in which firms interact with their markets by:

- The ubiquitous nature of the technology, which suggests that the e-business strategist can assume that each year more people will have Internet access
- Faster dispersal and greater availability of information
- Increased transparency and choice for the customer
- Far-reaching globalization resulting in a larger supply of products and services
- New suppliers entering with a focused e-strategy

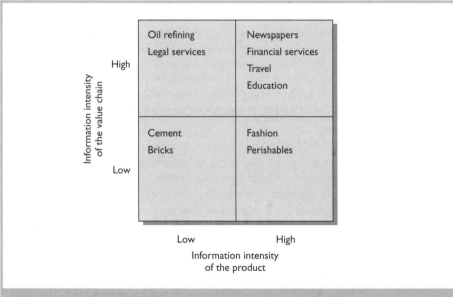

Figure 1.1 Information intensity matrix *(Source: adapted from Porter and Millar, 1985)*

■ New electronic services appearing on the market
■ Transformation of the sales channel; links disappearing in the traditional value chain

The necessity to improve return on investment, coupled with the high risk potential of investing large sums unwisely, has been a key stimulus in arousing interest in e-business strategy. The Internet, because of its low cost, global reach and adaptability, presents both a threat and an opportunity to current and aspiring e-business organizations. Although, firms could communicate and perform business together over vast distances prior to the availability of the Internet, the speed and distance at which transactions and communication can occur has now increased exponentially. For example, it is now possible to send data files overseas, have them processed (which can be overnight) and then receive updates the next morning. The Internet is also accelerating the pace at which products/services are changing. Those in top management are feeling the heat, as they realize there are innumerable ways to go and that the e-phenomenon will change business irrevocably. Matters are not helped by the blurring of traditional lines of business, erosion of boundaries between existing and new lines of competition. However, some firms have not fully exploited e-business as a strategic opportunity, let alone understood it, or adapted to it.

The World Wide Web is a global hypermedia network that provides users on computer networks with a simple yet cost-effective and consistent method of access to a variety of information sources. The Internet is the common link connecting computers, which enables users to access documents without needing to store a copy on their own computer. There are many transfer methods (such as Telnet and FTP protocols) to choose from and, without the World Wide Web, each computer would need to have access to every protocol to obtain every available document.

Another significant advantage of the World Wide Web is that, once information is available, it is accessible for any computer and authorized users should only have to use one simple program to access it. Web page authoring programs such as FrontPage Express (see www.microsoft.com/ms.htm for further details) make it easy for users to create and publish information onto the World Wide Web for others to access. Once established, material is made available to an international audience amounting to millions with no extra distribution costs. Also, editing of existing files is straightforward, as computers called file servers offer a common store of information, which may be used by client computers (client/server computing).

PROBLEMS OF THE INTERNET AND WORLD WIDE WEB

The Internet is like an overloaded highway that needs to be upgraded. But if this is done badly, the Internet's ability to support innovative, as-yet unimagined applications could be in jeopardy (*The Economist*, 2001). The Internet has begun to strain under the enormous weight of traffic that it has attracted. The Internet now needs an overhaul if it is to cope with the mushrooming demand from millions of additional computers, hundreds of millions of new users, the desire for ever-faster connections and an expected boom in access from mobile devices. While the original architectural structure has lasted surprisingly well, the time has come to improve the composition of the network itself, with emphasis on the software protocols on which it is founded.

There are currently two problems with the Internet, the mounting pressure to increase the number of addresses and the increasing requirement for networks to be scaled up to cope with faster connections in an efficient manner. If these two problems prove to be insuperable, the 'end-to-end' principle on which the Internet was founded could be under threat. End-to-end, in essence, is the idea that the network should be as dumb as possible, and just do one thing: send packets from one place to another, without discrimination.

The Internet is an interconnected collection of networks, which allow increasing numbers of people to communicate easily, quickly and cost effectively. To facilitate communication each computer connected to the Internet must have a unique Internet protocol (IP) address. This currently takes the form of xxx.xxx.xxx.xxx, where xxx must be a number from 0 to 255. For example, let us say that you wish to send a message to a colleague in another town and you dialled into your **Internet service provider (ISP)** from home and the message is to be relayed over the telephone line. The message needs to be translated from the alphanumeric text into electronic signals, transmitted over the Internet and then converted back into alphanumeric text. Underlying the flow of data is the networking infrastructure, where the ISP provides and maintains a pool of modems for customers. The backbone, which consists of high-quality fibre-optic cables, provides users with the opportunity to transfer files speedily. Naturally, as organizations become more dependent on the Internet, the ability to exchange large volumes of information in a relatively short period of time becomes increasingly important. On the Internet large chunks of data are known as packets.

Network reliability is a core issue for the e-business strategist. When users transmit text, the route of the data depends on the routers (packet switchers). When a packet reaches a router, the router looks for the IP address and then checks its routing table. If it is able to locate the network that contains the IP address, the packet is sent to that network. If the network is not located, then the router sends the packet on a default route, usually up the backbone hierarchy to the next router. This process will continue until the packet reaches a Network Service Provider (NSP) backbone, which holds the largest routing tables.

The above works well if you know the IP address of the computer that you wish to connect to. Otherwise, your Web browser needs to refer to the **domain name service** or DNS. The DNS is a distributed database, which keeps a record of computers' names and corresponding IP addresses on the Internet. Many computers host the part of the DNS database and software that allows users to access it. These computers are known as DNS servers, and individually they only contain a subset of the database. Like routers, if a DNS does not contain the domain name requested by another computer, the DNS server transfers the request to another DNS server.

The current specification for IP, called IP version 4 or IPv4, only allows for around four billion addresses. Internet experts have therefore proposed a switch from 32-bit addresses to 128-bit ones. Put simply, four billion addresses for each of four billion people on each of four billion planets in each of four billion galaxies. This should be enough to cope with the expected growth in the numbers of mobile devices, Internet-capable household appliances and so on for the next few millennia. The new protocol, originally known as 'next generation IP', was eventually named IPv6. (IPv5 was an experimental protocol that is no longer used.)

Another concern for the e-business strategist is the capacity or speed of data transfer (**bandwidth**). The term broadband describes a two-way digital service that transmits at least

Key Term...

Internet service provider (ISP)
An organization that has a permanent connection to the Internet and sells temporary connections to subscribers

Key Term...

Domain name service (DNS)
Service that translates domain names into IP addresses. However, because domain names are alphabetic, they are easier to remember, but the Internet is based on IP addresses. Therefore, when the user uses a domain name, a DNS service must translate the name into the corresponding IP address

Key Term...

Bandwidth
Relates to the volume of data that can be transmitted over the Internet in a fixed period of time. For Internet devices, which are digital, the bandwidth is usually expressed in bits per second (bps) or bytes per second. Conversely, the bandwidth for analogue devices is expressed in cycles per second, or Hertz (Hz)

1.5 Mbps in at least one direction. A useful comparison can be made with current dial-up modems, which currently handle 28.8 or 56 Kbps. While speeds of 28.8 and 56 Kbps are adequate for downloading still images and text, data-rich applications such as video-on-demand require broadband connections. It is also possible to be online all the time with broadband Internet access via cable modems. Cable modems allow high-speed data access to the Internet via a broadband network. The high bandwidth of broadband will allow customers 'continuous connectivity'. This means that once a computer is on, there is immediate Internet access. Moreover, there is no need for extra phone lines or having to break a data connection to make a telephone call.

The rise of broadband connections also complicates the picture, as many broadband providers now offer special content, such as movies and music on demand, to subscribers. The content is their main weapon for competitive advantage, so there is no incentive to supply rapid access to competing providers' content or networks, which is obviously opposing the notion of end-to-end. Another issue of concern is the idea of 'quality of service' (QoS). With high-bandwidth connections, consumers expect high levels of performance. Multimedia such as **streaming audio and video**, and Internet telephony, require a guaranteed minimum level of performance if they are to be effective. According to Vin Cerf, sometimes called the father of the Internet, there are two mutually exclusive approaches: make the whole network go faster, so that even the slowest link is acceptable, or introduce new protocols that allow users to negotiate a connection with a guaranteed quality of service.

One of the biggest advantages of the World Wide Web, that any given piece of information can be served from a single location, is also one of the biggest disadvantages. For example, a single point of failure will result in many documents being periodically (and sometimes permanently) inaccessible due to network or system problems. This is arguably one of the most frustrating features of the World Wide Web, since it sometimes makes the system as a whole unreliable. In addition to reliability issues, another major problem is the requirement for sufficient bandwidth to deliver information to everyone who requests it.

According to Berners-Lee (2002a, b) most knowledge is built on two pillars: semantics and mathematics. Computers have long been superior to people in processing data. However, search engines cannot tell the difference between a post code and a telephone number. To a computer perusing a travel site, a departure time of '09:05A' could just as easily mean '09.05 Australian dollars'. Berners-Lee suggests that, on the Semantic Web, words will be tagged in XML so that computers can tell what they precisely mean, with smart software programmes called 'agents' being able to grasp both the meaning and context. Computers that are equally adroit at dealing with language and reason will not just help people uncover new insights; they could blaze new trails on their own. Even with a fairly crude version of this future Web, mining online repositories for nuggets of knowledge would no longer force people to wade through screen after screen of extraneous data. Instead, computers would dispatch intelligent agents, or software messengers, to explore websites by the thousand and logically sift out just what is relevant.

WHAT IS THE DIFFERENCE BETWEEN E-COMMERCE AND E-BUSINESS?

Electronic commerce has been described in its most basic form as the paperless exchange of information using a variety of methods, which can include for example electronic data

---

Key Term...

Streaming audio and video
This is a technique for transferring data so that data can be processed as a steady and continuous stream. Streaming means that the client browser or plug-in can start displaying the data before the entire file has been transmitted

interchange (EDI). EDI has been used in retailing and automotive sectors for application-to-application interaction and has been successfully used to exchange data between organizations using a standard electronic format. Transactions include invoices, purchase orders, shipping notices and money transfers. The Internet has added another dimension, by not only supporting application-to-application electronic commerce, but also, and especially, person-to-person and person-to-application forms of e-commerce. E-commerce can also include email, electronic bulletin boards, fax transmissions and electronic funds transfer.

Timmers (2000) states that electronic commerce has existed for over 20 years and that electronic commerce is the means by which companies communicate via digital transactions. Kelly (1998) suggests that e-commerce possesses four attributes:

- Exchange of digitized information between parties.
- It is technology-enabled.
- It is technology-mediated.
- It includes intra- and interorganisational actitivities that support the exchange.

Nevertheless, the terms 'e-commerce', 'e-business', 'digital economy', 'Internet commerce' and a myriad of other terms and phrases are used to describe the current electronic business phenomenon. So what does it all mean? According to Tony Mellor of EDS Asia Pacific, all the phrases mean roughly the same. Mellor simplifies the electronic business phenomenon by dividing it into e-commerce and e-business. Electronic business includes e-commerce but also incorporates business being done throughout the entire value chain. According to Mellor, companies that have commenced trading electronically with their supplies have experienced a 20 per cent reduction in costs.

There are four basic categories of e-commerce. The business-to-business segment represents the full spectrum of e-commerce that can occur between firms. Significant advantages and costs savings can be obtained from transacting on the web and this segment has grown exponentially. This segment is becoming extremely competitive with the legacy firms fighting back. General Motors and Ford are currently transferring all their purchases to the Internet. The Internet has empowered the consumer in terms of price comparison and greater choice. In the B2C quadrant, organizations such as Amazon and Dell currently offer a wide variety of books and computers respectively at keen prices. Internet companies have also allowed consumers to transform the traditional revenue mix (Modahl, 2000). Consumers are now able to drive transactions the other way round. In the **C2B** segment, consumers can join together and present themselves as a buyer group to commercial organizations. Consumers are able to bid for airline tickets on priceline.com. The last segment of the matrix, **C2C**, reflects the added value offered by auction–exchange. Organizations like online auctioneers e-Bay are examples of the type of e-commerce that is available.

One of the earliest adopters of the term e-business was IBM. Previously, e-commerce was the buzzword used. The change in terminology made a shift in paradigm from just selling to making use of the convenience, availability and global reach of the technology. E-business is currently reshaping the business world as organizations discover the benefits of on-screen transactions (Harris, 1999). This is evidenced by the results of a survey of 500 large companies in which more than 90 per cent of top management believe that the Internet will transform or have a big impact on the global marketplace by 2001 (EIU and Booz Allen & Hamilton, 1999). However, the anticipated transformation has not been as drastic. PriceWaterhouseCoopers (2000) in their global CEO survey noted that 68 per cent

Key Term...

C2B
Consumer-to-business transactions between a consumer and business

Key Term...

C2C
Consumer-to-consumer transactions between a consumer and other consumers

of North American and Asian CEOs foresee major or at least significant Internet-related competition, while the corresponding figure for European and Latin American CEO was 56 per cent. It would appear that the intensity of e-business varies by region. E-business in the USA is soon expected to accelerate into a period of hyper-growth, with Britain and Germany two years later, and Japan, France and Italy a further two years behind. Businesses around the world are therefore on the verge of a revolution, as the Web shifts the power from the firm to the customer. Products and services can now be purchased by consumers who are able to obtain more information, and have consequently become more discerning.

The electronic communication revolution (telephone, TV and Internet) will mean that distance will no longer determine the price of communicating electronically (Cairncross, 1998). Adept use of e-commerce will become arguably the most important form of competitive advantage for businesses. It has the potential to create new business models and to find new ways of doing things (Cairncross, 1998). The benefits of e-commerce come not only from speeding up and automating a firm's internal processes but also from its ability to spread the benefits to other members of its supply chain. E-business will eventually be deployed throughout an entire industry's supply chain, linking manufacturers, assemblers, distributors, marketers and customers (King and Clift, 1999). A single press of a button triggers many processes throughout the chain. The provision of services will increasingly become more important than mere products. Web pages will deliver bespoke services, such as help for consumers in making their choices or inventory management for business partners. Fixed prices will give way to reflect true market worth, and firms will join together to make convenient packages for the customer.

King and Clift assert that most businesses will migrate to e-business in four stages:

1 Website: organizations make their presence in e-business. Attempts will be made to integrate their site's buying and selling processes into the organization's back office, customer and marketing systems.
2 Connect website to supply chain: involves connecting the website's capabilities to supply chains. For example, it is anticipated that the reduction in paperwork will reduce costs.
3 Form alliances: alliances will be formed to operationalize the new business model. Electronic share dealing on the Internet is an example of this.
4 Industrial convergence: E-business makes it possible for industries to combine expertise and produce package solutions.

The massive scale changes taking place in global markets now make it imperative that organizations (private and public sector) fully understand the business applications of e-commerce and are able to formulate, implement and evaluate corporate, business and operational strategies.

Definitions of e-commerce and e-business by academics and consultants vary. For example, Rayport and Jaworksi (2001) take a broad view of e-commerce by arguing that it involves the entire world of electronically based organizational activities that support a firm's market exchanges. Conversely, Kalakota and Robinson (2000) are of the opinion that e-business encompasses e-commerce and includes all internal and external electronically based activities. The GartnerGroup (www4.gartner.com) lists three types of e-commerce technology: sell-side (enables a company to sell its products to buyers), buy-side (allows internal employees to perform corporate procurement activities), and marketplace (electronic marketplaces bring multiple buyers and sellers together in a single Web application). For the purposes of this book, e-business encompasses e-commerce, but goes far beyond it to include the application of information technologies for internal business processes as well for the activities in which a company engages during commercial activity. These activities can include functional activities such finance, marketing, human resources management and operations.

MOBILE INTERNET

A mobile Internet connection is different from the fixed Internet in three important respects. First, a mobile phone is a far more personal device to its user than a PC. It tends to be used by only one person, who will have the phone with them throughout the day. Emails sent to a phone reach the person straightaway, whereas email messages that go to a PC may not be obtained as easily. Second, network operators can determine what menus and services appear on their users' mobile phones. PCs users have plenty of scope to alter settings, whereas on mobile phones all they can easily change is the ringing tone and the screen logo. The ability to design and set the starting page that users see when they connect to the mobile Internet is a big advantage, because it allows operators to direct traffic as gatekeepers.

The convergence of the two fastest-growing communications technologies of all time – mobile phones and the Internet – will, they say, make possible all kinds of new services and create a vast new market as consumers around the world start logging on from Internet-capable phones (Standage, 2001). It is anticipated that by 2004, the number of mobile-Internet users will rise to around one billion, from 200 million today. Indeed, despite the problems of **m-commerce**, it will not be long before the number of Internet-connected mobile phones exceeds the number of Internet-connected PCs. Nokia bullishly predicts that this will happen in 2002; Ericsson, another handset maker, says 2003; even pessimistic forecasts put the date at 2005.

It was these bullish projections that prompted mobile-network operators around the world collectively to pay more than $100bn in 2000 for licences to operate '**third-generation' (3G)**. Unlike existing second-generation (2G) systems, 3G systems can handle data quickly and efficiently alongside voice calls and are ideally placed to be used as one of the key technologies that will underpin m-commerce.

Unfortunately, the collapse of technology stocks, together with the debt incurred by telecommunications companies in buying their licences, has affected the 3G's future. This delay in 3G services has extended the payback period for telecommunications companies. The world's first 3G network was launched in Japan on October 2001, five months late; 3G networks are projected in other parts of the world, but will arrive much later than previously anticipated. Users' expectations have now been curtailed and, instead of wanting to watch video clips on the move, or videoconferencing on a train, they are concentrating more on commercial goals. These include using phones to access email, download news items and weather reports, and call up location-specific information. To generate some revenue, many operators have launched the so-called 2.5G networks, which allow continuous data connection. It will therefore probably be 2.5G handsets, rather than 3G ones, that will overtake PCs to become the world's most prevalent Internet-access devices. But, nevertheless, mobile phones will soon become the predominant means of access to the Internet.

Actual e-business may not amount to much in some countries at the moment but penetration rates are set to escalate with the International Data Corporation (IDC) estimating

---

Key Term...

M-commerce
Relates to online commerce performed from mobile phones or hand-held computers

Key Term...

Third generation (3G)
3G promised increased bandwidth (analogue phones formed the first generation and digital phones the second) for mobile communications technology. 3G systems can handle data quickly and efficiently alongside voice calls and was initially placed to be used as one of the key technologies that will underpin m-commerce

that 169 million Europeans will be online in 2003. This increase represents an annual growth of 33 per cent from present levels. It is anticipated that penetration will increase significantly due to lower priced PC, the disappearance of ISP charges and lower phone tariffs. PCs are currently the favoured route for accessing e-business. However, other electronic channel penetration is adding to the mix.

WHO IS USING THE INTERNET?

Trying to estimate the number of people online throughout the world is an inexact attempt at best. To make an estimate and forecast of Internet users for many countries is a daunting task. Ideally such data would be based on comprehensive surveys with standard methodologies and be performed on a periodic basis. However, such data do not exist and will not be available for a long time, as the majority of companies would not be able or willing to absorb the costs of such a survey. There are several surveys around, using all sorts of varying measurement methodologies.

For example, Nua (www.nua.ie) includes both adults and children who have accessed the Internet at least once during the three months prior to being surveyed. Where these figures are not available, Nua uses figures for users who have gone online in the past six months, past year, or whenever performed. An Internet user represents a person with access to the Internet and is not specific to Internet account holders. When the figure for Internet account holders is the only information available, this figure is multiplied by a factor of three to give the number of Internet users. When more than one survey is available on a country's demographics, Nua will take the mean of the two surveys or, in the case where Nua feels one study may be more comprehensive/reliable than the other, Nua will quote this figure over the other.

Internet Industry Almanac (www.c-i-a.com) collects available data on computer and Internet statistics from market research companies, associations, government agencies, computer companies and other sources. From these data it has created a large spreadsheet of historical data for 50+ countries and the worldwide estimate. To test the data it calculates computers per capita, Internet host computers per capita and Internet users per capita. These ratios tend to fall in ranges depending on a country's industrial, economic and political development. At a minimum these ratios show data points that need further checking and analysis. Internet Industry Almanac calculates the ratio between computers and Internet hosts and the ratio between computers and Internet users. These ratios are also helpful tools to spot anomalies in the data. It is speculative to project the number of Internet hosts and Internet users for year-end 2002, 2004 and 2005. To do so Internet Industry Almanac first projected the computers-in-use for each country. The increases in the installed base of computers per country happen at a reasonably predictable rate. Using four guidelines, the Internet host and Internet user projections can be summarized as follows:

- Projections are made from well designed and executed surveys. An increasing number of surveys are now available from government agencies in many countries.
- Estimates based on the number of Internet host computers. The Internet user/Internet host computer ratio can be estimated from previous survey data or by comparison with countries with similar Internet/computer industries.
- Estimates based on the portion of computers-in-use with Internet access. The computers-in-use/Internet user ratio can be estimated from previous survey data or by comparison with countries with similar Internet/computer industries.

■ Projections from the number of Internet access accounts and the average number of Internet users per account. Such data are available from ISP associations in a few countries.

In preparing the current estimates the first three methods are mainly used. Internet access account estimates from ISP associations are a promising methodology for the future, but few statistics are currently available. Industry Almanac defines an Internet user as any person over 16 who uses the Internet on a regular basis at least once a month. These numbers include business, educational and home Internet users.

So how many people use the Internet?

NUA reported that there are 513.41m Internet users (see Table 1.1). According to NUA's figure this shows a 35.9 per cent increase from September 2000. Table 1.2 breaks the 513.41m figure down by region. Canada and the USA have 35.2 per cent of the online market. Europe is in second place with 30.1 per cent of the online market with Asia/Pacific third with 28 per cent. According to etforecasts (www.etforecasts.com), the number of Internet users grew from 128m in 1997 to more than 533m in 2001. Much of the growth in Internet

Month	Number of Users, million	% of Population
August 2001	513.41	8.46
July 2001	507.92	8.37
June 2001	478.70	7.88
May 2001	462.57	7.62
April 2001	460.87	7.59
March 2001	458.11	7.55
February 2001	455.55	7.50
January 2001	455.55	7.50
December 2000	451.04	7.43
November 2000	407.10	6.71
October 2000	381.79	6.29
September 2000	377.65	6.22
(Source: Extracted from Nua February 2002)		

Table 1.1 Internet users online

Region	Number of Users, million	% of Total
Africa	4.15	0.81
Asia/Pacific	143.99	28.04
Europe	154.63	30.11
Middle East	4.65	0.91
Canada and USA	180.68	35.20
Latin America	25.33	4.93
World total	513.41	100.00
(Source: Extracted from Nua February 2002)		

Table 1.2 Internet users by region – August 2001

Internet Users	Number of Users, million	Share, %
1. USA	148 400	27.82
2. Japan	48 400	9.07
3. China	38 200	7.16
4. Germany	24 300	4.56
5. South Korea	23 800	4.46
6. UK	20 560	3.85
7. Canada	17 240	3.23
8. Italy	16 700	3.13
9. Brazil	14 190	2.66
10. France	12 360	2.32
11. India	9 950	1.87
11. Russia	9 950	1.87
13. Australia	9 050	1.70
14. Taiwan	8 670	1.63
15. Spain	8 110	1.52
16. Top 15 total	533 348	76.85
(Source: www.etforecasts.com Internet user forecast by country)		

Table 1.3 Top 15 Internet countries – Year end 2001

users is taking place outside the USA with Asia expecting to see strong growth in the next five years. It is anticipated that China will surpass Japan and become second to the USA in number of Internet users by 2003.

Table 1.3 shows the top 15 Internet users by country and, despite the USA having an overwhelming lead in Internet users with almost 28 per cent of total Internet users at year-end 2001, the USA is only ranked sixth in terms of Internet users per capita (see Table 1.4).

Sweden is the per capita leader with 546.31 Internet users per 1000 users with Iceland and Canada in second and third places, with 546.1 and 544.54 Internet users per 1000 respectively. Taiwan is in 15th position with 384.82 Internet users per 1000 people.

According to Internet Industry Almanac, the number of Internet users surpassed 530m in 2001 and will continue to grow strongly in the next five years (see Table 1.5). It is forecast that most of the growth will come from Asia, Latin America and parts of Europe. By the end of 2005 the number of worldwide Internet users will double to 1.12bn with increasing numbers of Internet users using wireless devices such as web-enabled cell phones and **Personal digital assistants (PDAs)** to go online. Wireless devices will be become supplemental to PC Internet access for most users in developed countries. It is projected that in countries with low Internet penetration many wireless Internet devices will be the primary Internet access devices. Despite the wireless Internet being a disappointment in 1999 and 2000 due to unrealistic expectations in Western Europe and the USA, it is projected that wireless Internet users will reach 48m in 2005.

Key Term...

Personal digital assistant (PDAs)

PDAs are hand-held devices that combine computing, telephone/fax and networking features. A typical PDA can function as a cellular phone, fax sender and personal organizer

Country	Internet Users Per 1000 People
1. Sweden	546.31
2. Iceland	546.10
3. Canada	544.54
4. Denmark	540.32
5. Norway	532.01
6. USA	520.52
7. Finland	516.38
8. Singapore	499.37
9. South Korea	497.91
10. Switzerland	466.85
11. Australia	464.34
12. Netherlands	447.29
13. New Zealand	410.39
14. Austria	394.80
15. Taiwan	384.82
(Source: www.etforecasts.com Internet user forecast by country)	

Table 1.4 Top 15 Countries in Internet users per capita – Year end 2001

Year-End	2001	2004	2007
USA			
Internet users, millions	149	193	236
Wireless Internet user share, %	4.5	27.9	46.3
Worldwide			
Internet users, millions	533	945	1 460
Wireless Internet user share, %	16.0	41.5	56.8
Asia-Pacific			
Internet users, millions	115	357	612
Wireless Internet user share, %	34.8	50.9	60.4
Western Europe			
Internet users, millions	126	208	290
Wireless Internet user share, %	13.9	49.6	67.0
(Source: Internet Industry Almanac, 2002)			

Table 1.5 Summary of Internet users by geographic region and projection for 2002–2007

UNDERSTANDING INTERNET CONSUMERS

Understanding Internet consumers is an important managerial activity. Websites like www.in2home.co.uk, which is owned by Thus (formerly Scottish Telecom) Internet Services, provided a variety of interesting content and links to websites containing information about fashion and beauty, health and fitness, kids and family, and leisure. As of 23:59 on 31 March 2002, the In2Home service ceased to operate as a result of changes that have taken place in the Internet Industry. The customer focus has changed towards serving customers looking for a premium Internet service, rather than the mass-market free-subscription model.

Older Internet consumers

In a study of older Internet users Trocchia and Janda (2000) observed that certain motivational and attitudinal characteristics distinguish older Internet users from their non-user counterparts. These observations have important implications for marketers as well as consumers.

Multiple reference groups

An interesting observation is the fact that older individuals possess multiple reference groups. Older adults compare themselves with their peers outside their age groups. For example, they make reference with professional groups, religious groups and interest groups. Therefore, organizations may use such references when designing marketing programmes. Instead of segmenting solely by age, a firm might consider the case where a retired accountant may feel compelled to keep up with his younger, Internet-using counterparts if he believes that they are still a part of his reference group. He may then use the Internet to stay abreast of current developments in the profession as well as to keep in touch with others in the field.

Technophobia

Compared to Internet users, non-users can exhibit an aversion to technology. This aversion is often attributed to misperceptions regarding the Internet's ease of use and potential benefits. A firm's marketing communications efforts should therefore focus on clarifying these misperceptions and stress the Internet's user-friendliness and functionality. Communications should focus on ease of use through the point-and-click features and menu-driven options.

Resistance to change

It was observed that non-users were found to possess greater resistance to change than users. Marketers might find it useful to minimize the differences between non-users' current activities and the corresponding activities that they could perform using the Internet. This should make the perceived potential adoption of the Internet seem like a less drastic change. For example, advertisements should be formulated portraying sending an email overseas as little different from conventional snail mail, but much more time-, cost- and labour-efficient.

Social interactions

Users made use of the Internet's ability to keep in close touch with family and friends. Non-users did not fully appreciate the Internet's capabilities in this regard. Interviews by Trocchia and Janda (2000) indicated that such Internet services as email, chat rooms and electronic greeting cards were viewed as having a positive impact on the quality of our informants' lives. In addition to maintaining existing social relations, the Internet strengthen social bonds. Internet marketers may therefore wish to use emotional appeals to promote their services. These promotions may include demonstrations of lively e-chatting between grandparents and grandchildren and electronic transmission of family photographs and greeting cards.

Bricks and clicks

Non-using informants expressed a preference for physical interactions with the interaction with sales staff. Compared to non-users, users appeared to be more comfortable with performing virtual activities such as email, online chatting, surfing the net and making online purchases. These activities were deemed less satisfying because they were thought of as less appealing than traditional methods. Internet marketers may therefore wish to lessen

Characteristics	October 2000, %	October 2001, %
Age in years		
16 to 24	82	87
25 to 44	60	69
45 to 54	50	58
55 to 64	28	37
65 and over	10	11
Gender		
Male	52	55
Female	39	51
(Source: National Statistics Omnibus Survey, October 2001)		

Table 1.6 Adults in the UK who have used the Internet by their characteristics

perceived differences between virtual and real-world transactions. One method of accomplishing this may be to emphasize the growing number of online transactions being performed through the Internet.

UK Internet users statistics

UK Internet statistics are produced by the Government (www.statistics.gov.uk) and they provide extremely useful data for organizations that wish to keep track of Internet users. Statistics are produced on:

- Households with home access to the Internet (split by region and income)
- Adults who have used the Internet by characteristics
- Adults who have used the Internet by social class
- Locations that adults have to access the Internet (for personal use)
- Adults who have accessed the Internet by purpose of Internet use
- Reasons for not using the Internet

In summary, some of the interesting observations include the fact that 39 per cent of all UK households have access to the Internet from home and the fact that for the 12-month period October 2000 to October 2001, the percentage of adults who accessed the Internet at some time increased from 45 to 53 per cent. Results also show the importance of understanding the profile of adults using the Internet. Table 1.6 shows that 87 per cent of users between the ages of 16 and 24 use the Internet and this drops to 11 per cent of users over 65. One of the most significant observations is the fact for the 12-month period October 2000 to October 2001, the percentage of females who accessed the Internet at some time increased from 39 to 51 per cent.

WHAT WILL BE THE MAJOR TRENDS THAT WILL IMPACT THE INTERNET?

Despite the velocity of technology change, one should not conclude that the Internet has now finished changing. The Internet, although a network in name and geography, is a creature of the technology, not the traditional network of the telephone or television industry. It will continue to change and evolve at the speed of the ever-changing computer industry.

1998–2001	2002–2006
Email proliferation	Web mobile phones
Free web browser	Broadband connections
Content explosion	Business-to-business e-commerce
Low-cost PCs	Wireless web content
Intranets for business users	M-Commerce (E-Commerce for mobile devices)
Web hosting services	
Business-to-consumer e-commerce	Application service providers (ASPs)
PC purchase rebates from ISPs	Web appliances
Business-to-business e-commerce	Declining and fixed ISP rates outside the USA
'Free' ISP rates in international markets	Hardware cost bundled in ISP rates
Web-driven productivity gains	E-Commerce-driven productivity gains
	Web interactive TV services
(Source: www.etforecasts.com)	

Table 1.7 Internet business drivers

It is now changing to provide such new services as real-time transport in order to support, for example, audio and video streams. The availability of pervasive networking (i.e. the Internet), along with powerful affordable computing and communications in portable form (i.e. laptop computers, two-way pagers, PDAs, mobile phones), is making possible a new paradigm of nomadic computing and communications.

Table 1.7 illustrates etforecasts' salient Internet business drivers for the period 1998–2001 and projections for the period 2002–2006. Apart from changing technology, the forces of change will impact the e-business strategist for the foreseeable future. Computer Economics has suggested that ten trends will impact on the Internet over the next five years (computereconomics.com). These are:

- Bands, channels, platforms and formats
- Cyber law and disorder
- Global response
- Linguistic and cultural diversity
- Privacy: a social and legal requirement
- Restricting access
- Strategic turmoil
- Surviving on a crowded Web – purveyor perspective
- Surviving on a crowded Web – user perspective
- Taxation of Internet commerce

SUMMARY

The period from October 1998 to April 2000 was the euphoric stage of the Internet bubble and there were several high-profile collapses, such as boo.com. Salient points of Chapter 1 are as follows:

What is the Internet?
The Internet Society is a good starting point for a review of the Internet as it has a useful website (www.isoc.org), which contains several articles documenting the developments of the Internet.

What is the World Wide Web?

The World Wide Web is one of the Internet's most popular services and began in 1990, when a collection of European researchers at Conseil Européen pour la Recherche Nucléaire (CERN) proposed that knowledge could be shared by linking documents contextually.

Benefits of the Internet and World Wide Web

The Internet, because of its low cost, global reach and adaptability, presents both a threat and opportunity to current and aspiring e-business organizations. The Internet is also accelerating the pace at which products/services are changing. The World Wide Web is a global hypermedia network that provides users on computer networks with a simple yet cost effective and consistent method of access to a variety of information sources.

Problems of the Internet and World Wide Web

There are currently two problems with the Internet, the mounting pressure to increase the number of addresses and the increasing requirement for networks to be scaled up to cope with faster connections in an efficient manner. One of the biggest advantages of the World Wide Web, that any given piece of information can be served from a single location, is also one of the biggest disadvantages. For example, a single point of failure will result in many documents being periodically (and sometimes permanently) inaccessible due to network or system problems.

What is the difference between e-commerce and e-business?

For the purposes of this book, e-business encompasses e-commerce but goes far beyond it to include the application of information technologies for internal business processes as well for the activities in which a company engages during commercial activity. These activities can include functional activities such finance, marketing, human resources management and operations.

Mobile Internet

PCs are currently the favoured route for accessing e-business. Mobile phones (m-business) are gaining market share. It is also possible to be online all the time with broadband Internet access via cable modems. Cable modems allow high-speed data access to the Internet via a broadband network. This means that once a computer is on, there is immediate Internet access. A mobile Internet connection is different from the fixed Internet in three important respects.

Who is using the Internet?

According to Internet Industry Almanac, the number of Internet users surpassed 530 million in 2001 and will continue to grow strongly in the next five years (see Table 1.5). By the end of 2005 the number of worldwide Internet users will double to 1.12 billion with increasing numbers of Internet users using wireless devices such as web-enabled cell phones and PDAs to go online. Interestingly, despite the wireless Internet being a disappointment in 1999 and 2000 due to unrealistic expectations in Western Europe and the USA, it is projected that wireless Internet users will reach 48 million in 2005.

Understanding Internet consumers

Understanding Internet consumers is an important managerial activity. The customer focus has changed towards serving customers looking for a premium Internet service, rather than the mass market free subscription model.

DISCUSSION QUESTIONS

1. What do you believe makes the Internet and World Wide Web similar to and different from previous innovations in commerce?

2. What do you understand by the term e-commerce? How does it differ from e-business?

3. Why is it important to understand Internet consumers? What are the penalties for getting it wrong?

ASSESSMENT QUESTIONS

1. The World Wide Web was developed from the bottom up by public-sector organizations rather than it being imposed by large multinational commercial organizations. What do you believe have been the significant implications of the bottom-up public-sector approach and how has this affected the rise of the World Wide Web?

2. Using evidence to support your views, how well is the Internet currently satisfying the needs of the female consumer? How does the need of the female consumer differ from that of the male?

3. The impact of the Internet on the commercial landscape is arguably on par with the industrial revolution that took place during the mid 18th Century. However, despite the well cited benefits of the Internet, together with the growth of Internet users, the Internet is beginning to strain under the enormous weight of traffic. You are required to discuss these major problems from the perspectives of business and society.

GROUP ASSIGNMENT QUESTIONS

1. Using any organization of your choice, together with relevant Internet material, write a short report that describes the actual benefits your selected organization has derived from using the Internet. Also outline how the ten Internet trends suggested by Computer Economics (2001) will affect your selected organization.

2. Using the UK Internet statistics produced by the UK Government (www.statistics.gov.uk) or any other country of your choice, you are required to analyse Internet User statistics for your selected country. For your selected country you are also required to outline how the Internet penetration rates are likely to change in the future?

3. In your opinion what has caused the disparity in Internet users as illustrated in Table 1.4? You are required to identify reasons why Internet users per 1000 people in Sweden, Iceland, Canada, Denmark and Norway are higher than in the USA?

MAIN CASE STUDY
SPECIAL REPORT – The Future of E-Business, by Robert D. Hof in San Mateo, CA, with Steve Hamm in New York, Business Week, 13 May 2002

How E-Biz Rose, Fell, and Will Rise Anew.
As in previous tech upheavals, solid expansion may come now that a shakeout has cleared the tracks

The economy is stuck in the doldrums, thanks largely to the broken promises of technology. Dazzled by seemingly limitless returns, bankers had funded hundreds of companies, all going after the same dubious markets. Heedless, individual investors clamored to get into the stock market, driving share prices to unheard-of levels. Soon, the overheated market crashed, turning the new heroes of business into goats and scoundrels. Now, disillusionment reigns, and nobody knows what's going to happen next.

Sound familiar? Maybe it's not as familiar as you might think. The year is 1850. The place is England. And the new technology is the steam locomotive. In a surprising number of ways, railroads were the Internet of 150 years ago. And not just because rails, like the Internet today, connected people and markets much faster than any previous method of transport. "Railway Mania" – as that short period of British stock market lunacy was called – was every bit as nutty as the Internet bubble. Hundreds of companies, many promoting rail lines between small towns, hawked stock well in advance of construction. It all fell apart in 1847, when railroad shares plunged 85% and hundreds of businesses, even banks, went belly-up.

What happened next is even more fascinating. After the bust, train traffic in Britain leveled off briefly, in 1848, before resuming a steady climb. By 1870, just two decades after the crash, railroads were carrying 322 million passengers a year, more than four times as many as in 1850. For all its pain, the bust cleared the tracks of speculative stock plays and swindles, leaving only the most solid companies to survive. The remaining companies, says W. Brian Arthur, an economist at the Santa Fe Institute, a think tank, went on to produce the industry's greatest growth and greatest impact on business and society.

For a rising chorus of economists and business historians, the railroad's parallels with the Internet are too striking to ignore. Defying the downbeat attitude toward the Net these days, they are making a bold prediction: The same decades-long build-out that marked the post-crash railroad revolution will play out during the Information Revolution, led today by the Internet. If they're right, e-business may well be poised for its own long, steady build-out for decades to come. "Up to now, it has been pretty hard going," says Andrew J. Ball, president of Webcor Builders, a San Mateo (Calif.) construction company that has struggled for years to link its partners over the Web. "Now is the time when we'll see the real advances."

History, however, is not destiny. For one thing, the Internet is only the latest development in the larger information-technology revolution, so it may not pack the wallop of railroads, electricity, or the automobile. And not all new technologies exhibit precisely the same patterns. Nuclear power, for one, has yet to return from its bust after the Three Mile Island accident in Pennsylvania in 1979. And to be truly pervasive, the Internet will require myriad supporting technologies and regulations to become universally useful. Railroads needed every accessory from the telegraph to toilets, the automobile's spread depended on the federal government funding interstate highways, and personal computers needed packaged software, the mouse, and more.

There's no guarantee these helper technologies or government aid will materialize for the Internet.

Most important, industry infrastructure and people's habits take years to change, no matter how compelling a new technology may be. The emerging Net-driven corporate model, which taps networks to co-ordinate a vast phalanx of partners, is so difficult to operate that even some of its most advanced proponents, such as Cisco Systems Inc., have stumbled. That's why many businesses remain hesitant to take the e-biz plunge. Nearly 90% of 1,026 companies surveyed by Forrester Research Inc. are doing some kind of e-commerce, but far fewer are doing the really big stuff: Only about one-third have supply-chain management projects or are running customer-relationship management programs – the most popular Net-connected projects today. "It will take a very long time before the economy wide effects of the Internet come through," says Chris Freeman, emeritus professor at Britain's University of Sussex and author of *As Time Goes By: From the Industrial Revolutions to the Information Revolution* (Freeman and Louca, 2002). "It requires a huge process of learning and cultural change."

For that reason, the next phase of e-business will be nothing like the dot-com era. For all its insanity and subsequent pain, that frenzy – like others in history – served a valuable purpose: The infrastructure for e-business was created with amazing speed. But the new era's motto is no longer "Get big fast." And it certainly isn't "Get rich quick." Instead, the new mantra is almost puritanical: "Work hard now." And it's not the financiers, whose momentum-driven reign on the Net has come to an end, who are writing the checks. With venture capitalists avoiding Internet business plans as if they were month-old herring, it's up to the folks who actually buy the stuff to drive it into widespread use.

Indeed, the e-biz build-out, if and when it comes, will be relatively slow, marked by further ups and downs. It isn't that innovative new technologies and ideas won't continue to bubble up. It's just that they won't produce upstarts with bottomless budgets and limitless goals. Much of the work will be aimed, instead, at helping existing companies use the Internet to cut costs, serve customers better, and open new markets. And because the new Net style will have to coexist for some time with old methods, the ultimate payoff in lower costs and greater productivity may still be many years away.

For both remaining dot-coms and traditional companies embracing the Net, that means a long period of developing and deploying the gritty stuff. There's much work to be done, from installing thousands of access points for wireless networks to hashing out arcane data-interchange standards and rolling out broadband links to the masses. "Everybody knows where this is going to end up: Business goes electronic," says Christian A. Larsen, CEO of online mortgage broker E-Loan Inc. "Now, it's really about putting our heads down. We've got a lot of wood to chop."

The notion that e-business is due for a comeback may sound daft. After all, many of the dot-coms are dead and gone. E-business leaders such as Amazon.com Inc. and Cisco face continuing doubts about their business models. Many traditional titans that bet on e-business, from Levi Strauss & Co. to ChevronTexaco Corp., stumbled in their online efforts. Even the term "e-business" is so discredited that General Motors Corp. (GM) – which incessantly plugged its e-GM unit from 1999 until folding it into its info-tech department last fall – now insists on calling its continuing e-business efforts "digitization." Growls James A. Champy, author of *X-Engineering the Corporation: Reinventing Your Business in the Digital Age* and chairman of Perot Systems Corp.'s consulting practice: "We're in a big stall."

Yet the lessons of history indicate that this holding pattern may not be permanent. It turns out that the similar dynamics of railroads and the Internet aren't simply an odd coincidence. According to Venezuelan economic researcher Carlota Perez, author of the upcoming *Technological Revolutions and Financial Capital: The Dynamics of Bubbles and Golden Ages*, the same pattern holds for three other tech-driven economic movements as well: the Industrial Revolution of the late 1700s in England, the age of cheap steel and electricity in the late 1800s in the U.S. and Germany, and the automobile and mass-production era starting about 1910. After a gestation period of a decade or more, the new technology usually sparks a boom followed by a sudden bust, leading to widespread doubts.

Today, says Perez, "the world is once again at a crossroads where explanations and guiding criteria are sorely needed." And that's where her work and Freeman's provide some possible answers. What typically follows these uncertain periods, in fact, is several decades of sustained build-out, in which the technology drives the entire economy and becomes essential to business and society. The key to seizing the opportunities is patience, say Perez and Freeman: Despite the rapid rise and collapse of the bubble, the cycle can take at least 50 years to play out from initial breakthrough to maturity.

The Internet's cycle may well prove shorter, since some economists think the Net's impact won't match that of the Industrial Revolution or the railroads. But it is clearly the latest technology to seize the banner of the Information Revolution – and perhaps the most powerful force yet, thanks to the instant, infinitely adaptable global connections it makes possible. Consider the longevity of the IT revolution's previous standard bearer: the PC. After Apple Computer Inc. popularized the device in the 1970s, the IBM PC sparked a mid-1980s boom. Overcapacity led to a wrenching shakeout in 1985, which killed countless PC and component makers. But after the bust, PC sales dipped only slightly. Then, in the next 15 years, they shot up eightfold, to 131 million units in 2000 – creating such new giants as Microsoft, Intel, and Dell Computer – before falling 4% last year.

All this suggests that the Internet – which wasn't widely used on a commercial basis until 1995 – has years to go before its ride is over. The latest data, in fact, show continued growth, even after dot-com shares started to crash in April, 2000. The number of Internet users worldwide is still rising – by 48% in 2000 and 27% in 2001, to more than 500 million people today, according to researcher IDC. And even as venture funding of Net companies fell 71% last year, IDC says Internet trade between businesses rose 73%, to $496 billion, and online retail spending rose 56%, to $112 billion, in the worst retail year in a decade. Even perennial cash incinerator Amazon.com turned its first-ever net profit in the 2001 holiday quarter.

Yet with e-commerce accounting for less than 2% of all trade, it's clear that the Net is still in the Model T stage. The build-out to come will take a winding path, often in fits and starts, as people, companies, and governmental organizations adapt their work and lives to take advantage of the new technologies.

First on the build-out agenda are myriad supporting technologies that make the Net easier to use. The electric ignition, for instance, banished the auto's cumbersome hand-crank starter. Likewise, broadband connections eliminate the dial-up-and-wait of modems, providing instant access that prompts people to meld the Net into their daily lives. "Technology has to be comfortable," says Arthur. Some new innovations promise to free people from mundane tech tasks altogether. As cheaper and smaller computers find their way into everything from air conditioners to factory robots, those devices can communicate directly with each other over the Internet. Wal-Mart Stores Inc., for instance, is experimenting with radio-frequency identification tags – tiny chips that soon will cost only a few cents. These let computers track products as they move from truck to warehouse to store – replacing repeated human scanning of bar codes.

The real imperative for the next few years, though, will be adapting new technology to people and their work, rather than forcing people to adapt to it. The emergence of packaged software made the PC easier to use by freeing people from having to learn programming. Similarly, so-called Web services are emerging that could make the Net a much smoother experience by essentially turning software into a service available online. Travel site Expedia.com, for example, recently introduced online alerts that find you via computer, cell phone, or pager if your flight is delayed, then let your family know when you'll land.

As the technology opens up new vistas, even greater changes will be needed. In a constant give-and-take with the new technologies, people and organizations inevitably must change how they do things to tap into the opportunities. That was how leaders previous tech revolutions leaped ahead. In the late 1700s, for instance, pottery entrepreneur Josiah Wedgwood pioneered productivity-boosting ideas in factory organization and the division of labor – not only building a company that endures to this day but spurring a wholesale change in manufacturing.

In the Information Age, the Net is accelerating the rollout of a new model: the networked corporation. Embodied by such leaders as Dell and Cisco, these corporations outsource whatever can be done better by someone else. But – ideally, at least – they keep an eye on what partners are doing by sharing information across entire supply chains linked over the Net. Dell, for instance, uses the Web to stay in touch with everyone from chipmakers and disk-drive producers to customers large and small. Keeping close tabs over the Net allows Dell to maintain just four days' worth of inventory, down from 32 days in 1995.

Yet this model is incredibly tough to execute. The evidence: Few corporations so far have fully embraced it. And some that have done so have a lot to learn. Cisco, for instance, missed a severe downturn in its business in late 2000 because its systems didn't recognize that customers had double-ordered as a way to guarantee delivery much-needed networking gear, which was in short supply. That led to losses and Cisco's first layoffs. The lesson here is that companies need to alter old processes and encourage their partners to do the same. It's always this way with tech revolutions, says author Perez: "Each involved profound changes in people, organizations, and skills in a sort of habit-breaking hurricane."

Consider the case of Boise Office Solutions. The office products subsidiary of paper giant Boise Cascade Corp. has moved successfully to the Net. Some 30% of its $2.5 billion in annual sales are online, and that's expected to rise to 45% this year. The result: savings of at least $585,000 a year so far, and each percentage point rise in online sales is expected to add $100,000 in additional savings. But Web sales created huge upheaval in the call-center operation, says David A. Goudge, senior vice-president for marketing at Boise Office Solutions. If the Web-sales estimates are even 1% off, the call-center unit suddenly can be way overstaffed – or understaffed – in turn forcing the call-center manager to change how the unit is run.

To help managers and employees deal with all the turmoil, Boise brought in consultant Peppers & Rogers Group to teach them how to deal with constant change. "We're handling nitroglycerin," says Goudge. "Don't underestimate the change in management needed to calm people down." He has that right. According to Forrester Research Inc., 40% of companies that adopted programs to manage the inevitable change in processes when they installed online purchasing systems reduced their costs. In contrast, only 3% of companies that didn't do so saved money.

Indeed, the people factor is usually a tougher problem than any technical difficulties. Online alcoholic beverage marketplace eSkye Solutions Inc., for instance, ran smack into the status quo, even though founder J. Smoke Wallin knew his stuff: He was the scion of a family that ran Indianapolis distributor National Wine & Spirits Inc. Both distributors and buyers liked the system's speed, but "these are busy people, and at the end of the day, the old system was easy," says Wallin. Last year, eSkye began selling software to manage online beverage procurement. Even so, he says, business is slow: "The biggest hurdle going forward will be getting people to change their behavior."

Most of the time, making such changes will simply take sheer dogged persistence. Gilbert Papazian II, CEO of South San Francisco (Calif.) produce distributor Lucky Strike Farms, was pitched by more than 30 dot-com produce marketplaces. At first, he threw them all out because they didn't know his industry. But Rob Bonavito, CEO of iTradeNetwork, kept coming back, begging Papazian to teach him the business. Papazian kept making suggestions until the dot-com finally developed a useful online system for produce buyers and sellers to streamline their transactions, reducing paper and fax transactions. Says Papazian: "Once I started using the system, it was great."

Still, some companies and industries simply don't want to adapt, often out of fear they will lose control of their business. The music industry, for instance, is waging war against everyone from file-sharing purveyors such as Napster and Kazaa to PC makers Apple and Gateway, which build machines that can download music and copy compact discs. Indeed, Hollywood's success in persuading the courts to clamp down on new technologies points up yet another brake on technology: law. In past tech revolutions, regulation often lags both technology and organizational change. In the PC era, it took the courts years to decide that software, and even the code embedded in chips, should be protected by copyright laws. But as Andrew S. Grove, chairman of chipmaker Intel Corp. says, useful "technology always wins in the end."

That's more likely to happen in the Internet's case once companies realize the Web is a tool to improve business processes – not a business unto itself. Citigroup blew more than $1 billion between 1998 and 2000 on e-Citi, a separate division charged with making the company a leading Net player. But the services never gained traction. One reason: e-Citi customers couldn't use Citibank teller machines. Last fall, Citi folded e-Citi back into the mother ship. Since then, Citi's online customer base has shot up 80%, to 10 million.

The rewards of e-business – along with all its wrenching change and hard work – are considerable. Already, a group of economists polled by the Brookings Institution last year estimated that the Internet is adding one-fourth to one-half a percentage point to productivity in the U.S. alone. Even one-third of a point over the next decade would add roughly $1,500 a year to the average American's annual income by the year 2010, according to Brookings economist Robert E. Litan. And the studies Litan cites don't measure convenience, greater choice, time savings, and other benefits.

Such numbers also fail to measure the transformative changes sweeping across business. There's a risk in assuming that current measures of benefits tell the whole story. Says Paul Saffo, a director at Institute for the Future, a Silicon Valley research group: "Applying metrics on this is like putting road signs on sand dunes." Fact is, for all the uncertainty today, the Internet and the network business model already are the common sense of commerce – even if not all businesses yet choose or know how to apply them. "I think the Internet is like electricity," says Dell CEO Michael S. Dell. Maybe that notion isn't common sense quite yet. But if history is any guide, it will be one day.

CASE QUESTIONS

Question 1 According to Chris Freeman, emeritus professor at Britain's University of Sussex, the Internet requires a huge process of learning and cultural change and it will take a very long time before the economy wide effects of the Internet come through. You are required to critically discuss whether you agree or disagree with this statement.

Question 2 What do you believe will be the real imperative for e-business organizations for the next few years? For example, how can they adapt new technology to people and work, rather than forcing people to adapt to it? You may find it useful to look at the travel site Expedia.com, which was cited in the case study as an example of an organization that had adapted the Internet to people through its online alerts, which can find you via computer mobile phone or pager.

Question 3 With e-commerce accounting for less than 2 per cent of all trade, the Internet is still in its infancy. Given the rise, fall and projected rise of the Internet what do you believe is the future prospects of e-business? You may find it useful to assess the prospects of e-business in a country of your choice.

MINI CASE STUDY I
The Next Web, by T. Berners Lee, Business Week, 4 March 2002

1. Jane asks her agent for help

Jane is planning a vacation in Fiji, and – thanks to the Semantic Web – her computer will make all the necessary arrangements. Her travel agent, built entirely from software code, will explore the Web, gather all the relevant information about airline schedules, condominium prices, and the merits of the different beaches, and return with Jane's digital tickets in hand.

2. The agent explores the Semantic Web

The agent's first stop is a virtual library, where he learns the terms and definitions used by airlines, ships, real estate agents, and car-rental services. Each industry uses its own definitions, written in a language called XML. Once he knows the appropriate 'tags' he can find the info Jane needs.

3. Going to meet the airline rep

Armed with his semantic data, Jane's agent is now ready to negotiate with the software reps on various airline Web sites. In addition to learning about fares and flight schedules, he picks up tidbits about alternative travel modes, such as cruise ships.

4. The right place to stay

After boning up on the various travel alternatives, the agent heads back to the library to read up on the semantics that describe condo rentals. Then he zips off to the Web sites of real estate agents handling properties on Fiji, including resort chains and time-shares. Since Jane's request included the words 'house' and 'condo', he knows to ignore any hotel offerings that don't include kitchens.

5. Now to cut the options

What emerges are a dozen candidate flights and scores of lodging alternatives. These can be juggled to yield thousands of combinations. Jane doesn't have the patience or time to explore them all – but the agent does. In a wink, he ranks all the possibilities based on priorities, such as maximum time spent on the beach. He picks five alternatives to show Jane.

6. Jane makes the final decision

She prefers air travel to cruises, so the agent dives back onto the Web to close the deal. He confirms some reservations, cancels others and pays the software agent at United Airlines. He concludes the deal for a condo and reserves a car for Jane – without waiting for her to ask – knowing she usually rents sporty two-door cars.

CASE QUESTIONS

Question 1 What do you believe are the main advantages of the Semantic Web?

Question 2 Do you feel that people in your country would be happy to use a travel agent built entirely from software code?

For a start, people are used to paying for it

How do you make money on the Internet? In the late 1990s, this was the question on everybody's lips. The answers bandied about included "building communities", "ensuring stickiness", "B2C", "B2B" and many others. Buzzwords came and went, and eventually nearly everyone went bust. The problem was that advertising revenue was insufficient to keep most sites running, and there was no standard way to charge for things on the Internet. There still isn't. Getting people to type their credit-card details into a web page raises security concerns, and makes purchases of less than a few dollars impractical. A handful of sites selling books, CDs, flights and holidays look as though they will survive. But most news and content sites are losing money, and many are now trying to introduce subscription fees. Many more have folded. Why should things be any different on the mobile Internet?

This will cost you

Last, and most important, people know that using mobile phones costs money, and there is a mechanism for the network operator to charge them for that use. What is more, users seem prepared to pay a "mobility premium" to do things while on the move. Sending an e-mail or instant message over the Internet from a PC is essentially free; sending a text message from a phone costs an average of 10 cents, but users are prepared to pay because they regard it as good value, or because it makes their lives easier. And even when text messaging is more expensive, people still use it. In some places, sending a text message home while "roaming" in a foreign country can cost as much as euro 1 (92 cents). Such charges are currently under investigation by the EU's competition commission. But compared with the cost and hassle of buying a postcard and a stamp, this still seems reasonable enough to many people. In short, if you have a mobile phone, the network operator knows who you are, where you are, can direct you to the portal of its choice, and can charge you money. This is a very different world from that of the fixed Internet.

Mobile has some drawbacks, of course. Mobile devices have more limited screens and keyboards than PCs, and slower connections. Also, says Niklas Savander of Nokia, mobility makes people much more impatient. Researchers have found that a five-second delay to access something on an Internet-capable phone seems far longer to users than a five-second wait to call up a web page. "With the same response time, people rate mobile as slower," he says. "So we have a slower connection, but users want a faster response."

For me, here, now

But the combination of personalisation, location and a willingness to pay makes all kinds of new business models possible. Tomi Ahonen, head of 3G Business Consulting at Nokia, gives the example of someone waiting at a bus stop who pulls out his Internet-capable phone to find out when the next bus will arrive. The information sent to the phone can be personalised, reflecting the fact that the user's location is known, and perhaps his home address too; so bus routes that run from one to the other can appear at the top of the list, saving the user from having to scroll and click through lots of pages and menus. A very similar service, which allows users to find out when the next bus is due by sending a text message from a bus stop, is already available in Italy.

Would-be providers of mobile Internet services cannot simply set up their servers and wait for the money to roll in, however, because the network operators – who know who and where the users are, and control the billing system – hold all the cards. This has changed the balance of power between users, network operators and content providers. On the fixed Internet, the network access provider acts as a "dumb pipe" between the user's PC and, say, an online bookstore or travel agent. The access provider will not know how the connection has been used, and there is no question of claiming a commission. Mobile network operators, on the other hand, are in a far more powerful position. "Wireless is a smarter pipe," says Chris Matthiasson of BT Cellnet. This means that operators are much less likely to be disintermediated.

Furthermore, unlike Internet access providers, wireless operators charge by usage, either for every minute spent online, or for every byte downloaded. This means they make money on transporting data come what may, so it makes sense to offer users the widest choice of content possible to encourage them to run up transport charges. That is how i-mode works; the vast majority of DoCoMo's data revenues come from transport, not the sale of content (though the firm does take 9% on the sale of other providers' content). A typical i-mode user spends ¥2,000 (about $17) per month on data-transport fees, and only ¥400 on content subscriptions.

Operators therefore generally offer a selection of approved services through their own chosen portal, and also give subscribers the option of going elsewhere. This is what AOL does with its dial-up Internet service; it offers services such as instant messaging, chat-rooms and e-mail, as well as access to the web. But surveys show that most users still spend most of their time within what used to be AOL's walled garden. The best way for operators to keep users within their walled gardens, says Katrina Bond of Analysys, is to offer attractive services. The fact that operators know who and where their users are – and may be able to keep this information to themselves – can give their home-grown or approved services a valuable advantage.

CASE QUESTIONS

Question 1 What can mobile operators do to drive traffic? How important is the relationship between content providers and operators?

Question 2 Why are mobile phone users willing to pay a "mobility premium" to do things while on the move?

NOTE

The Advanced Research Projects Agency (ARPA) changed its name to Defense Advanced Research Projects Agency (DARPA) in 1971, then back to ARPA in 1993, and back to DARPA in 1996. We refer throughout to DARPA, the current name.

REFERENCES

Afuah, A. and C.L. Tucci (2001) *Internet Business Models and Strategic Text and Cases*, McGraw-Hill Irwin, New York.

Berners-Lee, T. (2002a) The next Web, *BusinessWeek*, 4 March.

———(2002b) What is the semantic web? *Businessweek online*, Special report, 4 March.

Briones, M.G. (1999) Web future will revolve around individual users, *Marketing News*, vol. 33, no. 9, p. 28.

Cairncross, F. (1998) *The Death of Distance, How the Communications Revolution will Change our Lives*, Orion Business Books, London.

Computer Economics (2001) Forces of change 2001 update: Ten trends that will impact the Internet over the next five years, www.computereconomics.com.

Deise, M., C. Nowikow, P. King and A. Wright (2000) *Executive's Guide to E-business From Tactics to Strategy*, PriceWaterhouseCoopers, Wiley, New York.

The Economist (2001) Upgrading the Internet, from *The Economist* print edition, March.

EIU and Booz Allen & Hamilton (1999) See www.bah.com/e-business.

Freeman, C. and F. Louca (2002). *As Time Goes by: from the Industrial Revolution to the Information Revolution*, Oxford University Press, Oxford.

Harris, C. (1999) Banking restructuring in Europe, *Financial Times Survey: World Economy & Finance*, 24 September, p. XVIII.

Hoque, F. (2000) *e-Enterprise Business Models, Architecture and Components*, Cambridge University Press, Cambridge.

Kahn, R. (1972) Communications Principles for Operating Systems. Internal BBN memorandum.

Kalakota, R and M. Robinson (2000) *e-business 2.0: A Roadmap to Success*, Addison-Wesley, Reading, MA.

Kelly, K. (1998) *New Rules for the New Economy: 10 Radical Strategies for a Connected World*, Penguin Group, New York.

King, P. and J. Clift (1999) Time to distinguish between e-business and e-commerce, *FT Guide to Digital Business*, Financial Times, Autumn, p. 7.

Kleinrock, L. (1964) *Communication Nets: Stochastic Message Flow and Delay*, McGraw-Hill, New York.

Kozinets, R.V. (1999) E-tribalized marketing? The strategic implications of virtual communities of consumption, *European Management Journal*, vol. 17, no. 3, pp. 252–264.

Modahl, M. (2000) *Now or Never: How Companies Must Change Today to Win the Battle for the Internet Customer*, Orion Business, London.

Porter, M.E. and V.E. Millar (1985) How information gives you competitive advantage, *Harvard Business Review*, vol. 63, no. 4, pp. 149–160.

PriceWaterhouseCoopers (2000) *Inside the Mind of the CEO, The 2000 Global CEO Survey*, World Economic Forum, Annual Meeting, Davos, Switzerland.

Rayport, J.F. and B.J. Jaworksi (2001) *e-commerce*, McGraw-Hill/Irwin, New York.

Rich, M.K. (2000) The direction of marketing relationships, *The Journal of Business & Industrial Marketing*, vol. 15, no. 2/3, pp. 170–191.

Roberts, L. (1967) Multiple Computer Networks and Intercomputer Communication, ACM Gatlinburg Conference.

Standage, T. (2001) The Internet, Untethered, Mobile Technology Report, *The Economist*, 11 October.

Timmers, P. (2000) *Electronic Commerce Strategies and Models for Business to Business Trading*, Wiley, Chichester.

Trocchia, P.J. and S. Janda (2000) A phenomenological investigation of Internet usage among older individuals, *Journal of Consumer Marketing*, vol. 17, no. 7, pp. 605–616.

CHAPTER 2

THE IMPACT OF THE INTERNET ON BUSINESS RELATIONSHIPS

LEARNING OUTCOMES

When you have read and worked through this chapter, you will be able to:

■ Appreciate the e-business strategy revolution concept
■ Outline the changing relationships between organizations and suppliers
■ Outline the changing relationships between organizations and their customers
■ Outline the changing relationships within organizations
■ Give practical examples to illustrate the impact of the Internet on business relationships

INTRODUCTION

The first part of this chapter uses Gary Hamel's 'strategy as revolution' *Harvard Business Review* article as a way to get readers to be open-minded, so that they can appreciate and obtain value from e-business. Relationships are the central theme of the discussion with emphasis on the changing nature of the following key relationships: organization and supplier; organization and customer; and intra-organization relationships. It also introduces themes that are explored in greater detail in later chapters; strategy (Chapter 4) organization (Chapter 6) and marketing (Chapter 7).

THE E-BUSINESS STRATEGY REVOLUTION

The Internet has had a profound impact on business relationships at the corporate, business and operational levels. Success will be dependent upon management being open-minded so as to understand and derive real value from the Internet. Commentators, practitioners, consultants and academics have used the term 'revolution' to describe what is happening in this digital age. Consequently, senior management are grasping for ideas to liberate corporate values and produce more revolutionary strategies. Although published in the *Harvard Business Review* in 1996, Gary Hamel's 'strategy as revolution' is apt for the digital economy. Hamel identified three kinds of companies: rule makers; rule takers; and industry revolutionaries. Rule makers refers to organizations that built the industry. Rule takers refers to organizations who pay 'homage' to the industry pioneers. Industry revolutionaries refers to organizations that are intent on overturning the industrial order. Hamel argues that never have companies been more hospitable to industry revolutionaries and more hostile to industry incumbents. According to Hamel, strategy is revolutionary; everything else is tactics. The following ten principles can help an organization to liberate its spirit and produce more revolutionary strategies.

■ *Principle 1.* Strategic planning is not strategic. Strategy-making processes still tend to be reductionist, using simply rules and heuristics. The future is expected to be more or less like the present. Hence, only a small percentage of the industry norms are challenged, resulting in the strategy making being largely extrapolative.

■ *Principle 2*. Strategy making must be subversive. An industry revolution will only take place if the creators of strategy cast off industrial conventions. When these beliefs are relaxed, then new opportunities will present themselves.

■ *Principle 3*. The bottleneck is at the top of the bottle. As the external environment becomes increasingly turbulent, too much experience becomes a handicap and in some extreme cases even dangerous.

■ *Principle 4*. Revolutionaries exist in every company. At the middle management layer there are often staff who are straining against the bit of industrial orthodoxy. If top management does not let revolutionaries challenge from within, they will eventually leave and challenge you in the marketplace.

■ *Principle 5*. Change is not the problem; engagement is. When senior managers talk about change, they are really taking actions to pay for their past mistakes. All too often, the term change is synonymous with restructuring or reorganization.

■ *Principle 6*. Strategy making must be democratic. The capacity for creative thought is distributed at all levels in an organization. Hence the strategy-making process should involve staff at all levels. In addition senior managers must not be allowed to drown out new voices.

■ *Principle 7*. Anyone can be a strategy activist. Everyone has the potential to become a strategy activist. Traditionally, front-line employees and middle managers are inclined to regard themselves more as victims than as activists. They have little belief in themselves to shape the future of their organizations.

■ *Principle 8*. Perspective is worth 50 IQ points. There are four tasks to perform if an organization is intent on creating industry revolution:
  ■ Identify the unshakeable beliefs that cut across the industry.
  ■ Search for external discontinuities that might create opportunities to rewrite the industry's rules.
  ■ Understand fully its core competencies.
  ■ Use the above to identify revolutionary ideas.

■ *Principle 9*. Top-down and bottom-up are not the alternatives. A deep diagonal slice approach to strategy making will achieve diversity of perspective and unity of purpose.

■ *Principle 10*. You cannot see the end from the beginning. Senior managers must not be scared of an open and creative strategy-making process. Too much of a hard sell from the top will result in the organization pursuing incremental improvements.

CHANGING RELATIONSHIPS

The increasing importance of internal and external relationships is a paradigm shift in modern businesses. Individual firms no longer compete solely as autonomous entities, but collaborate with outside organizations. Competition is now multidimensional, with firms competing on a variety of business relationships (Lambert and Cooper, 2000). The Internet phenomenon is changing business processes in three areas and the key relationships can be summarized as follows:

■ Relationships between organizations and their suppliers
■ Relationships between organizations and their customers
■ Relationships within the organization

RELATIONSHIPS BETWEEN ORGANIZATIONS AND THEIR SUPPLIERS

Profitability is a function of demand and supply, which differ widely depending on the industry structure. In some sectors a small amount of excess capacity can trigger price wars, e.g. the oil industry. The relationship between the organization and its suppliers is increasingly becoming an important aspect of business success. To remain in the chain, firms do not just have to demonstrate the physical value they add, but also add value through their ability to manage their own suppliers (MacDonald, 2000). Traditional logistic practices are 'slow to die' among vendors, carriers and shippers (Lancioni, Smith and Oliva, 2000). The face-to-face contact is no longer required between carriers and shippers, as rate negotiations can be carried out electronically and at a lower cost.

Organizations that are able to manage the flow of goods, information and funds with suppliers will flourish and prosper. Conditions under which a supply group can be powerful include:

- Dominance by a few suppliers
- Non-availability of substitute products
- High differentiation by the supplier
- High switching costs for the buyer
- Threat of forward integration of suppliers

Supply chains are a network of organizations that are involved through upstream and downstream linkages in the different processes and activities that enhance value in the products/services produces for the customer (Christopher, 1992). Problems are created when each party in the supply chain attempts to reduce their own costs and transfer costs in the supply chain. Unfortunately, transferring costs either upstream or downstream is ultimately borne in the price paid by the end user. Emphasis should be placed on optimizing the entire supply chain in terms of value and minimizing it in terms of cost. Therefore, in competitive markets, it is imperative that each party in the supply chain view themself as a part of the whole. In fact, much of the reluctance to interface with other firms in the supply chain is breaking down (Lancioni, Smith and Oliva, 2000). Organizations are now sharing production-planning schedules with competitors. This improvement in attitude is due to a variety of factors.

Web technology presents the opportunity for suppliers to be linked online with substantial benefits accruing due to the seamless interaction of salient business processes. **Universal Product Codes (UPC), electronic data interchange (EDI)** and quick response (QR) were used during the 1990s in retailing. Retailers scanned UPC and orders were transmitted, via computer through EDI, resulting in QR inventory systems designed to provide product availability, while at the same minimizing cash tied up in inventory. Prior to the Internet, EDI systems were proprietary, being owned and operated by a retailer, a vendor or a third-party provider known as a **value added network (VAN)**. These systems tended to be rather expensive to develop and required a great deal of collaboration by all parties involved. In the third millennium, EDI data is being transmitted over the Internet through extranets. An extranet is a collaborative network that makes use of Internet technology to link the firm with their suppliers and customers. Extranets, unlike the Internet, are private and secure in that only certain parties can access them. Within the firm it is also possible to use intranets, which are secure communications systems that enable employees within a firm to communicate electronically. According

Key Term...

Universal Product Codes (UPC)
Universal product codes were the first bar code widely adopted and can be found on items purchased from retail organizations such as supermarkets

Key Term...

Electronic data interchange (EDI)
The electronic exchange of business documents between organizations in a standard format

Key Term...

Value added network (VAN)
Value added network is a private network provider that is used by a company to facilitate EDI

ILLUSTRATIVE EXAMPLE 1
Extracted from: Less Touch, More Value, by Andrea Williamson, Intel Corporation, Ascet, Vol. 4, 15 May 2002
Copyright with permission of Montgomery Research Inc., 300 Montgomery Street, Suite 1135, San Francisco, CA 94104. Tel. +1 415 397 2400;
www.mriresearch.com

Increasing the direct connections between business systems facilitates the move to requiring less touch in the supply chain and extracting more value out of the supply chain.

As more value is extracted from the supply chain, business systems become more automated, requiring less human intervention. What was once a person-to-person process is evolving into a machine-to-machine process. As internal systems become more automated and business processes between trading partners become more standardized, there will be fewer steps within the process, thus less "touch" will occur. Less touch means more value for the entire supply chain because all trading partners realize the efficiency and productivity gains possible in true electronic business systems. Intel Corporation is moving rapidly towards a more automated machine to machine, or business-to-business integration (B2Bi), environment.

CONNECTING POINTS

At Intel, there are more than 200 different touch-points occurring during business with customers and suppliers. A touch-point occurs when a person or separate system needs to get involved in making the business process complete. Each touch-point, therefore, has the potential to become an automated process, if the systems supporting the business process can start to communicate dynamically and automatically. For example, an order is placed using a machine-to-machine (M2M) solution. If that product is in constraint mode, the transaction process data falls out of the system and goes into a spreadsheet. Thus, the M2M solution failed due to business process. Somebody then needs to walk that spreadsheet through the system, which will involve more touch-points.

There are also judgment points involved in the course of doing business, which lead to high-touch interactions. Judgment points occur when a human being needs to make a judgment call before a transaction can continue, especially with sensitive materials and information. For example, Intel has a complex electronic information management system used to send confidential and sensitive documents to its customers. Many documents need an approval by a field sales person, or marketing manager, before the document can be sent to the customer.

There are plenty of internal processes that can hinder a company's ability to respond to itself, let alone respond to its trading partners in a timely manner. For instance, Intel has a goal to reduce by half the time it takes for a demand signal, or order process, to get through from a customer request to sending that request to a supplier. It currently takes hundreds of planners to work this manual process. Imagine the time to market and productivity savings that could be realized with internal automated processes in place.

SUPPLY CHAIN VALUE

These are all good reasons why Intel is finding ways to extract more value out of the supply chain by implementing operational efficiency improvements and increasing the speed of data and information across its e-business systems. The corporation is getting more value out of the supply chain by reducing time and costs in every e-business program. In addition, by sharing real-time data with customers and suppliers, and promoting and enabling standards, e-business value is shifting from competing businesses to competing supply chains.

Intel's goal is to double the e-business productivity gains realized over the past two years. They will achieve this through focusing on several things. One, by reducing internal planning touch points the corporation will run more efficiently. Two, with continued system integration, more trading partners can benefit from e-business programs. Three, cutting out the inefficiencies in the system means that Intel and its customers can spend more time on value-added activities. Employees have more job satisfaction when they are in more rewarding analytical (instead of task-oriented) jobs. The corporation experiences lower undesired turnover due to the automation of undesirable tasks.

to Cooke (1998), **collaboration, planning, forecasting and replenishment (CPFR)** takes EDI to a higher level. CPFR is basically an inventory management system for the sharing of information among channel members and is popular in the grocery and drug industries. The retailer sends requests to a manufacturer, who uses the data to construct a computer-generated replenishment forecast. This shared approach to replenishment provides benefits to both parties.

The whole supply chain is changing in terms of better information and the ability to aggregate scale. E-business has caused **Enterprise Resource Planning (ERP)** system suppliers to join forces with smaller software houses to produce their own web-enabling software. E-business is revolutionizing the way supply chains are configured and managed and, as a result, many chains are becoming virtual (Cahill, 2000). Deise, Nowikow, King and Wright (2000) state that corporate information systems are extending upstream to suppliers and downstream to customers' information systems through the use of e-supply chain. The term 'Buy-side' collaboration (suppliers, contract manufacturers, logistics providers) and 'Sell-side' collaboration (customers, channel partners, logistics providers) are used to distinguish the focus of the collaboration. Members of an e-supply chain can use technology collaboratively to improve key B2B processes in terms of speed, agility, real-time control or customer satisfaction. The e-supply chain is the communications and operations backbone of the enlarged supply network. E-business enables extended supply chains beyond an organization's boundaries, so virtual supply chains force greater co-operation between companies. These looser affiliations of companies, organized as a supply network enhance value added for all members and the benefits to be derived.

The growth of the Internet has presented significant opportunities for service improvement and cost reduction (Lancioni, Smith and Oliva, 2000) and these are summarized in Table 2.1.

Measuring supply chain performance

The Internet has made purchasing and selling online easier with product information now available at the click of a mouse. The growth of e-business has resulted in an increase in online purchasing traffic, as well as concerns regarding the logistics community's ability to meet **online fulfilment** needs. As a result, logistics providers have begun to explore ways to work more efficiently through established partnerships, better serving the needs of the market. It was eagerly anticipated that the Internet would transform logistics by making it

Key Term...

Collaboration, planning, forecasting and replenishment (CPFR)
A business model that takes a holistic approach to supply chain management

Key Term...

Enterprise Resource Planning
A term used for a broad range of activities supported by multi-module application software that assists organizations to manage salient business processes

Key Term...

Online fulfilment
Relates to the ability to promptly deliver what the online customer has requested

Opportunities

Online vendor catalogues from which buyers can find, select and order items directly from suppliers without human contact

The ability to:
   track shipments using a wide variety of modes
   contact vendors or buyers regarding customer service problems from late deliveries, stockouts
   reserve space in public warehouses for anticipated deliveries to market locations
   schedule outbound shipments from private and public distribution cetntres on a 24-hour basis
   provide 7-day/24-hour worldwide customer service
   receive orders from international customers
   check the status of orders placed by vendors
   place bids on projects issued by government and industry buyers
   notify vendors of changes in configuration of products that are produced to order
   pay invoices electronically and to check outstanding debit balances
   track equipment locations including rail cars, trucks and material handling equipment
   directly communicate with vendors, customers, etc. regarding supply issues on a 7-day/24-hour basis via email
   schedule more pick-ups and deliveries
   be more responsive to customer service problems
   reduce service costs and response times

(Source: Lancioni, Smith and Oliva, 2000)

Table 2.1 Opportunities provided by the Internet for supply chains

so much easier to match up shippers' loads with carriers' trucks. No longer would carriers have to take back empty trucks to their point of origin, since Internet technology would enable true just-in-time delivery. However, some commentators felt that e-commerce failed to live up to its hype. Nevertheless, in a study by the Logistics Research Group at Ohio State University in the USA, e-business has been cited as one of the most important factors that would influence the growth of logistics during the next decade (Frontline Solutions, 2001). Table 2.2 shows how the factors affect logistics growth.

Managers who are well versed in **supply chain management** are wrestling with the issue of performance because a generally accepted framework does not exist (Brewer and Speh, 2000). In an attempt to assist managers, Brewer and Speh introduced a modified version of the balanced scorecard. This new approach offers several primary benefits. First, it highlights the interfunctional and interfirm nature of supply chains and recognizes the need to ascertain the extent to which firms effectively work together and the extent to which functions are co-ordinated and integrated. Second, Brewer and Speh's framework will increase the chance that a balanced management approach is indeed practised within firms and among supply chain partners. The measures suggested may stimulate managers to create appropriate measures. Finally, the novel approach should help employees and managers focus attention on achieving goals that are superior to traditional measures.

Supply-chain financial metrics tend to focus on lower costs, higher margins, enhanced cash flow, higher revenue growth, higher rate of return on assets (Cooper and Ellram, 1993; Novack and Simco, 1991; Scott and Westbrook, 1991). The findings of a study by Pittiglio and McGrath (1997) to validate the relationship between supply chain integration and business

Key Term...

Supply chain management (SCM)
In its simplest form SCM relates to the management of the product, information and finances flows within an organization

Factors	
E-business/e-commerce	34%
SCM integration	26%
International	10%
Information technology	6%
Customer value	5%
All others	19%
Total	100%
(Source: Frontline Solutions, 2001)	

Table 2.2 Factors of logistics growth

success revealed that best-practice supply chain management companies have a 45 per cent total supply-chain cost advantage over their supply-chain competitors.

According to Kaplan and Norton (1996), traditional performance measures tell the story of past events. Strategy plays an important role in the choice of performance measures and the **balanced scorecard** created by Kaplan and Norton suggests that a balanced performance measurement system consists of four distinct areas; financial, customer, internal business process perspective and innovation and learning perspective. As a structure, the balanced scorecard methodology breaks the organizational goals down into vision, strategies, tactics and metrics. This is achieved by reviewing the corporate vision and strategy to ensure that they capture the leadership's true intent. Kaplan and Norton's notion of traditional performance is that it tends to be a lag rather than a lead indicator. Financial measures alone are inadequate for guiding and evaluating the journey that information age companies must make. The financial perspective is still important and can be used to check and balance. It must be borne in mind that the firm still has to ensure that the strategy formulation, implementation and execution are indeed contributing to the bottom line. The customer perspective should be viewed from that of the customer and not from that of the firm. The measures should capture customer opinion and should be able to affect the future. Measures used include: customer satisfaction; customer retention; new customer acquisition; product/service quality; response time; flexibility; and cost. In this section, managers must identify the internal business processes that are crucial to their organization. This commences with customer need and passes through the innovation phase of design and develop and then the operations phase of make, market and service. By looking at processes beyond operations, this enables the firm to understand long-term prospects. The learning and growth perspective enables managers to identify the organizational infrastructure that would best fit strategic goals. While the previous perspectives help the manager identify where the organization stands now and where it has to be in the future in order to be successful, this fourth perspective informs management how to get there.

The supply chain performance metrics advocated by Brewer and Speh (2000) are provided in Table 2.3. They show how the balanced scorecard could be used to enhance supply chain management.

ILLUSTRATIVE EXAMPLE II

Logistics.com named to Internetweek magazine's "Internetweek 100" for second consecutive year, by Kerry Weiss-Pena and Casy Jones, logistics.com, 18 June 2001

LOGISTICS.COM ONLY E-LOGISTICS COMPANY SELECTED

BURLINGTON, Mass. (June 18, 2001) – Logistics.com, Inc., the leader in transportation procurement and management technology, today announced that it has been named to *InternetWeek* magazine's "InternetWeek 100," for the second consecutive year. Logistics.com was the only e-logistics company to be recognized. Other companies named to the list include AT&T, Cisco Systems, Inc. and IBM; logistics industry powerhouses, such as CSX Corporation, Danzas/AEI Inc. and Union Pacific Corporation; and Logistics.com customers Airborne, Inc., Roadway Express, Inc., and Yellow Corporation.

"It's an honor to be selected to the prestigious InternetWeek 100 list for the second consecutive year and to be recognized along with other industry leaders as a preeminent e-business," said Kel Kelly, chief marketing officer, Logistics.com. "The e-Logistics industry has matured enormously since the last InternetWeek 100 was unveiled one year ago, and we are proud of the leadership position that we have established."

Logistics.com was selected for the InternetWeek 100 for its success in leveraging Internet technologies to deliver results and achieve tangible business benefits. "As e-business dollars remain tight amid the current economic malaise, InternetWeek 100 companies aren't necessarily the freest spenders or the most daring technology pioneers. However, all InternetWeek 100 e-businesses can point to tangible bottom-line results," according to *InternetWeek* Editor-in-Chief, Robert Preston. InternetWeek 100 is the premier ranking of the 100 most successful e-businesses as determined by *InternetWeek*'s extensive research. Based on rigorous, performance-oriented metrics and the percentage of total points tallied in the survey, the list identifies the top commercial web innovators in 10 major industry sectors: general manufacturing, chemicals and pharmaceuticals, consumer products, financial services, high technology, retail & distribution, media & services, transportation, travel & hospitality and Internet companies. Logistics.com was chosen in the Internet Companies category.

RELATIONSHIPS BETWEEN ORGANIZATIONS AND THEIR CUSTOMERS

E-businesses should understand the importance of identifying, categorizing, understanding, meeting and serving the customer. This approach places great emphasis on information gathering and marketing processes. However, to be truly effective, customer orientation must become the driving force of all existing and planned e-business activities.

Typical prime areas for customer orientation in e-businesses include:

- *Strategy.* Customer orientation requires that customer satisfaction be built into all e-business strategies.

Customer perspective	
Goals	**Measures**
Customer view of product/service	Number of customer contacts
Customer view of timeliness	Relative customer order response time
Customer view of flexibility	Customer perception of flexible response
Customer value	Customer value ratio
Internal business perspective	
Waste reduction	Supply-chain cost of ownership
Time compression	Supply-chain cycle efficiency
Flexible response	Number of choices/average response time
Unit-cost reduction	Percentage of supply chain target costs achieved
Financial perspective	
Profit margin	Profit margin by supply chain partner
Cash flow	Cash to cash cycle
Revenue growth	Customer growth and profitability
Return on assets	Return on supply-chain assets
Innovation and learning perspective	
Product/process innovation	Product finalization point
Partnership management	Product-category commitment ratio
Information flows	Number of shared data sets/total data sets
Threats and substitutes	Performance trajectories of competing technologies

Table 2.3 The supply chain metrics advocated by Brewer and Speh (2000)

- ■ *Competition.* Because of the increasing rate of change in business, management needs to be aware of how the competition, both current and emergent, meeting customer needs in order to differentiate and excel.
- ■ *Image.* Customer focus can have a profound influence on the company image. Everything from the company logo to website layout and design needs to be tailored to specific customer needs and expectations.
- ■ *Quality.* Emphasis should be placed on the interaction with customers and should prevail throughout the value chain.
- ■ *Culture.* The attitudes and opinions of all employees are important to customer orientation. Some e-business firms place importance in creating a unique organizational culture among staff, irrespective of whether employees interact with customers. Staff working in e-businesses are encouraged to be aware of the importance of customer value.

The marketing process basically involves understanding and segmenting the market, establishing a market position, analysing customer needs and preferences, producing a marketing plan and evaluating inputs with outputs. In the early period of the Internet the most visible aspect of this process was brand building. This took the form of marketing promotion in the form of advertising communications, public relations, information dissemination and customer 'awakening'. Unfortunately, it has become evident that true customer orientation requires a much deeper organizational starting point. Organizations need to co-ordinate business processes around the customer and to develop systematic ways of adopting, monitoring and improving online customer relationship-building and purchasing behaviours.

Relationship marketing

Some organizations that have embraced the Internet have placed emphasis on relationships and the resulting customization of product/services to meet specific needs of individual customers. This is dramatically altering marketing processes within all firms that have an e-business operation. Emphasis has now switched from mass production to individualized production. So, mass marketing has now given way to mass customization as firms attempt to make almost instant changes in the production process to individualize output in quantities as small as one. These changes, coupled with the emphasis on relationships, have endorsed the topic of **relationship marketing**. The drive towards mass customization will further drive relationship marketing with its associated demands for greater understanding of each customer within the seller's marketing umbrella. This additional emphasis will spur marketers and consultants to find new and better ways of gaining customer information and keeping it current as never before (Zieger, 1999).

The traditional mechanical approaches to information acquisition no longer apply in e-business, as new skill sets are required to understand the basic implementation of a concept with a subsequent measurement of results while controlling for extraneous variables. Transaction marketing permitted the measurement of defined activities that were readily apparent and relatively easy to measure. The movement to relationship marketing encompasses an entirely new set of concerns that are not as easily identified or measured. Firms can proceed by simply making their databases more rigorous, making their websites more user friendly and securing ever more expensive technology for tracking and measuring customer responses. In addition, organizations must make sure that they do not break any laws about what a company can have in its databases. Marketing now requires the expertise of other functions to effectively embrace cross-functional processes, which ultimately enhance customer relationships. It must be borne in mind that simply following the holy grail of greater understanding of customers and offering mechanical solutions for gaining that understanding will not lead to effective relationship marketing.

The most significant effect of e-business is to cut the cost of interaction, i.e. the searching, co-ordinating, and monitoring that people and companies need to do when they trade. This can be a significant activity in developed economies. E-business creates an ability to come up with better ideas faster and increases the velocity associated with dynamic industry change.

Recent research has revealed a gap between the horizontal and vertical support for relationship marketing among managers and the actual behaviours that are necessary to effectively implement changes (Rich and Smith, 2000). Relationships tend to be approached unsystematically and lack the level of financial investment to make them succeed. Organizations tend only to go for incremental infrastructure changes where they are required for the effective implementation of significant alterations to business processes (Morris, Brunyee and Page 1998). Database integration within a firm is frequently the first step in creating a usable source of customer information, although there is little current evidence that everyone is effectively performing such a function (Krol, 1999). Success depends upon achieving

Key Term...

Relationship marketing
A philosophy that seeks to ensure a favourable balance among the organization, quality and customer service

a balance between the sales effort and the other functional areas within the firm. Having strong relationships among functions delivers a sense of relationship between all parties involved, both internally and externally. Interestingly, the reward system has been found to impede team effort. Marshall (1996) asserts that until such time as an organization embraces a reward system for team effort, relationship development with customers will rarely be maximized.

Increasing numbers of companies are embracing and integrating electronic communications into their operations in an effort to strengthen their databases and enhance relationships. E-business allows a greater degree of intimacy with customer bases, but many companies are finding it difficult to deal with the crucial activity of two-way customer interaction (Donath, 1998). For example, prospects respond to website stimuli, but their requests for information are frequently ignored or at best not treated as a priority communication by the selling firm. Griffiths (1999) revealed in his UK study that companies fail to respond to nearly half of all requests for information received via the Internet. Another problem is that firms establish sound methodologies for gathering detailed information about prospects and customers in building databases but fail to exploit the data for building relationships. As Cahill (1998) noted, people tend to have relationships with people not solely with products. In addition, once the client database has been built, there is then the issue of keeping it up to date and maintaining quality (Dyer, 1999). Gummesson (1999) suggests that people's attitudes about technology must change.

In his book *Total Relationship Marketing*, Gummesson (1999) postulates that marketing needs rethinking from the traditional 4Ps to 30Rs (relationships). Gummesson categorizes the relationships into market and non-market:

Market relationships
- *Classic market relationships* – these include the supplier–customer dyad, the triad of supplier–customer–competitor relationships and the physical distribution network.
- *Special market relationships* – these include specific aspects of the classical relationships, such as the interaction in the service encounter or the customer as an affiliate of a loyalty programme.

Non-market relationships
- Mega relationships – exist above the market relationships. They provide the foundation for market relationships and concern society and the economy.
- Nano relationships – exist below the market relationships and concentrate on those relationships inside an organization. These include:
  - Market mechanism are brought inside the company.
  - Internal customer relationship.
  - Quality providing a relationship between operations management and marketing.
  - Internal marketing: relationships with the employee market.
  - The two-dimensional matrix relationship.
  - The relationship to external providers of marketing services.
  - The owner and financier relationship.

Avlonitis and Karayanni (2000) remain positive about the Internet, stating that the Internet should be used as a facilitator of market-oriented strategies, enabling interactive marketing and customized products for B2B transactions.

Key Term...

Customization

Customization allows website visitors to specify their own perferences

Key Term...

Personalization

Personalization does not rely on explicit user instructions, but uses artificial intelligence to identify patterns in customers' choices or demographics and to extrapolate projections from them

Customization versus personalization

The importance of **customization** has already been discussed in the previous section on relationship marketing. This section now considers the benefits of **personalization**. The difference between customization and personalization is that the former lets a website visitor specify his or her own preferences. For example, the MyYahoo feature at Yahoo.com allows users to instruct the website to display automatically the weather forecast for a specific location, to track their favourite shares, or to give prominence on the home page to specific sports news. Conversely, personalization does not rely on explicit user instructions. Artificial intelligence is utilized to find patterns in customers' choices or demographics and to extrapolate projections from them. One of the most popular examples is Amazon.com's personalized book and music recommendations.

It was anticipated that cash-rich time-poor Internet users would welcome organizations buying sophisticated software to make personalized pitches to them. However, website customers appear to be ambivalent about the benefits (Nunes and Kamil, 2001). According to Nunes and Kamil (2001), despite e-commerce, companies face a constant question: how much should they personalize their sites? After performing a survey of more than 300 online consumers, Nunes and Kamil found that, rather than have some state-of-the-art technology figure out their interests and surprise and delight them with products and services they would undoubtedly love, most consumers would prefer to customize website interactions for themselves.

It would appear that artificial-intelligence-based personalization of websites is not currently delivering on its promise and that user-performed customization has been under-rated by website architects and under-used as a way to provide value to customers. Therefore, the best strategy is not mutually exclusive and a combination of both personalization and customization may be more palatable to customers. For example, imagine a DVD seller asking after a purchase, 'Should we add this title to our growing knowledge of your interests to guide our future recommendations?' If the customer were offered the opportunity to decline future prompts, a customer might say 'no' and spare themselves further suggestions. Similarly, a website with personalization capabilities, which include the ability to identify patterns in the user's click-stream, might suggest a customization: 'We notice you frequently go from this home page to check the local forecast for Barbados. Would you like to include that information on this home page?'

Are customer relations really important?

Traditionally, it has been hypothesized that market-oriented firms seem to enjoy a higher level of business performance (Chang and Chen, 1998; Jaworski and Kohli, 1993; Ruekert, 1992), which may produce superior quality, enhanced productivity and stronger customer loyalty (Zeithaml, Parasuraman and Berry 1990). However, there is still some equivocality over the market orientation–performance relationship (Greenley 1995a; Caruana, Pitt and Berthon, 1998). Matters are not helped by a confusion of terminology (Gray, Matear, Boshoff and Matheson, 1998; Slater and Narver, 1998). For example, the terms marketing orientation (business philosophy) and market orientation (implementation of that philosophy), and customer-led (satisfying customer expressed needs) and market-oriented (satisfying customer latent needs) illustrate the need for precision. As a consequence of this confusion, existing research has not yet been able to construct a valid and reliable measure of market orientation (Kumar, Subramanian and Yauger, 1998; Gray, Matear, Boshoff and Matheson, 1998). In their conclusion Kumar, Subramanian and Yauger (1998) suggest that researchers may benefit by viewing market orientation as a configurational concept and then ascertaining how the differences in forms of market orientation affect performance.

Gray, Matear, Boshoff and Matheson (1998), citing Greenley (1995b), conclude that there may be different modes of market orientation, whereby different combinations of customers and competitor orientation, interfunctional co-ordination, responsiveness and profit emphasis levels may produce similar benefits.

Interestingly, in a strategic marketing planning–performance study Phillips, Davies and Moutinho (2001) concluded that the important issue is not whether strategic marketing planning affects performance, but rather what marketing capabilities are required to enhance performance. Therefore, in the digital age a key activity is to identify the essential e-marketing capabilities by evaluating and enhancing skills and competencies at the individual, group and organization levels.

Customer relationship management

According to Seybold (1998), on average US companies lose half of their customers within a five-year period and it can be five times as expensive to acquire a new customer as it is to retain existing customers (Reichheld, 1996). In addition, loyal customers are frequently willing to pay a higher price and be less price sensitive. So, customer loyalty can be employed as a good way of enhancing organizational profitability. Thus in today's e-business environment the ability to capture and maintain loyal customers is as important as sales revenues.

The Internet has rewritten the rules of engagement, but it has not meant that enhancing customer loyalty has led to more and increasingly profitable customers (Zingle, 2000). Zingle analyses some of the old rules of Customer Relationship Management (CRM) and presents a new view of redefining and building loyalty for the Internet age. The industrial model of CRM was a one-way command model and control conditions prevailed. The overall aim was to keep customers satisfied or 'happy' by seeking out customers and controlling the sales channels, products and services and balancing the conditions and mechanics of trade. The typical stages in a customer relationship are:

- Fulfilment – the company has what I want.
- Value – the price meets my expectations.
- Convenience – the product is easy to get.
- Trust – I am reasonably confident the product is reliable.

If a company is able to achieve the above four needs of a customer, the result is satisfaction.

According to Zingle, in an Internet-era world customer satisfaction is merely the beginning. Customer satisfaction is the price of entry. In an Internet-era world the stages change to:

- Satisfaction – my basic needs are met.
- Bonding – the company is acting in my best interests.
- Personalization – the company understands.
- Empowerment – the relationship is on my terms and under my control.
- Customer loyalty – has the company built up a reservoir of good will and am I deriving high value from the relationship?

According to Stone (2001), significant benefits can be achieved by e-CRM and he cites the example of IBM, which increased sales via the Web from $3 billion in 1998 to $23 billion in

1.	Frequent updates. Keep web pages up to date
2.	Attractive home page: Design home page that is attractive to users
3.	But do not overdo it: Too many graphics and sounds that take too long to load will scare e-customers away
4.	Easy customer contact: Make it easy for customers to contact you and respond in a timely fashion
5.	Provide a good response: Answer customer questions
6.	Anticipate questions: Use Frequently Asked Questions, or FAQ, as a menu choice
7.	Easy order, easy pay: Your e-commerce website should have an order form that is easy to use and has a secure pay system
8.	Be informative: Customers today are looking for solutions to problems, so tell them how your products and services provide those answers
9.	The electronic catalogue: As many as 90% of car buyers preshop for vehicles on the Net
10.	Follow up: Thank customers and verify that everything is to their satisfaction, but do so without irritating them

(Source: Bressler, 2001)

Table 2.4 Ten tips for keeping your customers from clicking away to the competition

2000. IBM also saw an increase from 14 million service transactions in 1998 via the Web to 99 million transactions in 2000. However, Bressler (2001) argues that sales are not enough, as smart marketers have long known the value of long-term customer relationships, and provides 10 tips for keeping your customers from clicking away to the competition (see Table 2.4).

Accenture (2000) surveyed more than 500 executives across six industries to understand what CRM capabilities would have the most impact and how they contributed to the bottom line. Their results revealed that CRM performance accounts for anywhere from 28 to more than 60 per cent of the variance in companies' return on sales (Ros) (see Table 2.5). In a study of the communications industry, Accenture reported that by improving performance in high-impact CRM capabilities, a typical communications company can add tens of millions and even hundreds of millions of pounds to the bottom line. Companies that are not investing in enhancing CRM capabilities are leaving profits on the table. Accenture has grouped marketing, sales and service capabilities into five areas on which a company needs

Industry	Return on sales (%)
Retail	28
Forest products	44
Pharmaceutical	47
Communications	50
Chemicals	52
Electronics & high tech	64
(Source: Acenture, 2000)	

Table 2.5 The variations in return on sales across six industries

Enhancing capabilities	$ m
Customer insight	**25**
Turning customer information into insight	12
Customer retention and acquisition	5.5
Measuring profitability	4.5
Segmentation	2.5
Customer offers	**19**
Strong value propositions	9.0
Managing products and service mix	5.0
New products and services	3.5
Brand management	1.5
Customer interactions	**42**
Customer service	13.0
Sales planning	7.5
Key account management	6.0
Advertising	6.5
Promotion	6.0
Channel management	3.0
High-performing organizations	**40**
Motivating and rewarding people	13.0
Attracting and retaining people	10.0
Building selling and service skills	9.5
Ability to change the organization	5.0
Building service culture	2.0
Enterprise integration	**17**
Partner and alliance management	9.0
E-CRM	8.0
(Source: Accenture, 2000)	

Table 2.6 Enhanced capabilities; improving capabilities from average to high in each area can improve ROS for a $1bn company by the amount indicated

to focus. Adopting a multiplier approach, Accenture has calculated the impacts on ROS on moving from average to high (see Table 2.6).

In his book *Loyalty Rules!*, Reichheld (2001) convincingly demonstrates that the more volatility the economy serves up, the more vital is the role loyalty plays in building effective, long-term, profitable relationships. Rigby, Reichheld and Schefter (2002) assert that successful CRM depends more on strategy than on the amount spent on technology. They believe that the only way to make CRM work is by taking the time to calculate customer strategy and to align business practices before implementing technology. They refer to four pitfalls to avoid.

Peril 1: implementing CRM before creating a customer strategy

Many CRM products claim they will automate the delicate and sometimes mysterious process of repelling low-margin customers and luring high-margin ones. Many managers mistake CRM technology for a marketing strategy. That is, they allow the technology to drive their customer strategy, or retrofit a customer strategy to match the CRM technology they've just purchased. To make matters worse, they then delegate customer relationship management to their Chief Information Officers. If CRM is to work technology that affects customers must always be aligned with an overarching strategy.

Peril 2: rolling out CRM before changing your organization to match

If a company wants to enhance relationships with its more profitable customers, it needs to first revamp the key business processes that relate to customers, from customer service to order fulfilment. Merely having a strategy is not enough, a CRM rollout will succeed only after the organization and its processes such as job descriptions, performance measures, compensation systems and training programmes have been restructured in order to better meet customers' needs.

Unless companies adopt customer-centric philosophies, change their structures and processes, and alter their corporate cultures accordingly, before the CRM project, it is unlikely to get off the ground.

Peril 3: assuming that more CRM technology is better

Given the vast sums of money spent on CRM, it would appear that CRM has to be technology intensive. However, evidence suggests that this is not necessarily the case. Customer relationships can be managed in many ways, and the objectives of CRM can be fulfilled without huge investments in technology simply by, say, motivating employees to be more aware of customer needs. Merely relying on a technological solution, or assuming that a high-tech solution is better than a low-tech one, is a costly pitfall. In fact, companies with well-functioning CRM programs perform simple tasks such as sending out thank you letters to customers.

Peril 4: stalking, not wooing, customers

If an organization wishes to attract more profitable and loyal customers, it needs to determine the kinds of relationships that are required to be successful. Such relationships will vary across industries, across companies in an industry, and across customers in a company. Unfortunately, managers sometimes ignore these considerations while using CRM, with disastrous consequences. They can end up trying to build relationships with the wrong customers, or trying to build relationships with the right customers, albeit the wrong way.

Relationships need to be viewed from two dimensions and if the organization attempts to build relationships with disinterested customers, they may be perceived as a stalker, annoying potential customers and turning them into vociferous critics. Managers should contact customers based on their customer strategy, not the CRM program.

RELATIONSHIPS WITHIN THE ORGANIZATION

The organization itself is the final piece in the jigsaw. The structure and culture of the organization may need reshaping as the firm migrates from traditional to e-business. Internally within businesses the communication between different functional areas, marketing, finance, human resources and IT, can be enabled and changed quite significantly by e-business. The redesign and automation of support processes can lead to lower capital and process costs by bringing resources online and by thorough outsourcing respectively. The organization is the mediating link between the supplier and customer. For all links to be effective there must be integrated processes and systems within an e-business. It is pointless trying to integrate across organizational boundaries if there are ineffective internal processes and systems. E-business enables collaboration across organizational boundaries, but, as has been explained in the previous section, one of the key blockers is the identification of costs and benefits to each organization.

In the digital era, it has been acknowledged that the intangible assets of an e-business firm will be key to both enhancing shareholder value and growing at an accelerated pace. Consequently, all functions are seeking to be at the forefront of internal discussions about the creation of value through leverage knowledge. Extending the work of Day (1994) by applying it to e-businesses, it is proposed that organizations in the knowledge era can become more market oriented by identifying, building and enhancing internal capabilities. Interestingly, the concept of capabilities dates back to Selznick (1957) and Penrose (1959). Unfortunately, the lack of understanding of capabilities has meant that in practice firms produce lengthy lists of strengths and weaknesses.

Capabilities are complex bundles of skills and accumulated knowledge, exercised through organizational processes that permit firms to co-ordinate activities and make use of their assets (Day, 1994). Capabilities and organizational processes (see Figure 2.1) are closely interweaved, due to the fact that it is the capability that enables the activities in a business process to be carried out. A key driver of performance and growth of today's firms resides in the capability of the organization, which in turn depends on the capability of its functions. The competitive marketplace brings a high demand and premium for talent, so people are placing a great deal of value on working in an environment where their capabilities can be developed.

Saint-Onge (2000) proposes a knowledge capital model, which reinforces the difference between organizations competing in the industrial and digital ages. In the former age physical assets played a prominent role in value creation. In the digital age, intangible assets represent the most important source of value creation. Saint-Onge's model provides a new perspective with which to create a knowledge-intensive enterprise. Managing the knowledge capital of the firm involves systematically developing, maintaining, leveraging and renewing its intangible assets. Intangible assets can be categorized into three elements: human capital, customer capital and structural capital.

	Individual Capability	Organizational Capability	Knowledge Architecture	Strategic Capabilities Unit
Domain				
Purpose				
Roles				

Figure 2.1 Strategic capabilities: a matrix for defining a new mandate and structure (*Source: Saint-Onge, 2000*)

Human capital can be defined as the capabilities of employees in an organization that are required to provide solutions to customers' needs. Individual capabilities are composed of attributes, competencies and mindsets.

Customer capital can be defined as the sum of the customer relationships with emphasis on the depth (penetration), width (coverage), length (durability) and profitability of the organization's relationship.

Structural capital can be defined as the organizational capabilities (strategies, structures, processes and culture) necessary to meet market requirements. It is anticipated that these capabilities can be developed into core competencies of the organization.

This chapter has illustrated the remarkable augmentation of the Internet. A salient issue is the issue of determining the appropriateness of traditional organizational dimensions when implementing a new e-business model. From a commercial perspective organizations must internally redesign, recalibrate and even restructure key organizational dimensions. Organizations operating in the new economy must align themselves internally with the demands that the dynamic environment imposes on strategic behaviour. A good example of this is that, despite making a significant investment in their e-business strategies and IT, some managers remain unclear about how to adapt their organization. The Internet creates opportunities for new forms of arranging work, such as collapsing boundaries with suppliers, with customers and within the organization, but in a competitive environment it is imperative for management to identify the key attributes and processes required for competitive advantage. However, there is still a paucity of systematic studies of the e-phenomenon and even fewer that explore the role that structural and process variables play in the design of e-commerce organizations (Geisler, 2001).

SUMMARY

Conceptually, some industries appear ideally suited to e-business because of their intangible nature and information nature. However, e-business is a complex fusion of strategic planning processes, enterprise applications and organizational structure, which if incorrectly aligned can destroy shareholder value. E-business mandates rethinking and repositioning and changes the nature of the communication and interaction between almost all parties involved in the value chain. Traditional strategy formulation is no longer apt for the digital age. Hamel's (1996) strategy revolution appears to be a good starting point, as it forces the individual to be open-minded about the Internet.

This chapter takes the view that performance and ultimate success of an e-business is dependent upon deep relationships. These relationships can be summarized into three: relationships with suppliers; relationships within the firm; and relationships with customers.

Relationships between organizations and their suppliers

E-business enables extended supply chains beyond an organization's boundaries, so virtual supply chains force greater co-operation between companies. Organizations that are able to manage the flow of goods, information and funds with suppliers will flourish and prosper. Conditions under which a supply group can be powerful include:

- Dominance by a few suppliers
- Non-availability of substitute products
- High differentiation by the supplier
- High switching costs for the buyer
- Threat of forward integration of suppliers

Relationships between organizations and their customers

E-businesses should understand the importance of identifying, categorizing, understanding, meeting and serving the customer. This approach places great emphasis on information gathering and marketing processes.

Typical prime areas for customer orientation in e-businesses include:

- Strategy
- Originality
- Image
- Quality
- Culture

Relationships within the organization

Internally within businesses the communication between different functional areas, marketing, finance, human resources and IT, can be enabled and changed quite significantly by e-business. The organization is the mediating link between the supplier and customer, of which human, capital, customer capital and structural capital are the salient attributes.

DISCUSSION QUESTIONS

1. Examine Hamel's 10 principles in his strategy revolution. To what extent, if at all, do you agree that they are apt for the digital age?

2. What business relationships have benefited the most from the Internet to date? Is this likely to continue in the future?

3. Is CRM really new or is it merely an old tendency or trend coming back from the era prior to mass production? What do you understand by the term e-CRM?

ASSESSMENT QUESTIONS

I. Using academic papers, books, press articles and relevant Internet material, write a short report which describes the problems experienced by logistics organizations as they embrace the Internet. You may find it useful to visit the Institute of Logistics and Transport web site (www.iolt.org.uk).

2. Using British Airways (www.britishairways.com) or another organization of your choice as an example, you are required to evaluate the impact of the Internet on traditional relationships. Your discussion should be focused around one of the three relationships, with suppliers, within the organization or with customers.

3. According to Seibel's vice President for European Marketing Phil Robinson, 'The reasons CRM is in huge demand, the reason people buy these applications, is that they impact the bottom line directly. Corporates used to justify an investment in ERP based on reducing costs. CRM is a fundamental case. It is about increasing revenues and profit and that is a very good story.' Critically evaluate this statement. Do you believe that CRM is really new or is it an old tendency or a trend coming back from old times and customs before mass production?

GROUP ASSIGNMENT QUESTIONS

I. The growth of e-business has resulted in an increase in online purchasing traffic, as well as concerns regarding the logistics community's ability to meet online fulfilment needs. You are required to identify examples of how logistic organizations have met or exceeded fulfilment needs.

2. Using the work of Brewer and Speh (2000), you are required to use Kaplan and Norton's (1996) Balanced Scorecard framework and illustrate, using any appropriate organization of your choice, how the balanced scorecard could be used to enhance supply chain management. You should develop a balanced scorecard. It should include:
- Vision statement and overall goals and objectives
- Objectives for each perspective
- Measures for each perspective (two to five measures)
- Description of the types of targets that would be used for each measure

3. In his book *Loyalty Rules!*, Reichheld (2001) convincingly demonstrates that the more volatility the economy serves up, the more vital the role loyalty plays in building effective, long-term, profitable relationships. Rigby, Reichheld and Schefter (2002) assert that successful CRM depends more on strategy than on the amount spent on technology. They believe that the only way to make CRM work is by taking the time to calculate customer strategy and to align business practices before implementing technology and they refer to four pitfalls to avoid.

   Using any organization(s) of your choice, you are required to look for examples for each of the four perils highlighted by Rigby, Reichheld and Schefter (2002).

MAIN CASE STUDY
Creating an Effective Customer Relationship Strategy in a Digital World, by Cheryl Bowden, BEA Systems, www.crmproject.com, CRM Project, Vol. 2, 15 August 2002. Copyright with permission of Montgomery Research, Inc. www.mriresearch.com

By learning from customer responses – and applying that knowledge – Marketing can increase its overall effectiveness and market penetration.

With the accelerating pace of technology change, shrinking product lifecycles, commoditization of products and services, and hyper-competition, companies are struggling to maintain a competitive advantage. In this environment, one sure way to achieve a sustainable advantage is by knowing your customers better than your competition and acting on this knowledge faster and more effectively. Through BEA WebLogic Personalization Server™, BEA WebLogic Commerce Server™ and BEA Campaign Manager for WebLogic™, BEA is extending its industry-leading BEA WebLogic E-Business Platform™ with the infrastructure and management tools that businesses need to effectively manage customer relationships for higher sales, greater loyalty, lower customer acquisition costs, and improved profits – in short, a sustainable competitive advantage.

The Competitive Edge of eCRM

The rules of the game have changed for Customer Relationship Management (CRM). Customer demand for increased value, greater convenience, and more control over products and services, along with heightened pressure from competitors, have increased customer acquisition costs and decreased customer and brand loyalty. At the same time, advancements in technology have enabled the cost-effective distribution of huge amounts of customer data, the delivery of customized products, and the efficient use of interactive channels. These technology developments are creating major opportunities to collect and use customer information to gain a better understanding of customer needs and to strengthen customer relationships. To take advantage of these opportunities and address the escalating demands of customers, companies are shifting the focus of their efforts to adopt a customer-centric approach. Product excellence, innovation, and operational efficiency are still important; however, successful companies are building on these existing business strengths as they shift their attention to their customers.

eCRM, and the effective use of customer information, is quickly becoming the key driver of growth and profitability. As a result, an increasing number of companies are migrating more of their investment dollars to eCRM solutions. Worldwide, investment in eCRM solutions will reach $11 billion to $14 billion annually by 2003, according to IDC and Forrester. And the payoff is significant. A Jupiter Communications survey of companies who have implemented eCRM solutions found that, on average, companies were able to recover their investments in seven months. Even more impressive, the average return after one year was 300%. Examples of early movers in embracing eCRM who are reaping significant benefits include: Cisco Systems automated customer interactions with its one-to-one website, saving $270 million in annual operating expenses and significantly reducing the time required to place an order.

Amazon.com was able to achieve a repeat purchase rate of 78%, more than double the industry average, by building one-to-one relationships with its customers and targeting their individual needs. This customer loyalty has enabled Amazon to remain a viable e-commerce company at a time when so many other dot-coms have failed. Sears demonstrated the cross-channel benefits of eCRM by increasing Web shoppers' subsequent offline purchases by 27%. To achieve positive results like these from their eCRM efforts, companies must develop a comprehensive strategy for managing and utilizing customer knowledge. This strategy should include three key objectives:

- Know Your Customer
- Reach Your Customer
- Grow Your Customer

Know Your Customer

Know Your Customer is about understanding your individual customer's value and needs. This understanding comes only from collecting information that customers provide in their interactions with your company, and developing a 360-degree view of customer behavior across all touch points. As you begin a dialogue with individual customers, you create a learning relationship with your customers; each interaction becomes an opportunity to build and extend your relationship with that customer. The more extensive the learning relationship, the more invested the customer becomes in the relationship and the more difficult it will be for the customer to switch to a competitor.

Reach Your Customer

Reach Your Customer is about reaching the right customers with the right offer at the right time through the right channel. Based on your knowledge of each customer, you are able to reach specific customers with targeted offers, information, products, and services. You reach each customer with a personalized message based on his or her needs, behaviors, and value.

Grow Your Customer

Grow Your Customer refers to your company's ability to effectively execute Marketing strategies based on your knowledge of customer share and customer lifetime value. You must use scarce investment dollars to target your efforts to your best, most valuable customers. Increasing the total value of your customer base by retaining and growing your best customers, is significantly less expensive than trying to generate the same amount of value by acquiring new customers. Focusing on your best customers requires you to re-examine and re-allocate total Marketing and sales investments from less profitable customers and the acquisition of new customers. For some companies, knowing, reaching and growing customers will be an extension of the way they operate today. For others, it will require a dramatic shift in the way they interact with customers. To maximize the effectiveness of its eCRM efforts, each company will need to optimize its people, processes, technology, and customer knowledge.

The Challenges for Marketing

This increased focus on customers significantly impacts the organization, especially the roles and responsibilities of the Marketing department. Marketing has always played an important role in defining customer strategy, but now Marketing must leverage customer knowledge throughout the enterprise to effectively anticipate and deliver to customer needs. This requires Marketing to manage integrated campaigns that extend beyond standard Marketing functions and encompass sales, service, and fulfillment functions. This creates several challenges for Marketing:

Integrated Customer Relationship Strategy

In order to manage integrated campaigns, Marketing is quickly finding itself the focal point for developing and managing an integrated customer relationship strategy to connect all the customer touch points in the organization. Specifically, this requires Marketing to develop a strategy for proactively collecting and managing customer data across the enterprise, develop specific campaigns and programs to increase the enterprise's knowledge of customer needs and values, and then leverage customer information effectively to deliver customized products and services to meet individual customer's needs.

Marketing Accountability

The combination of a highly competitive business environment, scarce Marketing resources, and new advances in technology is creating a situation where Marketing is being held to new levels of accountability. Marketing is held responsible for the success of both the overall customer relationship strategy and the success of specific eCRM initiatives.

Marketing is charged with developing highly targeted strategies that focus investments on the best opportunities, in order to minimize costs and maximize ROI. Similar to mutual fund managers, who seek to maximize the performance of their investment portfolios, Marketing managers must try to maximize the value of their customer portfolios. Marketing managers must measure the value of individual customers as well as the success of Marketing campaigns targeted to specific customer segments.

Marketing will need to be able to provide answers to questions like these:

- What percent of revenue is attributable to the top 20% of customers? The top 10%?
- What is the average lifetime value of my customer base?
- Are there unprofitable customers, with whom the cost to service is higher than the revenue received?
- What is my current share of the customer? How can I increase my share of the customer for my best customers?
- Did unit margins per customer increase based on cross-sell and up-sell programs?
- Did customer satisfaction increase? Did customer loyalty increase?
- What is my return on investment for specific campaigns?

Effective Use of Technology

Central to the ability to develop and implement a customer relationship strategy and measure its performance is the effective use of technology. As technology changes at a rapid pace, it is much harder to implement complex solutions that support an integrated, multi-channel eCRM environment. Organizations have tried putting together several technologies to create an overall solution, only to find that the systems and applications do not play well together.

To build a proper infrastructure with management tools to support, monitor, and refine customer strategies requires the Marketing department to partner more closely with the information technology (IT) department. Marketing must understand that it needs to effectively communicate its complex requirements and strategy to IT. IT, in turn, must understand what is required to create and maintain the robust environment that will support the overall strategy.

Additionally, IT is expected to support the selection and implementation of the best management tools that not only provide an integrated solution, but also leverage prior and future IT investments. For both IT and Marketing, resource constraints make it critical that the technology solution enables Marketing to manage its increased responsibilities with minimal intervention and assistance from IT.

BEA's Infrastructure Solution

BEA is helping companies implement effective customer relationship strategies by providing the infrastructure and management tools to enable companies to use customer knowledge for competitive advantage. The BEA WebLogic E-Business Platform, with more than 9,400 customers worldwide, is the infrastructure of choice for the Internet economy. With BEA WebLogic Server™, the market-leading Java application server, at its core, the WebLogic E-Business Platform enables companies to collaborate in real-time with customers across the entire customer life cycle, and adapt quickly to the fast-paced changes of the business environment. Moreover, the WebLogic E-Business Platform provides the foundation for a unified view of the customer across the enterprise by easily integrating with new and existing applications.

For example, Charles Schwab & Co. uses the WebLogic E-Business Platform to deliver world-class services through its Internet site.

We rely on our premier technology partners such as BEA to develop the solutions that allow us to deliver products and services to our customers, providing them with the very best possible investment experience at Schwab. Schwab has deployed one of the largest and most robust technology infrastructures in corporate America, and we require industrial-strength application server technology that our employees and customers can count on to deliver the very best levels of service in the most demanding conditions. – Dawn G.Lepore, Vice Chairman and Chief Information Officer, The Charles Schwab Corporation

Now, BEA has extended its industry-leading e-business platform to enable Customer Relationship Management on the Web and through other channels with BEA WebLogic Personalization Server, BEA WebLogic Commerce Server, and BEA Campaign Manager for WebLogic.

To enable businesses to meet the significant challenges in becoming a customer-centric organization, BEA and its partners provide a complete solution to accomplish the following:

Integrate and Leverage Customer Information

A customer-focused strategy requires the ability to integrate and leverage customer information from across the enterprise. Information on customers resides in numerous financial applications, customer service systems, sales applications, and Marketing databases in different areas of the company. In addition, customer information is continually collected from Web, sales, service, and support interactions. The result is that, in most enterprises, customer information is distributed across multiple geographies, systems, and formats – preventing a company from gaining the understanding of its customers needed to effectively reach and grow them. BEA provides the ability to integrate enterprise applications, including back-office systems and Web applications, to create a unified view of the customer across all touch points. BEA enables you to leverage this integrated customer information through multi-level analysis of customer profile information – analysis that provides the knowledge about and insight into customer behaviors and needs, which is necessary for identifying significant Marketing opportunities and to be able to define the products and services required to meet these needs. For example, if you know that an online customer who calls your service center after the sale is less likely to complete a transaction online again, you can offer a specific incentive to encourage the customer to go back online.

Maximize Value of Customer Relationships

Once you are able to leverage customer information, the next step is to turn the information into knowledge and the knowledge into actionable programs that increase the value of your customers.

BEA extends a company's ability to build profitable customer relationships by enabling marketers to create, refine, and execute targeted Marketing campaigns and promotions to stimulate awareness, interest, and action. BEA Campaign Manager for WebLogic was designed with the business user in mind, providing a flexible and easy-to-use interface to reach customers through personalized Marketing campaigns. Personalized campaigns create opportunities to grow customers by enabling cross-sell and up-sell offers and promotions and extensive multi-action campaigns targeted to your most valuable customer segments. BEA WebLogic Personalization Server and Commerce Server provide the foundation for personalizing individual customer inter-actions and for creating a consistent and compelling customer experience that keeps your customers coming back. Customers gain access to personalized products, services, and information when and where they need it – an important component for retaining and growing a loyal customer base and maximizing the value of your customers.

Increase Marketing Efficiency

Maximizing customer relationships necessitates that you also minimize internal costs through effective use of Marketing resources, including people, process and technology. An effective eCRM solution empowers Marketing to reach customers quickly, easily and efficiently.

BEA gives marketers the ability to design and execute highly effective campaigns that generate higher returns at less cost than a traditional mass Marketing approach. Measuring Marketing initiatives and customer responses and behaviors allows Marketing to carefully analyze campaign results, redirect Marketing dollars to the best opportunities, and justify Marketing budgets with strong results.

Increasing the effectiveness of Marketing initiatives comes from developing repeatable processes that generate predictable results. By learning from customer responses to targeted efforts and being able to apply what is learned to a wider audience of customers, Marketing can increase its overall effectiveness and market penetration.

Empowering Marketing Efforts

Changes to the competitive landscape have accelerated in the last several years, forcing companies to focus on customers and customer relationships in order to maintain a competitive edge. As organizations embrace eCRM as a solution to this imperative, they face new challenges. The Marketing function in particular needs to make significant adjustments to develop and implement customer-focused strategy and programs.

BEA is continually improving the industry-leading WebLogic E-Business Platform to address the challenges created by focusing on customer relationships. BEA's solution empowers business users with the infrastructure and management tools needed to effectively manage customer relationships. The combination of BEA WebLogic Personalization Server, BEA WebLogic Commerce Server and BEA Campaign Manager for WebLogic gives Marketing the ability to quickly turn the challenges of eCRM into long-term competitive advantage.

CASE QUESTIONS

Question 1 What are the theoretical benefits of eCRM?

Question 2 What has made the BEA WebLogic E-Business Platform, with more than 9400 customers worldwide, become so popular for organizations that wish to collaborate in real time with customers across the entire customer life cycle? You may find it useful to visit the BEA website (www.bea.com).

Question 3 What do you believe are the salient issues for organizations that wish to become a customer-centric organization? How does BEA help organizations maximize the value of customer relationships? You may find it useful to visit the BEA website (www.bea.com).

MINI CASE STUDY 1
Danzas AEI named top logistics e-business company by Internet Week magazine, www.danzasaei.com, 15 June 2000

Darien, CT (June 15, 2000) – Danzas AEI said today it has been named by *Internet Week* magazine as the transportation logistics industry's premier e-business provider in the publication's first-ever survey of top 100 U.S. e-business companies. According to the "InternetWeek 100" survey, Danzas AEI e-business services were superior to those offered by FedEx Corp., UPS and the U.S. Postal Service, among others. The survey selected the top 10 U.S. e-business providers in each of 10 industries.

According to *InternetWeek*, Danzas AEI's e-business success is based on "giving customers what they demand: the latest and most detailed information on materials being transported or (on) inventory being managed." Danzas AEI's "Web and legacy applications offer customers everything from simple access to the status of a shipment to end-to-end supply chain management," the magazine said.

"We are honored to receive this award from such a respected publication," said John L. Luludis, Danzas AEI vice president and chief information officer. "We believe it validates the soundness of our e-business strategy, which is to offer a robust fulfillment platform that facilitates the international movement of goods purchased online."

"The core challenge facing global e-business companies today is providing customers with the "landed cost" of an international transaction," said Eric S. Vargas, Danzas AEI, vice president, logistics applications. The "landed cost" is the total cost of an international transaction after shipping; customs and other charges are factored in. "International shipping is a complex process that requires a knowledge of global transportation and distribution patterns, an array of tax and customs regulations, and trade-related issues unique to each country," said Vargas. "E-businesses and their customers need to be aware of the rules that govern their transactions. They also must know the transaction's 'landed' cost, which involves more than just shipping charges." Vargas cited a survey by leading Web consultant Forrester Research that 46 percent of total orders placed on the sites of 50 companies were rejected because the orders came from foreign consumers. The survey findings were reported in a separate story in

InternetWeek.

"We believe the success of our e-business model stems from our vast experience serving global markets and our powerful IT applications that allow e-businesses and their customers to quickly obtain the information needed to make an intelligent and cost-effective business decision."

"Our e-business model was not based on a 'build-it-and-they-will-come' approach," said Luludis. "We started by surveying our customers, asking them about their e-business plans, and the needs and expectations of their customers. We then built our system around those responses. It is truly a customer-centric e-business strategy. That is why it works."

Danzas AEI's e-business model operates as "AEI Interactive," a robust online applications suite that mirrors the global transaction process from the initial purchase order to final delivery of the finished goods. "AEI Interactive" includes LOGIS-GLOS® an order management system; ShipAEI® a tool for customers to book and trace shipments; a web-enabled warehouse management system to monitor inventories across Danzas AEI's global network, and an online U.S. customs brokerage tool to manage the processing and release of imported goods at ports-of-entry. "AEI Interactive" is designed to link with customers' back-office systems to support the seamless processing of critical shipping and trade data. Danzas AEI also offers a comprehensive online "Global Resource Guide" that provides users with critical trade data in an easy-to-understand format.

Danzas AEI recently unveiled LOGIS-XM® an exception management tool that tracks each shipment, alerts the customer to those shipments that fail to meet in-transit benchmarks or "exceptions" and prompts the user to take immediate corrective action. This tool also consolidates historical data so that it can be analyzed to improve distribution flow.

CASE QUESTIONS

Question 1 Briefly outline what you believe were the important factors that enabled Danzas AEI to be named the top logistic e-business company by *InternetWeek*?

Question 2 Why has Danzai AEI (www.danzas.com) maintained its position as a top logistic e-business company? With emphasis on any specific market, Europe, North America or Asia, you are required to analyse the Ryder organization (www.ryder.com) and its strengths and weaknesses.

MINI CASE STUDY II
UK struggles to see benefits of e-business, Institute of Logistics and Transport, www.iolt.org, UK, 6 April 2001

Both the private and public sector in Britain are struggling to close the gap between e-business hype and real business benefits, according to a survey released today, *The E-Business Report, 2001* surveyed more than 1,000 public sector organisations and private companies between May 2000 and February 2001. It reveals business applications are delivering greater efficiencies for companies in the vanguard of e-business, but increased revenue is proving elusive.

The research was designed to gauge how the Internet is changing management practice in a wide variety of organisations. It was conducted by the University of Birmingham's Centre for Business Strategy and Procurement on behalf of the Chartered Institute of Purchasing & Supply (CIPS), the Institute of Management (IM) and the Institute of Logistics and Transport (ILT). The CIPS, IM and ILT have a combined membership of 100,000 organisations and private companies. The survey showed those fastest to take up e-business are experiencing real tangible benefits. Nevertheless take-up is slow, and much-heralded fundamental changes to business processes have not materialised, in many cases due to unrealistic expectations or lack of an overall e-strategy.

Key findings by business functions

Sales and Marketing
- 33% of "early adopters" claim the Internet has allowed them to enter new markets
- 53% reported improvements in supply chain efficiency as a result of adopting e-business strategies
- 43% report increased sales
- 53% believe sales will primarily come from the Internet in the future
- 47% of internet use was in B2B applications compared to 25% for B2C

However:
- Only 20% of respondents in sales and marketing said they are using the Internet, and 80% of this group admitted it was for information gathering and communication rather than transactions
- Only 11% see any value in e-marketplaces with buyer power being the main concern

Supply Chain
- 67% report reductions in input costs, 39% in purchase costs and 33% report improved purchasing terms all leading to a leaner organisation
- Over 51% also report increases in speed of delivery

However:
- Nearly two thirds, 61% see no increase in revenue
- Although e-business is reducing transaction costs and purchase prices for 67% of users, 77% of respondents have not adopted an e-supply strategy, suggesting the benefits to purchasing professionals are still not fully apparent

Internal Organisation
- Less than half, 46% of respondents claim their organisations have any e-business and e-organisation strategies and 56% are not clear when or whether their company will develop a clear e-business strategy

- 63% do not believe they have necessary IT skills and 63% report being unable to keep up with the pace of IT change
- 93% perceive no threat to their job function from e-business, and 89% expect no threat to their own jobs. However, 60% expect improvements in operational efficiency, which may suggest a reduction in companies' headcount in the long-term.

Commenting on the findings, Professor Andrew Cox, Director of the University of Birmingham's Centre for Business Strategy and Procurement, said: "Everyone expected the Internet to bring major benefits for UK business but actually we've seen only modest savings. Aside from reduced transaction costs and lower purchase prices in the supply chain, companies that have been quicker to take-up e-business aren't yet reporting significant benefits.

Professor Cox said: "The goal of integrated supply-chains may not be achievable beyond a few key industry sectors. It is possible that more time is needed to realise the benefits, or current expectations are too high. Many people are adopting a wait and see strategy, they want proof of full benefits before adopting new technology. The truth may be that e-business works for some sectors, like retail and wholesale, where significant improvements in logistical cycle times have been achieved, but for many sectors it is not realistic to expect a truly integrated supply chain function with benefits to all parties."

CASE QUESTIONS

Question 1 According to the results of the *E-business Report, 2001* the take-up of e-business is slow and the much-heralded fundamental changes to business processes have not materialized, in many cases due to unrealistic expectations or lack of an overall e-strategy. Using the findings of *The E-Business Report, 2001*, you are required to critically discuss this statement with emphasis on business functions.

Question 2 Do you feel that the findings of The *E-business Report, 2001* are specific to the UK or can the findings be generalized to other countries? You should use examples to illustrate your views.

REFERENCES

Accenture (2000) The CRM Project, http://wolfe.crmproject.com.

Avlonitis, G.J. and D. Karayanni (2000) The impact of Internet use on business to business marketing, *Industrial Marketing Management*, vol. 29, no. 5, 441–459.

Bressler, M (2001) Internet CRM must have human touch, *Marketing News*, vol. 35, no. 22, 42.

Brewer, P.C. and T.W. Speh (2000) Using the Balance Scorecard to measure supply chain performance, *Journal of Business Logistics*, vol. 21, no. 1, pp. 75–88.

Cahill, D.J. (1998) Relationship marketing? But all I really wanted was a one-night stand, *Marketing News*, vol. 32, no. 19, September, p. 4.

Caruana, A., L. Pitt, and P. Berthon (1998) Excellence-market orientation link: Some consequences for service firms, *Journal of Business Research*, vol. 45, pp. 5–15.

Chang T.-Z. and S.-J. Chen (1998) Market orientation, service quality and business profitability: a conceptual model and empirical evidence, *The Journal of Services Marketing*, vol. 12, no. 4, pp. 246–264.

Christopher, M. (1992) *Logistics and Supply Chain Management*, Financial Times/Pitman Publishing, New York.

Cooke, J.A. (1998) VMI: Very Mixed Impact, *Logistics Management & Distribution Report*, vol. 31, p. 51.

Cooper, M. and L. Ellram (1993) Purchasing and logistics strategy, *International Journal of Logistics Management*, vol. 42, no. 2, pp. 13–24.

Day, G.S. (1994) The capabilities of market-driven organisations, *Journal of Marketing*, vol. 58, October, pp. 37–52.

Deise, M., C. Nowikow, P. King and A. Wright (2000) *Executive's Guide to E-Business From Tactics to Strategy*, PriceWaterhouseCoopers, John Wiley & Sons, New York.

Donath, B. (1998) Slow e-mail response rate torpedoes marketing efforts, *Marketing News*, vol. 32, no. 18, August, pp. 5–6.

Dyer, J. (1999) Making the most of your client database, *Chartered Accountants Journal of New Zealand*, vol. 78, no. 8, September, pp. 73–74.

Frontline Solutions (2001) E-business to influence logistics, vol. 2, no. 3, p. 1.

Geisler, E. (2001) Organising for e-business: the implementation of management principles in electronic commerce, *Portland International Conference on the Management of Engineering and Technology*, Portland, Oregon, 29 July–2 August.

Gray, B., S. Matear, C. Boshoff and P. Matheson (1998) Developing a better measure of market orientation, *European Journal of Marketing*, vol. 23, no. 9/10, pp. 884–905.

Greenley, G.E. (1995a) Market orientation and company performance: Empirical evidence from UK companies, *British Journal of Management*, vol. 6, pp. 1–13.

———(1995b) Forms of market orientation in UK companies, *Journal of Management Studies*, vol. 32, no. 1, pp. 47–66.

Griffiths, A. (1999) Clients miss Internet chance, DMA claims, *Campaign-London*, January, p. 8.

Gummesson, E. (1999) *Total Relationship Marketing*, Butterworth-Heinemann, London.

Hamel, G. (1996) Strategy as revolution, *Harvard Business Review*, vol. 74, no. 1, pp. 69–82.

Jaworski, B.J. and A.K. Kohli (1993) Market orientation: antecedents and consequences, *Journal of Marketing*, vol. 57, January, pp. 53–70.

Kaplan, R.S. and D.P. Norton (1996) Using the balanced scorecard as a strategic management system, *Harvard Business Review*, vol. 74, no. 1, pp. 78–92.

Krol, C. (1999) A new age: it's all about relationships, *Advertising Age*, vol. 70, no. 21, May, pp. S1, S4.

Kumar, K., R. Subramanian and C. Yauger (1998) Examining the market orientation-performance relationship: a context-specific study, *Journal of Management*, vol. 24, no. 2, pp. 201–233.

Lambert, D.M. and M.C. Cooper (2000) Issues in supply chain management, *Industrial Marketing Management*, vol. 29, pp. 65–83.

Lancioni, R.A., M.F. Smith and T.A. Oliva (2000) The role of the Internet in supply chain management, *Industrial Marketing Management*, vol. 29, pp. 45–56.

MacDonald, A. (2000) E-business driving the virtual supply chain, *In the E-business Report*, Intentia/PA Consulting Group, London.

Marshall, G.W. (1996) The folly of rewarding A while hoping for B, *Marketing News*, vol. 30, no. 23, November, pp. 6–9.

Morris, M.H., J. Brunyee and M. Page (1998) Relationship marketing in practice: myths and realities, *Industrial Marketing Management*, vol. 27, no. 4, July, pp. 359–371.

Novack, R. and S. Simco (1991) The industrial procurement process: A supply chain management perspective, *Journal of Business Logistics*, vol, 12, no. 1, pp. 145–167.

Nunes, P.F. and A. Kamil (2001) Personalisation? No thanks, *Harvard Business Review*, vol. 79, no. 4, pp. 32–33.

Penrose, E.T. (1959) *The Theory of the Growth of the Firm*, Basil Blackwell, London.

Phillips, P. A., F. Davies and L. Moutinho (2001) The interactive effects of strategic marketing planning and performance: A neural network analysis, *Journal of Marketing Management*, vol. 17, no. 1–2, 159–182.

Pittiglio, R. and T. McGrath (1997) *Integrated Supply Chain Management Benchmarking Study*, http://strategic.ic.gc.ca/ssg/bs00164e.html.

Reichheld, F.F. (2001) *Loyalty Rules!* Harvard Business School, Cambridge, MA.

Rich, M.K. and D.C. Smith (2000) Determining relationship skills of prospective salespeople, *Journal of Business and Industrial Marketing*, vol. 15, no. 4, April, pp. 241–259.

Rigby, D.K., F.F. Reichheld and P. Schefter (2002) Avoid the four perils of CRM, *Harvard Business Review*, vol. 80, no. 2, pp. 101–108.

Ruekert, R.W. (1992) Developing a market orientation: an organisational strategy perspective, *International Journal of Research in Marketing*, vol. 9, pp. 225–245.

Saint-Onge, H. (2000) Strategic capabilities: shaping human-resource management within the knowledge-driven enterprise, http://knowinc.com/saint-onge/library/strategic.htm.

Scott, C. and R. Westbrook (1991) New strategic tools for supply chain management, *International Journal of Physical Distribution and Logistics Management*, vol. 21, no. 1, pp. 23–33.

Selznick, P. (1957) *Leadership in Administration*, Harper & Row, New York.

Seybold, P.V. (1998) *Customer.com*, Time Books, New York.

Slater, S.F. and J.C. Narver (1998) Customer-led and market-oriented: Let's not confuse the two, *Strategic Management Journal*, vol. 19, pp. 1001–1006.

Stone, M. (2001) *The Returns to Transformed Customer Contact Management*, IBM Global Services.

Zeithaml, V.A., A. Parasuraman and L.L. Berry (1990) *Delivering Quality Service*, The Free Press, New York.

Zieger, A. (1999) Customization nation, *Incentive*, vol. 173, no. 5, May, pp. 35–40.

Zingle, T. (2000) *The death of customer satisfaction – CRM in the Internet Age*, White Paper, http://zingle.crmproject.com/.

CHAPTER 3
E-BUSINESS RISK MANAGEMENT

LEARNING OUTCOMES

When you have read and worked through this chapter, you will be able to:
- Understand the basics of traditional risk management
- Understand the basics of e-business risk management
- Understand how to integrate e-business risks
- Formulate e-business risk management strategies
- Appreciate the concept and difficulties of e-cash
- Measure and monitor e-business risks

INTRODUCTION

The concept of **risk management** in an e-business environment is becoming an increasingly significant relevant concept in a number of ways. Chapter 1 discussed the advantages and disadvantages of the Internet and, if we look back with hindsight, risk management was not as prominent as it should have been. The first wave of dot.coms frequently entered into the unknown, after making major investments in new products or new markets. With the increasing number of online transactions, both private- and public-sector organizations need to embrace the Internet. For example, from a supplier perspective, suppliers have realized that the Internet continues to shift power from the seller to the buyer irreversibly and that they need to leverage their core competencies and develop effective risk management strategies.

This chapter seeks to highlight some of the salient **e-business risk management** issues relating to technology, competition, suppliers and customers. While each industry typically faces different types of risk, which makes it hard to generalize, this chapter considers an industry where the ability to manage risks is paramount. In the banking and insurance industry, the ability to manage risks is crucial and, in the absence of such a capability, losses can be huge or even lead to bankruptcy. This chapter assumes that risk is not always a good thing and a priority for senior management is that it needs to be managed. In finance programmes the term 'risk versus return' is often cited. Traditional attitudes about risk were focused around the mathematics of the chance that an outcome other than expected will occur. In finance, investment risk is related to the possibility of actually earning a return other than expected – the greater the variability of the possible outcomes, the riskier the investment (Brigham, Gapenski and Ehrhardt, 1999). An alternative way of describing the spread of outcomes (risk) is the standard deviation. The standard deviation is merely the square root of the variance (see Brigham *et al.*, 1999, p. 165 for a worked example). It must be borne in mind that, when looking at the variance, management are not indifferent between positive and negative outcomes. For example, if the returns are greater, all stakeholders can benefit; however, if the returns are less than expected, the organization's going-concern assumptions are at risk.

Systematic approaches to risk assessment and risk control became prominent during the last decade because of changing attitudes to risk, contemporary pressures in managerial

Key Term...

Risk management
A method that adopts an enterprise approach to monitoring and managing risks, associated with competition, the organization, suppliers and customers

Key Term...

E-business risk management
E-business risk management incorporates risk management and adopts a broader perspective by focusing on technology risk

decision-making and the demands of corporate governance (Hunt, 2000). The importance of how senior management should manage business risks in their entirety and should review on a regular basis the effectiveness of risk evaluation and control processes has been highlighted by the Institute of Chartered Accountants (1999). Prior to this, the Cadbury Report (1992), which addressed the area of financial probity, defined risk management as financial control. Risk management has therefore become an important managerial concern for financial and non-financial institutions. The goal for risk managers is to create policies and procedures that create trust by providing security, reliability, effectiveness and compliance.

WHY IS E-BUSINESS RISK MANAGEMENT IMPORTANT?

Running any business naturally entails taking risks. Various commentators have suggested that satisfactory performance will not emerge from a total risk-eliminating strategy; some risk is inevitable. Key decisions have to be made to ensure that the corporations get it right. Will they make the right choice when it comes to investing in e-business or will they destroy shareholder value? This is the challenge for the strategist.

During the last couple of years dynamic dot.coms have captured public imagination through the creation of revolutionary business models. Unfortunately, within a 12-month period things that started so well ended rather abruptly. The Internet bandwagon was on a roll, gathering momentum by blind faith in the new economy. The Swedish online fashion retailer Boo.com was the first high profile dot.com to fall and other failures are shown in Table 3.1. Given that there is an extremely narrow line between success and failure, it would be fatuous to ignore any lessons that could be learned from these failures? A brief review of some of the high profile casualties provides a useful starting point.

In the UK, during 2000 almost half a billion pounds was lost by **venture capitalists** who were anticipating a **bull** Internet **stock market**. Unfortunately, Internet-based stocks turned markets around the globe into **bear markets**. The scale of write-offs sent shockwaves throughout the investment community, which deepened the depression among dot.com firms hoping that 2001 would provide the light at the end of a dark tunnel. At the start of the 2000, everyone wanted to have a business interest in the Internet; by the end of the year there was a great deal of activity to reduce Internet exposure. In all, £1bn was invested by venture capitalists on high-tech companies in 2000. A 55 per cent fall in 2001 in the value of the TechMark, the stock exchange for technology-related companies, had a profound effect on venture capital success rates, as it soon became clear that the bulk of the businesses would not be able to float to give any return on investment. Alarmingly, the £500m spent on bad investments does not take into account the hundreds of millions of pounds established companies have pumped into their own Internet projects from internally generated funds. Most, including Granada, IPC and News International, have sought to incorporate new media, and many have had to rethink their Internet investment strategies.

Matters are not helped by the fact that even successful online ventures have to retrench staff. Problems have also affected *The Wall Street Journal* (WSJ.com). At the end of March 2001, *The Wall Street Journal* (WSJ.com), which was one of the world's most successful online news operations stunned the troubled online content market by revealing it was about to lay off staff. *The Wall Street Journal* is one of the few newspapers to have made positive cashflows from its online operations. WSJ.com has been one of the Web's most successful subscription services organizations and was long the envy of Internet content

Key Term...

Venture capitalists (VC)
Venture capitalists provide investment expertise with entrepreneurial skills to deliver funding to organizations well positioned for fast growth that have the potential to deliver outstanding returns to investors

Key Term...

Bull stock market
This occurs when stock markets such as the FTSE100 are rising

Key Term...

Bear stock market
This occurs when stock markets such as the FTSE100 are falling

Company	Service	Strength	Weakness	Registered subscribers
Boo.com	Clothing retailer. The Titanic of dot.com start-ups. Boo promised it all. Free shipping and free returns, a site in seven languages and 18 countries	They looked good; well at least picture editors thought so	Boo.com spent investors' money with zeal but generated little revenue. Got carried away by affluence – money was lavished on transatlantic flights and numerous other perks. Website launched six months late. Lots of technical problems	Unknown
Boxman	Pan-European retailer of CDs	Was in the top three of European online CD retailers	Had ambitious expansion and acquisition plans. Got too far ahead of itself, assuming further fundraising would be easy	Unknown
Breathe	Started out as a free Internet access provider. Followed Freeserve into unmetered access and moved heavily into mobile Internet services	Provided a good service and had built up a good brand name	Built its strategy around WAP, which has been slow to take off	More than 500 000
ClickMango	Health and beauty site	Had Joanna Lumley as its public face. Founders were very frugal	Run by two young inexperienced public schoolboys, trying to compete in a very small marketplace. Monthly turnover was only £4000. The health e-retail market failed to take-off	Not many
Thestreet.co.uk	Financial news website	Had lots of money and what seemed to be a successful US business behind it	The needs of financial news community were already being catered for by other websites and publications. Thestreet.com's falling valuation and a new strategy to save cash; getting the business to profitability	180 000
Letsbuyit.com	Founded by Swedes in 1999, Letsbuyit.com, like Boo.com, expanded at a rate of knots across Europe. Described as a 'co-buying' network, the idea was that consumers would group together to secure bulk discounts on products. By the end of 2000, it was operating in 14 European countries, but sales were abysmal	'In-yer-face' advertising did lead to widespread awareness of the brand name, although no one actually knew what Letsbuyit.com did	The curse of the Swedish dot.coms. Letsbuyit's imminent failure can be put down to three factors: bad timing, over-ambition and a questionable business model. Letsbuyit worked on minuscule margins	100 000

Table 3.1 A summary of some early dot.com failures

ILLUSTRATIVE EXAMPLE 1
Breathe problems with free Internet users, Breathe.com

In July 2000, Breathe.com, the Internet service provider (ISP), told at least 500 users of its free service they must start paying because they are using it too much. The service, launched in April 2000, gave users free access to the Internet for 24 hours a day for life for a one-off fee of £50. However, despite paying the one-off fee of £50, the 500 highest users were told that they were that their level of use put "the service at risk" and the ISP had the right to disconnect them.

Sean Gardner, chief operating officer at Breathe.com, said it was a 'tough decision', but defended the decision by saying that at least half of the 500 customers thrown off the free service were business users. This therefore provided opportunities for domestic customers. He said: 'The spirit of the offer was access at any time, but it was not intended to be used 24 hours a day. A small number of users were significantly affecting the quality of the service for the other 49 500.' Breathe.com also has more than 200 000 users for its standard pay-by-the-minute service. The 500 removed from the free service were offered their £50 fee back as call credits for the paid-for service.

Less than three months after acquiring the Internet service provider operations of breathe.com for £1.4 million in January 2001, Great Universal Stores (GUS) closed its Breathe.com business. After burning £35 million cash in 18 months and accumulating £50 m debts, due to a high-profile television advertising campaign, the receivers were called in December 2000. GUS sought to use breathe.com's mobile Internet access technology to boost its own online shopping operations. This move totally ignored an Internet access business with 400 000 registered subscribers.

---

suppliers the world over (including FT.com). WSJ.com's Internet service has more than half a million subscribers, who pay £41 per year for the online service or £20 if they already subscribe to *The Wall Street Journal*. The subscription-based news model was one of the most successful on the Web. According to its parent company, Dow Jones, job cuts are expected as part of a move to save Dow Jones £40m over the next year by reducing the media giant's overall headcount of 8500.

Research by MediaGuardian.co.uk into dot.com deaths revealed where most of the £500m was squandered. The results show an estimated £332m being frittered away on high-profile Internet companies. With losses of £100m plus, Boo.com was a significant Internet casualty.

Nua

Nua was a leading provider of enterprise web publishing solutions in the **knowledge management** marketplace. Nua's customers were large organizations that wanted to create value and profit from their information and knowledge (http://www.nua.ie/products/index.shtml). Nua also established itself as an online publisher – with Nua Internet Surveys, New Thinking, Making it Work, and Net Style, Nua's ideas and thinking reach over 250 000 people worldwide on a weekly basis (http://www.nua.ie/nkb/index.cgi).

However, on Tuesday 27 March 2001, Nua Ltd went into receivership. Gerry McGovern managing director of NUA had little option but to close his Internet business. Nua's corporate slogan 'profit from knowledge' failed to materialize and Nua collapsed with debts of

---

Key Term...

Knowledge management (KM)

Knowledge management embodies organizational processes that seek synergistic combination of data and the information processing capacity of information technologies, which can be enhanced through creative strategies

---

ILLUSTRATIVE EXAMPLE II
Beenz.com puts up 'for sale' sign, Amy Vickers, www.mediaguardian.co.uk, Thursday 29 March 2001

Online loyalty points service Beenz.com is up for sale, becoming the latest casualty of the internet recession. The company, which operates an internet "loyalty points" service, initiated yet another round of redundancies, leaving the company with just 80 employees worldwide – down from 260 at its peak a year ago.

A spokesman for the company refused to say how Beenz.com had managed to burn through £56m in two years, nor give details of how much cash Beenz.com had left in the bank.

"The only thing I can add is that they are keeping their options open," said the spokesman.

Beenz.com's board of directors has been looking at ways of restructuring the business since its troubles were first rumoured last November. Chief executive officer Charles Cohen told MediaGuardian.co.uk in December he was conducting a three-month review and would not rule out a strategic partnership with an offline company taking a stake in the business. In a statement today, Beenz.com said it was already "in discussions with several potential strategic partners".

The latest round of job cuts have hit the London office the hardest, although the company will continue to run global networks from its London base.

Unfortunately on 18 October 2001, the following statement was issuers by beenz.com.

BEENZ.COM INC. IS DISSOLVED
New York (October 18, 2001)
beenz.com inc. announced today that it has filed a 'Certificate of Dissolution' with the State of Delaware. The Board of Directors and Stockholders of beenz.com inc., in accordance with the provisions of Section 275 of the General Corporation Law of the State of Delaware, authorized the preparation and filing of the Certificate of Dissolution effective as of October 11, 2001. As of that date the corporation ceased to conduct business and all rights and franchises of the corporation under Delaware law were thereby surrendered.

Those wishing additional information can contact the Division of Corporations of the Secretary of State of the State of Delaware.

---

around £500,000. This is in stark contrast to the fact that Nua was once touted as a US$1bn float. At the time of the collapse, Nua cited eight reasons to buy Nua Publish. These included:

■ A unique publishing system that ensures web content is professionally presented every single time.
■ The bespoke Nua Publish Methodology ensures that designs are successfully implemented so that they meet client needs.
■ The Nua Publish Standards ensure that all content is presented in accordance with industry best practice for presentation and accessibility.
■ There is no need for client downloads or tricky installations. Contributors just need a web browser to work with Nua Publish.
■ Is more efficient to implement because it is a highly configurable an 'out of the box' product.
■ Is a more cost-effective investment than other 'heavy duty' **content management** platforms, while delivering similar key benefits and more.

Key Term...

Content management
In the broadest terms, content management is a systems-based approach to indexing content, ensuring that it can be accessed through all platforms and providing direct publishing mechanisms

- Less after sales support is required and therefore Nua Publish is cost-effective to maintain because there are fewer ongoing training and technical support issues.
- Nua Publish supports tailored learning modules that teach how to create great content for websites.

So what can be learned from the above failures? The above cases no doubt produced business plans but with hindsight there was obviously something missing. A traditional business pays much attention to profits but the first mover dot.coms ignored this issue. There would also appear to have been scant attention to revenue streams. After a 12 month period, the bubble burst and dot.coms have to show potential providers of finance where and how the revenues are to be generated and how the cost base is to be managed. It is no good simply to focus attention on cost reduction. Forecasting revenue in a new market is more difficult to predict and model. This chapter speculates that effective risk management can help e-businesses avoid some of the problems experienced after the hype of the first wave of e-business. The rest of this chapter attempts to demonstrate the need for new forms of risk management thinking in an e-business environment.

ORGANIZATIONAL WIDE E-BUSINESS RISKS

E-business risk management is a phenomenon that has become increasingly important because of the limitations of technology. Insuretrust.com defines the term e-business risk management as the 'organizational strategies that incorporate all reasonable efforts to preserve the integrity of information assets and corporate intangible assets'. The surge in new electronic technologies has created the need for an organization to draw together all the risks that it faces. Traditionally, risk management practices were contrived functionally with, for example, the finance director handling credit risk and foreign exchange risk, the human resources director handling employment risk and the marketing director handling product market risk. Techniques such as integrated risk management offers a new approach to enhancing shareholder value (Meulbroek, 2000). Basically, integrated risk management is the identification and assessment of the aggregated risks that affect shareholder value and the implementation of an appropriate strategy to manage them. Integrated risk management can be approached from three dimensions:

- Modifying the business processes
- Changing capital structure
- Employing targeted financial instruments (such as futures, forwards or options)

Kazim (1999) has eloquently stated the risks of inertia as '... the cost of experimentation in an e-business enabled world, where alliances are rapidly becoming common, is significantly lower than doing nothing at all'. One of the biggest problems would appear knowing what to do. According to a survey by the Confederation of British Industry and PwC 'the (financial service) industry is grappling with the extent of the challenges presented by e-business and what exactly its response should be'.

E-business risks can be classified as strategic risk, which can then be broken down into business and non-business risk. Figure Q3.1 (given in Assessment Question 2) provides an illustration of the individual risks that together make up the e-business risk environment. At the company level, strategic risks can be categorized into e-business risk and non-e-business risk. It must be borne in mind that some of the boundaries of the risk categories are blurred. E-business risk is caused by the fact that the firm is in business to create a competitive advantage and create added value for stakeholders. This risk depends upon product market risk, economic risk and technological risk. Non-e-business risk is a product of event risk and financial risk. Given the turbulent nature of the technology sector, the threat of event risk becomes greater. Financial risk is symmetrical as the outcomes can be either a performance gain or a loss.

Strategic risk

According to Smith (2000), e-business brings new risks, whether it is embraced or not. There is much concern about online security. Serious as this issue is, there are some fundamental risks that should be considered. These include not doing anything at all, getting the strategy wrong and getting the implementation wrong.

Not doing anything at all

New and existing competitors can quickly alter the competitive landscape by delivering greater service excellence throughout the supply chain. This provides substantial benefits to those who are able to enhance customer value. These benefits have been explained in Chapter 2. An organization that suffers from a deterioration in customer relationships can suffer permanent damage to its reputation. Those e-businesses that are successful will be able to recruit and retain the most talented employees. Conversely, those firms that are unsuccessful are unlikely to attract or retain key employees. Some e-businesses that have not articulated their strategy may find it hard to attract and retain strategic partners.

Getting the strategy wrong

Chapter 2 explained the impacts of the Internet. So, if it is assumed that the Internet does impact the firm, most senior managers will need to formulate and implement an e-business strategy. As previously discussed, poor strategy can lead to corporate collapse. Smith (2000) asserts that management must understand their business. A good SWOT analysis (i.e. one that is customer orientated) is a solid base to start from. Chapter 4 addresses the strategic planning issues for e-business. The organization should take the opportunity to totally revisit what they do. Consideration should be given to core competences, contacts, alliances and other intangible assets. It is essential that the strategists appreciate what their business means to stakeholders. E-business represents an opportunity to organizations but it must not be seen as a panacea. In the rush to the e-business marketplace, the softer organizational issues such as power and culture should not be dismissed. The concept of power in an organization can be viewed in several ways. For example, power in the social world can be a term given to a facet of human relationships, and hence discussed with regard to relationships between people. Alternatively, power can be seen as a personal trait or power can be viewed as a consequence of position within a hierarchy. Organizational culture can be at odds with the immense changes created by e-business. Strain can be placed on the three layers of organizational culture, values, beliefs and the taken-for-granted assumptions (Schein, 1985). On a much wider dimension culture can relate to the individual person, functional department, professional institution and industry. Velocity in e-business should be matched with good decision-making ability. First-mover advantage was cited in the early days as a prerequisite for competitive advantage. However, when the bubble burst, providers began questioning the decision-making ability of the senior management team.

Getting the implementation wrong

E-business is re-shaping the IT of many organizations. The transformation is much more pervasive and complete than it has been in the past. E-commerce is only a small part of a much larger transformation, which involves how organizations interact with one another and how they use the ubiquitous Internet infrastructure. Different types of strategic change and different approaches to managing strategic change were evident within traditional organizations. However, with the development of e-business, there is need for new approaches to strategic change. Smith (2000) anticipates several implementation risks. There is a need to communicate e-business strategy and strategic objectives effectively in order to inform both internal and external key stakeholders.

Prior to the digital age, it was possible to have face-to-face meetings with colleagues to discuss the progress of projects. However, now with teams being scattered across towns, counties or continents, it is becoming popular to visit project members virtually rather than physically. Project managers have to deliver products and products in a much shorter time frame. In order to satisfy the on-time and within-budget goal, new project management techniques have become critical for successful implementation. Internet project management techniques are characterized as complex as a result of high speed, high change and high uncertainty.

Another problem organizations should avoid is promising more than they can deliver. During the Christmas 2000 period several high-profile firms received harmful publicity by not being able to satisfy customers in terms of back-office order fulfilment. In the UK, retailer Toys'R'Us had to close down its website well before 25 December.

Business risk
Product risk

Management needs to carefully consider the advantages and disadvantages of any particular strategy to develop new products. Prospects for those organizations that are able to digitize their products would appear to be favourable, but one should not ignore the risk and reward trade-off. Even those firms like insurers, who are of course used to dealing with risk and have built up expertise, have experienced problems in trying to generate sustainable e-business models. The e-business phenomenon alters the picture and it is crucial that decision-makers apply a systematic approach to product development. While it may be attractive to create a broad e-product line, many firms have found that in terms of cash flow it is expensive, risky and potentially unsustainable in the medium to long term.

The Ansoff (1987) product matrix tool can be used to illustrate the risk in product innovation. The presumption is based on the observation that taking an organization into a new commercial territory has risk associated with it. New products are more risky than traditional ones, as are new markets. Moreover, the combination of new products for new markets can be extremely risky. Managers should consider the product matrix when appraising new investments, as well as the best estimate of the measure of risk versus return.

In an e-business environment it may well be that only some of a selected number of e-commerce options can be implemented due to resource constraints. Figure 3.1 illustrates the product/market matrix that can assist identifying new strategic options to existing products. Moreover, the product risk can be enumerated, as each grid gives some indication of the risk associated with each option. In the example shown risk increases through options I to IV. In addition, e-business can be used to support a given product-market 'cell' in many different ways, for example by providing a new distribution channel and by allowing e-commerce transactions. These opportunities present a third 'dimension' of the matrix, providing a 'cube' of possible e-business opportunities. These can be prioritized, using appropriate risk techniques and using qualitative criteria.

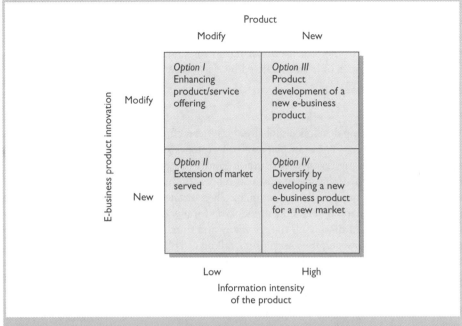

Figure 3.1 E-business market/product options (*Source: Adapted from Ansoff, 1987*)

Economic risk

The economy of any country plays an important factor in the management of e-business risks. For example, lower interest rates will tend to lead to narrower margins, as prices are transparent in an e-commerce environment. Organizations have had to reduce costs and redesign products. The general response to these trends has been a shift towards a customer-focus strategy. Previous preoccupation with product and market share has been expanded to include the best way to enhance customer loyalty and retention ratios. Another salient economic risk is the fluctuation of exchange rates. Management needs to appreciate the sources of exchange risk due to the fixed and floating exchange rates and the constant pressure for purchasing-power parity (Higson, 1995).

Technological risk

Technology and systems are central to e-businesses. Any e-business needs to construct a clear blueprint for constructing the IT platform. The risks of getting this wrong could be so great as to lead to the eventual demise of the business. Matters are not helped by paucity of available skilled labour resources in the IT industry. The ability to attract and retain key IT employees is a strategic issue. Matters are not helped by the lack of people being trained to respond to the needs of the rapidly changing e-marketplace. Despite governments around the world relaxing the restrictions on work permits, the job market for IT experts is global, so the problem will not go away as a result of a change in entry policy.

Non-business risk

Event risk

The consequence of a catastrophic business event poses a challenge to senior management. There is a need to fund measures that reduce the impact of catastrophes and provide financial protection to all stakeholders. According to Kunreuther (2000) the financial costs of natural disasters are increasing in size and public profile. Traditionally, it was felt that truly devasting events were so rare that organizations were unwilling to insure and take basic precautions against them. Now risk managers are looking to protect themselves with financial instruments, such as Act of God bonds. In terms of financial control, the enormity of the debts left by the collapse of Barings in 1995, $1.1bn of losses incurred by Daiwa bank in 1995 and £90m of losses incurred by Natwest Markets in 1997 indicate the seriousness of event risk.

Legal risk

While case law is being developed globally at an increasing rate, legal risk is an important issue for organizations. For example, as a consequence of the dot-com bubble bursting, scores of companies are franticly revising their exit strategies. E-business companies are facing the fact that the first wave of business models founded on advertising revenues and affiliate referral programmes do not automatically translate into millions of pounds. Senior management and shareholders alike are looking for a way out. The way out, however, is usually in the form of dissolving the company and moving on, or attempting to sell the remaining assets. However, the assets of the failing or failed dot-coms are ripe for the harvest. While both personal and intellectual property assets are now in abundance, and often available at a deep discount, buyers must not become enamoured and engage in hasty and potentially problematic transactions. Management that is considering entering into any agreement for the purchase of assets of a failed e-business should keep three goals in mind:

- Acquire ownership interest in the targeted assets.
- Ensure full delivery and transfer of the targeted assets.
- Do not take on hidden obligations or liabilities that were not supposed to be part of the deal.

The excitement of gaining a potentially new website and domain name at a low price can quickly diminish if the acquiring firm inadvertently assumes the seller's liabilities and contractual obligations.

Reputation risk

This risk is created by the chance of a fall in earnings or capital arising from negative public opinion. As previously discussed in Chapter 2, good relationships are the conerstone of delighted customers. In the worst scenario this could lead to litigation, financial loss or harmful publicity. Reputation can be become impaired even if customers suffer no actual damage. For example, if a computer hacker breaks into a website and makes alterations, the organization could suffer substantial damage to its reputation, although no customer may have suffered any pecuniary loss. Managerial justification for gaining customers through different customer loyalty programmes is that customer satisfaction and loyalty can have a positive influence on long-term financial performance. Additionally, the elements in achieving higher revenue – via customer retention are:

- Base revenue – the longer one can retain the customer, the more money one may make.
- Cost savings – customers appear to cost less to be served.
- Price premium – customers may pay more for one's product.
- Acquisition cost – customers are willing to cross-sell and up-sell themselves.
- They tend to generate recommendations (Reichheld, 1996). On these grounds it is not surprising that so many e-businesses have embarked on customer loyalty programmes, usually targeted at specific segmentation.

Disaster risk

Some organizations may feel that truly devastating events are so rare that it is not worth insuring or taking simple precautions against them. However, given the high-profile casualties of the Internet, it would be prudent for senior management to take advantage of IT developments and risk assessment methodologies. IT systems are now fast enough and powerful enough to create sophisticated models for estimating the risks associated with corporate collapse.

Regulatory risk

Despite certain markets, such as financial services and telecommunication, being traditionally regulated, the degree and form has diminished. Multilateral trade agreements have helped e-business escalate in previously regulated markets and this has led to widespread differential pricing. Two notable examples of trade agreements include:

- The World Trade Organization (WTO) Information Technology Agreement (ITA) of 1997, which eliminated tariffs on a range of Information and Communication Technology (ICT) products necessary for e-commerce, including computer hardware, computer software, telecommunications equipment, semiconductors and other electronic components and equipment by 1 January 2000. By 13 September 2000, the ITA had 42 participants, accounting for 93 per cent of trade in information technology products.
- The Agreement on Basic Telecommunications (ABT) of 1997, which saw 69 countries make commitments to allow foreign companies to supply telecommunications services in their markets, most of which had until then been state-owned monopolies. The ABT is estimated to have opened up 95 per cent of the world telecommunications market to real competition, encouraging investment in new technologies and promoting pro-competitive regulatory principles. The ABT has contributed to a fall of costs associated with telecommunications services, which has made previously unattractive markets attractive for global organizations.

Financial risk

One of the most important financial objectives for any organization is to create value. Unfortunately, since the ancient Greeks and perhaps even before, the notion of value has had a complex history. Accountants are still trying to grapple with defining the term value in its broadest sense. Debate has taken place on the link between the economic and ethical aspects. This in turn has made it difficult to identify, measure and communicate value-added activities throughout the organization. In finance, an organization only adds value for its shareholders when equity returns exceed equity costs (Black, Wright, Bachman and Davies, 1998). In economic terms an organization's specific competitive strategy is to develop and sustain a competitive advantage in its chosen market place so that it can earn a super profit, i.e. above normal rate of return (Ward, 1993). Figure 3.2 illustrates the options available for creating a sustainable competitive advantage.

When an organization operates in the financial markets it experiences three main categories of risk. These categories are market risk, credit risk and operational risk (Hussain, 2000). Market risk is the risk that the value of a contract, financial instrument, asset or portfolio will alter as economic conditions alter. Factors that affect organizations include changing interest rates, currency exchange rates, liquidity of financial markets and environmental events. Credit risk can be explained as the possibility that a counterparty will fail to honour an obligation to a financial institution. This relates to both settlement and pre-settlement credit risk for all customers. Operational risk can be explained as everything that is not market

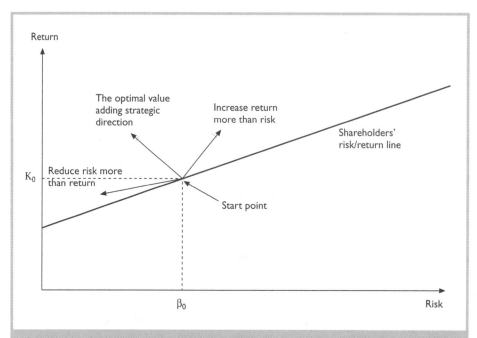

Figure 3.2 Economic value-adding strategies. Any strategy that moves the company to a point below the shareholders' risk/return line reduces shareholder value

and credit risk. Operational risk, which incorporates security risk, is one of the most frequently mentioned risks in connection with the Internet. Security problems are not new risks, but transacting online poses new issues.

STRATEGIC E-BUSINESS RISK MANAGEMENT

The scope of strategic e-business risk management is much wider and inclusive than traditional forms of technology security. Issues relating to technology security are discussed in much greater depth in Chapter 11 and related to the integrity of information assets. To be successful in an e-business environment it is necessary to cope with new forms of environment risk, e-business model risk and decision-making risk. These risk areas increase the level of uncertainty facing managers and consequently e-business strategy should be dynamic. It is also desirable that the e-business strategy is in alignment with strategic action and that those responsible for e-business strategy formulation and implementation ensure that they understand the key 'enabling relationships' through the supply chain.

Given the fact that e-business strategy needs to be continuously refined to adjustments in the external and internal environment, strategic dissonance theory, postulated by Burgelman and Grove (1996), can be applied to the e-business environment (Jagannathan, Srinivassan and Kalman, 2001). Burgelman and Grove (1996) provide a useful framework for the continuous refinement of strategy in a digital environment. This theory may be particularly relevant to e-business organizations as it has been noted that, in every dynamic industry, alignment between an organization's strategic intent and strategic action is not enduring. Inevitably, strategic actions will tend to either lead or lag strategic intent, which creates the divergence between intent and action and causes strategic dissonance. From a management perspective, strategic dissonance is a crucial issue, as failure to keep in alignment could place the organization at risk. Burgelman and Grove (1996) refer to the term 'strategic inflexion point', which describes the giving way of one type of industry dynamics to another. Therefore, monitoring risk becomes a key competence, as managers have to understand the e-business equilibrium and anticipate the next 'Internet inflexion point'. As senior management seek to create shareholder value, effective strategic e-business risk management represents a way for organizations to withdraw capital from non-efficient assets and to redeploy it in those assets that add value. Reaching an investment decision requires recognition of several factors, some of which include:

■ Is the quality and integrity of the data sufficient to make pertinent e-business related decisions?
■ How much resource should be allocated to each area of the e-business operation?
■ Is the e-business organization's response to major changes in the environment compatible with the new emerging e-business environment?
■ Is the e-business organization capable of evaluating the inherent risks during the decision-making process?
■ Does the e-business operation operate within a zone of accepted risk exposure?

IS THE ORGANIZATION READY FOR E-BUSINESS?

As it is important to minimize risk whenever possible, it is good practice to focus on the external business environment. In order to make sensible e-business strategic decisions, organizations should focus on the e-business environment and assess the various underlying details that, when considered together, produce a definitive picture of the environment. A useful methodology has been proposed by McConnell International (www.mcconnellinternational.com), which, in collaboration with www.witsa.org, considered the importance of seizing the opportunity of global e-readiness in terms of e-business risk. Mconnell International global e-readiness methodology involves rating by key attributes (see Table 3.2). The results of the tool combine a dynamic evaluation of the relevance and accuracy of available quantitative and qualitative data. This includes understanding a myriad cultural, institutional and historical factors relevant to the actual situation in each country. The ratings measure status and progress on five interrelated attributes:

■ Connectivity
■ E-leadership
■ Information security
■ Human capital
■ E-business climate

Connectivity
Potential e-business organizations need to be able to exchange information, goods and services on a global basis and have access to affordable information and communications technology and services, reliable electrical power and a reasonable transportation system. While connectivity by itself is an important first step, it must be borne in mind that it is not a sufficient condition for participation in the networked economy.

E-leadership
A nation's progress in a digital economy depends on alliances between government and the commercial sector to develop solutions that are sensitive to the specific needs of each

Key Attribute	Key Elements
Connectivity – are networks affordable and easy to access and use?	Availability of wireline and wireless communication services Level and depth of computing in businesses, homes and at schools Affordable and reliable networked access, including the cost of service, downtime and the amount of data sharing among users Conducive IT infrastructure, i.e. reliable electricity supply and efficient transportation systems within country
E-leadership – is e-business a national priority?	Enthusiasm of government towards the creation of an e-society Implementation of e-government processes Strength of e-commerce alliances between business leaders and government Government making sure that e-commerce is available for members of the society
Information security – can reliance be placed on the processing and storage of networked information?	Sophistication of laws safeguarding intellectual property rights Level of electronic privacy legislation Effectiveness of the legal framework to deal with computer-related crimes
Human capital – are there appropriate people available to build knowledge-based society?	Evidence of a knowledge-based society Appropriate culture and creativity within the country that leads to information sharing within the society IT-literate and efficient workforce
E-business climate – is the business climate conducive to the digital age?	Healthy competition among communication and information services providers Evidence of political stability, financial soundness, transparency and predictability of government decisions Evidence of financial and personal participation by foreign investors in ICT firms Financial systems having the sophistication to cope with electronic business transactions

(Source: McConnell International, 2000)

Table 3.2 E-business readiness attributes

market. However, without commitment between government and business leaders to create conditions favourable for e-business, progress will be slow and uneven. The preferred environment is created by the government adopting an inclusive style for all members of the population, but at the same time protecting consumer interests.

Information security

One of the most cited concerns of consumers is that of security. Therefore, prior to an explosion of online transactions the level of information security that an emerging market can achieve is important. Trust is at the root of the problem. Inadequate or obsolete laws or weak enforcement to protect those who create, maintain and disseminate information make an uncongenial environment in which to conduct e-business. The development of the software industry can be stunted by the poor protection of intellectual property. Inadequate protection of online personal data creates barriers to information exchange. Failure to recognize electronic signatures or to permit the use of encryption lessens consumers' trust.

Human capital

Organizations are competing globally fiercely for skilled IT people. Shortages are greatest in four areas: managers capable of completing complex e-business projects; strategists who understand government regulation's tendency to dampen business cycles, particularly in a fast changing technology environment; local content creators' awareness of the Internet's potential; and, software, hardware and communications architects/engineers. Obviously, to maximize the take up of e-business the government needs a population that has access to, and is able to use, the Internet.

E-business climate

While the previous four criteria can each contribute and enhance the quality of the e-business climate, the last criterion is not a combination of the other four. E-business is conducted in a complex context of regulatory policies and institutional arrangements that set the rules for the competitive marketplace. Interestingly, where policies and practices encourage e-business, performance outcomes will be higher. Where true competition is stifled or the rule of law is perceived to be weak, potential investors demand greater returns premiums for risk.

SUMMARY

This chapter assumes that risk is not always a good thing and a priority for senior management is that it needs to be managed. In finance programmes the term 'risk versus return' is often cited. Traditional attitudes about risk were focused around the mathematics of chance that an outcome other than expected will occur. In finance, investment risk is related to the possibility of actually earning a return other than expected.

Organizations are now expected to demonstrate higher levels of understanding of risk management. Risk management has moved beyond financial control and now encompasses the entire organization. It is important to adapt financial econometric models to the complex business environment. The challenges include e-business, death of distance, deregulation and more demanding consumers. When these are combined together, they form the competitive landscape for the new economy.

Why is e-business risk management important?

Running any business naturally entails taking risks. Various commentators have suggested that satisfactory performance will not emerge from a total risk-eliminating strategy; some risk is inevitable. Over the last few years dynamic dot.coms have captured public imagination through the creation of revolutionary business models. The collapse of the Swedish online fashion retailer Boo.com, which was the first and highest profile to fall, started to pave the way for other dot.com failures (see Table 3.1).

Organizational wide e-business risks

E-business risk management is a phenomenon that has become increasingly important owing to the limitations of technology. Insuretrust.com defines the term e-business risk management as the 'organizational strategies that incorporate all reasonable efforts to preserve the integrity of information assets and corporate intangible assets'. The surge in new electronic technologies has created the need for organizations to draw together all the risks that it faces.

Is the organization ready for e-business?

As it is important to minimize risk whenever possible, it is good practice to focus on the external business environment. In order to make sensible e-business strategic decisions, organizations should focus on the e-business environment and assess the various underlying details that, when considered together, produce a definitive picture of the environment. A useful methodology has been proposed by McConnell International (www.mcconnellinternational.com), which, in collaboration with www.witsa.org, considered the importance of seizing the opportunity of global e-Readiness in terms of e-business risk.

DISCUSSION QUESTIONS

1. Do you believe that e-business risk management is important? How does it differ from traditional forms of risk management?

2. What do you believe are the most important risks facing managers in an e-business environment? In your opinion does the importance vary by industry?

3. First-mover advantage was cited in the early days as a prerequisite for competitive advantage during the first wave of e-business. However, the early dot.coms had problems balancing decision-making tempo with risk. What do you believe are the salient lessons learned from seeking first-mover advantage?

GROUP ASSIGNMENT QUESTIONS

1. Using any company in Table 3.1, which provides a summary of some early dot.com failures, you are required to critically evaluate the events that led to the organization's demise. What lessons could be learned? What are the implications of your findings in terms of risk management?

2. Using the work of McConnell International (2000), which identifies e-business readiness attributes (see Table 3.2), you are required to assess the e-business risk in any organization of your choice in seizing the opportunity of global e-readiness.
You may find it useful to focus on connectivity, e-leadership, human capital and e-business climate.

3. The Ansoff (1987) product matrix tool can be used to illustrate the risk of product innovation. The presumption is based on the observation that taking an organization into a new commercial territory has risk associated with it. New products are more risky than traditional ones, as are new markets.

You are required to explain how managers should consider the product matrix when appraising new e-business investments. You will find it useful to illustrate your answer with an organization of your choice.

ASSESSMENT QUESTIONS

1. E-business risk management is a phenomenon that has become increasingly important owing to the limitations of technology. Insuretrust.com defines the term e-business risk management as the 'organizational strategies that incorporate all reasonable efforts to preserve the integrity of information assets and corporate intangible assets'.

You are required to outline how an e-business manager should preserve the integrity of information assets and corporate intangible assets.

2. With the development of e-business, there is need for new approaches to strategic change. Smith (2000) anticipates several implementation risks. There is a need to effectively communicate e-business strategy and strategic objectives to inform key stakeholders both internal and external.

Using Fig. Q3.1 you are required to focus on the e-business risks and explain how any organization of your choice is addressing these threats.

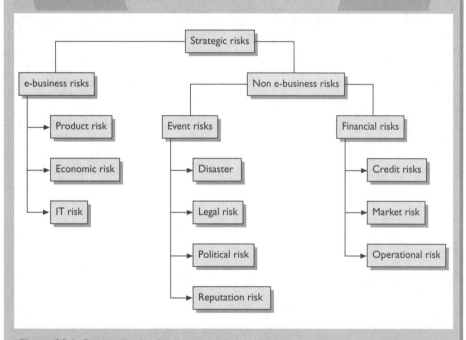

Figure Q3.1 Organizational-wide e-business risks

3. Using Table 3.2, critique the different approaches to e-leadership in two countries of your choice in terms of the work of McConnell International (2000). You are required to outline the relative strengths and weaknesses of the state of e-readiness.

MAIN CASE STUDY
Risk Management in the Internet Age, by J. Quinn, Bank Accounting & Finance, vol. 14, no. 1, pp. 33–37, 2000

The patterns of business-to-business (B2B) relationships and transactions are being fundamentally reshaped by the revolutionary impact of Internet-enabled commerce. As a crucial enabler of B2B activities, the corporate-lending and risk-management sector must respond to that set of radical transformations.

This article will describe the new risk-management topography of the rapidly evolving world of business-to-business e-commerce. The article looks at several ways in which developments in B2B e-commerce will have a dramatic impact on corporate lending and risk management. We begin by focusing on the avalanche of data that is being generated as a result of the explosive growth of B2B e-commerce. We then describe the stages of development through which risk-management processes will evolve in connection with B2B e-commerce. Then, we examine specific risk-management challenges and opportunities that are arising in connection with new patterns of B2B transactions. This will include discussion of the following:

- opportunities that are likely to arise in connection with not only improvements in traditional data but also the ability to tap new, nontraditional information;
- the impact that these changes can be expected to have on corporate-credit products, processes, and market segments.

New opportunities for savvy mining of B2B e-commerce data

Widely accepted projections estimate that, by 2004, B2B e-commerce will represent upwards of $2.5 trillion in transactions. The huge volume of these electronically mediated transactions means that there are opportunities to capture and to analyze enormous quantities of detailed transactional data about the interactions between B2B buyers and sellers. In some important ways, the situation that is emerging in today's corporate-credit sector can be compared to the transformations that shook up the consumer-credit sector during the late 1980s and early 1990s. Back then, a new breed of credit card issuer – including MBNA, First USA, Capital One, and Advanta – burst onto the scene and grabbed dominant shares of the market from the incumbent lenders. A major part of their success was driven by their aggressive and savvy use of new consumer data that had become available to which they then applied sophisticated new predictive modeling and data-driven risk-profiling techniques. The computer-based tools enabled credit-card issuers to do a better job of identifying prospective customers and to precisely evaluate the risk of those potential customers. Lenders were also able to use these new data to tailor offerings to match customers' predicted needs and to significantly refine their pricing to match an individual's risk profile.

These applications of new information radically reshaped the consumer-credit sector a decade ago. In the case of today's corporate-credit markets, look for analogous opportunities to arise in connection with the data that can be extracted from electronically mediated B2B transactions. This will include far-reaching changes in processes and products, as well as important opportunities for lenders and investors.

Stages of the credit-market evolution

To better understand the opportunities and challenges connected with this reshaping of the way in which corporate-credit risk and corresponding debt is priced and traded, it helps to think of it as unfolding through a process of three distinct, but related, steps. First, the creation of online B2B exchanges that match buyers and sellers of goods. This stage is in the midst of rapid development. It includes a significant and accelerating number of vertical (for example, automotive, chemicals, agriculture) and horizontal (for example, maintenance, repair, and operations [MRO], used capital equipment) electronic markets that have been established in the past 6 to 24 months.

Second, the addition of a first generation of credit decision and payment mechanisms to the B2B exchanges. These mechanisms would serve to link goods and payment exchange into a single transaction. Just as in the first step, this area is showing accelerated activity and includes initiatives from emerging financial intermediaries such as eCredit and Tradesafe.com. ECredit, for instance, is beginning to offer credit-risk analysis, credit for buyers, payment processing, escrow services, and receivables management. Additional capabilities to watch for include credit default insurance, insurance and warranties covering physical goods, and delivery of credit-risk derivatives to facilitate global trade. Other early entrants include Actrade, CapitalStream, ETime Capital, and i-escrow. Most of these players have arrived in the past 3 to 12 months.

Third, the emergence of a new breed of financial data providers. These new data providers take the new data that can be harvested from the activities that have been enabled in the first two steps. These data then could be used to reshape the corporate credit markets. These types of initiatives are still in a very early stage of development and will require addressing the following issues related to the data themselves: type (for example, receivables, payables, inventory); quality (for example, real-time, standardized); quantity (that is, many exchanges); and privacy (for example, permission based to facilitate specific credit transactions). Financial institutions need look no further than their own evolutionary history of standardization in the equity markets, bond markets, and retail consumer mortgage lending markets to see what lies ahead for corporate debt.

Improvements in traditional data: frequency, accuracy, and standardization

As these stages unfold, it will be imperative that institutions look to radically reshape the corporate-credit process. Today, credit-risk evaluation methods rely heavily on nonstandard data collected directly from corporate borrowers and on period-based data collected from third-party rating agencies or other market-data providers. These nonstandard or stale data are then used to support decisions affecting the origination, monitoring, and trading of corporate debt. Specific examples of these collection and analysis activities include:

- due diligence repeated by underwriters, syndicate members, and investors;
- ongoing collection and analysis of financial data to support credit-risk review, margining, debt covenant monitoring, and agency ratings.

In contrast, the new approach to credit-risk evaluation will be based on real-time, standardized information (for example, quality of sales, earnings before interest, taxes, depreciation, and amortization [EBITDA], payables, receivables) specific to a given corporation or sector that will be available from e-commerce sources. For instance, the limitations of today's data and tools means that companies of similar size, industry sector, and location currently tend to be evaluated by a single standard as though they all represented roughly the same level of credit risk. In contrast, the detailed data that e-commerce will make available will make it possible to develop new risk-analysis tools that will allow lenders and traders to do a better job of determining the credit risk of a particular company, and they then will be able to price loans or debt accordingly. It also will be possible to take transactional data and begin to correlate them – in almost real time – with industry or geographic economic variables and then to do value-at-risk modeling that will make it possible to assess how a company's risk profile is changing over time.

And, with regard to timeliness, lending and investing decisions for basic corporate loans currently can take weeks; complex international transactions often take 6 to 12 months. In the future, real-time, standard data will accelerate the due diligence conducted by lenders and investors, and it will reduce the cost to monitor credit risk once debt has been issued.

The impact of new sources and uses of nontraditional data

In addition to the refinement of traditional types of data that have been used in the past to inform corporate-credit decisions, there also will be opportunities to tap new sources of data. For instance, not only will there be more timely access to traditional data, but also it will be possible to get access to what might be thought of as behavioral or performance data for corporate customers. In effect, it will be possible to start scoring companies much the way that info-savvy consumer-credit institutions score their prospective customers for credit cards. Some of the data that could be extracted from B2B transaction databases could include:

• How often does this company come to the market?
• How many customers does the company have?
• Is the company's customer list increasing or decreasing?
• How concentrated is the company's business?
• How concentrated is the business of the customers of the company?

And, in fact, a similar analysis also might be done regarding the suppliers to a company.

Moreover, there are some very interesting ways in which lenders might be able to incorporate information about characteristics of specific suppliers or customers with whom the company is doing business. For example, analysis of e-commerce data might indicate that a company that is seeking credit suddenly has begun to sign contracts with customer companies that are – based on an analysis of electronic data – known for dragging out their payments to suppliers. This could be a sign that the company is struggling to pump up its sales figures and, consequently, is lowering the standards that it uses for screening customers.

Or the company might begin using suppliers who provide lower-quality products or materials that are especially attractive to companies that are struggling and, therefore, trying to cut short-term costs – again, perhaps, recognized through analysis of electronic data. This would be the analog of the way that a credit card company can make use of behavioral information that can flag when a consumer is undergoing financial distress. Yet another way of examining the data might be in terms of the distribution of a company's business by industry or by geography. For instance, analysis of data extracted from electronic transactions might be used to get a fairly good sense of how geographically concentrated the company's business is. How global, say, are they in their sales efforts? This information could be used to develop a much more precise level of currency, foreign exchange, and/or political risk connected to a company.

More generally, these and other opportunities will arise as a result of the greater ease and more timely access that e-commerce provides to transaction-generated data. And, in the end, this means that savvy lenders will be able to get a much clearer picture of the creditworthiness of a company and of the level (and nature) of risk that the company represents.

One likely way in which the evolution of corporate-credit processes might begin to unfold would be through a collaborative initiative between, say, a mutual fund and an organization that is applying the new risk-analysis tools. In this situation, the mutual fund might be seeking to buy loans that fit a specific profile that is based on traditional credit-risk information. The new credit-analysis capabilities then would take online data and use them to identify the best risks among the pool of companies that traditional analyses would rate as identical. These data-driven insights would make it possible to differentially underprice the market rates on the loans to these cream-of-the-crop risks, and the analysts and the mutual fund then would have the opportunity to split the spread for those loans.

Over time, the growth in this type of savvy utilization of e-generated data inexorably would pull the credit markets toward the new mode of operation.

Impact on products, processes, and market segments

Just-in-time financing: the use of working capital on a transaction-by-transaction basis versus revolving lines of credit

Consider the ways in which these types of data-enhanced capabilities will have an impact on today's corporate-credit origination process, making it possible to more accurately evaluate deal flow and affect decisions about which deals to pursue most aggressively. We will see deals that are structured and priced based on a specific borrower's real-time, digitized financial data as opposed to market comparables. This improved granularity in data will allow savvy lenders to identify mismatches between risk and will result in competitive pricing that will translate into improved performance of a lender's portfolio and the performance of their syndicate investors.

Benefits in corporate-credit origination do not need to be limited to lenders and investors, however. Borrowers stand to gain from shortened deal-origination cycles as well. Today, for example, small and midsize companies are forced to bundle their origination activity into larger offerings with components (that is, tranches) set up to cover short-, mid-, and longer-term capital needs. A more efficient process will allow businesses to take a more incremental, just-in-time approach to borrowing.

Extending credit to small and midsized business

The new data will be a particularly powerful tool when applied to currently underserved small-to-midsize companies and private companies. Even though these companies represent more than half of the U.S. economy, often only limited and imperfect information is available about them. This means that they have tended to fly below the radar screens of credit-rating agencies or other market data providers. New benefits now can be delivered to these small- and mid-cap players:

- reduced transaction costs (through reduction in the effort and time required to do the deal);
- reduced cost of capital (through reduction in the premium paid to lenders to compensate for lack of transparency and liquidity);
- increased liquidity (through improvement in the efficiency in matching a borrower's risk profile with an investor's risk appetite or desire for certain cash flows).

Aligning risk-management services with new patterns of B2B transactions

The explosive growth in B2B e-commerce also is creating a new set of challenges and opportunities directly as a result of the major changes that are under way in the patterns of B2B relationships and transactions.

Consider the impact of one of the most powerful transformative characteristics of the World Wide Web: the way in which the Web makes it possible to link up buyers and sellers who previously never would have been able to find one another, much less engage in business transactions. The most obvious effect of this is the way it is giving boost to international interaction and trade. The VerticalNet B2B exchange, for example, reports that fully 40% of the visitors to its multitude of industry-specific sites come from outside the U.S.

Even before the explosion of B2B e-commerce, the need for new risk-management services to support growing global trade has been on the rise. For example, between 1995 and 1998 the worldwide export credit insurance market expanded by 57%, which was double the rate of growth in world trade, which itself rose twice as fast as global output.

New services just announced by the Coface Group, a leading provider of export insurance headquartered in France, provide an early example of an effort to meet global-trade needs. More specifically, the new services offer to certify, secure, rate, and guarantee B2B trade over the Internet. This will allow banks, businesses, and virtual markets to assure the successful completion of the contractual obligations through the following steps:

• verifying the identities of the parties in an electronic transaction;
• establishing their delegations and contractual authorities;
• protecting against the repudiation of the transaction by either party.

Coface also has launched @rating, a tiered classification system that distinguishes among companies according to their ability to honor their commercial obligations. Other insurers are certain to launch similar kinds of services, and entirely new kinds of technology-enabled mechanisms also will emerge. One intriguing possibility: a B2B-community-based service that would rate B2B buyers and sellers, much like eBay participants already rate the partners with whom they have traded on the (primarily) consumer-to-consumer eBay exchange.

It also is important to remember that, whether or not the participants in these e-enabled B2B transactions actually are located at opposite points of the globe from one another, these new-to-one-another buyer–seller relationships are going to require a corporate-lending and risk-management infrastructure that can handle the torrent of risks that accompany business transactions between new trading partners.

Conclusion

The bottom line: Structural shifts are beginning to reshape the corporate lending and risk-management landscape, and enormous opportunities will be available to those who will manage to be the first to get a sense of the new lay of the land.

Overall, the real-time, standard data generated as a byproduct of the B2B exchanges will create opportunities for borrowers, lenders, and investors to exploit market inefficiencies and to extract benefits through reduced transaction costs and greater risk transparency. Big rewards await those savvy players who move swiftly to take advantage of these new data sources. And the key to their success will be their ability to quickly invent new tools that enable them to identify and take advantage of risk/return gaps before the general market competes away the opportunity.

It is important to emphasize that, as significant as first-mover advantages are in virtually every e-arena, they are likely to be even more accentuated in this sector. The looming transformation of corporate lending, risk management, and investment banking will be a complicated, multistage process. This means that enormous advantages will accrue to those who move early, who experiment shrewdly, and who are the quickest to gain understanding of how to effectively address the issues – and seize the opportunities – that will arise at each step of the evolution.

CASE QUESTIONS

Question 1 How have the patterns of B2B relationships and transactions been reshaped by the revolutionary impact of Internet-enabled commerce? What are the implications for the discipline of risk management?

Question 2 How has the Internet reshaped the consumer-credit sector? What are the new techniques available for B2B credit-scoring?

Question 3 Do you believe that first mover advantage is available in the credit-scoring sector? What are the risks of being first to market?

MINI CASE STUDY 1
Where did it go wrong for Clickmango.com?, by Sally Whittle, From Computing, August 2000

Toby Rowland, Clickmango's founder and chief operating officer, has news for those eager to write off the business. "We haven't thrown in the towel yet," he said.

Still, the outlook is bleak. Since April, when the company began looking for £10m to fund its international expansion, Clickmango has been turned down by 75 potential investors and suffered the humiliation of being refused a £300,000 bridging loan by its lead investor. The firm now has enough cash to survive for just six weeks.

So what went wrong? Last October, it took eight days for Clickmango to secure £3m in venture capital funding from Rothschild Capital and Atlas Venture. It recruited 80 staff from companies including Oracle, Disney and AOL, and roped in actress Joanna Lumley as its spokeswoman.

Costs were modest, with the vendor spending just £250,000 on marketing, and it focused on developing partnerships that would not cost it a lot of money, including a recently signed deal with Hotmail.

The website cost less than £1m to set up, while running costs were about £100,000 per month – even though burn rates of five times that sum are not unusual. Weekly sales were £2000 and growing at 20 per cent, while the company had a healthy six figure sum in the bank. Good – but not good enough.

Timing is everything
"I can't help thinking it's all about timing," said Rowland, his voice hoarse from phone calls with bankers, partners and customers. "We timed it wrong, and I don't think we're the only ones."

According to Matthew Nordan, director of European research at Forrester, Rowland is right. "We're going to see the trickle of dotcom failures become a flood," he warned.

"The climate is much tougher, and companies have to offer something not just good, but unique."

A report by PricewaterhouseCoopers earlier this year suggested that as many as 60 per cent of UK dotcoms would require additional financing before the end of the year. If Clickmango's example is anything to go by, those companies will find it hard to obtain.

Rowland's problems started when technology stocks crashed in April. Investor sentiment began to turn against business-to-consumer (B2C) startups, and was hardened by the collapse of boo.com in May. "That's when we made our mistake," said Rowland. "We waited until the service had launched before looking for funding, but the market had crashed and it was very difficult to find investors."

In the following weeks, Rowland learned a painful lesson. "The venture capitalists and investors are only interested for as long as they see a fast financial exit. I understand that much better now."

With the value of US sites such as Mother Nature and PlanetRX collapsing, investors were wary of companies with poor flotation prospects.

Rob Zegelaar, senior principal with Atlas, said: "We didn't see that a loan would help it raise the finance needed to build the business." In other words, Atlas didn't believe that Clickmango could raise the capital necessary for a sale or initial public offering (IPO), and so cut its losses.

The natural answer

Other B2C companies have been more fortunate, however. Competing health site Thinknatural raised £6m only weeks before the market crashed. "It's valued at five times more than US companies generating millions of dollars," said Rowland. "It's untenable, but [the valuation] gave it a platform to get more investment."

Thinknatural has since signed partnerships with the Kingfisher Group, which will sell its products in Superdrug stores, and Zoom.co.uk, the online arm of retail group Arcadia.

But an application by Kizoom.com for £5m in venture capital funding was turned down in May. The company, which provides wireless transport information, was lucky to find £500,000 from private investors, which kept it afloat long enough to sign an exclusive deal with Railtrack.

Damian Bown, Kizoom's founder and chief executive, said: "Venture capitalists didn't want to know, and didn't believe we could get partnerships." Today, Kizoom has access to 500,000 Railtrack customers every month, and plans to approach the venture capitalists again later in the year.

Without such capital, however, Clickmango found itself unable to attract similar partnerships despite five weeks of negotiations with high street giant Boots. "Even bricks and mortar investors watch the markets closely because they like to think that they have the option to run the business or to IPO it," Rowland explained.

But while bricks and mortar companies are sitting back and enjoying the Schadenfreude, Rowland believes people are missing the point. "No-one can say the business didn't work," he said. "We were only given three months to prove it."

In these tough times, however, it's easy to forget that many companies are making a roaring success out of their web ventures. AOL's quarterly cash flow is more than $1bn, and Amazon's run rate is more than twice that. But it's not surprising that these dotcom successes are peppered with many others sliding towards ruin.

It seems that revolutions must always consume their first and most passionate advocates.

Clickmango.com – the rise and possible fall

- **June 1999** Robert Norton, former head of ecommerce at AOLUK, and Toby Rowland, head of data mining at Disney, conceive of a natural health site.
- **October 1999** The two 30-year-olds secure £500,000 from Rothschild Capital and £2.5m from Atlas Venture.
- **November 1999** The company moves from its one-room office to London's fashionable Brick Lane. Rowland negotiates a rent reduction.
- **December 1999** Rowland hires a feng shui consultant for the office who positions his desk facing the wall. Norton pays an undisclosed amount for an inflatable pink and green boardroom.
- **January 2000** Actress Joanna Lumley helps Clickmango launch in the UK and France, with 80 employees.
- **April 2000** With £1m in the bank, Clickmango begins negotiations for a second round of funding, with the aim of raising a further £10m. Existing investors decline to take part.
- **May 2000** Norton devotes himself to full-time fundraising, while Rowland runs the business. The company signs its 900th supplier.
- **June 2000** Clickmango closes its French operation, and approaches Atlas Venture for a £300,000 bridging loan.
- **July 2000** The bridging loan is refused. Clickmango enters into negotiations with Boots, and says it will stay open until at least September.

CASE QUESTIONS

Question 1 Despite prudent financial expenditure and weekly sales growing at 20 per cent, why was Clickmango experiencing difficulties?

Question 2 While bricks and mortar companies are sitting back and enjoying the Schadenfreude, Rowland believes people are missing the point. 'No-one can say the business didn't work,' he said. 'We were only given three months to prove it'. Do you agree with this statement? You should illustrate your views with appropriate examples.

MINI CASE STUDY II
Clickmango shuts up shop, by James Middleton, uk.internet.com, 5 September 2000

The death knell has finally sounded for struggling online health and beauty retailer Clickmango, which announced today that it would be shutting up shop on 11 September. The death knell has finally sounded for struggling online health and beauty retailer Clickmango, which announced today that it would be shutting up shop on 11 September.

Clickmango earned an eleventh-hour stay of execution last month as it attempted to conclude negotiations with one of many "blue-chip white knights" who had made approaches to acquire or invest in the company, according to co-founder Robert Norton.

However, Norton said the decision has now been taken to close the company "rather than risk insolvency". He said the closure would allow Clickmango to meet contractual obligations to creditors and staff.

"We have had a great deal of support over recent months and it is extremely important that we honour our agreements," he said.

Norton claimed that Clickmango had received "a number of offers" since the announcement last month and had spoken to all of those who had shown an interest in acquiring or investing in the business, but to no avail.

Employees have been given 30 days' notice, and only a skeleton staff remains behind to finish shutting down the business.

The site, fronted by *Absolutely Fabulous* star Joanna Lumley, was launched on 11 April this year. It will stop taking orders on 11 September and will be taken down the next day.

CASE QUESTIONS

Question 1 Clickmango earned an eleventh-hour stay of execution last month as it attempted to conclude negotiations with one of many 'blue-chip white knights' who had made approaches to acquire or invest in the company, according to co-founder Robert Norton.

What do you understand by the term 'blue chip white knight?' Do you think that a 'blue chip white knight' would have been able to keep Clickmango trading for the next two to three years?

Question 2 What do you think are the salient lessons learned in the demise of Clickmango?

REFERENCES

Ansoff, I. (1987) *Corporate Strategy*, revised edn, Penguin, London.

Black, A., P. Wright, J.E. Bachman and J. Davies (1998) *In Search of Shareholder Value: Managing the Drivers of Performance*, FT Pitman Publishing, London.

Brigham, E.F., L.C. Gapenski and M.C. Ehrhardt (1999) *Financial Management: Theory and Practice*, 9th edn, Dryden Press, Orlando, FL.

Brown, G.W. (2000) Seeking security in a volatile world, Mastering Risk, part 4 of 10, *Financial Times*, 16 May, pp. 2–4.

Burgelman, R.A. and A.S. Grove (1996) Strategic dissonance, *California Management Review*, vol. 38, no. 2, pp. 8–28

Cadbury Report, The (1992). *The Financial Aspects of Corporate Governance*, December, Gee, London.

Higson, C. (1995) *Business Finance*, 2nd edn, Butterworths, London.

Hunt, B. (2000) Issues of the moment the rise and rise of risk management, Mastering Risk, part 10 of 10, *Financial Times*, 27 June, pp. 2–4.

Hussain, A. (2000) *Managing Operational Risk in Financial Markets*, Butterworth-Heinemann, Oxford.

Institute of Chartered Accountants (1999) *Internal Control: Guidance for Directors on the Combined Codes*, ICAEW, London; www.icaew.co.uk/internalcontrol.

Jagannathan, S.R., J. Srinivassan and J.L. Kalman (2001) *Internet Commerce Metrics and Models: in the New Era of Accountability*, Prentice Hall PTR, Upper Straddle River, NJ.

Kazim, A. (1999) The impact of electronic business on the insurance industry, *Insurance Digest*, PriceWaterhouseCoopers, London, Spring, pp. 4–7.

Kunreuther, H. (2000) Seeking succour from the rising costs of catastrophe, Mastering Risk, part 9 of 10, *Financial Times*, 20 June, pp. 2–4.

McConnell International (2000). *Risk E-business: Seizing the Opportunity of Global E-readiness*, in collaboration with World Information Technology and Service Alliance.

Meulbroek, L. (2000) Total strategies for company-wide risk control, Mastering Risk, part 3 of 10, *Financial Times*, 9 May, pp. 2–47.

Quinn, J. (2000) Risk management in the Internet age, *Bank Accounting & Finance*, vol. 14, no. 1, pp. 33–37.

Reichheld, F.F. (1996) *The Loyalty Effect*, Harvard Business School Press, Boston, MA.

Schein, C. (1985) *Organisation Culture and Leadership*, Jossey-Bass, San Francisco, CA.

Smith, D. (2000) E-business risk management, *Computer Law & Security*, vol. 16, no. 6, pp. 396–398.

Ward, K. (1993). Accounting for a sustainable competitive advantage, *Management Accounting CIMA*, vol. 71, no. 9, p. 36.

CHAPTER 4
STRATEGIC PLANNING FOR E-BUSINESS ORGANIZATIONS

LEARNING OUTCOMES

When you have read and worked through this chapter, you will be able to:

- Appreciate the importance of strategic planning
- Understand the problems with traditional strategic planning systems
- Understand the problems of measuring strategic planning effectiveness
- Formulate e-business strategies
- Appreciate the need for e-business strategy to create value
- Identify European Internet main players
- Appreciate the importance of e-business strategy formulation and implementation in the service-sector, manufacturing and public-sector environments

INTRODUCTION

In contrast to much of the early thinking about **e-business strategy**, as highlighted in Chapter 1, the Internet has not changed the fundamentals of business and corporate strategy, as the essence of commercial business is still the generation of value by offerings to customers (Mathur and Kenyon, 2001). Nevertheless, evidence over the last two years would suggest that some investments in e-business have been rather imprudent with the business proposition being in some cases weak. This has resulted in e-business strategic plans being founded on optimism and hope rather than on solid business propositions and sound strategies. This chapter seeks to provide a basic understanding of formulating, implementing and evaluating e-business strategies and considers **deliberate** rather than **emergent e-business strategies** (see Mintzberg and Walters, 1985 for a discussion about emergent strategies).

Adopting the philosophy of Mathur and Kenyon (2001), this chapter starts off by considering the fundamentals of traditional **strategic planning**, by asking the question 'Why perform strategic planning?' and then considers problems with traditional strategic planning systems. **Strategic planning effectiveness** is proposed as a way of enhancing business performance. Some recent insights of e-business strategy academic literature are used to outline current themes. A review of European Internet main players is performed to outline developments in Europe. The chapter concludes by briefly looking at e-business activities in manufacturing and public-sector environments.

WHY PERFORM STRATEGIC PLANNING?

During four decades of empirical research, strategic planning has proven to be an essential prerequisite in successful organizations. Although this has not always been revealed in

Key Term...

E-business strategy
The online strategy used to connect with customers, partners and suppliers and the transformation of existing business processes to enhance shareholder value

Key Term...

Deliberate e-business strategy
A deliberate e-business strategy is one that has been conceived by the top management team as a planned systematic response to the turbulent environment facing the e-business organization

Key Term...

Emergent e-business strategy
An emergent e-business strategy is one that evolves from lower down the organization without team management intervention

Key Term...

Strategic planning
Strategic planning involves the entire process of defining the future direction and character of the organization, and of attempting over an adopted timetable to attain the desired state to accomplish related goals and outcomes.

Key Term...

Strategic planning effectiveness
Planning; formality, participation, sophistication and thoroughness are important attributes of strategic planning effectiveness

empirical research, positive planning–performance studies outnumber negative ones. The 1990s have seen a variety of empirical studies that have reported the benefits of strategic planning (see Phillips and Moutinho, 2000 for a review of the literature). As a consequence of squeezing costs, downsizing and shaving seconds from cycle time during the last recession, strategic planning is now in vogue, but with new definitions. The philosophy of this chapter is that a good e-business strategy can be developed from a good strategic planning system. Naturally, over time the focus of the planning process needs to change.

Budget-based strategic planning has been replaced with flexible new approaches and new processes to identify and build core competencies for the digital economy. Organizations can secure themselves a healthy competitive position in the third millennium by formulating strategies that can be implemented in the marketplace. During the earlier stages of the Internet several e-business consultants stated that the 'strategic planning process should be 10 per cent planning and 90 per cent implementation' It was now no good spending six to nine months trying to formulate the best strategy and then leaving the client to deal with the problem of implementation. The e-business landscape is changing at such a rate that in a short period of time dot.coms have moved through the entire e-business cycle and, instead of being in a position to challenge legacy firms, they are now battling for survival. A significant statement was made by UK's *The Times* newspaper on Saturday 19 May 2001, which reported that the bullish projections of £1000 billion in e-commerce revenue in Europe by 2004 will not materialize. Moreover, dot.com entrepreneurs have learned the painful lesson that the Internet is just another communication and distribution medium. The Internet now places the power back with the bricks-and-mortar companies. As a result of the changing landscape, *The Times* newspaper stated that it was to end its specialised e-business page and return e-business coverage to its rightful place – on the traditional business pages.

For effective decision-making, the management team must be truly integrated. It is important to co-ordinate strategic activities across multiple strategic business units and functions. To achieve this integration, management must confront many challenges. Economic power has now shifted from the organization (i.e. supplier and producer) to the consumer. Consumers are the judges of what makes up a quality product and/or service. Therefore, the challenge is to create consumer value. An effective strategic planning system could create the framework that allows management to create added value. Strategic planning systems can assist organizations with strategy formulation and implementation. Moreover, an effective strategy process leverages core competencies and affords the flexibility to recognize and exploit external opportunities.

This book asserts that the solution to some of the above problems can be determined through the design and implementation of an effective strategic planning process. To illustrate this we shall briefly review some of the strategic planning systems literature.

PROBLEMS WITH TRADITIONAL STRATEGIC PLANNING SYSTEMS

Phillips and Moutinho (1998) in their study noted that organizations with ineffective strategic planning systems (SPS) suffered four major problems:

- Strategic planning process is biased by the budget process.
- There is a performance gap between those firms that do and those that do not encourage strategic thinking.

- There is a lack of objective data for decision-making.
- There is a lack of marketing/finance techniques for non-routine decision-making.

Strategic planning process biased by the budget process

Budget-based planning is more of a control mechanism and is deficient in that it does not fully consider the immediate strategic question concerning target markets, service levels and competitor analysis, let alone the longer-term strategic issues of environmental change.

Performance gap between those firms that do and those that do not encourage strategic thinking

Not only did some organizations consider and answer the question 'Shall we adopt a strategic management process?', but more importantly they were continually trying to ascertain what processes are appropriate. The benefits were encouraging with indications that best practice is linked to superior performance.

Lack of objective data for decision-making

Many participants complained that their existing information system did not provide them with adequate 'hard' data required for strategic decision-making. Traditional systems were excellent at transaction processing but were unable to provide management with strategic information, which tended to be of a qualitative nature.

Lack of marketing/finance techniques for non-routine decision-making

Beyond basic marketing and financial techniques there was a general distrust of the managerial tools and techniques used in best-practice organizations. Thus, instead of beleaguered managers trying to adapt to the external environment by using more sophisticated techniques, many placed reliance on gut feeling. Unfortunately, as a consequence of the insular approach many organizations displayed the following symptoms:

- Lower levels of performance
- Lack of a SPS that translates strategy into action
- Lack of focus on appropriate measures beyond traditional financial measures
- Accounting myopia

The changes previously discussed are leading to new and greater demands on strategic planning systems. We have now probably reached the stage where every corporate strategist is currently preoccupied with trying to determine how value can be created from an e-business environment. Moreover, given that several high-profile Internet companies are cash negative and loss making, e-business strategic decision-making is that much more difficult. So, given that the sole purpose of strategic planning is to improve strategic performance, improving, assessing and monitoring the effectiveness of the e-business strategic planning process would appear to be a key managerial task. However, anecdotal evidence would suggest that many e-business firms do not perform the task adequately.

The traditional approach to evaluating the effectiveness of the strategic planning process within an organization is measured in terms of its corporate strategy meeting and exceeding the needs of all stakeholders. However, measuring the effectiveness of the nature of e-business strategic planning in firms, as opposed solely to measuring performance outcomes, is problematic. First, given the time lag between strategy formulation, implementation and improvement, how do managers determine at an early stage when and where the strategic planning process is weak? Second, how do managers measure the qualitative or intangible attributes of the strategic planning process? Third, how can strategic planning effectiveness be expressed for internal and external benchmarking?

Despite the improvement in planning scales used by academics, the tendency is still to treat planning in terms of a single dimensional perspective. For example, some studies have measured strategic planning solely in terms of: formality (e.g. McKiernan and Morris, 1995); comprehensiveness (e.g. Fredrickson, 1984); sophistication (e.g. Robinson and Pearce, 1988); and length of planning horizon (e.g. Rhyne, 1986). Strategic planning is a multidimensional construct covering all functional areas of the organization. Firms should therefore try to identify the most important attributes of e-business strategic planning. Finding the variables that reflect good planning should be the thrust of strategic planners. This multidimensional approach has been the thrust of the SPS literature. However, as succinctly stated by Greenley (1993, p. 3):

> " improved management effectiveness through strategic planning may lead to improved performance, but this will depend on the ability of managers to address the range of internal and external variables that impinge on performance. "

The need for a multidimensional approach to conceptualization and measurement of planning systems dimensions has been highlighted (e.g. Yasai-Ardekani and Haug, 1997). Given the shift in the SPS literature from one-dimensional to multidimensional perspective, managers might find it useful to adopt the SPS approach as the organizing framework. Contingency theory argues that the design and use of systems is contingent upon the context of the organizational setting (Hofer, 1975). This assumes a match between the strategic planning system and the contextual contingency variables, which are hypothesized to lead to sustainable competitive advantage. Assuming that there is more than one way to develop and implement strategy, the key to effective e-business strategic planning is to get the best fit between the organization's culture, capability, external environment and desired performance goals.

MEASURING STRATEGIC PLANNING EFFECTIVENESS

Strategic alliances in the emerging digitized global economy are becoming increasingly dependent on information and communication technologies for co-ordinating their organizational activities. Controlling globally distributed, networked, multi-partner enterprises is a major governance challenge. Maximizing shareholder value by leveraging new digitized technologies as an enabler is perceived to be an important way forward for improving organizational effectiveness and gaining strategic (and operational) business advantage. An effective strategic planning process has been found to be associated with higher levels of business performance (Phillips, Davies and Moutinho, 1999).

Phillips (1996) identified four crucial characteristics of strategic planning effectiveness – formality, participation, sophistication and thoroughness, which were found to be positively and significantly related to the dimensions of efficiency, effectiveness and adaptability.

Planning formality
Formal strategic planning is an explicit and ongoing organizational process, with several components, including establishment of goals and generation and evaluation of strategies. However, as most organizations are engaged in strategic planning, with the advent of the Internet corporates need to develop more rigorous methods for gauging the formality of the strategic planning process.

Planning participation

Participation has been identified as an important component of the planning process. Senior management must be committed and believe that the Internet presents a business opportunity rather than merely treat it as a defensive mechanism. Once senior management have embraced e-business, then it becomes easier to gain ownership and commitment from employees.

Planning sophistication

Several planning–performance studies have successfully examined the relationship between sophistication and performance (Phillips and Moutinho, 2000). Sophistication has been defined in many ways. These include: structured strategic plans; structured operational plans; intuitive plans; and unstructured plans. In another study sophistication was defined as high, moderate and low, while in a third study churches were designated as informal planners, operational planners or long-range planners.

Planning thoroughness

In today's tumultuous environment it seems logical that executives would benefit from obtaining guidelines or benchmarks associated with best-practice business strategic planning. By comparing such information with their own planning practices, managers could incorporate good practices used by other organizations into their own business. The identification and implementation of such key characteristics would cause an organization to develop better strategic plans. These critical planning procedures can be evaluated by the measure of thoroughness.

These four high-level factors are by no means exhaustive (Phillips and Moutinho, 2000). However, based on previous research, together with the fact that organizations were at the 'end of the beginning', they capture a set of attributes that provide a useful first step for measuring strategic planning effectiveness. Individually, these attributes can assist managers by providing the catalyst for continuous improvement in strategic planning, formulation, implementation and evaluation. Collectively, the attributes can assist in the development of 'turnaround' strategies to maximize planning effectiveness.

DEVELOPING THE E-BUSINESS STRATEGY

In Chapter 1, the public-sector origins of the Internet were highlighted. However, considerable attention is now being paid to private-sector organizations that are actively exploring and exploiting the potential of the Internet and associated technologies (Doherty and McAulay, 2002). The difference between offering an online and offline product/service is highlighted by the fact that in an offline environment it is normal to identify one or two critical benefits. However, in an online world, a firm must develop a wide array of benefits. Rayport and Jaworski (2001) postulate that senior management must complete three sequential tasks when considering an online offering:

- Identify the scope of the offering.
- Identify the customer decision process.
- Map the offering to the consumer decision process.

The new millennium has seen the rise and fall of 'dot.com' firms, coupled with hype and disappointment over what the Internet will bring to business. While investors may now have taken a dislike to Web-based firms, problems of embracing or responding to the Internet remain a challenge for managers of established firms (Loebbecke and Powell, 2002). For today's e-business organization, it may be simple to set up a Web presence, but it has proved difficult to create a sustainable online business. Just a few years ago, being first to the marketplace was viewed as a prerequisite to success. Despite acknowledging the merits of speed, Bates, Rizvi, Tewari and Vardhan (2001) cite proponents who stated that 'you have to act; you can't afford to think about it'. Bates *et al.* (2001) concluded that, gripped by a misunderstanding of competitive dynamics, dot.coms squandered their ample but not limitless resources.

Table 4.1 shows how the Internet has created a market for **e-services**. The categories of hosted (rented) applications, online services, content providers and providers of physical goods present an array of opportunities for entrepreneurs. Oliveira, Roth and Gilland (2002), developing the e-service theme, pose an interesting question by asking 'How can business performance of e-service companies be improved in today's knowledge-based economy?' They propose a model that links the e-service company's knowledge-based competencies with their competitive capabilities. From a synthesis of the current literature, their analysis suggests that services that strategically build a portfolio of knowledge-based competencies, namely human capital, structural capital and absorptive capacity, have more operations-based options than their counterparts who are less apt to invest.

E-service Categories	Definition	Examples
Hosted (rented) applications	Central server-based software application wherein significant or total functionality and features are delivered via Internet connection. Usually purchased on a pay-per-use or subscription basis	Accounting Time and expense tracking Business planning Sales automation Intranets Project management
Online services	Corporate and personal services enhanced and facilitated through Internet based communication	Banking Human resource management Website monitoring Online learning
Content providers	Commercial information sources, utilizing the Internet to provide subscription-based delivery of digital media or content	News Financial information Research Audio Video
Providers of physical goods	Delivery of final physical goods enhanced and facilitated by Internet-based communication. Internet may enable easier communication or facilitation of delivery or may allow customization of final physical goods	Printed material Purchase or rental of entertainment media Consumables

(Source: At Your e-Service, http://www.atyourservice.com/)

Table 4.1 What are e-services?

Key Term...

E-services
A business concept developed by Hewlett Packard, e-services is the idea that the World Wide Web is moving beyond e-business and e-commerce. Instead of solely focusing on the issue of completing sales on the Web, organizations are now providing services for businesses or consumers using the Web

A useful checklist has been proffered by Hayes (2000) who cites seven steps to e-business success. These are as follows:

- Start high – radically change your business do not simply develop a fancy website.
- Think fresh – think outside of the black box.
- Know your market – understand the needs of your market.
- Set vision – set a long-term vision.
- Define strategy – define, prioritize and select e-initatives.
- Create – transform the business through a set of corporate initiatives.
- Refresh regularly – remember speed, innovation and change are important.

Analysing the e-business environment

According to Porter (2001) the Internet has not created new industries except for hi-tech, such as online auctions and digital marketplaces, but the greatest impact has been its ability to reconfigure existing industries. A good example is the part-time MBA programme market. Schneider (2001) highlights the availability of MBA programmes that enable students to work while they study. **Web-enabled courses** mean that business schools can expand distance learning and at the same time maintain healthy margins. Porter (2001) asserts that his five-forces framework (Porter, 1980) can be used in an e-business environment. The following five underlying forces can determine e-business industry attractiveness: threat of substitute product/service; bargaining of suppliers; barriers to entry; bargaining power of buyers; and rivalry among existing competitors.

Key Term...

Web-enabled courses
The provision of education courses over the Internet, which can mean that business schools can expand distance learning and at the same time maintain healthy margins, due to low distribution costs

Threat of substitute product/service

The Internet provides opportunities to organizations by boosting an industry's efficiency in various ways and increasing the overall size of the market relative to traditional substitutes. There could be product-for-product substitution, where there is a replacement of traditional products due to technology innovation. For example, fax being a substitute for the postal service and then email for fax. The proliferation of new enhanced technology offerings such as VOD (video on demand), MP3 and digital wide-screen televisions, are now competing as generic substitutes for traditional furniture and other available household expenditure. Nevertheless, online firms must beware of the threat of obsolescence, the ability for customers to switch to substitutes at a click and the cost structure of their product/service.

Bargaining power of suppliers

The importance of understanding the bargaining power of suppliers has been previously discussed in Chapter 2. The Internet widens access to suppliers and this has increased the bargaining power over suppliers. It must not be forgotten that at the same it provides suppliers' access to more customers. One of the earlier threats of the Internet has been disintermediation, where only those parties who are perceived to be adding value would remain in the value chain. Internet procurement and digital markets improve the efficiency of the marketplace, but, as procedures lead to standardized products, this reduces differentiation.

Barriers to entry

During the first wave of the Internet rush, one of the most hyped benefits was the economies of scale that could be achieved through the ubiquitous appeal of the Internet. These unit-cost reductions would lead to lower prices to consumers and firms would benefit from a disproportionate increase in sales volumes. However, this attracted new forms of competition to a whole range of industries. For example, in traditionally regulated markets, efficiency was not a primary concern for senior management. In some markets, insurance firms made used of part-time salespeople who would sell insurance inefficiently in addition to their full-time job. Now with some markets becoming deregulated, strategists within overseas corporations can quickly spot market inefficiencies. The Internet reduces the need for a direct sales force and more efficient distribution channels can be designed.

Bargaining power of buyers

The Internet has tended to standardize products and one of the reasons for e-business failures is that markets have become crowded. Buyers have more power when products are undifferentiated, so the strategist must bear this in mind when assessing industry attractiveness. If there are few buyers and they are concentrated, this reduces switching costs, as organizations have little option but to negotiate with a buyer. Several organizations have created e-markets where buyers specify their requirements and potential suppliers have to bid for contracts.

Rivalry among existing competitors

Competitive intensity varies by market. In those markets where products/services can be digitized, strategists have to engage in regular and extensive monitoring of primary competitors. The Internet reduces the differences among competitors, as offerings are hard to keep proprietary. This in turn focuses attention on price. Any change in price by an organization can result in a simultaneous reaction from a competitor. Strategists also need to be aware of new forms of competitors; the Internet widens geographic coverage and simultaneously increases the potential for new players in the marketplace. With some of the earlier revenue projections of the Internet not materializing, e-business organizations that are looking for growth in sales volumes have to win sales from competitors. This has increased the threat of rivalry and it is perhaps another reason why there have been so many Internet casualties.

Porter's (1980) five-forces model is a useful tool to use in analysing the environment, but the user should not see the tool as a panacea. The e-business environment is rapidly changing, so forces may move from high to low or vice versa much more quickly than a new model is formulated. The model does not place emphasis on the customer, but assumes that all aspects of the microenvironment are vital. Given the importance of the customer, as seen previously in Chapter 2, this is a major concern. The Internet has made organizations place emphasis on collaboration and co-operation. The five-forces model also overlooks the role of people and how they interact within organizations. Given the fact that issues relating to culture and internal competencies can affect strategy, this can represent a significant barrier to a successful strategy implementation.

What are the strategic options?

According to the previous chapter the risks of doing nothing are perhaps too large to contemplate, so the strategist needs to pursue an appropriate strategy. The response from organizations has been predictably mixed, with earlier e-business strategies being defensive. The collapse of Internet stocks has led analysts to suggest that e-business firms pursue more innovative strategies. An organization's strategy can have three domains: entrepreneurial, relating to how the organization orients itself to the marketplace; administrative, embracing how the organization attempts to co-ordinate and implement its strategies; and technical, referring to the IT and business processes used to produce the organization's products and services. There are at least three strategic options available, defender, attacker and reaction.

Defender

This type of strategy (Miles and Snow, 1978) appears suitable for a firm that seeks to obtain cost advantages. However, in an e-business environment there are two problems with this type of strategy. First, low cost advantage is at best value neutral in the medium term. Salomon Smith Barney (1999) supports this assertion, by saying that, despite the cost advantages being highlighted in insurance research studies, lower costs will result in lower prices. In a transparent environment, customers can quickly obtain the lower prices for identical products. In addition, Web insurance may become less profitable than in a bricks and mortar environment. A worst-case scenario would be the defender firm having nothing left to defend.

Attacker

The earlier pioneers of the Internet were those firms that were aggressive in outlook, and pioneering in their quest for new product/market segments. They sought to create new business models that embraced the Internet, the idea being that the seamless integration of its value chain offered a competitive advantage that is hard to dislodge.

Reactor

The reactor realises that changes are taken place in their market place but reacts by doing nothing (Miles and Snow, 1978). Comments from various commentators in the early days of the Internet that if your business does not go online, then your organization risks becoming history suggested that this strategy is one to be avoided. However, given the prominence of clicks and bricks, a one hundred per cent presence on the Internet is not always necessary.

Internet portfolio analysis

At their most basic, organizations consist of a bundle of projects, and a failure to invest systematically can lead to an organization investing a large amount of cash in ill-fated Internet initiatives. According to Booz Allen & Hamilton (2001), organizations that are successful in developing new lines of business have a clearly articulated portfolio strategy that covers the following considerations:

- Type of business opportunity
- Capital investment parameters
- Degree of operational involvement
- Link with core business
- Pipeline objectives

This is perhaps timely, because the time has come when managers should be using rigorous screening processes when selecting which projects to back. Booz Allen & Hamilton postulate that there is a clear distinction between how corporate venture groups and independent incubators screen new business opportunities. The former groups focus on synergy with core assets while the latter emphasize intra-portfolio synergies, market dominance and the management team. This is illustrated in Table 4.2.

A comparison of classical portfolio planning and Internet portfolio planning is illustrated in Table 4.3. Tjan (2001) cites the example of Sun Microsystems, who decided that they were going to place their entire business onto the Internet. However, the company had more than 100 live Internet projects that spread over five separate online stores. This wide array of Internet initiatives confused all stakeholders and also wasted cash. Using Sun Microsystems as an example, Tjan proposes a framework that has been used widely.

Criteria	Corporate VC/Incubator	Independent VC/Incubator
Strategic	Leverage core assets	Intra-portfolio synergies
Competitive	Competitive in target space	Industry leader
Industry	Industry-related	Growth markets/industries
Management	Industry expert	Experienced business builder
Financial	Low risk, material return	High risk, high return
(Source: Booz Allen & Hamilton, 2001)		

Table 4.2 Screening criteria for new projects

As risk is inherent in all business projects, Tjan suggests that companies often make one of three mistakes when making investment decisions.

Let a thousand flowers bloom
Venture capitalist and organizations were guilty of being too scared to be left out of the Internet by spreading cash too wide and thin. It can be healthy to experiment but to invest in all projects in the hope that a few will flourish is dangerous.

Bet it all
An antithetical approach to letting a thousand flowers bloom is the bet-it-all approach. Instead of throwing money at a wide variety of projects, management decides to devote all cash resources to a single initiative. The unpredictable nature of Internet means that the downside risk is to lose it all.

Trend-surf
In periods of uncertainty it is all too easy to follow the crowd in the race to the next big thing. This tendency has been used by many Internet investors to supply funds to the latest trend that has evolved, from websites to B2C sites, B2B markets, m-commerce and storage. With a few notable exceptions too much money gets invested and then lost in too few opportunities.

Classical Portfolio Planning	Internet Portfolio Planning
Used in mature markets	Used in rapidly evolving e-markets
Used in long-term planning process, five- to ten-year cycles	Used in shorter cycles with an iterative planning process
Emphasis on the interaction between industry growth and market position	Emphasis on measuring project viability against company fit
Mainly a corporate planning tool	Used at corporate and strategic business levels
Inherent weaknesses for new business creation	Sound tool for evaluating new venture innovation and validation
Focus on capital resource allocation	Greater strategic emphasis on resource allocation
(Source: Adapted from Tjan, 2001)	

Table 4.3 Comparison of classical portfolio planning and Internet portfolio planning

As discussed in Chapter 3, it is prudent to adopt a portfolio approach, where investments are made in a variety of projects representing different levels of risk and return. At the start of the Internet hype it was perhaps justifiable to invest in a collection of Internet projects. It was assumed that even a single success would outweigh the losses of all the failures. However, in reality given the cash 'burn rate' of loss-making investments, it is advisable for organizations to use much more disciplined procedures. Tjan (2001) proposes an Internet portfolio approach.

Traditional two-by-two planning matrices, such as the Boston Consulting Group growth/share, assume that two factors define a business position in the marketplace. The first, relative market share, is the ratio of the share of the organization's products/services to the share of the market leader. The second, market growth rate, is the growth rate of the product/service category. Figure 4.1 illustrates the categories of star, problem child, cash cow and dog. While the technique is taught on business programmes around the globe, there are several problems associated with the matrix, which are now compounded in e-markets. The definitions of both the market and its growth rate were difficult enough in traditional markets and, although the BCG matrix has merits in its simplicity, it has some severe weaknesses. In digital markets much of the data relating to markets and growth rates is unavailable. Thus, qualitative data must be taken into account. Tjan (2001) replaced the dimensions of market growth rate and market share with the qualitative dimensions of business viability and business fit. **Viability** is a proxy for the quantitative data on invest-ment pay-off and fit measures the degree to which an investment complements existing processes, capabilities and culture. By considering all Internet initiatives in terms of via-bility and fit, a firm can think practically and holistically about its digital portfolio. Figure 4.2 illustrates the Tjan's Internet portfolio map. Tjan, citing the example of Universal Soda, illustrates metrics for viability and fit:

Key Term...

Viability
A proxy for the quantitative data on investment pay-off

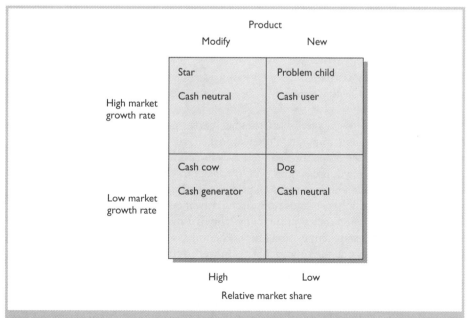

Figure 4.1 The growth share matrix (*Source: adapted from Boston Consulting Group – see Johnson and Scholes, 2001, pp. 170–172 for background to the growth share matrix*)

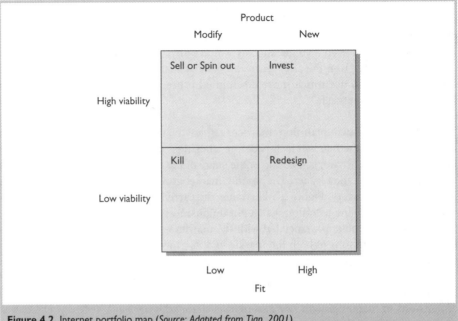

Figure 4.2 Internet portfolio map (*Source: Adapted from Tjan, 2001*)

- ■ Viability
  - ■ Market value potential
  - ■ Time to positive cash flow
  - ■ Personnel requirement
  - ■ Funding requirement

- ■ Fit
  - ■ Alignment with core capabilities
  - ■ Alignment with other company initiatives
  - ■ Fit with organizational structure
  - ■ Fit with company's culture
  - ■ Ease of technical implementation

The spectacular collapse of several Internet businesses has clearly led to the euphoria for first-mover advantage to evaporate. Porter (2001) suggests that negative profitability was perhaps a consequence of too much attention being placed on what the Internet could do and on unrealistic growth projections. There was optimism that the Internet would create new forces that would enhance industry profitability. It was anticipated that the Internet would increase switching costs and create strong network effects, which in turn would result in first movers obtaining robust profitability. The first movers would maintain their competitive position by establishing strong new-economy brands. Unfortunately, this has not transpired frequently and the concept of first-mover advantage needs closer examination.

Switching costs relate to the costs incurred by a customer in changing from one supplier to another, which include contractual issues and learning how to use the new product or service (Porter, 2001). Switching costs move in the opposing direction to customers' bargaining power and the barriers to entry into an industry rise. It was thought that switching costs on the Internet would raise them substantially, but this has not transpired. Companies

were expected to create such a tailored offer, better service and greater purchasing convenience, which buyers would be loath to forfeit. However, in reality, switching costs are likely
to be lower, not higher, on the Internet than they are for traditional ways of doing business,
including approaches using earlier generations of information systems such as EDI. On
the Internet, buyers can often switch suppliers with just a few mouse clicks, and new Web
technologies are systematically reducing switching costs even further.

Products or services become more valuable as more customers use them and experience a
network effect. Network effects are insufficient in themselves to provide barriers to entry, as
they must also be proprietary to one company. The first wave of Internet applications, such
as email, displayed network effects and, where such effects are significant, they can create
demand-side economies of scale and raise barriers to entry. The ubiquitous nature of the
Internet with its common standards and protocols makes it difficult for one company to
capture the benefits of a network effect. Porter (2001) cites American Online as an organization that has managed to protect its online community, but this is an exception, not the
rule. Moreover, if a company is able to control a network effect, the effect often reaches a
point of diminishing returns once there is a critical mass of customers. Internet brands
have proved expensive to build and matters are not helped by a lack of physical presence
and lack of human association.

Building an e-business strategy is slightly different from building a business strategy for a
traditional business. The sheer immensity and diversity of both the potential benefits and
problems related to e-business make it rather difficult to get a firm grip on how to tackle
salient corporate-level issues. The challenge is to fully understand and exploit e-business
potential without losing sight of the core strengths and differentiators within a particular
product or service. The strategist should draw up a checklist of questions that, if addressed,
would assist the organization through the e-business planning process. These could include:

- How will e-business fit into corporate strategy?
- Do we need to create a separate division or company for the proposed e-business project?
- Do we fully understand the opportunities and threats arising from e-business?
- Can we establish barriers to entry and where will be the greatest e-business impact on our value chain?
- Who will be the likely new competitors in the e-business market?
- Which of our current and future products/services are best suited to e-business?
- How will our e-business affect organizational structure, operational processes, regulatory and tax status?
- What market are we targeting? B2B or B2C – or a combination?
- Do we have the cash reserves to sustain a period of negative cash flow?
- Have we established a senior steering group to monitor, co-ordinate and assess future e-business developments?

There are very few theoretical frameworks that truly help practising e-business managers
understand and craft a winning strategy (Bruun, Jensen and Skovgaard, 2002). Willcocks
and Plant (2001), who were searching for B2C e-business initiatives with common paths
and practices, noted two themes. First, the movement towards online was an evolutionary
process for bricks-and-mortar companies. Second, it involved planning and flexibility in a turbulent market and technology environment. To help managers move from traditional to
e-businesses, Hackbarth and Kettinger (2000) proposed a methodology that charts the path
to effective digital business strategy. Their four-stage methodology makes use of SWOT
analysis and each stage has its own activities, tasks and outputs.

Hackbarth and Kettinger suggest that e-business strategies pass through three levels of increasing complexity, which they categorize as experimentation, integration and transformation. Table 4.4 illustrates the three levels of e-business. According to Hackbarth and Kettinger, many companies are at the experimentation stage, whereby individual departments have taken the initiatives to embark on isolated Internet applications. Unfortunately, these projects are not tightly linked to corporate strategy or a companywide e-business strategy. Many industry pioneers (e.g. Wal-Mart, Cisco and Tesco Stores) have successfully moved to level II (integration). At the integration phase organizations have linked e-business strategy to corporate strategy, albeit the former being subservient to the latter. Performance benefits accrue mainly through cost reductions and revenue growth. A core competence in having business processes that are tied directly to the bottom line and a culture that uses the IT advancements to maximize efficiency produce a sustainable competitive advantage. To get into the third phase, level III companies have used e-business strategy to drive corporate strategy. Companies extend inter-enterprise process linkages between suppliers, customers and partners to create seamless partnerships. Emphasis is placed on sharing and trust. The new value chain presents new commercial opportunities to the organization. Intangible assets give the e-business strategy its strength and flexibility. A level III organization makes use of 'e-breakout strategies' to create longer-lasting relationships with customers, exploit intellectual capital and leverage co-operative relationships with competitors. To attain the win–win approach, the firm must continually anticipate and respond

	Level I Experimentation	Level II Integration	Level III Transformation
E-business strategy	No e-business strategy	E-business strategy supports current corporate strategy	E-business strategy supports breakout corporate strategy
Corporate strategy	E-business strategy not linked to corporate strategy	E-business strategy subservient to corporate strategy	E-business strategy is a driver of corporate strategy
Scope	Departmental/ functional orientation	Cross-functional participation	Cross-enterprise involvement (interconnected customers, suppliers and partners)
Payoffs	Unclear	Cost reduction, business support and enhancement of existing business practices, revenue enhancement	New revenue stream, new business lines, drastic improvements in customer service and customer satisfaction
Levers	Technological infrastructure and software applications	Business processes	People, intellectual capital and relationships co-operation
Role of information	Secondary to technology	Supports process efficiency and effectiveness	Information asymmetries used to create business opportunities

(Source: Hackbarth and Kettinger, 2000)

Table 4.4 Three levels of e-business

to strategic threats and capitalize on market opportunities. Hackbarth and Kettinger call this the essence of the 'strategic e-breakout methodology'.

To migrate from level I to level II it is necessary to understand salient business processes. Moving from level II to level III requires not only an understanding of the business processes but also relations with suppliers, customers and competition. The customer/supplier life cycle provides a good way of isolating buying and selling activities so as to understand better the interrelationships between customers' and suppliers' business processes and their touchpoints in the organization (Kettinger and Hackbarth, 1997). The strategic breakout methodology follows four stages: initiate, diagnose, breakout and transition.

Stage I. Initiate
■ Outline project scope.
■ Identify project stakeholders.
■ Determine project schedule.
■ Project workplan.

Stage II. Diagnose – industry analysis
■ Conduct industry competitive assessment.
■ Benchmark e-business technology.
■ Assess industry business partnership.
■ Industry opportunity and threat rankings.

Stage II. Diagnose – company analysis
■ Business strategy assessment.
■ Identify current business strategy rankings.
■ Assess firm capabilities related to its customers.
■ Assess firm capabilities related to its suppliers.
■ Assess firm business partnerships.
■ Assess firm e-business technology.
■ Firm strengths/weaknesses rankings.

Stage III. Breakout
■ Evaluate firm strategic SWOT assessment.
■ SWOT assessment matrices.
■ Brainstorm breakout strategies.
■ Finalize e-business breakout strategy.

Stage IV. Transition
■ Analyse the gap between breakout strategy and current strategy.
■ Plot e-business transition strategy including recommended courses of action and milestones.
■ E-business transition strategy.

The process is completed by Hackbarth and Kettinger's change readiness assessment, which assesses the readiness of a company to adopt and implement the transition strategy. Organization factors such as organizational structure and culture may be difficult to alter and must be incorporated into the e-business strategy process.

E-BUSINESS STRATEGIES FOR VALUE CREATION

Key Term...

Value proposition
The value proposition requires management to consider three items: (i) choice of target segment; (ii) choice of focal support; and (iii) explanation why the firm's offering is better than competitors

Despite the collapse in share prices of Internet related stock during 2001, the primary goal of most management teams is to increase shareholder value through favourable movements in the traditional financial indicators of revenue and profits. Managers are faced with the basic choice of targeting a small market of a few customers with high profit potential, or focusing on a mass market of many customers with lower profit potential. Unfortunately, if managers get it wrong, profits are at best low and the customer value proposition deteriorates quickly. Creating value is about designing future competitive offerings for financial success (Mathur and Kenyon, 2001) and the challenge for managers is to beat the competition by providing more value.

The question whether firms compete on value propositions or value clusters has been raised by Rayport and Jaworski (2001). According to their theory, value proposition requires management to consider three items; choice of target segment; choice of focal support; and an explanation why the firm's offering is better than competitors. The value-cluster approach suggests that, as a result of the customization capabilities available to e-commerce firms, multiple segments of customers can be addressed with a variety or combination of benefits offered.

Key Term...

Value cluster
The value cluster approach suggests that as a result of the customization capabilities available to e-commerce firms, multiple segments of customers can be addressed with a variety or combination of benefits offered

In their survey of 30 European e-commerce companies, Zott, Amit and Donlevy (2000) identified two main strategies for value creation for e-commerce. These are the efficiency of the business model and the degree that the business model creates stickiness. In their case analysis, Zott, Amit and Donlevy (2000) observed that companies within their sample were able to enhance transaction efficiency by:

- Improving the supply chain by reducing supplier cost and integrating vertically
- Providing a broad product and service range
- Simple transactions for the consumer
- Quickening the process and providing the consumer with greater time
- Reducing the asymmetry of information knowledge among members of the supply chain

Key Term...

Fit
Measures the degree to which an investment complements existing processes, capabilities and culture

In addition, Zott, Amit and Donlevy (2000) identified some effective means by which their sample created stickiness. These include:

- Reward customers for loyalty.
- Personalize the product or service offering.
- Create virtual communities.
- Develop ways of building trust.

It is anticipated that companies that score high in the two categories of efficiency and stickiness are more likely to create value. Zott, Amit and Donlevy (2000) noted several areas of best practice, but there were wide variations in the degree to which the e-commerce organizations had achieved efficiency and stickiness in their business models. Several organizations displayed strengths in certain facets of the multi-component constructs, such as in building trust in the transaction, allowing the consumer to save time and finding ways of attracting and keeping the consumer. However, the sample organizations did not make use of the full spectrum of multi-component constructs available for value creation. Lesser-used strategies include: decreasing asymmetry of information between players; making the transactional context more convenient for the consumer; making greater use of loyalty programmes; and virtual communities.

ILLUSTRATIVE EXAMPLE 1
This Egg Is on a Roll, by David Fairlamb, Business Week, 1 March 2001

THE BRITISH CYBER BANK IS TURNING A PROFIT IN A SECTOR MANY THOUGHT HAD DIED WITH THE DOT-COMS

Online consumer sales, online lending, online banking. Didn't all of that explode with the dot-bomb? If it did, somebody forgot to tell Paul Gratton. He's the CEO of Egg PLC, a London-based Internet financial services company that is rolling along very nicely, thank you. In the four years since it hatched, the online bank has attracted more than 2 million customers. Last year it generated revenues of $132 million, almost 10 times as much as in its first full year of operation. And on Feb. 25, Egg announced its first profit-making quarter – $5.7 million for the final three months of 2001.

Contrast that with the dismal situation at most European Internet banks, such as Germany's troubled Consors Discount-Broker and Italy's Bipop. They're losing money by the bucketful. "Egg is one of the very few leading lights in a troubled sector and is now ready to expand abroad," says Remus Brett, senior analyst in London with Forrester Research Inc., a Cambridge (Mass.) research firm. On Jan. 29, Gratton paid $8 million for Zebank, the loss-making online-finance operation of France's Groupe Arnault.

KEEPING THE PACE

Egg's evolution into Europe's premier online bank was something of an accident. It was set up in 1998 by Prudential PLC, the British insurer that still owns 79% of its shares, as a telephone-based bank. But the high interest rates it offered depositors drew so much business that its call centers were swamped. Management pushed new clients onto its Web site. Since then, Egg has run a series of promotions to keep old customers and win new ones, including 0% interest for six months on newly issued credit cards.

Its online store, where customers can buy everything from ready-to-wear clothes to fossils – using Egg credit cards – is surprisingly successful. Gratton notes that last summer the bank sold more cases of wine than investment products.

So far, so good. But Egg will find it harder and harder to maintain its momentum and justify its current $1.7 billion market capitalization. Other banks, online and off, are aggressively trying to poach Egg's credit-card customers with lower interest rates. Egg's bad-loan provisions, which jumped from $53 million in 2000 to $97.2 million last year, could sap profitability.

"KEY TO SUCCESS"

And there are big question marks over the move into France. "France is not like Britain," warns Patrick Frazer, a retail banking specialist with Lafferty Group, a London financial-research firm. "It will be harder to bring in new customers and to earn as much from them."

Gratton, who just bought himself a 16th-century mansion in Derbyshire, is not worried. "The key to success is a strong brand name and a broad range of services to cross-sell," he says. Egg has clearly achieved the first. One recent survey showed that 88% of Britons polled knew Egg's name. That kind of brand recognition for such a young company is hard to beat.

ILLUSTRATIVE EXAMPLE II
Time for charities to take on the Net challenge, by Joe Sexton,
http://society.guardian.co.uk, 20 July 2001

Joe Saxton (head of voluntary services for the Future Foundation) explains how a new taskforce is to look at how the voluntary sector can use the internet to greater effect

There are very few functions that charities and community groups carry out that cannot be enhanced, improved, developed or made more cost-effective by the use of the internet. Despite all the hype and counter-hype, dot.com flotation and share price collapses, the internet is a very powerful communications tool for not for profit organisations.

For a large multi-national charity such as the Salvation Army, central co-ordination of hardware and a template allows local corps to have excellent websites by simply adding their own content.

For an organisation like the British Epilepsy Association, the internet lets them run a discussion group and put people with epilepsy in touch with each other as never before.

Angell Town, a deprived estate in south London, is using the internet to train young people and eventually plans to wire up every flat on the estate, so doctors and school are all contactable by email.

While the potential is great, most organisations are far from realising it to the full. The barriers, particularly for small and medium sized charities and community groups, can be substantial. How does an organisation with only 10 members of staff, let alone one or two, find the expertise to develop its own website to the full?

For many organisations, a website is not a tool for liberation, but a millstone which needs constantly updating and redesigning.

It is to try to tackle these issues that a number of organisations are coming together to create a taskforce which will look at the common needs of charities and community groups and act as a catalyst for change.

A range of proposals have already been made and the response to these already indicates that two areas stand out as particularly important: influencing government to do more and better sources of information so that organisations aren't constantly reinventing the wheel.

The desire to get the government to do more isn't a plea for special treatment but to get a chunk of the resources that the public and private sector are already receiving. I'm delighted to say that the Office of the E-envoy and the active community unit are keen to work with the taskforce (and other groups) to do more.

While the taskforce will have some core tasks, there will be other activities which we will support as they are driven forward to groups of energetic individuals or organisations.

One excellent suggestion is a group to look at how the sector can make the most of digital television. Another suggestion is to develop the use of the internet for cost-cutting and virtual mergers, so that organisations can act separately to the outside world, but pool core functions or even just combine purchasing power behind the scenes.

EUROPEAN INTERNET MAIN PLAYERS

The Internet has had a rather short, but well documented, history. The largest companies in each value network segment have tended to originate from North America. Cisco Systems (www.cisco.com), AOL/TimeWarner (www.aoltimewarner.com), Charles Schwab (www.schwab.com), IBM (www.ibm.com), MCI worldcom (www.worldcom.com) were the earlier market leaders in their respective segment, these being e-commerce, content aggregators/creators, market makers, service providers and backbone operators respectively (Afuah and Tucci, 2001). There has been much activity in the European stock markets and in Table 4.5 a review of major European Internet firms is given, using data originally obtained from the GlobalNetIndex, which was compiled by GlobalNetFinancial. com-NewMedia Investor on behalf of GlobalNetFinancial.com Inc. This website is no longer active, but, given the turbulent nature, it would be a useful exercise to chart the progress of the firms during 2001 and 2002.

Company	October 2000	Activity in 2001
Affinity Internet UK (www.affinity.uk.com)	Affinity Internet Holdings is the operator of the VIP own-brand Internet access service that provides the content and infrastructure for a variety of organizations	Turnover up for 2001 of £52.8m up 366% from 2000
Autonomy Corp UK (www.autonomy.co.uk)	Autonomy applies its world-leading neural network and digital signalling processing technologies in three different markets: knowledge management; new media; and e-commerce	Unaudited fall in revenue of 19.6% from $65.4m to $52.6m for 2001
Baltimore Technologies UK (www.baltimore.com)	Baltimore Technologies is a UK based e-security company, that develops enterprise and e-commerce security systems and providing advice, product training and support for its hardware and software products	Revenue for the 2001 was £39.2m
Brokat Infosystems (www.brokat.com)	Brokat has quickly developed into one of the world's leading suppliers of secure solutions for e-banking, e-brokerage and e-payment. Its solutions are based on the modular e-services platform brokat twister	DATA Design AG (www.datadesignag.com) took over the financial section of Brokat
Comdirekt Bank (www.commerzbank.com)	Codirekt is an online brokerage house, of which 18.15% was floated, the rest of the share capital being owned by Commerzbank (60.5%) and T-online (21.35%).	Difficult trading environment which led to a restructuring of business units. Profit from ordinary activities fell from €67.3m in 2000 to €12m in 2001
Consors Discount (www.consors.de)	Consors Discount became Germany's pioneer discount broker. Abandoning rigid commissions and introducing execution-only broking, the business model was attractive to active private investors	Most difficult year, which led to a loss of €126m. Net income fell from €52.7m in 2000 to €40.4m in 2001. Net commission fell from €229m in 2000 to €125m in 2001

Table 4.5 The constituent members of the Leaders Index as of 9 October 2000

Company	October 2000	Activity in 2001
Direkt Anlage Bank (www.direktanlagebank.de)	This online banking and brokerage business has a strong base in the B2B and B2C markets.	In wake of the merger with Self Trade SA in 2000, the Group now operates in five European countries: France, Germany, Spain, Switzerland and the UK. Commission income fell by 35.5% to T€89,708
Distefora (www.distefora.com)	Distefora Holding AG is the parent company of the Distefora group with interests in Internet services, mobile information, navigation and cable networks. Distefora provides an added-value venture capitalist role by promoting innovation, looking for competition and actively shaping new Internet trends	Sold ISION Internet AG, as part of a comprehensive restructuring, which partly contributed to a fall in sales revenues from TCHF 192,578 in 2000 to TCHF 75,204 in 2001
Easynet Group UK (www.easynet.com)	Easynet activities focus on the supply and development of Internet and telecommunications infrastructure, encompassing residential consumer connections to high-capacity digital leased lines. High-quality Internet access is complemented by a variety of services including technical support, software development, consultancy and e-commerce	Revenue increading by 89% to £78.7m in 2000 from £41.7m in 2000
Egg UK (www.egg.com)	The insurance group Prudential floated off a quarter of its Internet bank called Egg. Egg provides a variety of financial services online including banking, investing, and insurance	Revenue increasing by more than 100% to £189.4m in 2001, from £93.2m in 2000.
Exchange Holdings (www.moneyeXtra.com)	A joint venture between Origo services, a firm set up by 20 leading insurance firms to co-ordinate and streamline third-party distribution of life assurance and pension products, and AT&T Istel; the group offers online financial information to business across the eXweb and to consumers through www.moneyeXtra.com	The Exchange was acquired by Marlborough Stirling plc in 2001.
FI System (www.fisystem.fr)	The FI system group consists of FI system, Coplanet, Probase and In Fine Conseil and operates as a Web agency. FI system is involved in Internet and intranet site consultancy, creative design and technical implementation	Total interim turnover for 2001 was €48m.
Framtidsfabriken (www.framtidsfabriken.com)	Swedish company, Framfab offers digital services based on Internet technology and develops sustainable e-business strategies. Long-term business partners add specialist know-how in IT consulting and integration as well as software development	Suffered a steep dive in demand which resulted in a series of non-recurring effects of an action programme and divestiture of operations totally SEK 493m in 2001. EBITA fell from − SEK 415m in 2000 to −SEK 1,007m in 2001

Table 4.5 continued

Company	October 2000	Activity in 2001
Freeserve UK (www.freeserve.co.uk)	Freeserve, which is 82% owned by Dixons, was the first free ISP and provides its customers with a full range of content channels from its portal. Interestingly, the firm acquired a US$1m stake in GlobalNet financial.	Acquired in February 2001 by the French company Wanadoo (www.wanadoo.com). In addition to the extensive France Telecom marketing network, Wanadoo now benefits from the broad market reach of the Dixons Group, which markets Freeserve solutions
GEO Interactive Media (www.geo.co.il)	Emblaze systems, formerly GEO Interactive Media, wants to light a fire under the current product/service offerings	Changed name to Emblaze Sysyems Ltd. In December 2001, recognized that the marketplace was undergoing financial trauma. The group growth, which resulted in a loss of $29.1m. Sales fell from $30.7m in 2000 to $23m in 2001
GFI Informatique (www.gfi.fr)	GFI Informatique is an IT service company that offers expertise in system engineering and integration, software applications, consultancy and new technologies. The group is actively involved at all stages in the information system life cycle, designing, producing, implementing and administering high-valued applications	The 2001 turnover for the GFI Informatique Group has been fixed at €607.3m with 18.5% growth compared to 2000. The Group has realized an organic growth of 11% and has had particular success in France, Italy, Spain and Portugal
GFT Technology (www.internetprofi.com)	GFT Technologies provides an array of product packages and services based on fixed time/fixed price for customized solutions in the areas of Internet, e-commerce, customer relationship management and supply chain management	2001 was one of the hardest years in GFT's 15-year history. The company underwent a merger with the Emagine Group, and reported a loss for the first time since breaking into profit in 1994. The end of year deficit for the new group amounted to −€2.28m
Icon Medialab (www.iconmedialab.com)	Icon Medialab offers interactive solutions within the field of interactive digital communication, including Web design, CD-ROM/DVD production, technology and business consulting	Business technology solutions suffered a downturn in 2001 and the company was subsequently restructured, returning sales of SEK 1186.3 million. In January 2002, it merged with Lost Boys, an Internet solutions company based in The Netherlands
ID Media AG (www.i-dmedia.com)	ID Media is a full-service marketing and communication agency. It consists of four divisions, Cycosmus, Living-Screen, ID services and ID-TV	I-DMedia AG's total 2001 turnover fell short of the 2000 total by 44%. Its net revenues amounted to DEM K 43,612. It now focuses in two divisions – e-marketing solutions, and systems and technologies
Information Highway (www.infohwy.se)	Information Highway's mission is to develop Web-based business development, which can help those firms that have made a strategic choice to strengthen the competitiveness of their business operations through e-commerce	Information Highway Information Highway merged with Connecta in 2000, owned by Adcore, and all divisions of the Information Highway group have now ceased to trade

Table 4.5 continued

Company	October 2000	Activity in 2001
Intershop Communications AG (www.intershop.de)	Intershop is an experienced vendor of standard software for sell-side e-commerce applications. Most of the business revenue is derived from software licences. About two-thirds of licence revenues are generated by e-commerce solutions for Telcos and hosting ISPs	As companies cut their spending on technology, Intershop reduced its workforce, restructured the organization and concentrated on expanding their product portfolio. Total revenue for 2001 was €68.7m, compared with €123m in 2000
Pixelpark AG (www.pixelpark.com)	Pixelpark AG is a multimedia company providing products and services encompassing e-commerce, e-marketing, convergence and knowledge management	Pixelpark was restructured during 2001, withdrawing from Eastern Europe, the UK and Spain, and failing to operate at a profit in the fourth quarter of the year. Focusing on services and solutions, PixelPark reported total revenue at €81.3m in 2001
Ricardo De (www.ricardo.de)	Ricardo De is Germany's first and largest online auction site	The Ricardo.de portal is one of many portals in the pan-European auction community, QXL ricardo, offering its services in 12 countries
T-Online International (www.t-online.de)	T-Online is an ISP subsidiary of Deutsche Telekom. It has over 50% of the German market and is the country's most visited portal. The site offers a variety of services, including news, SMS messaging and e-commerce on its site	In the 2001 financial year, positive business performance meant a significant increase in T-Online Group revenues, with a year-on-year increase of 43% to €1.140bn. The company aims to achieve top three status as a European Internet media network
Terra Networks (www.terralycos.com)	Terra Lycos, formerly Terra Networks, wants to break new ground and devour the competition on the Internet	Terra Lycos is now a global Internet group with a presence in 42 countries in 19 languages, reaching 116m individual users per month worldwide. Its revenue reached €694m in 2001
Tiscali (www.tiscali.it)	Tiscali originated in Cagliari, but now has operations across Italy. The company offers free Internet access across Italy alongside a core telephony service	Tiscali has 7.3m active users, and has become one of Europe largest Internet companies. The company offers Internet access, content business services and communications. Its revenues have grown to €635.7m in 2001
WM-Data (www.wmdata.com)	This Nordic computer-services company provides computer solutions for administrative systems	WM-Data has divested some of its operations to focus on its core businesses: solutions and value-adding services. Although the company failed to grow in 2001, sales reached €1294.6m in 2001

Table 4.5 continued

E-BUSINESS STRATEGY IN THE MANUFACTURING SECTOR

The ability to digitize products has been one of the main reasons why the Internet e-business has taken off in some sectors. The Internet has affected the manufacturing sector, but research focusing on distinguishing the hype from the reality has been lacking. In an attempt to address this, IBM commissioned Benchmark Research Ltd to survey 300 medium-sized UK manufacturing businesses to investigate the industry's current aspirations and objectives in relation to e-business.

Key questions asked in the survey include:

■ To what extent are companies committed to e-business?
■ What are the key drivers underpinning e-business investment?
■ Which business functions are driving e-business investment?
■ What is the main focus of e-business projects?
■ What are the main difficulties anticipated in implementing e-business strategy?

The survey revealed that more that 86 per cent of UK manufacturers see e-business as important to the future health of their organizations. Managers placed emphasis on knowing how their e-business processes compared with competitors. Only 1 per cent of companies in the £10m to £49m category had a fully defined e-business strategy and 63 per cent had taken no action. In the sample of companies with a £50m+ turnover, 9 per cent had a fully defined e-business strategy and 22 per cent had taken no action. UK manufacturers would

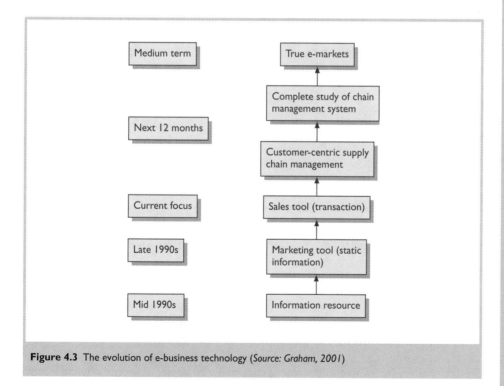

Figure 4.3 The evolution of e-business technology (*Source: Graham, 2001*)

appear to be customer orientated, as the top three business drivers of e-business investments were: improve customer communication; improve customer service; and improve supplier communication. The sales and marketing department was the most influential department in e-business investment. The only other functions that had a significant influence over investment were the IT function and the Board. The main focus of e-business projects was supply-chain integration with emphasis on customer orientation. IBM speculated that perhaps manufacturers strive to achieve a greater relationship orientation with key supply-chain partners. Another goal was to integrate IT systems. The single most significant difficulty was persuading senior management to support/fund the project. This finding might be a reflection of the fact that a large number of companies have not formulated an e-business strategy. Matters are also not helped by the 'IT technophobia' of some senior management in the UK.

IBM speculates that the Internet will remain a powerful sales and marketing tool, providing opportunities in the area of customer relationship management. The emergence of the supply-chain tool will lead to improvements in the customer-biased form of supply chain management, albeit at a slower pace than customer-focused relationships. Extrapolating past events into the future, IBM forecasts that e-business technology will be critical in the medium term in true e-markets. Figure 4.3 illustrates the evolution of the information resource from the mid 1990s to true e-market.

E-BUSINESS STRATEGY IN THE PUBLIC SECTOR

In the UK the Government has embarked on a programme of work to ensure that it becomes a world leader in the knowledge economy revolution. Each month, the e-Minister and the e-Envoy, Patricia Hewitt and Andrew Pinder at the time of writing, provide a joint report to the Prime Minister. These reports set out the progress that has been made in taking forward the UK Online Strategy that provides details of significant developments and issues. The reports emphasize five main areas of the strategy:

- Modern Markets
- Confident People
- Successful Business
- Government Online
- World Class Supply

The Office of the e-Envoy is responsible for getting the UK online, ensuring that the country, its citizens and its businesses derive maximum benefit from the knowledge economy.

To achieve this aim, the e-Envoy has three core objectives:

- To make the UK the best environment in the world for e-commerce by 2002
- To ensure that everyone who wants it has access to the Internet by 2005
- To make all Government services available online by 2005

The Office is organized into three main groups of e-commerce, e-government and e-communications. The e-commerce group is tasked with enabling e-commerce for the UK as a whole by developing an e-commerce framework that is conducive to developing a confident and skilled population. It is expected that this will be achieved by helping individuals and businesses get the skills and access to the technologies they need and closely monitoring e-commerce activity. The e-government group is to ensure that the quality and efficiency of government services is transformed through the use of electronic delivery. The Government has made a commitment that all government services will be accessible electronically by 2005. The e-Government group is specifically responsible for the development of the ukonline.gov.uk Citizen Portal, the Government Gateway and the Knowledge Network. The e-communication group seeks to ensure that the government has a first-class Internet presence, and that all its services are online by 2005. The Group exists to co-ordinate, develop and improve e-communications throughout government.

The UK Home Office (2001) has prepared an initial e-business strategy, which demonstrates two important points. The Home Office recognizes the fundamental importance of e-business in enhancing the future provision of services and in meeting its targets. In addition, the Home Office has a commitment to work with private-sector partners in the delivery of IS/IT to develop new e-business solutions. Some important contracts have been awarded for the delivery of IS/IT and business change in the core Home Office (the Sirius programme), for IT infrastructure and services in the Prison Service (Quantum) and for call centre services to add to passport issuing and printing services in UK Passport Agency. This greatly enhances the capability to deliver a clear programme of e-business initiatives to improve the delivery of services.

The Home Office vision statement is:

> " By the end of 2005 to enable all appropriate Home Office services to be accessible electronically wherever they are required. Services will be delivered through a variety of channels including Internet, digital TV and call centre technologies. The delivery channels will reflect the needs and preferences of our customers and stakeholders and our commitment to best value. We will also take steps to consult the public as part of our policy development and delivery. "

Although the Home Office is a public-sector organization, there are similar powerful drivers to those in the private sector that change business practice. Rising expectations of customers mean that it is necessary for Government departments and other public-sector organizations to work together effectively to respond to satisfy customer needs, both current and potential, through improved access to a wider range of service choices.

By July 2001, 47 per cent of services were capable of being delivered electronically with a target of 95 per cent by 2005. The Home Office recognizes that e-business should not be merely an add-on to current methods of working, but should become an integrated way of how businesses plan and deliver services to the customer. Making it happen will involve an e-business programme that spans three dimensions of the strategy:

■ Delivering services to customers
■ Working with partners
■ Modernizing internal systems and processes

SUMMARY

Despite the growth of e-business not meeting the early projections made by respected analysts, the e-business revolution is impossible to ignore. Traditional strategic planning systems that have served organizations well during the last decade are now obsolete. If it is assumed that strategic planning is a good thing, then the challenge for e-businesses is to design an effective planning process that quickly leads to implementation. Unfortunately, the drive for speed makes the strategist skip essential activities in the drive for success.

Why perform strategic planning?

During the initial research performed for this book, several e-business consultants stated that the 'strategic planning process should be 10 per cent planning and 90 per cent implementation'. Moreover, dot.com entrepreneurs have learned the painful lesson that the Internet is just another communication and distribution medium. The Internet now places the power back with the bricks-and-mortar companies. As a result of the changing landscape, *The Times* newspaper stated that it 'ends its specialised e-business page and returns e-business coverage to its rightful place: the business pages'.

Problems with traditional strategic planning systems

Phillips and Moutinho (1998) in their study noted that organizations with ineffective SPS suffered four major problems:
- The strategic planning process is biased by the budget process.
- There is a performance gap between those firms that do and those that do not encourage strategic thinking.
- A lack of objective data for decision-making.
- A lack of marketing/finance techniques for non-routine decision-making.

Measuring strategic planning effectiveness

Strategic alliances in the emerging digitized global economy are becoming increasingly dependent on information and communication technologies for co-ordinating their organizational activities. Maximizing shareholder value by leveraging new digitized technologies as an enabler is perceived to be an important way forward for improving organizational effectiveness and gaining strategic (and operational) business advantage. An effective strategic planning process has been found to be associated with higher levels of business performance (Phillips, Davies and Moutinho, 1999).

Some recent insights of e-business strategy

In Chapter 1, the public-sector origins of the Internet were highlighted. However, considerable attention is now being paid to private-sector organizations that are exploring and exploiting the potential of the Internet and associated technologies (Doherty and McAulay, 2002). While investors may now have taken a dislike to Web-based firms, problems of embracing or responding to the Internet remain a challenge for managers of established firms (Loebbecke and Powell 2002). For today's e-business organization, it may be simple to set up a Web presence, but it has proved difficult to create a sustainable online business. The Internet has presented a variety of new strategic options to organizations. However, it has not changed the fundamentals of corporate strategy. The essence of any e-business is still the generation of value by offerings to customers. If enough customers buy the offering, rather than competing substitutes, above the breakeven price, then value will be enhanced.

European Internet main players

There has been much activity in the European stock markets and there have been notable successes and failures during the last two years. Despite the current problems with the financial service organizations in Germany, online brokerage firms have been successful.

E-business strategy in the manufacturing sector

The ability to digitize products has been one of the main reasons why e-business has taken off in some sectors. IBM commissioned Benchmark Research Ltd to survey 300 medium-sized UK manufacturing businesses to investigate the industry's current aspirations and objectives in relation to e-business. The survey revealed that more that 86 per cent of UK manufacturers see e-business as important to the future health of their organizations.

E-business strategy in the public sector

The UK e-government group is to ensure that the quality and efficiency of government services are transformed through the use of electronic delivery. The e-communication group seeks to ensure that the Government has a first-class Internet presence, and that all its services are online by 2005. The group exists to co-ordinate, develop and improve e-communications throughout government.

DISCUSSION QUESTIONS

1. Do you believe that e-business strategy is different from traditional business strategy? If you feel that it is, why is this the case? If not, provide reasons for your views.

2. Discuss the reasons why you believe strategic planning is important for any aspiring e-business organization. In your opinion which traditional strategy frameworks are useful for the e-business strategist?

3. How should corporations deal with the need for speed in e-business? What are the potential pitfalls? How can they be avoided?

ASSESSMENT QUESTIONS

1. Using Porter's five-forces framework, analyse the e-business environment of an industry with which you are familiar. You are required to write a short report, which details the strength and weaknesses of each of the five forces.

2. The Office of the e-Envoy is responsible for getting the UK online, ensuring that the country, its citizens and its businesses derive maximum benefit from the knowledge economy. To achieve this aim, the e-Envoy has three core objectives:
• To make the UK the best environment in the world for e-commerce by 2002
• To ensure that everyone who wants it has access to the Internet by 2005
• To make all Government services available online by 2005

You are required to evaluate the success of The Office of the e-Envoy in meeting the above three core objectives.

3. Using any industry of your choice, you are required to write a report that outlines how the Internet has affect the traditional business strategy process.

GROUP ASSIGNMENT QUESTIONS

1. What do you understand by the term e-service? Using At Your e-Service (www.atyourservice.com) or any other e-service organization, you are required to outline how the Internet has created a market for the organization's core e-services.

2. Select one organization from the European Internet main players list in Table 4.5. Critically evaluate the development of the organization since October 2000. What have been the major internal and external challenges facing the organization?

3. Table 4.4 illustrates the three levels of e-business. According to Hackbarth and Kettinger (2000), many companies are at the experimentation stage, whereby individual departments have taken the initiative to embark on isolated Internet applications. Unfortunately, these projects are not tightly linked to corporate strategy or a company-wide e-business strategy. Many industry pioneers (e.g. Wal-Mart, Cisco and Tesco Stores) have successfully moved to level II (integration).

Using the framework of Hackbarth and Kettinger (2000), you are required to critically discuss the above statement that many industry pioneers (e.g. Wal-Mart, Cisco and Tesco Stores) have successfully moved to level II (integration).

MAIN CASE STUDY
Extracted from "Bloody but Unbowed", by Stephen Baker, with contributions from Ariane Sains and Emilie King, Business Week e-biz, 19 March 2001

Ola Lauritzson's startup ran out of gas. Here are the lessons to be learned

His university classmates in Stockholm still remember Ola Lauritzson as the guy who wore a coat and tie to class while the others were decked out in grunge. And it was the fresh-faced Lauritzson, president of the Young Shareholders' Assn., who was first in line to hobnob with Sweden's captains of finance and industry when they called on Stockholm's elite School of Economics. Lauritzson had a plan. In the spring of 1998, the 24-year-old set out to revolutionize European finance through the Internet. He just needed a few million dollars. For that, he cold-called the financiers he had been cultivating and gave many of them their first dot-com pitch. His vision sold. Within a year and a half, Lauritzson raised $12 million to piece together his dream. It was an Internet service called EPO.com, which he hoped would become synonymous with "electronic public offerings." The goal was to reach out to tens of millions of new investors, bypassing the Old-Boy networks that had long locked up capital in Europe, to allow regular folks to buy shares in initial public offerings. The Internet service also would allow them to invest across borders – still a rarity in Europe.

Living on airplanes and a diet of junk food, Lauritzson crisscrossed the Continent getting regulatory approvals and signing up prospective IPOs. "It was a land grab," he recalls. He sprinted – but not fast enough. In mid-2000, the markets turned chilly. In

December, his $12 million spent and venture investors in flight, he sold EPO to a well-funded British rival, EO.

New order

Today, the once high-flying CEO has become an employee of the British company, a manager of marketing. As Lauritzson's former rivals revamp the operations he raced at such cost to establish in Stockholm, Paris, and three other European cities, he has time to ponder a decade of lessons crammed into a frantic two years. The clearest one, perhaps, is that upstarts should sidestep battles with Old Economy titans. In his drive to create an electronic investment bank, says his new employer, EO CEO John St. John, "Ola was holding a huge sign up to the whole financial world: I'm trying to destroy your livelihood." That's not the kind of message the Establishment likes to see. In the end, the financial powers prevailed over Sweden's Internet interloper.

The lessons extend far beyond a 26-year-old's advanced degree in hard knocks. Indeed, Lauritzson's travails provide keys for deciphering Europe's Internet economy – and debunk many of the myths that led to the ephemeral burst of dot-com euphoria. For starters, while the Net promised to transcend Europe's national boundaries, Lauritzson was smashing into them time and again. Getting regulatory approval in each market took weeks, even months. Europe's borders, in effect, stretch high into cyberspace.

And how about the notion that small, tech-savvy markets such as Sweden could produce an e-business elite that would storm the Continent? That myth crumbled as well. In the dot-com desolation of Stockholm, it's all too clear how illusory the notion was. Of the estimated 1,000 Swedish Internet startups gobbling up investment capital just a year ago, nearly half have shut their doors or sold out.

As Lauritzson learned, rich markets with deeper pools of capital provide safer harbors in stormy times. That's why so many Swedish entrepreneurs have found refuge in Europe's biggest Net economies – Britain and Germany. Even Sweden's marquee Net flops – fashion e-tailer boo.com and music seller Boxman.com – moved from Stockholm to London as they waged their losing battles to survive. "I see more of my Swedish friends here than in Stockholm," Lauritzson says, reaching for a plate of sliced tuna at a sushi shop in London's Soho district.

Boy wonder

Gloom aside, Lauritzson's adventure also debunks the current wisdom that Europe's Net economy was merely a digital mirage. True, for many students, B2C now means "Back to Consulting." Yet Lauritzson and thousands like him who jumped into the Net economy are sticking it out, working at survivor companies. More important, the Net bubble provided a generation with a chance to do something nearly unprecedented in Europe: launch a company as a young person. Many of these entrepreneurs will be back, smarter and more focused, to take on the next stage of Europe's high-tech advance.

Lauritzson, for one, didn't need the Net economy for his launch as an entrepreneur. He'd been at it more than half his life. As a 9-year-old in the southern Swedish town of Helsingborg, he started a company to collect recyclable cans – and had the gumption to sell shares in the ragtag outfit to neighbors. Lauritzson soon saw that the several hundred dollars he picked up from investors would produce scant returns in the can business. He invested the funds in the stock market, turned a profit, and distributed the proceeds to shareholders.

Later, in high school, Lauritzson went international. Ordering rain ponchos from Hong Kong, he customized them with logos for schools, rock bands, and small companies and sold them in Sweden. The project went awry when he lost track of a shipment in a Shanghai warehouse, wiping out most of his profits. "My big mistake was doing it all from Sweden," Lauritzson says. "I should have traveled to China."

That taught him to think big. Indeed, big thoughts took root in 1995, when, as a 21-year-old, he read about Spring Street Brewery Co. Spring Street founder Andrew D. Klein raised $1.6 million by reaching out to retail investors through their pokey 9,600-baud modems. That experience provided the spark for Wit Capital Corp., the online investment bank Klein founded in 1996. In Stockholm, Lauritzson sat down to write a master's thesis on the Internet in capital markets – and developed it into a business plan.

In the spring of 1998, when Lauritzson began raising funds for EPO.com, Europe's Internet was in diapers – at least two years behind the U.S. And the rush of capital that briefly transformed Stockholm into a Nordic clone of Silicon Valley was a year and a half away. "It was still Old Economy," he recalls.

Warp speed

But Lauritzson believed those Old Economy types could be wooed with the right pitch. He aimed at the very top of Sweden's Establishment: Bjorn Sprangare, who once headed Sweden's largest insurer and now works for the King of Sweden, serving as governor of the 400-year-old Royal Palace perched at the edge of Stockholm's historic center. "[Lauritzson] was a persuasive young man," Sprangare says. "He still is." After one lunch with Lauritzson, Sprangare bought a small share and provided an entree into Sweden's business elite. Lauritzson tapped Sprangare's contacts for a quick $2 million in friends-and-family funding. Money in hand, he hired three staffers, rented office space, and set to work developing systems for Internet IPOs.

Lauritzson's vision extended far beyond establishing a successful dot-com company. EPO.com, he believed, was going to be a revolutionary force in Europe – giving birth to a broad equity culture. European IPOs have long been cozy affairs limited to select groups of insiders. Last year, retail investors gained access to a measly 10% of Europe's $200 billion market for initial public offerings – barely one quarter of the rate in the U.S. And few Europeans have a chance to invest in IPOs outside their home markets. This limits opportunities for investors and handicaps European startups. After all, Silicon Valley highfliers such as Cisco Systems Inc. and Yahoo! Inc. likely wouldn't have grown as rapidly without access to funds outside of California. The fractured IPO market boxed in generations of startups and "kept Europe down," says Roel Pieper, who oversees the European operations of New York-based Insight Capital Partners. "But when these national markets go Continental, watch out."

Investors wanted in on these new markets. If Europe was years behind America, dot-com backers had a chance to stake out early positions for the Continent's cyber-Gold Rush. It was just a question of finding the next Amazon.com and Yahoo. And where better to start than Sweden? The country had more Net surfers per capita than the U.S. and was a leader in what looked like the next great Internet frontier: wireless. Venture-capital groups ranging from Japan's Softbank to Bernard Arnault's Europ@web rushed into Stockholm, showering money on such outfits as boo.com, Boxman.com, and a constellation of wireless Web startups.

The tables had turned. Forget chasing Sprangare's contacts. Lauritzson now was receiving cold calls as investors clamored for a piece of EPO. In January, 2000, he accepted $10 million in financing from a consortium including Credit Lyonnais, BancBoston Capital's venture division, and a unit of Arnault's group.

The key was to move quickly. Even while writing his thesis, Lauritzson knew he would need to set up investment banking operations in all the major markets. But these administrative chores proved to be complex and time-consuming. Getting government approval to sell stock consumed eight months in Britain alone. What's more, he needed a computer system to send out prospectuses, take orders, and complete secure online transactions. "At this point, the priority was speed, marketing, and technology," he says. Money was the least of his concerns.

Even as Lauritzson raced to build the company, EPO was making its push into Europe's exploding IPO market. In 2000, EPO acquired 80,000 retail customers – investors eager to receive online prospectuses and a chance to buy shares of the upstarts. And EPO, while it never became the end-to-end investment bank that Lauritzson envisioned, eventually had a hand in 33 IPOs. Toon Bouton, CEO of Swedish recruiter Jobline International, recalls meeting with EPO about an offering as the markets were plunging in September. The decline didn't appear to faze Lauritzson and his colleagues. In fact, they sometimes got so excited about the IPO that Bouton had to cut short the discussions. "But then they got back to earth, they stuck to the plans and were very professional." The result: Jobline raised $83 million, $3 million more than expected in a rough market.

Still, EPO barely earned back a fraction of Lauritzson's investment. He declines to release results, but sources close to the company say it was on track for revenues in the millions, mostly from customer commissions. What business EPO had was largely in its Nordic stronghold.

Competition was growing in burlier markets to the south. Racing ahead in Germany was VEM – a German acronym for "Virtual Offering Firm." It was handling retail offerings for dozens of companies listing in the Neuer Markt, Europe's hottest bourse at the time. America's Wit Capital, Lauritzson's original inspiration, also was planning a push into Europe. And investment banks such as Goldman Sachs and Merrill Lynch were exploring partnerships for selling IPOs to Europe's online investors. Although the online IPO market reached only $500 million in 2000, or 0.25% of Europe's offerings, "it was in everybody's plans," says a banker at Goldman.

Lauritzson moved into large, high-ceilinged quarters at Riddargatan 17, a former optics factory in downtown Stockholm. He hired Andersen Consulting, now Accenture, to build his Internet exchange system. Andersen put a 20-person team on the job, creating a system that could easily handle the kind of business volumes Lauritzson dreamed of. But the work cost EPO a precious $2.5 million. "If we had that money, we could have moved into Spain," Lauritzson says.

Early on, his plan was to enter all the key markets within a year. This turned Lauritzson into a dot-com nomad. At least once a week, he would wake at 3:30 a.m., catch a predawn flight from Stockholm to London, work a marathon day in Britain, and return to Sweden at 2 a.m. He made similar treks to France, Italy, and Spain – and gained nine kilos from eating junk food on the run.

White hot

His biggest challenge was Germany, Europe's leading market. Without a powerful position there, he had little hope of prevailing as Europe's online IPO heavyweight. He decided that he lacked the time to build German operations from scratch and pushed instead to merge with market leader VEM. Last March, Lauritzson flew to Munich and sat down for talks with 31-year-old Andy Beyer, who had founded VEM just as Lauritzson was launching EPO.

Fueled by the white-hot Neuer Markt, Beyer was on track to earn revenues of $3.2 million in 2000, and had built his company into a larger operation than EPO. Lauritzson convinced Beyer that EPO needed Germany and that VEM couldn't last long without the rest of Europe. On Apr. 18, the two announced a merger agreement. Surprisingly, it would leave Lauritzson as CEO, though EPO shareholders would control only 42% of the combined company. VEM consented to the arrangement when EPO's prospects looked rosy, but Beyer's board soon had misgivings. "It was the issue of who would be in control," Beyer says.

That issue loomed larger as the Internet economy started to swoon. The first warning sign on the Continent came from boo.com, which had spent lavishly to become the most recognizable dot-com brand in Europe. After burning through $120 million in 16 months, boo.com on May 17 declared bankruptcy. At that point, the equation turned. Money mattered again, and dot-coms shifted their focus from eyeballs to burn rates. Equally worrisome, a tumble in the markets threatened to reduce the flood of IPOs to a trickle, slamming EPO's revenue. Lauritzson rushed to cut expenses, pulling back from Spain and slowing down in France.

Meanwhile, a deep-pocketed rival was taking shape in London in a glass-walled office just half a block from Piccadilly Circus. There, a group of seasoned investment bankers became the nucleus of EO. The group was led by John St. John, a former co-head of global equities at Lehman Brothers, along with colleagues from Dresdner Kleinwort Wasserstein, Morgan Stanley, and BNP Paribas. When EO opened its doors on June 1, its bash drew a Who's Who of British finance and politics, including then-Cabinet member Peter Mandelson.

While Lauritzson was attempting to build an empire on vision and technology, EO benefited from stronger links to money. In addition to its web of connections and friendships in London's financial district, the City, the British company received backing from venture capitalists NewMedia Spark PLC, lodged in the same building. Spark was heading into the downturn with a comfortable $100 million in cash. And the VC group knew a bit about the electronic IPO market. It had offered funding to Lauritzson in 1999 – but he already was negotiating with others. "I didn't need it at the time," Lauritzson says.

Money talks

St. John, who jumped from Lehman Bros. to EO in the spring of 2000, could see that investors already were fleeing from business-to-consumer dot-coms. He carefully steered in the other direction. Instead of becoming an online investment bank, threatening to snatch customers and deals from the incumbents, EO would simply sell a service: It was to be an online bridge between investment banks and retail brokers. Within months, St. John's bet seemed to pay off as EO signed partnerships with UBS Warburg, Barclays Bank, and Charles Schwab.

Lauritzson now says that his new colleagues overstate the contrast between their model and his. "It was more a difference in marketing," he says. EO's far bigger advantage boiled down to cash – something St. John doesn't contest. EO was swimming in it; Lauritzson wasn't even wading. In November, after months of haggling, VEM in Munich called off the merger with EPO. The two companies, it now seems clear, had radically different views of the deal. VEM's Beyer regarded it all along as a takeover by the German company – one in which the Swedes refused to cede control. EPO board member Sprangare says the company wasted precious time trying to patch differences that were irreconcilable. The breakup spooked Lauritzson's venture investors, who abandoned him in December with only a few days of funding left. This news traveled fast to the glass house in London, where EO had just received a fresh $15 million in funding from its backers – enough to carry it for 18 months.

Except for money, Lauritzson had nearly everything EO lacked: organization, government permits, some 80,000 customers, and a $2.5 million trading system. But without investor support, his negotiating position was weak. "We offered him what we thought was a fair price," St. John says with a smile, "and he accepted." The terms of the stock-for-stock deal are confidential, but sources close to EO say that Lauritzson and fellow EPO investors are left with only a sliver of EO.

Don't cry for Lauritzson. He holds shares in EO, which he expects will pay off richly when Europe's IPO market recovers. And he admits he's already mulling new plans, probably still focused on finance and the Internet, but this time launched from London. This Swede, after all, is a serial entrepreneur. That's a new breed in Europe. And like the rest of his class, Lauritzson is emerging smarter than ever from the dotcom crash – and battle-hardened too. He'll be back.

CASE QUESTIONS

Question 1 What do you understand by the term electronic investment bank? How was the philosophy of the electronic investment bank different from a traditional investment bank?

Question 2 Why did so many Swedish Internet entrepreneurs seek refuge in Britain and Germany?

Question 3 From an e-business strategy perspective what do you believe were the salient lessons that Ola Lauritzson learned as CEO of EPO.com?

MINI CASE STUDY I
E-Books: Still a Niche Market, by META Group analysts David Cearley, Val Sribar, Dale Kutnick, Timothy Hickernell, Elizabeth Sun, and William Zachmann, META Group Special for CNETNews.com, 3 May 2001

News Peg: E-books are a tough sell, Gemstar-TV Guide International's Chairman and CEO Henry Yuen told analysts this week, saying his company has outsold all of its competitors combined by moving just 60,000 reading devices since late fall. Yuen added that his company now offers 4,000 book titles for its REB1100 and REB1200 e-book devices.

Situation analysis

The e-book market is currently hampered by immature, expensive technology and a limited market of people willing to consider reading books on electronic devices rather than on paper. This market remains mired in its first generation, where the main users are either technophiles or users with highly specialized needs who are willing to put up with technical inadequacies and high cost.

During the next two to three years, we expect the e-book market to evolve into its second generation, with products achieving a somewhat wider appeal. In three to five years, we anticipate better, lower-cost technologies, more research into form factors, and the advent of faster wireless technology to support on-demand access to e-books. Furthermore, we expect growth in the number of people who are comfortable with handheld devices in general to invigorate this marketplace. Until we reach this third-generation stage, however, e-books will remain a niche market.

The leading edge of the e-book market is exemplified by companies such as Gemstar, which sells dedicated devices specifically for reading books, and Adobe and Microsoft, which provide font display and format technology. Dedicated devices provide a better display, but few people are willing to spend significant money for a device that displays only books, with a significantly inferior user experience and little or no savings on content compared to "real" paper books.

"E-books will become more prevalent as the cost of the reading devices goes down," says META Group analyst Elizabeth Sun. "However, at $200–$700 each, these devices are still too expensive for the average consumer, thereby limiting widespread acceptance."

We believe that, to reach a general consumer audience, e-book readers must provide a form factor capable of displaying legibly (and in various lighting situations) the equivalent of at least one full paperback page (and preferably two). It must cost considerably less than present readers, provide significantly longer battery life and, when closed for carrying, be no larger than a paperback book. Display readability must be equivalent to a printed book page. Incremental advances in technology as well as emerging new technologies in the laboratory, such as "electronic paper," may provide the basis for this kind of third-generation device. However, such a device is unlikely to appear before 2005.

Another approach to e-books leverages the burgeoning personal digital assistant (PDA) market. These devices can use software from companies such as peanutpress.com (recently acquired by Palm), Adobe, and Microsoft to provide reader capabilities for Palm and Pocket PC platforms. Currently, these software "readers" are typically free of charge, enabling PDA devices to add e-book functionality at no additional cost.

Because PDAs fulfill multiple functions beyond acting as an e-book reader, users are willing to spend more money on these devices. However, the consumer market for PDA-based e-publishing is severely limited by the small screen sizes and displays of current PDA form factors, which make reading these books difficult.

For instance, PDAs' screen size is much too small to support speed-reading techniques, and display readability is worse than a portable computer display, much less a printed book. However, during 2003/04, we expect these technologies to have a strong adoption rate in corporations, partly to support e-publishing.

The Tablet PC platform due to be released by Microsoft at the end of 2002 is another possible avenue for e-publishing delivery. The Tablet PC is expected to have all the functions of a laptop packed into a system the size of a clipboard. It will be an 8.5×11-inch notebook that is expected to weigh between 1 and 1.5 pounds. Initially, Tablet PCs will be priced as a high-end notebook computer replacement. Manufacturers may also choose to make a limited version that provides only reader functionality.

The evolution of devices is only part of the e-book equation. Currently, the content value of an e-book and paper book are equivalent. Development of hybrid content models that bring together text and audio (and possibly video) could provide a unique experience not available to readers of paper books.

Meanwhile, the latest Microsoft print display technology provides much better display than previous electronic technologies. And voice synthesis software, already available for the PC and laptop form factors, could be added to book readers and PDAs to enable them to read books aloud to users. If offered at the right price point, this would expand the audience for e-books. Indeed, we expect this "book on tape" functionality applied to e-books to be a key driver in expanding the market for second-generation e-books during the next two to three years.

Content distribution mechanisms have also been slowly evolving. Books offered by commercial sites, such as peanutpress.com, are typically two-thirds the cost of the paper editions and include books by top-selling authors, such as Stephen King.

Many classic books no longer under copyright are available for free as text files, which can easily be downloaded from the University of Pennsylvania (http://digital.library.upenn.edu/books/), University of Virginia (http://etext.lib.virginia.edu/ebooks/ebooklist.html), Project Gutenberg (http://www.gutenberg.org), and AOL's PDA library. These text files can easily be converted to formats readable in PDAs. Additionally, huge numbers of electronic texts available in Adobe PDF format can now be read on Palm OS devices using Acrobat Reader.

However, e-book content distribution currently is often playing catch-up in an attempt to match the library of titles and points of distribution available for paper books. To differentiate and add unique value, e-book content vendors will need to look outside this model. The emergence of pervasive computing technologies to embed systems into automobiles (such as GM's OnStar or XM Satellite Radio), hotels, and airline clubs provides new potential distribution points.

Downloading an e-book that can be listened to in the car, then downloaded to a handheld device and possibly uploaded and even printed, could provide a degree of flexibility that attracts a broader user base. In the future, readers could conceivably use holographic projection or heads-up displays onto glasses to project the image of book pages, creating a much larger "display" than any pocket-sized screen could produce.

However, we caution that such hybrid distribution models, like hybrid content models, are in the conceptual stage and unlikely to emerge until 2005 – if ever. During the next few years, technical users and higher-educational institutions will be the initial adopters for e-book technologies. In the meantime, Global 2000 companies must develop a strategy of storing and securing content to be distributed in multiple environments.

We believe that e-publishing of nonfiction books (rather than fiction) will develop via hybrid paper/electronic forms during the next five years, particularly in academia. E-publishing can be used to provide frequent updates to paper-based textbooks as well as multimedia materials and hypertext links to support non-linear learning, recognizing that different students learn in different methods and at different speeds.

User action

Companies with intellectual content in electronic form that may want to distribute it in formats readable on PDAs or specialized book readers should treat this as a niche consumer market for the next five years. However, e-book publishing will become a useful alternative to paper publishing for reaching targeted business audiences equipped with PDAs, either as a pure e-publishing or hybrid publishing effort.

For instance, companies can send updates to paper technical manuals to field technical staff via e-publishing. Therefore, companies may want to track e-publishing along with other aspects of pervasive computing, and eventually may find e-publishing to be an effective means of distributing some intellectual property to specific target audiences.

CASE QUESTIONS

Question 1 Identify the key strategic e-business issues facing publishers who wish to exploit the Internet. What are the major barriers to the growth of the e-book?

Question 2 Do you agree with the assertion that e-publishing of non-fiction books (rather than fiction) will develop via hybrid paper/electronic forms during the next five years, particularly in academia. How could e-publishing assist an e-business strategy student in their studies?

MINI CASE STUDY II
Ten handy hints: How to be an e-manager, The Economist, 9 November 2000
© *The Economist Newspaper Limited, London*

Across the desk of anybody writing about management these days pours a torrent of books about running an e-business. Most start off by saying that everything is different—and then talk as though everything was much the same. It is true that the Internet changes the skills required from managers, but not fundamentally so. Anyone who is a good manager can also become a good e-manager.

However, some qualities have become even more important than they used to be. Here, for any manager too busy wrestling with the Internet economy to plough through the literature, are the top ten things you need.

1. Speed

The list could, perhaps, stop right here. Being quick is more important than being large—indeed, large companies find it hard to be speedy. "There are very few things that the Internet slows down," reflects the MIT Media Lab's Mr Schrage. "Companies that take three or four months to reach a decision find that others have redesigned their websites in that time." Production cycles grow shorter; consumers expect service around the clock; companies do things in parallel that they would once have done sequentially. One way to be speedy is to avoid big-bang decisions. Internet-based technology can help. At Oracle, Gary Roberts, head of global information technologies, points out that Internet applications tend to be smaller than yesterday's proprietary systems, and the software is faster to develop. But speed is also a matter of a company's decision-making processes. Bureaucracy is a killer.

2. Good people

Human beings are the most important of all corporate inputs. Companies need fewer but better people: "celebrity teams," as Novell's Mr Schmidt puts it. Employees with new talents, skills and attitudes must be made to feel at home. Completely new jobs have sprung up in the past three years: content manager, information architect, chief e-business officer, chief knowledge officer. Companies need new ways to hire and—trickier—retain these people. They also need new ways to measure their performance.

3. Openness

The open nature of the Internet drives its success. The economic rewards that come from belonging to a large network will ensure that the new standards that emerge will remain open. In addition, as the Paris-based OECD pointed out in "The Economic and Social Impact of Electronic Commerce", a prescient study published last year, "Openness has emerged as a strategy." Many e-businesses allow their partners, suppliers or consumers an extraordinary degree of access to their databases and inner workings. To allow another business inside the corporate machine in this way requires trust, and a willingness to expose your weaknesses and mistakes to the world.

4. Collaboration skills

The Internet creates many new opportunities for teams and companies to work together. Only as companies learn new ways for their own people to collaborate do they begin fully to realise the opportunities to work with customers, suppliers and partners. Teams may be separated by time zone or by geographic distance, or they may work for different employers: the spread of outsourcing means that companies manage many more alliances. That calls for a different approach from that required to manage competition.

5. Discipline

Can that go with creativity and openness? It has to: "The Internet is all about discipline, protocols and standard processes," insists UTC's Mr Brittan. When a software program replaces human action, the garbage-in–garbage-out principle applies. Unless companies carefully specify the parameters of a procurement order, for example, it makes no sense to invite tenders in an electronic marketplace. Companies need to insist on a standard look and feel for their websites to avoid confusing customers; and they need to insist on common practices within the company on such issues as purchasing to reap real productivity gains from the Internet.

6. Good communications

Given the pace and complexity of change, communicating strategy to staff matters more than ever. Few grasp the Internet's breadth of impact. Communications can no longer be confined within the company, or even within the country. What a company thinks of as external information can turn into the internal sort, and vice versa.

7. Content-management skills

All those websites that companies design to reach their staff, their customers or their corporate partners almost always start off by carrying far too much information. Companies are not used to being content providers, and the people who know most about the subject on the site frequently do not, or cannot, manage the site. IBM's Mr Martinez recalls asking the manager of one of his company's intranet sites who its audience was, and what they needed to know. "We took 80% of the information off the site, use rose 3,000%, and the cost of running it fell dramatically." Many corporate managers are simply not used to expressing themselves clearly and concisely.

8. Customer focus

New opportunities have opened for companies to deepen their relations with customers. The emphasis has shifted from recruitment to retention, from the commodity to the service and from the mass market to the personalised. Companies are concentrating less on product and process management and more on the customer, treating each as an individual and trying to provide him with precisely the product he wants. This shift, made possible by enriched communications, is altering the whole shape of many companies. On the organisation charts that managers love to draw, the long shapes of product-related "silos" are now criss-crossed with a matrix of lines of functional responsibility. An executive in charge of retail banking or light trucks, for example, might also be in charge of monitoring fulfilment across the business.

9. Knowledge management

The communications revolution has raised the importance of pooling the skills and knowledge of a workforce. The development of sophisticated databases and intranets makes it possible for companies to build a core of knowledge that they can draw upon across the globe. But this is not easy. Managing workers of this kind requires a new sensitivity. Getting intelligent people to share what is in their heads takes more than mere money or clever software—although both can help.

10. Leadership by example

Plenty of bosses, especially in Europe and Asia, do not know how to use the Internet, and wear their ignorance as a badge of honour. But chief executives who have never done their own e-mail, or bought something online, or spent an evening or two looking at their competitors' web sites, are endangering their businesses. "Top-level management must spend real political capital to create an e-business," insists Forrester's Mr Colony. That is unlikely to happen if they have no first-hand experience of what the transformation is all about.

Armed with these ten essentials, old-economy managers should see the challenge ahead for what it is: the most revolutionary period they have ever experienced in corporate life. It will be frightening and exhausting, but it will also be enormously exciting. It may even be fun.

CASE QUESTIONS

Question 1 During the first wave of the Internet 'being quick is more important than being large – indeed, large companies find it hard to be speedy'. With hindsight do you agree with this statement? How should managers balance decision-making tempo with the risk of making the wrong decision? Is this an issue for all industries?

Question 2 By referring to an e-business organization with which you are familiar, benchmark the CEO against some of the attributes listed in the above article. Do you agree with each of the ten desired qualities? Are there any other attributes that you feel are important?

REFERENCES

Afuah, A. and C.L. Tucci (2001) *Internet Business Models and Strategies: Text and Cases*, McGraw-Hill Irwin, New York.

Bates, M., S.S.H. Rizvi, P. Tewari and D. Vardhan (2001) How fast is too fast? *The McKinsey Quarterly*, vol. 3, pp. 52–61.

Booz Allen & Hamilton (2001) *e-Business and Beyond: Organizing for Success in New Ventures*, Booz Allen & Hamilton Inc., www.bah.de/content/publikationen_events/sK_viewpoints.asp.

Bruun, P., M. Jensen and J. Skovgaard (2002). E-marketplaces: crafting a winning strategy, *European Management Journal*, vol. 20, no. 3, pp. 286–298.

Doherty, N.F. and L. McAulay (2002) Towards the formulation of a comprehensive framework for the evaluation of investments in sell-side e-commerce, *Evaluation and Program Planning*, vol. 25, pp. 159–165.

Fredrickson, J.W. (1984) The comprehensiveness of strategic decision process: extension, observations, future directions, *Academy of Management Journal*, vol. 27, pp. 445–446.

Graham, P. (2000) *E-business Strategy for Manufacturing Growth*, IBM, Global Midmarket Business.

Greenley, G.E. (1993) *Research on Strategic Planning and Performance: A Synthesis*. University of Birmingham Working Paper (ISBN 0 7044 1273X).

Hackbarth G. and W.J. Kettinger (2000) Building an e-business strategy, *Information Systems Management*, Summer, pp. 78–93.

Hayes I.S. (2000) Se(7)en steps to e-business success, *Software Magazine*, vol. 20, no. 1, pp. 24–28.

Hofer, C.W. (1975) Toward a contingency theory of business strategy, *Academy of Management Journal*, vol. 18, no. 4, pp. 784–810.

Hofer, C.W. and D. Schendel (1978) *Strategy Formulation: Analytical Concepts*, West, St. Paul, MN.

Home Office (2001) *e-Business Strategy*, www.homeoffice.gov.uk/ebusiness/stratman.pdf.

Johnson and Scholes (2001) *Exploring Corporate Strategy, Text and Cases*, 6th edn, FT Prentice Hall, Harlow.

Kettinger, W.J. and G. Hackbarth (1997) Selling in the Era of the 'Net': integration of electronic commerce in small firms, *Proceedings of the Eighteenth International Conference on Information Systems* Atlanta, Georgia, pp. 249–262.

Loebbecke, C. and P. Powell (2002) E-business in the entertainment sector: the Egmont case, *International Journal of Information Management*, vol. 22, no. 4, pp. 307–322.

Mathur, S.S. and A. Kenyon (2001) *Creating Value: Successful Business Strategies*, Butterworth-Heinemann, Oxford.

McKiernan, P. and C. Morris (1994). Strategic planning and financial performance in UK SMEs: does formality matter? *British Journal of Management*, vol. 5, pp. 31–41.

Miles, R.E. and C.C. Snow (1978) *Organisational Strategy, Structure, and Process*, McGraw-Hill, New York.

Mintzberg, H. and J.A. Waters (1985) Of strategies, deliberate and emergent, *Strategic Management Journal*, vol. 6, no. 3, pp. 257–272.

Oliveira, P., A.V. Roth and W. Gilland (2002) Achieving competitive capabilities in e-services, *Technological Forecasting and Social Change*, vol. 69, no. 7, pp. 721–739.

Phillips, P.A. (1996) Strategic planning and business performance in the UK hotel sector: Results of an exploratory study, *International Journal of Hospitality Management*, vol. 15, no. 4, pp. 347–362.

Phillips, P.A., F. Davies and L. Moutinho (1999) The interactive effects of strategic planning on hotel performance: A neural network analysis, *Management Decision*, vol. 37, no. 3/4, pp. 279–288.

Phillips, P.A. and L. Moutinho (1998) *Strategic Planning Systems in Hospitality and Tourism*, CAB International, Oxford.

—— —— (2000) The Strategic Planning Index (SPI): A tool for measuring strategic planning effectiveness, *Journal of Travel Research*, vol. 32, no. 2, pp. 369–379.

Porter, M.E. (1980) *Competitive Strategy*, Free Press, New York.

—— (2001) Strategy and the Internet, *Havard Business Review*, March, pp. 63–77.

Rayport, J.F. and B.J. Jaworksi (2001) *e-commerce*, McGraw-Hill/Irwin, New York.

Rhyne, L.C. (1986) The relationship of strategic planning to company performance, *Strategic Management Journal*, vol. 7, pp. 423–436.

Robinson, R.B. and J.A. Pearce (1988) Planned patterns of strategic behaviour and their relationship to business-unit performance, *Strategic Management Journal*, vol. 9, pp. 43–60.

Salomon Smith Barney (1999) *Net Winners and Losers, The Impact of the Internet on European Insurance*, Industry Report, October.

Schneider, M. (2001) MBA for working stiffs, *BusinessWeek*, 26 March, pp. 74–78.

Tjan, A.K. (2001) Finally, a way to put your Internert portfolio in order, *Harvard Business Review*, February, pp. 76–85.

Willcocks, L.P. and R. Plant (2001) Pathways to e-business leadership: Getting from bricks to clicks, *MIT Sloan Management Review*, vol. 42, no. 3, pp. 50–59.

Yasai-Ardekani, M. and R.S. Haug (1997) Contextual determinants of strategic planning processes, *Journal of Management Studies*, vol. 34, no. 5, pp. 729–767.

Zott, C., R. Amit and J. Donlevy (2000) Strategies for value creation in e-commerce: best practice in Europe, *European Management Journal*, vol. 18, no. 5, pp. 463–475.

CHAPTER 5
E-BUSINESS MODELS

LEARNING OUTCOMES

When you have read and worked through this chapter, you will be able to:
- Appreciate the importance of disruptive technologies
- Understand the difference between traditional and new economies
- Understand the various e-business models being used
- Appreciate the importance of pricing
- Understand the concept of e-finance
- Understand the concept of online retailing
- Appreciate the importance of integrating existing information communication technology systems with new applications

INTRODUCTION

The evolution of research focusing on **e-business models** has gathered pace. From its beginnings as a sure way of making money, organizations now realize the importance of meeting initial market expectations. A continual failure to meet projections will create a lack of confidence among shareholders, which will ultimately lead to a re-adjustment in shareholder value. This chapter focuses on e-business models and provides theory to reinforce the value to readers. The chapter commences by considering the term **disruptive technologies**. Eleven types of e-business models are assessed with illustrative examples. No type of business model, irrespective of the technology behind it, can be successful if it does not, in the end, generate revenue. Thus, the generation of cash is an imperative for any e-business model, so Internet pricing and e-cash are evaluated. Online retailing is used as an example of the operational issues of an e-business model. The importance of integrating existing ICT systems with new applications is highlighted. The chapter ends by discussing the important role now played by **middleware**.

DISRUPTIVE TECHNOLOGIES

The Internet has created the opportunities for organizations to develop new business structures and processes. This has been illustrated by Graham (2001), who highlighted the difference between the traditional and net generation business structures (see Fig. 5.1). During the early stages of e-business, it was felt that those organizations that achieved first mover advantage would continue to achieve sustainable competitive advantage. Unfortunately, organizations are continually faced with the need to make e-business model adjustments. Therefore, there is a need to be able to successfully transform existing business models to keep ahead. According to Seybold (2000), there need to be at least three factors present. First, it is necessary to create an executive team that has vision and flexibility with relevant expertise, backed by providers of financial capital who are willing to support the business beyond the short term. Also, maintaining deep relationships with suppliers and customers will enable the firm to reduce procurement cost and improve the product/service offering. The ability to invest heavily at the outset in a well-thought-out, robust, scalable

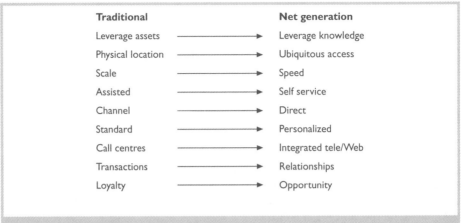

Traditional		Net generation
Leverage assets	→	Leverage knowledge
Physical location	→	Ubiquitous access
Scale	→	Speed
Assisted	→	Self service
Channel	→	Direct
Standard	→	Personalized
Call centres	→	Integrated tele/Web
Transactions	→	Relationships
Loyalty	→	Opportunity

Figure 5.1 New economy business structures 2000 & beyond (*Source: Adapted from Graham, 2001*)

and fully functional infrastructure and business processes with a customer focus will enhance the probability of success.

The changing business environment has meant that managers need to appreciate the necessity for change. Organizations can capture value from IT in two basic ways; by incorporating technology into existing businesses or by launching new products/services that exploit IT. Technology changes taking place in the external environment can be viewed as another form of disruptive technology. Christensen (1997) coined the term 'disruptive technologies' to describe the innovations that create a new market through the creation of a new product or service. One of the most salient characteristics of sustaining technological innovations is that they reinforce a firm's or industry's value and capture systems (Casillas *et al.*, 2000). The Internet is a prime example of a disruptive technology for organizations and industry sectors. Firms like eBay, Freeserve and T-Online International are examples of organizations that have taken advantage of the disruptive technology phenomenon. Competitive advantage has been derived in part from technology-supported systems with new forms and more efficient relationships. Good alliances and partnerships with outside parties, as well as co-operation amongst teams within the firm, would appear to be crucial factors in the design and implementation of sustainable technological improvements. However, there is also the danger than some organizations could learn faster and use stealth tactics to become a competitor.

Measurement of the impact of technological innovations can be illustrated by the technology S-curve (Christensen, 1997). Figure 5.2 shows the relationship of benefits to time. During the early stages there are minimal benefits realized in the development process. There is an improvement breakthrough during the middle stages and then, after the inflection point, the rewards switch from accelerating to diminishing. The inflection point is important, since when this point is reached technological innovation adopts a different posture.

If it is assumed that the Internet can be viewed as a disruptive technology, then it is important to appreciate the idiosyncrasy of virtual markets. Virtual markets can be characterized by three unique attributes – **reach and richness** (Evans and Wurster, 1997) and **digital representation** (Zott, Amit and Donlevy, 2000).

Key Term...

Reach and richness
The new economics of information has altered the trade-off between reach and richness. Traditionally business strategy either could focus on 'rich' information, customized products and services tailored to a niche audience, or could reach out to a larger market, but with watered-down information that sacrificed richness in favour of a broad, general appeal. Now organizations can obtain high levels of reach and richness

Key Term...

Digital representation
Denotes the absence of physical contact in a virtual market, which can be a barrier to purchasing

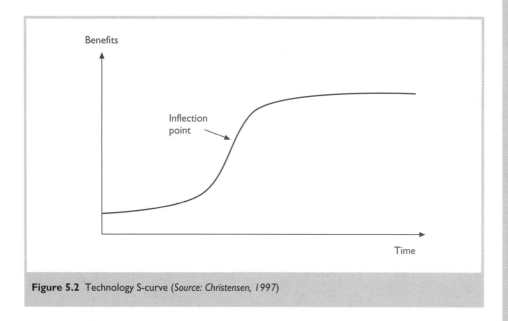

Figure 5.2 Technology S-curve (*Source: Christensen, 1997*)

Reach can be explained by the ability of the Internet to connect a large number of players and products, that is, to connect numerous suppliers, consumers, vendors and, indirectly, competitors and providers of complementary services (Zott, Amit and Donlevy, 2000).

Jupiter MMXI, which is a division of Jupiter Media Metrix, provides European website ratings based on a sample of Web surfers in various European countries. Web surfers have meters on their computers, which monitor the sites they visit. This metered information is compiled to produce Jupiter MMXI's European results. Only home computers are monitored in all countries except Sweden, where results are from both home and work computers.

The top 10 UK and global domains for the month of March 2002 are shown in Tables 5.1 and 5.2. In Table 5.1, it can be seen that MSN-Microsoft sites have a larger digital reach than Yahoo sites (69.2 and 42.6 per cent respectively). In this instance, reach refers to the percentage of home Web surfers (audience) estimated to have visited each site during the month. As a Web surfer may visit more than one site, the combined totals exceed will 100 per cent. Table 5.2 shows that MSN and Yahoo are the first and second top global domains in the UK with 60 and 42.4 per cent digital reach respectively.

The Internet supersedes physical boundaries and the cost of physical goods and services crossing geographical borders is greatly reduced. Instead of having to acquire physical premises, a vendor can connect to consumers anywhere in the world. The consumers themselves are presented with fewer temporal and spatial restrictions. Richness occurs in a virtual marketplace since relationships can be greater, deeper and quicker than in traditional markets. Technology provides players in a virtual market with additional knowledge. This mitigates the threat of information asymmetry between buyers and sellers. Buyers can obtain more information about potential purchases in virtual markets, which makes them more informed when making choices. Nevertheless, despite the advantages of reach and richness, Zott, Amit and Donlevy (2000) postulate that impersonal, electronic networks have drawbacks. They use the term digital representation, which denotes the lack of physical contact. Not being able to touch or feel, or to enjoy some of the

Top 10 Properties in the UK				
Rank February 2002	Rank March 2002	Domain Visitors	Unique Media (000)	Digital Reach (%)
		Total Digital Media	15 844	100.0
1	1	MSN-Microsoft sites	10 969	69.2
2	2	Yahoo sites	6 749	42.6
3	3	AOL Time Warner Network	6 294	39.7
4	4	BT sites	4 624	29.2
7	5	Google sites	4 596	29.0
5	6	Ask Jeeves Inc sites	4 036	25.5
6	7	Wanadoo sites	3 997	25.2
8	8	BBC sites	3 859	24.4
9	9	Amazon sites	3 287	20.7
11	10	Friendsreunited.co.uk	2 543	16.1
(Source: http://uk.jupitermmxi.com/data/thetop.jsp)				

Table 5.1 Jupiter MMXI top ten properties in UK, March 2002

Top 10 Global Domains in the UK				
Rank February 2002	Rank March 2002	Digital Media Visitors Reach (%)	Unique Visitors (000)	Digital Media Reach (%)
		Total Digital Media	15 844	100.0
1	1	MSN	9 511	60.0
2	2	Yahoo	6 722	42.4
3	3	Microsoft	5 962	37.6
4	4	Passport	5 393	34.0
7	5	Google	4 596	29.0
5	6	AOL	4 369	27.6
6	7	Askjeeves	3 985	25.1
10	8	BBC	3 774	23.8
8	9	Freeserve	3 738	23.6
9	10	Lycos	3 324	21.0
(Source: http://uk.jupitermmxi.com/data/thetop.jsp)				

Table 5.2 Jupiter MMXI top ten global domains in the UK panels, August 2001

social aspects of shopping, can become a barrier to purchasing. The failure of boo.com could be in part to do with the fact that consumers were not able to touch or try on clothes. However, if online transactions are quick and easy and supported with online communities and virtual storefronts, digital representation could be converted from a commercial threat into a business opportunity.

Senior managers who are faced with technological low-cost innovations brought about by the Internet have to understand how disruptive technologies threaten the sustainable competitive advantage of organizations within an industry. Moreover, the impact on a firm will depend upon the homogeneity of competitors and the nature of the industry. While organizations are continually scanning the external environment to anticipate new forms of disruptive technologies, it is also necessary to prepare the firm, strategically, operationally and organizationally, to compete in new and different market (Casillas *et al.*, 2000). Failure to incorporate the necessary changes into business processes will lead to a collapse in revenue and ultimate failure of the business model.

E-BUSINESS MODELS

The first wave of Internet start-ups comprised the dot.coms, which were launched to take advantage of the wealth of opportunities provided by the Internet. Dot.coms operated mainly on the Internet and were perceived to be dynamic with projected high exponential growth rates. This was also backed up with valuations that were at best optimistic. Despite possessing existing clients, relationships, brands and market share, 'bricks and mortar' companies were compared to dinosaurs that were about to become extinct. The collapse of several high profile dot.coms provided bricks and mortar with the opportunity to enhance their online presence by transforming into 'clicks and mortar' businesses. Events have now turned full circle, with high-profile dot.coms like Amazon investing in physical assets such as storage units in an effort to compete with traditional book retailers.

Nevertheless, despite the above chain of events, traditional business principles still apply. For example, the good use of information, the quality of data and the efficiency of business processes are components that are useful and necessary for a business to function effectively. However, in the new economy, the advent of information and transaction exchanges via the Web presents new opportunities for businesses. With the advent of the Internet, organizations have sought to create novel ways of interacting with members in the value chain. Sustainable relationships in the value chain are created when value is provided for all members in the value chain. It is therefore important for any strategist to appreciate that the economic environment is in a continued state of metamorphosis. This presents a challenge, and an understanding of e-business models allows the analyst to understand better what is going on in the e-business. The adoption of a successful e-business model may make it possible to increase competitiveness in the marketplace.

New business models have appeared on markets, modifying the nature of company internal and external business processes. These new forms of conducting business have affected traditional management techniques taught on management courses and no sector has been left untouched. In this new context, it is important to acknowledge the importance of e-business models. They are the new key to increasing a company's competitiveness in the marketplace by improving its current value added. One must not lose sight of the fact that any typology of e-business models should be viewed as only a guide, 'purely' explaining how business can be performed on the Internet.

Many e-businesses are struggling to address the most basic conundrum: What is the most appropriate e-business model? Strategists are experimenting with different formulae in different contextual settings. Some are incorporating e-business throughout the organization. Some have tried to create e-business strategic business units, and then spin them off as separate online entities. Others are investing in or merging with Internet start-ups. Some are trying to move their business to the Web. However, the evidence to date indicates that there is no simple prescription. Companies operating in the same sector, of the same size or with similar organizational cultures are finding that one e-business strategy does not fit all. Naturally, when an e-business is performing successfully, it is usually loath to risk any of its 'first-mover' advantage by letting others obtain its secrets.

Many companies are carefully quickly trying to leverage their traditional IT and business strengths, such as ERP systems or a smooth-running physical logistical distribution network, as e-business building blocks, not barriers.

As the new economy evolves, current and aspiring managers of e-businesses need to understand the full spectrum of opportunities and how competitors are responding to e-business. Given the complex systems of players and how they function, e-business models need to incorporate the contextual environment. It is important to bear in mind that any typology of e-business models should be viewed as a guide to describing a variety of the models. In reality, a model that incorporates features of several business models is often cited as best practice. After analysing more than 700 online organizations, Martinez (2000) observed some patterns in online business models. While there was some commonality among business models in terms of geography, industry, company size or type of e-business (B2B or B2C), a distinction can be made by their primary focus. Authors such as Rappa (2000) and Timmers (2000) have identified several generic e-business models. The following sections provide an outline of the various e-business models currently used.

Portals

During the initial days of the Internet, e-commerce was the bull's eye and **portals** were the arrows to shoot. Websites such as Yahoo (www.yahoo.com), Excite (www.excite.com), Lycos (www.lycos.com and Freeserve (www.freeserve.com) were the first stop for users going online. Analysts projected revenues based on banner advertising being strategically placed on websites. It was anticipated that users would click through to electronic stores. Venture capitalists were happy to provide portals with cash, with organizations impressing venture capitalists in their 'elevator pitches'. Table 5.3 shows that the top 10 Internet categories according to Jupiter MMXI for the month of March 2002 were portals, which obtained a digital media reach of 78.8 per cent with a corresponding figure of 77.8 per cent for ISPs.

Previous chapters have already highlighted the fact that the bullish Internet revenue projections never materialized. According to Booz Allen & Hamilton between October 1999 and October 2000, click-through rates fell by more than 40 per cent, with less than 0.2 per cent of page visitors clicking on banner ads on leading portal sites. However, Rozanski and Bollman (2001) still view portals as a potentially valuable marketing medium if used effectively. To generate profits, marketing professionals should favour brand building via traditional techniques such as reach, frequency and creativity. Instead of relying on sponsorship, broadband multimedia advertisement format, co-branding and co-retailing, firms should banish the banner and brandish the brand.

The portal was the first model of the Internet. The popularity of portals was such that frequently 60 per cent of Internet sessions include a stop at a portal, which makes some sites

Top 10 categories in the UK				
Rank February 2002	Rank March 2002	Domain	Unique Visitors (000)	Digital Media Reach (%)
		Total Digital Media	15 844	100.0
1	1	Portals	12 480	78.8
2	2	ISP	12 333	77.8
3	3	Services	10 595	66.9
5	4	Corporate presence	9 423	59.5
6	5	Search/navigation	9 075	57.3
4	6	Entertainment	8 952	56.5
7	7	Retail	8 628	54.5
8	8	Directories/resources	7 335	46.3
9	9	Application	7 097	44.8
10	10	Business/finance	6 528	41.2
(Source: http://uk.jupitermmxi.com/data/thetop.jsp)				

Table 5.3 Jupiter MMXI top ten categories in the UK, March 2002

more popular than some traditional broadcast networks (Rozanski and Bollman, 2001). The enthusiasm towards the portal business model led to some dot.coms being valued on unsustainable price earnings ratios. Yahoo, which was valued at $300 m prior to its IPO in 1996, achieved a market capitalization as high as $85 bn.

The disproportionate influence of portals in the new economy can be illustrated by looking at the UK unique audience statistics data collected by Nielsen/NetRatings (www.nielsen-netratings.com) for July 2002. The top 10 Web properties at home (Table 5.4) are headed by MSN with a unique audience of 7.7m and a reach of 47.6 per cent. In tenth place is Ask Jeeves with corresponding figures of 2.9m and a reach of 17.5 per cent. When figures for home and at work (Table 5.5) are compared, MSN remains in pole position with unique audience of 11.2m and a reach of 52 per cent. In tenth position is Lycos Network with unique audience of 4.3m and a reach of 20 per cent.

E-tailing

E-tailing is a popular model utilized by retail organizations for transactions with other companies. Organizations can act as intermediaries between producers and potential buyers to create added value. They manage the platforms where their virtual brochures are presented. E-commerce enables good effective management practices since managers can use technology to make faster business decisions, such as the selection and realization of products and rates. In this type of model, prices are determined by the firm but variations are allowed according to predefined criteria. However, only certain categories will work; commodity products, such as travel, PCs, electronics, software, grocery, books, ticketing, specialty gifts and music, are ideal. Shopping-guide.co.uk is a useful website that provides useful independent information e-tailing.

In February 2001, John Lewis (www.john-lewis-partnership.co.uk), a leading UK high-street department store chain and owner of Waitrose supermarkets, announced the acquisition

Key Term...

E-tailing
An e-business model that retail organizations use to transact online

Property	Unique audience	Reach (%)	Time per person
1. MSN	7 744 967	47.55	0: 39: 55
2. Yahoo!	5 853 182	35.94	0: 33: 50
3. Microsoft	5 257 586	32.28	0: 09: 34
4. Google	5 203 317	31.95	0: 14: 07
5. AOL Time Warner	5 089 615	31.25	0: 18: 38
6. Wanadoo	4 540 003	27.88	0: 14: 12
7. British Telecom	3 938 964	24.18	0: 19: 11
8. Amazon	3 365 390	20.66	0: 15: 13
9. BBC	3 068 266	18.84	0: 19: 49
10. Ask Jeeves	2 846 107	17.47	0: 10: 30

(Source: Neilson/netRatings, http://epm.netratings.com/uk/web/NRpublicreports.toppropertiesmonthly)

Table 5.4 Top 10 Web properties for the month of July 2002 (home)

Property	Unique Audience	Reach (%)	Time per Person
1. MSN	11 149 704	52.12	0: 42: 46
2. Yahoo!	8 732 691	40.82	0: 39: 16
3. Microsoft	8 230 436	38.47	0: 09: 30
4. Google	7 889 188	36.88	0: 20: 59
5. AOL Time Warner	7 244 167	33.86	0: 21: 18
6. Wanadoo	6 470 891	30.25	0: 13: 23
7. Amazon	5 417 681	25.33	0: 16: 00
8. British Telecom	5 397 384	25.23	0: 20: 22
9. BBC	5 279 082	24.68	0: 40: 40
10. Lycos Network	4 261 283	19.92	0: 08: 54

(Source: Neilson/netRatings, http://epm.netratings.com/uk/web/nrpublicreports.toppropertiesmonthly)

Table 5.5 Top 10 Web properties for the month of July 2002 (home and work)

of buy.com (UK), a leading UK Internet retailer of technology, software and office products. Following a successful trial of John Lewis online in the run-up to Christmas, the company decided to launch its department store Internet offer based on the buy.com technology and customer service platform. John Lewis continued to develop the existing buy.com business in parallel with the John Lewis online business itself. The two businesses have their own distinct websites.

However, as a result of combining the John Lewis name, product range and retail experience with buy.com, the department store can take a leading position online. In acquiring buy.com, John Lewis has secured a proven technology and customer service solution, an experienced management team and a rapidly growing e-commerce business.

Buy.com was launched in the UK in March 2000, and was the fourth most visited e-tail website in the UK in December 2000, with over 550 000 unique visitors and attracted more than 80 000 customers in the UK, with high levels of customer loyalty. New customers were being added at a rate of 3000 per week.

Auction

The **auction** model plays an intermediary role between buyers and sellers. This model of one seller to one broker to many buyers is more concerned with filling a gap in the marketplace than with mere content. Communication is faster and made easier, as it takes place in real time between buyers and sellers. This model eliminates both the distance and time and allows a continual updating of catalogues without the expensive printing costs. Access is provided to a wide variety of goods and services, grouped together by areas of commercial activity or personal interest. The exchange of goods can be provided via negotiation or bargaining between two entities or a group of organizations. It is relatively easy to operationalize the auction e-business model as there are very few restrictions placed on organizations. In addition to their pure form, auctions can take several forms: reverse and Dutch. In the most basic form of auction, the price is revealed at the moment the transaction takes place and the bidding can go up or down in a B2C environment. Auctioning for the lowest bid can be performed between companies in a B2B environment where firms are competing with each other to offer the lowest price for a certain type of product. This model is appropriate for organizations that offer customized, perishable or special products or services that would be difficult to order via a catalogue. Auctioning for the highest bid is possible when companies are looking for something rare on the market or when there is a shortage of substitutes. In a reverse auction, the buyer proposes a price that they are willing to pay for a good or service. It is then left up to the seller whether to fulfil the order from potential buyers.

Value chains

This business model groups together partner companies that consult each other through an organized process in the making of a product with very high added value. The main objective is to maximize the creation of added value through an efficient operational process. These partnerships meet the specific needs of third parties by offering customized products. These types of firms do not use online intermediaries, such as content aggregators, in their e-commerce processes. Instead, they attempt to build and maintain their own e-commerce infrastructure. A company usually co-ordinates and applies a strict control of activities and is then able to determine the cost of the entire system. However, the challenge is how the benefits can be shared out among all partners. This model of one seller to many buyers can be effective if the firm can create channel strategies that incorporate e-business with traditional channels.

Barter

The barter model allows goods and services to be exchanged without money. The Internet enables a business owner to barter tangible or intangible products with another company. For example, a company can make its warehouse space profitable by offering another company the possibility of storing its products there temporarily. Or a company that manufactures wooden furniture can barter sawdust and old wood with a company that produces plywood. The second variation of this model is the most virtual. In this case, companies or people with access to this e-business model are members of different associations or companies. This type of site favours shared expertise and knowledge. For instance, a computer programmer with difficulty in finding a solution to a code can go to a 'community alliance' site that is specialized in computers, communicate with other programmers, answer questions (if possible) and find a solution to his or her problem. Participants often give their codes for free in exchange for another service.

ILLUSTRATIVE EXAMPLE I

Freeserve: The online auction, extracts from www.freeserveauctions.com

---

The UK ISP Freeserve has a variety of online auctions everyday at www.fsauctions.co.uk. These include:

- Reserve price
- Dutch
- English
- Fixed price
- Quick win

RESERVE PRICE

A reserve price is the lowest price at which a seller is willing to sell an item, even though the opening bid price may be much lower. If the bidding does not meet or exceed this price, there is no transaction. The reserve price is never disclosed to potential buyers. If the maximum bid is higher than the seller's reserve price, the bid is set at the reserve price by Freeserve's automatic bidding software, or at the lowest winning price above the reserve price. If the bid is lower than the reserve, it will be displayed as entered. Those bids above the reserve price are marked with a status of 'winning' and the bids below the reserve price are marked 'losing.'

DUTCH

A Dutch auction is a multiple-item listing. The main difference between Dutch and multiple-quantity English is that, with Dutch, all winning bidders get their items at the price of the lowest winning bid. Additionally, automatic bidding or reserve price can not be used with Dutch.

For example, a Dutch Auction has 20 items for sale. The opening price for the items is £15.00 each. After the listing opens, 40 people place equal bids for the items at £15.00 each. If the listing were to close at this point, the first 20 people to bid would be declared the winners, because earlier bids take precedence over later bids of equal amount and quantity. However, just prior to the listing closing, a new bidder places a bid of £45.00 for one of the items. Because this person has the highest bid, they will obtain one of the 20 items listed. The remaining 19 items are won by the first 19 Bidders who bid at £15.00. However, because all bids clear at the lowest winning bid, the person who bid £45.00 will only be required to pay £15.00 for the item. By bidding over opening price, late bidders can essentially knock the earlier low bidders out of the running.

ENGLISH

An English auction can be used for either a single item or multiple items. With English listings, the price is raised successively until the listing closes. Potential buyers must use the next highest bid increment when making a bid. The high bidder(s) at that time are declared the winners and each bidder is required to pay the seller the amount of their winning bid. The bids are sorted in order of price and quantity of items bid for, and then the time bids are placed.

FIXED PRICE

A fixed price listing auction is where sellers sell their items at one low price available to buyers until the item sells out or the listing closes. As long as there is quantity available for an item, buyers can purchase the listed item at the sale price. Fixed price listing purchases are binding commitments. After a buyer makes a purchase, the order is processed immediately and cannot be cancelled.

QUICK WIN

A quick win auction is similar to the English auction, but it is only valid for single items. With quick win, the seller sets a threshold price. If a bidder matches the threshold price, the listing closes immediately and that bidder is declared the winner.

The Linux.co.uk website is a good example of the community alliance model. Linux, which offers a new alternative for a server operating system, is in competition with Microsoft. However, Linux is unique as it seeks to use the computer community's knowledge by offering the possibility to share knowledge and it allows a number of computer programmers to have access to its code. As described earlier, the strength of this e-commerce business model is to use the Web's advantages, on-line discussions (chat) and email, to bring specialists and their experiences closer together on a website that favours exchanges. This system can be used for social purposes, but it is particularly appreciated for technical support purposes.

Buying groups

This model is a buying group for several business owners, which allows greater negotiating power. The model is especially useful for the smaller business unable to get the benefits of economy of scale. When businesses are joined together into a buying group, the new entity plays the role of intermediary for research and negotiation with suppliers. It can also provide the distribution of product catalogues as well as the management of commercial and financial transactions and the delivery of merchandise.

LetsBuyIt.com (www.letsbuyit.com) has developed a pan-European e-business based on a buying group model. The model is called co-buying and offers LetsBuyIt.com members an opportunity to aggregate their demand for a product or service in order to achieve favourable purchasing terms. The idea is to bring together a group of people who want the same product so as to gain negotiating and purchasing power via economies of scale.

LetsBuyIt.com deals with suppliers, thus eliminating costs relating to overheads and so enabling them to deliver brand-name merchandise at much lower prices. In addition, to supply chain efficiencies, prices are driven down by members gaining power by forming groups. Added-value services are provided by allowing members to recommend products or services for online co-buys on the website and thus help LetsBuyit.com identify new co-buys.

Integration

Integration can either be vertical (according to a specific industry or market) or horizontal (according to an organizational function or process). A differentiation strategy is required if the website is to attract and retain new and existing buyers and sellers. If successful, the integration e-business model can generate significant growth and generate margins as high as 85 per cent.

Vertical integration

Vertical integration is predominantly present within a vertical market or a concentration of industries. Firms that employ this model provide industry specific goods and services and make company interrelations easier within the sector. This business model is often called a hub. The main challenge for vertical integration is the difficulty in diversifying activities and making them reach other horizontal markets, since expertise and interrelations are specialized in one domain. To remain a dominant force, vertical integrators must focus on building deep relationships with all parties of the supply chain. The ability to provide a 'one-stop' marketplace environment that offers a variety of products and useful content is a critical success factor.

Moreover (www.moreover.com) is an organization that provides news via its Dynamic Information Management system, which is able to monitor and retrieve online information that changes too quickly for traditional technologies to capture. Moreover's proprietary technology is designed to extract, filter and integrate dynamic content in real time. The result for clients is continuous access to the most relevant and timely information from a variety of online sources, delivered efficiently to corporate intranets and portals. Companies use Moreover's Connected Intelligence (CI) suite of customized products to gain agility and flexibility in fast-evolving environments where being well informed is essential to gaining a competitive advantage.

Horizontal integration

In contrast to vertical integration, some organizations provide services across different types of industries. Horizontal integration allows expertise in a standardized process to be exploited in different companies operating in different industries. The term 'functional hubs' is used to describe this situation, where firms are providing the same function across different industries. Firms employing horizontal integration are able to generate profits from the sale of back-office processes, in addition to transaction fees from the online market. For instance, success can be achieved through standardization, the horizontal integrator's process knowledge and workflow automation expertise. The main challenge of horizontal integrators will be to develop and provide personalized distribution functions for a specific industry. Obviously, success is dependent upon the commonality of business processes among buyers and sellers. If potential organizations are unable to use their intermediary for the majority of transactions, they need to be able to maintain some traditional processes.

Employease (www.employease.com) is working to inspire human resource managers, through the use of the Internet, to become more strategic and play a bigger, more important role in the success of their organizations. The company is also helping human resource managers inspire the human capital within their organization by providing an Internet business service for managing and communicating information on human resources, employee benefits and payroll. Major benefits cited by Employease include the avoidance of the high cost of traditional software and can be illustrated as follows:

- No installing hardware or software
- No configuring hardware or software
- No maintaining hardware or software
- No upgrading hardware or software

All of the above can be achieved through a Web browser and Internet connection. Employers are brought together via the Employease Network, which contains the B2B network for employee information. Adopting a bottom-up approach as an Internet Business Service,

Employease helps employers and service providers avoid the cost and complexity associated with traditional software. Benefits accrue straight to the bottom-line from the Employease Network by reducing administrative costs, improving service to employees and increasing focus on strategic human resources. Service providers benefit from the Employease Network by improving customer service, reducing operating expenses and delivering new services.

Infomediary

During the first wave of the Internet, companies playing the infomediary role were thought to become the custodians, agents and brokers of customer information, marketing it to businesses (and providing them with access to it) on consumers' behalf, while at the same time protecting their privacy (Hagel and Singer, 1999). According to Hagel and Singer, infomediaries tend to fall into two broad categories: entrepreneurial, Internet-based companies, and larger, more-established companies operating in traditional markets.

Instead of relying on selling and buying products on the Internet, some firms are able to trade by collecting valuable information about consumers and their buying habits. Infomediaries can combine a number of functions and act as one-stop shops, which can act as either competitors or partners to traditional intermediaries.

An example of an infomediary is your mortgage (www.yourmortgage.co.uk), which is a website that informs users of all they need to know about mortgages. Yourmortgage acts a one-stop shop about mortgages and introduces the user to a range of calculators, online quotes and lenders.

Affiliate

This e-business model provides traffic and potential commerce to transactional sites. During the early days of e-business, company valuations were in some cases based solely on the number of eyeballs visiting the website. Attracting customers to a specific website can be costly, so, if potential customers were effortless brought to a website and a small payment made for each sale, both parties would benefit.

The main participants in a revenue sharing program are merchants and affiliates. A merchant is an online retailer who has products or services for sale. An affiliate is a website owner who places merchant promotions on their site and makes a commission when a sale is generated from their website.

A useful website that provides details about a broad range a affiliates opportunities is www.affiliate-scheme.co.uk. There were 663 affiliate schemes available in June 2002:

- Affiliate directories and portals (24)
- Business opportunities (69)
- General links (8)
- Network marketing schemes (20)
- UK-based affiliate programmes (204)
- US, Canada and European affiliate programmes (288)
- Web master resources (20)
- Website promotion and marketing (30)

Subscription

If a website possesses high-value-added content, Internet users may be willing to pay to view content online. Unfortunately, after the availability of free content it is providing increasingly difficult to get Internet users to pay. Nevertheless, subscription sales are fast becoming one of the favoured revenue models for Internet commerce, especially in those firms operating in the media sector. Firms are now trying to balance free content, which drives up volume and revenue, with premium content or services that are available to subscribers. A good example of an organization facing the dilemma of subscription is FT.com, the online version of the *Financial Times*.

In April 2002, FT.com unveiled details of a new subscription packages for its Web content after several months of speculation about the planned cost of services. The *Financial Times* introduced a two-tiered subscription package, charging its users £75 or £200 a year.

Latest news, access to the week's analysis and comment, including one Lex comment column a day, and a searchable seven-day archive will remain free, along with personal finance and investment news. For a subscription fee of £75 a year, users can access five years' worth of *Financial Times* newspaper archives online, as well as viewing pages of the print edition of the *Financial Times* the night before publication. For £200, users get all of the above plus access to financial information on 18 000 listed companies over the world and a press archive from more than 500 news sources.

Community

The spirit of a community and relationships between its members can be the foundations for a valuable business asset. Internet users are sometimes prepared to invest in time and emotions, if it is felt that they fulfil a particular need. The community model takes advantage of this investment to build up and maintain user loyalty (as opposed to high traffic volume). The users of the website who visit continually offer opportunities for using some of the previous e-business models discussed. These can include advertising, infomediary and subscription models. Village UK (www.ivillage.co.uk) is a 24-hour online resource and community for women and is a leading website for women in the UK. In just over a year from launch, ABC electronic revealed that for the month ended 31 January 2002, iVillage UK had 541 596 unique users and 6 930 538 page impressions, which were higher than for handbag.com and femail.co.uk.

iVillage.co.uk is firmly backed by two industry giants, iVillage Inc. and Tesco, and its success is attributed to what differentiates it from other women's propositions, specifically community, online information resource and campaigns.

Community

With over 74 message boards ranging through breast cancer support, recipe ideas, birth stories and coping with abuse, the website has an extremely effective community model.

Online information resource

The site has over 3000 articles covering all aspects of life, as well as on-call experts and interactive tools. Content is user driven and delivered in response to issues raised by the iVillage UK community, ensuring that the site continues to grow and is dynamic.

Campaigns

By harnessing and supporting campaigns that affect the UK's female population, such as Domestic Abuse, Get Out of Debt, Breast Cancer Support and Shape Up Challenge, the site provides a much needed voice for women. As a media business, money is made through advertising, sponsorship and some paid-for services.

INTERNET PRICING

The growth of the Internet has been phenomenal, with the number of hosts, the number of users and the amount of traffic doubling approximately every year since 1988 (Mason, 2000). Unless, there is an unlimited supply of bandwidth at or near zero cost, there needs to be a service model and pricing mechanisms for allocating network resources that reflect consumers' valuations and social costs of congestion, given traffic characteristics and bandwidth availability (McKnight and Boroumand, 2000).

Unfortunately, there is a fixed supply of bandwidth and this presents two major problems for Internet users. The first relates to the new applications with high bandwidth requirements. For example, a one minute Internet telephone call uses 500 times the capacity of a comparable email, while one minute of video covering the same paragraph uses 15 000 times as much capacity, which is the equivalent of sending more than 10 000 pages of text. The second difficulty relates to the aggressive protocols to transport delay-intolerant traffic.

Among the marketing-mix variables, price can affect the bottom line directly, so it is advantageous to create strategies that avoid intense pricing, which can destroy profits. According to Odlyzko (2001), there are recurring patterns in the histories of previous communication, including ordinary mail, the telegraph, the telephone and now the Internet. The dominant theme has been that, for each new service, there has been an increase in quality and a fall in prices; then usage increases to generate more sales revenue. Oldyzko postulates that as services become less expensive and are more widely used, there is less need to segment the market, and thereby to extract maximal revenues and to maximize the utilization efficiency of the infrastructure. Instead, customer yearning for simplicity becomes foremost.

Economics is a suitable theoretic discipline to use as a managerial aid when managers are faced with how to allocate efficiently the scarce resource (the Internet). In an attempt to optimize shareholder value, a variety of Internet pricing proposals have been advocated with the 'smart market' and 'Paris metro pricing' being two well-cited proposals. Mackie-Mason and Varian's (1997) 'smart market' involves a zero usage price when network resources are not congested. When network resources are congested, packets are prioritized according to bids attached to them by users. Instead of paying the amount that users bid, a price is charged based on the highest bid for the priority packet that is not transmitted. Economists favour this model as the outcome is the classic supply-equal-demand level of service, where the equilibrium price, at any point of time, is the bid of the marginal user (McKnight and Boroumand, 2000).

Odlyzko's (1997) 'Paris Metro' Internet pricing proposal assumes that networks are partitioned into separate logical networks (like compartments on a train) with different usage charges applied on each sub-network. Despite having no guarantees of service quality, some users are happy to pay more for less crowded networks.

Internet service providers (ISPs) are currently looking at the issue of usage pricing versus flat-rate pricing. While usage pricing was the norm, the emerging consensus in the market place is for dial-up access to the Internet with a flat-rate pricing structure with unlimited access for a fixed monthly fee. One of the major attractions of flat rate pricing for users and service providers is its simplicity, which reduces risk and administrative costs. Flat-rate costs also reduce transaction costs for users and this predictability of income and cost flows is attractive to both parties. Flat-rate services provide service providers with the potential to bundle products/services. Bundling can enhance revenue as the strategy of offering several products/services for a single price is attractive to users. However, the decision whether to offer flat or metered rates to users needs to be determined using a systematic financial approach. For example, if customers are willing to pay a sum of money, in excess of cost of the service, then customers should be given what they desire. If the willingness to pay flat rates is too low, offer only measured rates (Odlyzo, 2001).

In an effort to deal with the problems of the 'smart market', a team of researchers (Shenker, Clark, Estrin and Heroz, 1996) have postulated a new pricing paradigm of 'edge pricing'. Shenker *et al.* highlight three weaknesses:

- Marginal cost prices may not cover total cost.
- Congestion costs are inherently inaccessible to the network and are not ideal to use as a basis for pricing.
- Optimality (efficiency) is not the only structural goal and some of these goals are incompatible with the global uniformity required for optimal pricing schemes.

The edge pricing approach incorporates two approximations. The first is to replace the current congestion condition with the expected congestion condition. The second is to replace the cost of the actual path with the cost of the expected path, where the charge depends only on the source and destinations. McKnight and Boroumand (2000) conclude that, while over-provisioning remains 'best practice' for many applications, over time new pricing mechanisms will be required by new business and consumer services. This suggests that ISPs e-business models need to be sensitive to the economic issues of Internet pricing.

E-CASH

The lack of widespread adoption of **e-cash**, partly due to the strength of traditional credit and debit cards, has led to demise of firms such as beenz.com and flooz.com. The old adage that the strength of any currency is only as good as the number of places that accept it and people who use it is a timely reminder. Digicash (www.digicash.com) was another failure and collapsed in 1998, but its technology and concept is maintained by eCash (www.eCash.com). The eCash Internet Payment Processing Works as follows:

1 A customer places an order at the merchant's website.
2 The merchant securely transfers order information to eCash over the Internet via a proprietary Electronic Commerce Messaging Protocol (ECMP). ECash receives order information and performs the requested services simultaneously.
3 ECash then routes the transaction authorization request through a payment processor to the appropriate card system.
4 The card system makes contact with the issuing bank (customer's bank) to request transaction authorization.
5 The issuing bank returns authorization to the card association or, if the transaction is not authorized, eCash returns a message to the merchant's system, to be requestioned or cancelled.
6 ECash receives transaction authorization and, if physical fulfillment is requested, sends an ECMP EDI message to the merchant or distribution centre authorizing order fulfillment. The merchant or distribution centre sends eCash an ECMP fulfillment notification to permit settlement and eCash sends a settlement request to the issuing bank (customer's bank). If

authorization is for the sale of a digitally delivered product or service, the settlement request is synchronized with the authorization.

7 The issuing bank approves the transfer of money to the acquiring bank (merchant's account).

Smartcards

Smartcards are credit-card-size plastic cards with a 'brain' on them, the brain being a small embedded computer chip. This card-computer can be programmed to provide security and convenience to individuals and businesses to perform tasks and store information. The JavaCard introduced by Schlumberger (www.smartcards.net) and submitted as a standard by JavaSoft is an important development in smartcard technology. Schlumberger was the first JavaCard on the market and the company is the first JavaCard licensee. JavaCards enable secure and chip-independent execution of different applications.

The development of an alternative payment systems to credit cards was an aspiration for several organizations. These were initially focused on those transactions where the amount was for micropayments or for electronic coinage, such as downloading an online daily newspaper, where the overall cost was too small to be effectively paid for by credit card.

Electronic payments systems can be categorized into two, non-credit or pre-paid systems (e.g. Ecoin, www.ecoin.net) and post-paid or credit-based (www.Pay2see.com) systems (Chaffey, 2002). Nevertheless, the problem of paying for items purchased online is one of the obstacles to e-business growth. Herbst (2001) suggests that there are two important themes in e-finance:

- Use of computers on the Internet to augment or substitute for traditional transactions that would otherwise be done in person, by mail, telephone or fax.
- Using the Internet to revolutionize traditional financial intermediaries, as well as monetary, tax and privacy issues.

Internet augmentation/substitute for traditional transactions

Online banking

The Basel Committee report on banking supervision defines electronic banking as the provision of retail and small-value banking products and services through electronic channels. Therefore, the definition covers direct deposits, ATMs, credit and debit cards, telephone banking, as well as electronic bill payment and Web-based banking (Pennathur, 2001). Electronic banking systems can be either 'closed' or 'open'. Closed systems restrict access to participants bound by agreements on the terms of membership, such as the access to the website by members. Open systems have no such membership restrictions. Websites may be viewed as informational (information only is provided) or transactional (user interaction is allowed).

The digital age presents a new and exciting way of conducting business. Yet the new marketplace has a unique underlying structure and represents an interplay of internal and external forces that few bank managers understand. Nevertheless, the Internet is gaining popularity as an additional distribution channel in the banking sector (Jayawardhena and Foley, 2000). Internet banking demonstrates the most significant technological revolution since the development of the ATM (Chou, 2000). Banks are able to provide cost-effective home banking services, such as a variety of banking, bill-payment and money-management services 24 hours a day, seven days a week. In the world of Internet banking there appears not to be a difference between serving one customer or one million customers (Chou, 2000). Electronic commerce seems to lower transaction costs (Bakos, 1997) and increases the economics of scale, scope and speed in processing banking services to the market (Llewellyn, 1997). Several academics and practitioners predict that a fundamental restructuring of the value chain in the banking industry will take place, where vertical integration will appear to shift to vertical disintegration and outsourcing (Llewellyn, 1997; Evans and Wurster, 1997; Hagel, Hewlins and Hutchings, 1997). The value chain is now best viewed as a 'value network' (Stabell and Fjeldstad, 1998; Andersen Consulting 2000). Disintegration of vertical integrated value chains in banking offers cost efficiency and added flexibility (Andersen Consulting, 2000). Hence, Vernon (2000) argues that one of the main ways to compete in the Internet banking market is to retain current customers and to gain new customers. Customer services play a major role in this contest, where building customer loyalty appears to occur through building the relationship between customers and banks (Furash, 1999).

Moving from the traditional market place to an electronic market reduces the cost consumers pay to search for information about products in the market (Bakos, 1997), and hence enhances the information stream to the patrons. The reduction of the search cost is believed to reduce loyalty and it may well be argued that it will change the effect of search cost on loyalty to that of other determinates (Methlie and Nysveen, 1999). High search costs are assumed to make it expensive for customers to shop around for the best offer in the market (Methlie and Nysveen, 1999). The implication of this is that it is costly for the customer to find alternative brands or suppliers. A barrier like search cost appears to be formidable in business-to-business markets, but it has also played an important role in the consumer market as well (Fornell, 1992), e.g. within the market place of bank services it has traditionally been intricate to search for information among suppliers in order to make comparisons. Introduction of the electronic market place, however, appears to make it effortless for the patrons to 'click around' on the Web, and hence it is easy to search for information and make comparisons (Chou, 2000). Nevertheless, when it is costly for the consumers to find alternative brands, they keep on using the same brand or the same supplier. This implies that high search cost leads to high conative loyalty. Stated differently, customers intend to keep on using the bank in the future, for the reason that it is costly to search for other information. However, customers are probably not satisfied with the situation where it is difficult to find alternatives and, as a consequence, with having limited flexibility to select a supplier (Methlie and Nysveen, 1999).

In contrast to Sweden and Finland, the UK and Germany have seen aggressive price competition with emphasis on deposit and savings products, which has led to a low margins. However, in terms of users Western Europe dominates online banking, Table 5.6 illustrates how the rest of world is expected to accelerate in its growth.

Region (millions of users)	2000	2001	2002	2003	2004
Western Europe	18.6	28.0	37.8	47.7	57.9
United States	9.9	14.7	17.1	20.4	22.8
Japan	2.5	6.5	11.9	19.6	21.8
Asia-Pacific (excluding Japan)	2.4	4.4	6.8	9.8	13.8
Rest of the world	1.0	1.7	3.1	5.1	6.1
Total	34.4	55.3	76.7	102.6	122.3
(Source: International Data Corporation)					

Table 5.6 Western Europe dominates online banking, 2000–2004

Region	2000 (%)	2001 (%)	2002 (%)	2003 (%)
France	0.5	3	5	13
Germany	1	4	11	16
Italy	0.5	2	4	8
Netherlands	1	4	11	16
Spain	0.5	3	7	12
Sweden	1	7	16	25
Switzerland	1	4	10	17
UK	5	9	16	25
(Source: Lafferty Publications, November 2001)				

Table 5.7 Penetration of online credit cards in Europe, 2000–2003

Online credit card payment

Table 5.7 shows how the Lafferty Group (2001) projects the penetration of online credit cards in Europe. The growth in Sweden from 1 to 25 per cent by 2003 is indicative of the fact that almost 60 per cent of the online population visited finance sites in May 2001 (Jupiter MMXI, 2001).

Brokerage transactions

The success of Charles Schwab, which was a discount broker turned online trading firm, demonstrated the potential of a multichannel hybrid strategy. As a result of Internet-based industry innovations, discount brokerages in Europe have helped create a new equity culture (Lund, 2000). German banks have created one of the most successful infrastructures for online brokerages. For example, in Germany there were no discount brokers until 1994, when Consors (www.consors.de) and DAB (www.dab.com) opened, currently the second and third largest brokers. German online trading accounts have grown from to 1.7m, approximately 40 per cent of the European market and are expected to triple to 5.1m by 2003 (*Online Finance Europe*, 2000).

Investment research

As a consequence of e-business fundamentally reshaping the financial services industry, Europeans are moving towards a more 'equity' culture rather than a pure saving culture. This has led investors to perform research into companies that they are considering for purchase or sale. Organizations such as Hemscott have evolved, which offer a range of information services and bespoke research, both online and offline. Hemscott's Media Services comprise www.hemscott.net , which is a leading financial portal for professional investors, business professionals and private investors.

Filing of tax returns

The UK Government (http://www.e-envoy.gov.uk) has set itself the goal that, by 2002, its citizens will be able to electronically submit self-assessment tax returns (see www.cabinet-office.gov.uk/moderngov/new_modgov.htm for latest details relating to Modernising Government). To achieve this electronic service delivery standard, the Inland Revenue created the Electronic Business Unit to 'focus on the delivery, promotion, support and development of electronic business'. Unlike other electronic tax filing systems, the system enables the citizen to file a return from any computer as authentication is linked to the citizen not the computer. More than 50 000 individuals registered to use the new service during the first two months and an integrated marketing campaign has played a key part in creating awareness for the new service.

Internet-based electronic exchanges

These include innovations like the NIPHX (www.niphx.com) electronic exchange, which creates a market of buyers and sellers of small capitalization stocks. Another example of an Internet-based electronic exchange is onExchange's (www.onexchange.com) trading and clearing system, which provides a comprehensive suite of integratable modules that span account management and multiparameter trade matching; real-time clearing, settlement and delivery tracking; and flexible product authoring. The system is designed for the Internet and the system is browser-based, built entirely with state-of-the-art Web-based technology. To allow maximum flexibility, technology components can be licensed as a complete system or as subsystems.

ONLINE RETAILING

The diffusion of Internet shopping is happening with remarkable speed and, as a result, it is forecast to reach critical mass in the near future. According to De Kare-Silver (2000), new technologies such as Web-enabled mobile phones, Web and digital TV, interactive kiosks etc. will make visits to the shops increasingly unnecessary. As these services develop, people will be able to order from their home or any place they can make an electronic connection.

Traditionally, retailing has been a one-to-one experience whereby consumers tend to shop at stores that are most conveniently located for them. However, e-commerce has reduced

	Conventional Media				New Media		
	Catalogue	Direct Mail	TV Shopping	Tele-phone	WWW	Email	Newsgroup ads
1. Comparison							
Easy to compare between competitors					+		+
Easy to share experiences with other customers							+
2. Product Extensive assortment	+				+	+	+
Extensive product information	+	+			+	+	+
Samples can be distributed		+			+		
3. Time Immediate delivery					+	+	+
Available 24h/day	+	+			+	+	+
Time pressure when buying			+	+			
(Source: Salste, 1996)							

Table 5.8 New media versus conventional media

the importance of store location. Specifically, consumers are no longer constrained by physical considerations because they can choose from a large number of 'cyberstores', to which they have access through their Internet connections (Dadomo and Soars, 1999). Moreover, to a great extent, in-store retailers have placed their highest priorities on operational concerns, rather than on customer management. Consequently, in-store shopping has gradually become an impersonal and unexciting experience for consumers, who have started seeking alternative shopping experiences. As a result, non-store retailing forms have emerged, such as telemarketing, catalogues and, increasingly nowadays, electronic shops. These developments have resulted in the decline of the in-store retailer's market shares and profitability. Burnett and McCollough (1994, p. 452) have described non-store shopping as 'a phenomenon where the primary shopping and purchase task takes place at a site other than a traditional retail setting, and is, therefore, primarily the responsibility of the consumer'.

By comparing the traditional in-store retail formats it is possible to identify several advantages of Internet shopping, major benefits that Internet shoppers are experiencing, as well as the impact that these benefits have on consumer behaviour. A comparison between conventional and new media is shown in Table 5.8 and these can be summarized as:

- Convenience
- Product assortment
- Comparison shopping
- Product price

Convenience

Convenience is highly related to general predisposition toward acts of shopping by individuals. Studies of catalogue and telephone shopping have indicated the role of convenience-orientation as a significant predictor of in-home shopping behaviour by customers. Shopping convenience includes the time, space and effort saved by a consumer and it also includes aspects such as an ease of placing and cancelling orders, returns and refunds, timely delivery of orders (Gehrt, Yale and Lawson, 1996).

The perceived convenience offered by Web vendors is a significant factor in influencing the decision to purchase at home (Swaminathan, Lepkowska-White and Rao, 1999). Specifically, consumers who shop on the Internet do not have dressing, travelling, walking, looking, waiting and carrying inconveniences. In addition, consumers are able to shop 24 hours a day and also can order products from any location in the world (as long as they have an Internet connection). Several studies have shown that the need for convenience positively affects the frequency and the size of purchases on the Internet (Greenfield Online, 1999; Swaminathan *et al.*, 1999).

Product assortment

From a buyer's perspective, the advantages of shopping on the Internet go beyond simple convenience, to the ability to find a wide variety of products. Specifically, because supply is not so much bound to geographical areas and because customization is easier with certain products, product assortment on the Internet is significantly increased. There is also the potential of wider availability of hard-to-find products and wider selection of items due to the width and efficiency of the channel (Hoffman, Novak and Chatterjee, 1997). Moreover, the special features of the Internet, like affordable targeted marketing, which facilitate the promotion of unique products for various market niches, enhance the product assortment (O'Connor and O'Keefe, 1996).

Comparison shopping

Nowadays, comparison shopping tools like 'shopping robots' have caused significant changes to the current retail environments by shifting the power of price control from the retailer to the purchaser and, at the same time, moving both of them towards a global marketplace for goods and services (El.Pub, 2000). Specifically, the ability of the Web to amass, analyse and control large quantities of specialized data in a few seconds can enable comparison shopping and speed the process of finding items (Wallace, 1995). In other words, the Internet empowers consumers with more information than they could possibly get by cruising shopping malls by car. Moreover, the capability of searching for goods on hundreds of Web sites puts unprecedented pressure on Web retailers to beat their competitors' prices (Turban, Lee, King and Chang, 2000).

Product price

As previously mentioned, the Internet provides consumers with information that allows price comparisons. This has a subsequent effect on the level of competition that exists in a certain retail environment. Consequently, increased competition among online vendors who try to attract potential buyers, and other cost saving factors like shortened distribution channels, lead to lower prices (Alba *et al.*, 1997).

Moreover, while online operations of established retail stores currently attempt to avoid price wars, new entrants to electronic commerce have adopted a policy of selling goods at a loss in order to attract consumers and build a brand name in the hope that they can make profits in the near future (Li, Kuo and Russel, 1999). Of course, it is consumers who have benefited from initiatives like these because they can obtain products at very low prices.

ILLUSTRATIVE EXAMPLE II
Online shoppers choose price over convenience, by Andrew Edgecliffe-Johnson, Carlos Grande and Alexandra Harney, FTIT, http://specials.ft.com/ftit, 20 February 2002

Online retailers around the world grew up a lot last year, but they also began to encounter some of the problems associated with more mature markets. After the over-hyped surge in all things e-commerce in 1999 and the painful shake-out in 2000, 2001 was less dramatic for e-tailing stocks. There were still casualties, such as Webvan, the US online grocer, which closed its virtual doors last July.

Others managed to pass symbolic milestones, such as Amazon.com and Priceline.com, which each reported their first slender quarterly profits unexpectedly early.

The predominant theme of the year was slowing sales growth, however, as the novelty of a start-up industry wore off and its members began to feel the economic pressures weighing on their offline rivals. Investors became more confident about which e-tailers would survive, but debates about their future growth prospects remain unsettled.

The US online retail market grew by 20 to 25 per cent in 2001, to $32bn, according to Goldman Sachs. That growth was well above that witnessed by traditional retailers in a recessionary economy, but well below the hopes analysts had a year ago. Jupiter Media Metrix now expects US growth in the 20 per cent range for 2002.

In the less-developed markets of Europe and Asia, many e-tailers are seeing stronger growth, but analysts expect their sales growth will also decelerate in 2002. There are some disappointing signs for e-tailing bulls in the US model. US consumers are shifting spending online more slowly than expected, with little sign of a mass online market developing as internet access broadens to different demographic groups.

Internet users spent 13 per cent of their holiday budgets online last Christmas, according to Nielsen/NetRatings. That was little changed from the 12.4 per cent share that online retailers took a year before. "We continue to believe that we have not reached the mass market for online shopping," says Anthony Noto, e-commerce analyst with Goldman Sachs. "We see broadband-at-home access as a key catalyst to re-accelerate sales by 2003."

Wider access to fast internet connections should have other benefits, according to Sean Kaldor, chief analyst at NetRatings. "E-tailers are designed for a 56k world. The growth of broadband will make new features, such as three-dimensional images of goods, easier to offer," he says.

For now, the evidence suggests that online shoppers are more concerned about price than about new features or convenience – the advantage which e-tailers once thought would allow them to charge more than offline stores. Ford Cavalleri, leader of the commerce and content practice at Aventis, says: "What really attracts people to buying online? You can make the convenience argument, but most of the time it's price."

Amazon.com, one of the few global names in online retailing, has made the same discovery. Jeff Bezos, its founder, has committed the group to an "everyday low pricing" model that would not look out of place at Wal-Mart. He has also begun to tackle customers' aversion to shipping charges by waiving these on orders above $99.

Non-US e-tailers may have to follow suit. Bob Mann, associate partner of Accenture, reviewed websites around the world over the holiday season and says: "We were surprised there weren't more promotions such as free shipping."

The price pressures have been driven in part by the growth of established US discounters such as Wal-Mart and Target Online. Stephen DiMarco of Compete, a Boston-based advisory company, notes that the growth in discounters' traffic was higher than at other online stores before Christmas.

Comparison shopping is also becoming an entrenched trend. "More customers are looking at one product on two sites, then opting to buy on the cheaper site," Mr DiMarco says.

Lower prices and other promotions have only been possible because of the cost-cutting that was a theme across the industry in 2001. As analysts reined in their expectations for the industry's growth, so executives realised that the infrastructure they built early on was, in many cases, more than they needed.

Better-looking bottom lines are an unintended consequence of the industry's inefficient beginnings, Mr Bezos says: "During the first four years of extraordinary growth we did not have time to operate efficiently."

"Clicks and mortar" retailers – those with physical and online stores – are meanwhile finding different types of saving. Tom Stemberg, chairman of Staples, says the US office supplies chain can afford to carry less inventory in its stores now that it can direct shoppers to its website. "We've been carrying ribbons for typewriters we sold 15 years ago," he says. "Previously, we could not have got rid of that item. Now we don't have to carry that inventory."

Clicks and mortar retailers are gaining ground on the "pure play" pioneers around the world. Growth from high-street retailers' sites was a key factor in the healthy order volumes seen in Europe at Christmas.

GUS, the UK owner of retail brands from Argos catalogues to Burberry fashion, increased e-commerce sales by two-thirds to £48m in the three months to December 31. Other European retailers are still investing in online operations. John Lewis, the UK department store group, launched its new site in October using transaction technology developed by Buy.com, the internet retailer whose UK operations it bought a year ago. John Lewis averaged 1,000 orders a day in November and December – a step change from peak orders achieved by Buy.com. And Amazon's German and UK operations were among the company's fastest-growing divisions.

Such evidence is necessarily piecemeal and comes against a background of strong general consumer spending in Europe. It is, however, supported by claims from Verdict, the retail consultancy, that retailers have geared up fulfilment operations to cope with an expected increase in home delivery.

Among Europeans, the online shopping habit has taken strongest root in the UK, according to NetValue, the web research group. Almost 68 per cent of UK web surfers visited retail sites at Christmas, compared with 62 per cent of Germans and 40 per cent of Swedes. NetValue estimates UK websites also convert more browsers into shoppers than other European sites.

Despite the growth in volumes, the key question remains the profitability of providing online shopping channels. Tesco.com, the biggest online grocer, is not in profit on its non-food sales.

Murray Hennessy, managing director of John Lewis Direct, which runs the group's web and catalogue units, says measuring profitability for clicks-and-mortar sites relies not just on the stand-alone economics of an e-commerce division, but on gauging those buyers who browse online and shop in the store. For many European retailers, that remains one of the challenges in 2002.

In Asia, meanwhile, the challenge is one of expanding the number of sites on offer, as much as the number of shoppers. Enthusiasm for e-commerce is still rising in Japan, a country with only about 22m fixed-line internet users where shopping online still has a certain cachet. "As Japan's internet population continues to grow, online retailing grows with it," says Shogo Noguchi, internet analyst at Goldman Sachs. A recent survey by Macromill, a market research group, showed that more than 80 per cent of Japanese internet users shop online.

But most of the money spent online flows to just two companies. Rakuten, Japan's homegrown answer to Yahoo, is the country's leading internet retailer. It expects net losses in the year ended December 31 to have shrunk to about ¥2.7bn,compared with a ¥9.51bn net loss last year.

Although Rakuten will not announce official results until later this month, Mr Noguchi expects the highly acquisitive company will have racked up sales of about ¥15bn in the last three months of the year.

Yahoo Japan, the other main recipient of Japanese online spending, has seen similar growth. It increased non-consolidated pre-tax profits by 38 per cent quarter-on-quarter, to ¥3.05bn in the three months to December 31.

The fact that most online purchases are still made with these two companies is perhaps an indication of the immaturity of the Japanese market.

Many online retailers maintain that the entire industry remains in its earliest stages – and not just in Japan. "I believe it is still so early," says Amazon's Mr Bezos. "Less than 1 per cent of commerce is being done online. I've long held that should be 15 per cent." He adds: "This is still 'day one'. We may not be at the Kitty Hawk stage, but nobody has even thought of the DC9."

What does the future hold for online retailing?

Both online retailers and physical retailers are facing interesting challenges as the online retailing market matures (Enders and Jelassi, 2000). Nevertheless, the online retailing market will continue to grow rapidly, with IDC (www.idc.com) predicting that by the end of 2002 more than 600m people worldwide will have access to the Web, and they will spend more than US $1 trillion shopping online. It is anticipated that once consumers get over their security and privacy issues, e-commerce will rival offline purchase. According to IDC, e-commerce grew to $600bn in 2001, a 68 per cent increase over 2000.

US residents perform more shopping online than those of any other country (the USA now accounts for 40 per cent of all money spent online), but its growth rate is decelerating. By 2006 the figure is expected to drop to 38 per cent as Asia and Western Europe increase their online spending. The sheer population of the Asia region is driving growth of about 89 per cent. The euro is fuelling a rise of 68 per cent as price transparency is enhanced.

B2B sales are expected to continue to dwarf B2C, with B2B accounting for 83 per cent of online sales in 2002 and 88 per cent in 2006, according to an IDC study. An interesting point to bear in mind is that the average B2B transaction is far higher than a B2C transaction, but given the increasing numbers of online consumers, B2C should not be ignored.

Therefore, it can be seen that, despite the failure of some online retailing models, the online market will evolve rapidly. Organizations should identify the lessons learned from previous flawed business models, prior to embarking on new online strategies. Rasch and Litner (2001) of the Boston Consulting Group (www.bcg.com) sought to understand how consumers and consumer companies have been using the online distribution channel.

After surveying nearly 12 000 European Internet users and performing one-on-one interviews with consumers in their homes, as well as with senior executives of organizations that are exemplars of online and multichannel retailing, BCG drew five conclusions:

- The online market, despite being in its formative years, is expected to grow rapidly over the next few years. Online spending in Europe only accounts for 1.5 per cent of total consumer spending. In the US the corresponding figure is approximately 2 per cent.
- An online distribution channel has a profound influence on consumers' offline behaviour. Thirty-seven per cent of all Internet users who browsed online before purchasing offline indicated that browsing online helped during the research process. Eighty-five per cent mentioned that they bought offline the brand and product that they identified online and 35 per cent bought from the merchant they found online.
- The Internet will widen the gap between winners and losers among established retailers and manufactures. Those retailers that have a large offline presence and are able to manage the Internet channel successfully will obtain above normal market share.
- Focusing on the most profitable customers will create a disproportionate amount of value. The top 20 per cent of online purchasers in a category account for a disproportionately large share of total online spending in that category.
- Organizations that meet the online expectations of their core customers will earn a big payoff, which will translate directly to the bottom line. According to the results satisfied customers spend 71 per cent more and transact two and a half times more often than dissatisfied ones.

CONSTRUCTING THE E-BUSINESS INFORMATION COMMUNICATION AND TECHNOLOGY (ICT) ARCHITECTURE

The integration of legacy systems and e-business technology can have a short payback. So it is imperative to integrate existing ICT systems with new (often front-office) applications and, to make these accessible for the Internet, 'Enterprise Application Integration (EAI)' and 'Web-enablement' are essential. This means that flexible and efficient communication between the front and the back office is indispensable. This communication, whether running synchronously or asynchronously, must be not just fast but especially safe. A robust and open architecture is a critical success factor in the implementation of large and medium-sized ICT and e-business projects. Scalability, extensibility, data consistency and the choice from 'best-or-broad' solutions are crucial factors in the design of an architecture that is (safely) accessible from the Internet and open to tomorrow's technologies and applications.

Good integrated architecture ensures:

- Flexible integration of the relevant applications and their data
- Fast ICT reaction to new and changing e-business processes
- Filtering and routing of information between internal and external users
- Accurate real time information for Web-based applications
- Improved data consistency and reduced data redundancy
- Integration of new and innovative technologies with the existing application portfolio
- Capitalization of earlier ICT investments

The introduction of the Internet means that ICT is an important link between strategy and the organization, touching all aspects of business operations. Efficient communication between the applications that support these business operations is essential. Arguably, this is only possible within an open and completely integrated architecture.

In his book, Hoque (2000) focuses upon the crucial issue of merging the forces of business and technology. He uses the term e-enterprise to mean an enterprise that has successfully put the two together. Figure 5.3 illustrates the framework for e-enterprise architecture. Using the universal symbol for infinity, Hoque envisages e-enterprise business and technology development being evolutionary. The e-enterprise architecture must embrace an interactive approach, which makes changes in a single part of the systems, yet remains conscious of the whole. The enterprise architecture can be divided into seven distinct elements.

- E-business models. These explain the high-level shape of the e-enterprise derived from the core marketing and financial model, inter-enterprise touch point examination, ownership and resource analysis.
- E-process models. These address the need to create new internal organizational processes that leverage the Internet and are composed of business entities, user-cases, inter-organizational processes, reusable business processes and business components.
- E-application models. These focus on design issues rather than on the implementation point of view. These types of models consist of a detailed application definition, user-interface mockups, applications specifications and business rules. In addition, blueprints are helpful for enhancing reusable functionality and application components in the final platform.
- E-application rules. These determine the final application by utilizing business and application logic for the rule engine, application framework and component software.
- E-application distribution/integration. This provides developers with the ability to allocate application resources across the network using multiple application servers, distributed object

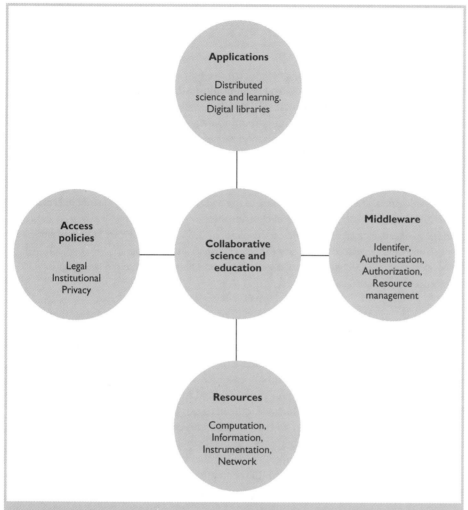

Figure 5.3 The relationship between middleware and the technical and policy components of an IT system required to work with it (*Source: www.nsf-middleware.org*)

architecture, technology components, middleware and enterprise application integration (EAI) software.

■ E-data. This is an abstracted data component that manages data for the entire platform. The e-data layer includes application data, data management systems, data warehouses, legacy data and enterprise resource planning (ERP)/material requisition planning (MRP) data repositories.

■ E-network. This refers to the network infrastructure for the e-enterprise platform, typically driving network security solutions, encryptions, connectivity tools, network operating system (NOS) system analysis and management tools.

MIDDLEWARE

It should be borne in mind that no e-business model will work without getting the right integration between existing and new programmes in an organization. If a company buys the best Web shop and cannot integrate it with the existing administration systems they already have, they will not get the desired return on investment. Organizations no longer have to invest in complete ERP systems, but can use middleware to integrate different systems.

Middleware is software that connects two or more otherwise separate applications across the Internet or local area networks. An excellent introduction to middleware is provided by the The Internet2 Middleware Initiative (I2-MI), www.internet2.edu/middleware/, which is working toward the deployment of core middleware services at Internet2 universities. The term middleware refers to an evolving layer of services that resides between the network and more traditional applications for managing security, access and information exchange to:

■ Allow educators, scientists and engineers, to use and share transparently distributed resources, such as computers, data, networks, and instruments.
■ Develop effective collaboration and communications tools such as Grid technologies, desktop video and other advanced services to expedite research and education.
■ Develop a working architecture and approach that can be extended to the larger set of Internet and network users.

Interoperable middleware between organizations is a particular need of further and higher education. For examples, scientific researchers need to have their local middleware work with that operated by national scientific resources, such as supercomputing centres, scholarly databases and government scientific facilities and laboratories. Advanced network applications will transform instructional processes, but they will depend on middleware to function. The fact that higher education is global in structure stimulates the need for interoperable standards and products. Middleware services deployed across industry and higher education institutions can work seamlessly together to verify students' electronic identities, permit remote access to libraries and deliver streamed-video classroom content. The students do not need to remember a large number of usernames, passwords or account numbers, because the institutions and their constituents trust open standards for authentication, information sharing and privacy management.

Middleware makes resource sharing seem transparent to the end user, providing consistency, security, privacy and capabilities. Figure 5.3 illustrates the relationship between middleware and the technical and policy components of an information technology system that are required to work with it.

SUMMARY

The evolution of research focusing on e-business models has gathered pace. From the beginnings of e-business as a sure way of making money, organizations now realize the importance of meeting initial market expectations. A continual failure to meet projections will create a lack of confidence among shareholders, which will ultimately lead to a re-adjustment in shareholder value. This chapter focuses on e-business models and provides theory to reinforce the value to readers.

Disruptive technology

Trying to use the disruptive technology of the Internet to gain competitive advantage during turbulent environments has proved problematic. The Internet supersedes physical boundaries and the cost of physical goods and services to cross geographical borders is greatly reduced.

Instead of having to acquire physical premises, a vendor can connect to consumers anywhere in the world.

E-business models

Many e-businesses are struggling to address the most basic conundrum: What is the most appropriate e-business model? Strategists are experimenting with different formulae in different contextual settings. Some are incorporating e-business throughout the organization. Some have tried to create e-business strategic business units, and then spin them off as separate online entities. Others are investing in or merging with Internet start-ups. Some are trying to move their business to the Web. However, the evidence to-date indicates that there is no simple prescription.

E-cash

Electronic cash can be broadly defined as tokens of value and digital coins or other digital tokens of value (e.g. 'digital cheques'). The lack of widespread adoption of e-cash, partly due to the strength of traditional credit and debit cards, has led to the demise of firms such as beenz.com and flooz.com. The old adage that the strength of any currency is only as good as the number of places that accept it and people who use it is a timely reminder. See Digicash (www.digicash.com).

What does the future hold for online retailing?

The online retailing market will continue to grow rapidly, with IDC (www.idc.com) predicting that by the end of 2002 more than 600m people worldwide will have access to the Web, and they will spend more than US $1 trillion shopping online. It is anticipated that once consumers get over their security and privacy issues, e-commerce will rival offline purchase. According to IDC, e-commerce grew to $600bn in 2001, a 68 per cent increase over 2000.

Constructing the e-business information communication and technology (ICT) architecture

A robust and open architecture is a critical success factor in the implementation of large and medium sized ICT and e-business projects. Scalability, extendibility, data consistency and the choice from 'best-or-broad' solutions are crucial factors in the design of an architecture that is (safely) accessible from the Internet and open to tomorrow's technologies and applications.

Middleware

It should be borne in mind that no e-business model will work without getting the right integration between existing and new programs in an organization. If a company buys the best Web shop and cannot integrate it with the existing administration systems they already have, they will not get the desired return on investment. Organizations no longer have to invest in complete ERP systems, but can use middleware to integrate different systems.

DISCUSSION QUESTIONS

1. Why is it important to critically assess e-business models? How do they differ from traditional business models?

2. What do you understand by the term portal? Why are they such a popular e-business model?

3. Why has the concept of e-cash failed to gain significant momentum over the Internet?

ASSESSMENT QUESTIONS

1. According to Rappa (2000) 'e-business models are perhaps the most discussed and least understood aspect of the Web'. Do you agree with this proposition? What evidence do you have to support your point of view?

2. It has been argued that 'e-business is not an option; it is driving the new economy and has significantly affected all industries'. You are required to state in your views the relative strength and weaknesses of this proposition.

3. Kalakota and Robinson (2001) argue that 'one of the best assets for online selling is an offline store'. Critically evaluate this statement, using relevant examples to support your discussion.

GROUP ASSIGNMENT QUESTIONS

1. Christensen (1997) coined the term 'disruptive technologies' to describe the innovations that create a new market through the creation of a new product or service. One of the most salient characteristics of sustaining technological innovations is that they reinforce a firm's or industry's value and capture systems (Casillas *et al.*, 2000).

You are required to critically evaluate the above statement. Do you believe that the Internet is a prime example of a disruptive technology for organizations and industry sectors?

2. Using any suitable e-business operation, you are required to perform a strategic analysis of the selected e-business model(s). In addition, you are to critique how value has been created by the implementation of the selected e-business model.

Using real-life examples to support your thoughts, critically evaluate the statement by McKnight and Boroumand (2000) that due to the 'Internet benefits of interoperability, statistical sharing and (usually) positive network externalities, providers of new applications and services will attempt to create new markets for their services, through the Internet, even if the underlying technical architecture of the Internet is not intrinsically designed to support such services'.

MAIN CASE STUDY
E-strategy brief; Siemens – electronic glue, The Economist, 31 May 2001
© The Economist Newspaper Ltd, London

There is an old saying in German business: "If Siemens only knew what Siemens knows." It sums up both the strengths and the weaknesses of this huge German electronics and electrical-engineering company. On the plus side, the company is renowned for the technical brilliance of its engineers. If somebody at Siemens has a question, somebody else in the company is likely to know the answer.

The difficulty lies in putting the two together. Siemens is a sprawling conglomerate with more than a dozen business units that make almost everything from light bulbs to power-generation equipment. It operates in 190 countries and employs 470,000 people. In such a vast empire, useful knowledge is easily wasted.

Heinrich von Pierer, Siemens's chief executive since 1992, has a favourite example of how much Siemens could gain by exploiting its knowledge to the full—or could lose if it does not. Siemens Malaysia wanted to bid to supply a high-speed data network linking Kuala Lumpur and its swanky new airport, but lacked the necessary know-how. Somebody thought to check the "sharenet", an internal system on which knowledge is posted for use throughout the company, and found that Siemens was already working on a similar project in Denmark. The people in Malaysia were able to adapt what had already been done there, and won an order for a pilot project. In future, proclaims Mr Pierer, his company hopes to be able to say: "Siemens knows what Siemens knows."

The key to this change is e-business. Siemens is spending euro 1 billion ($860m) in a bid to turn itself into an e-company. Or should that be an e-conglomerate? In effect, Siemens's investment is a huge bet on the idea that modern information and communications technology can knit the different parts of its far-flung empire into a more coherent whole.

Conventional wisdom speaks against conglomerates. Financial markets dislike them, rating conglomerates' shares up to 20% below what they think is the value of the sum of their parts. Usually, investors prefer to take on a mixture of risks of their own choosing, by buying the shares of different companies, rather than accepting the pre-packaged choice of a chief executive.

Such investors listen sceptically when conglomerates defend themselves. Opportunities for cross-selling or cost sharing are rarely as extensive as the bosses like to imagine. Increasingly, companies have bowed to market sentiment, defined a "core" business and sold the rest. Even Siemens has narrowed its scope, selling most of Epcos, a components manufacturer, and a minority stake in Infineon, a semiconductor maker, in the past couple of years.

Can Siemens confound convention? Not long ago, it would have seemed an unlikely Internet pioneer, for all its technical brilliance. It lacked the informality and flexibility of smaller, younger companies. One joke about Siemens has it that a new-born baby found on the steps of its Munich headquarters could not possibly have had anything to do with the company—because never in its life has it created something new in as short a time as nine months.

It has not even been much good at making money. Peter von Siemens, a member of the founding family who sits on the supervisory board, is said to have remarked that the prospect of returns like Siemens's would not entice a greengrocer to open a shop.

The company has not lost the ability to disappoint. It mistimed its big push into mobile-phone production and had to junk the optimistic forecasts that it was making only a few months ago. Its mobile-phone business lost euro 143m in the three months to March. Its information and communications division has announced 8,000 job losses so far this year.

For all that, Siemens is generally in better shape than it was. Its net profit margin, a feeble 2.6% in 1995–96, had perked up to 4.3% (after stripping out extraordinary gains) by 1999–2000. In large part, that was the result of new management techniques, introduced by Mr von Pierer, that were once unthinkable. Around 60% of managers' pay is now performance-related. Many employees qualify for share options.

The chief executive is also trying to loosen the company's old, stuffy culture. Siemens people nowadays work in smaller groups. An e-mail about Siemens's e-business initiative that Mr von Pierer sent last summer to all employees elicited "thousands" of replies. Would past Siemens bosses have asked for advice from the ranks? Albert Goller, head of the company's "centre of e-excellence" at Munich airport, says: "To be fast is more important than to be perfect." Would past Siemens managers have said that?

Such willingness to shake up the organisation ought to mean that Mr von Pierer makes a decent return on his euro 1 billion. Academics and businessfolk have found that investment in information technology works best when it goes hand-in-hand with organisational change. Erik Brynjolfsson, an economist at Massachusetts Institute of Technology who has looked into the effects of IT investment on the productivity and profitability of firms, has found that the return is far bigger in companies that are also prepared to change work practices, strategies and the products and services they sell. Investment in IT and "organisational" investment complement each other: each feeds the return on the other.*

Taking things apart

The danger lies in using IT purely as a way of doing more cheaply the same old things in the same old ways: processing information more cheaply in the same departments, or automating an otherwise unchanged production line. One top executive at a big high-tech company says that companies have to be prepared "to take things apart". Customer information, for example, should not be jealously guarded by the sales and marketing departments, but shared with production departments too. It is not enough for chief executives to understand what has to be done. They have to make sure that change is forced through: often, that means getting involved in details.

Siemens's bosses seem to be in tune with all this. Mr von Pierer talks of the necessity of having an "e-mindset". Mr Goller says: "For me the Internet is about two parts. One is the technology part and the other is the mindset, how we view our business."

In practice, Mr von Pierer's plan has four elements. The first is knowledge management—of which the sharenet is an example. The second is online purchasing. At the moment, electronic buying accounts for 10% of Siemens's euro 35 billion annual procurement bill. The plan is to raise this to 50% within three years. Most of the savings are expected to come from the exploitation of scale, pooling the previously fragmented demands of several purchasing departments for office equipment, furniture and so on into a single stream, using a company-wide platform called click2procure.

The third element is Siemens's dealings with its customers. Mostly, these are other companies, not retail customers. From about 20 countries, you can click on "buy from Siemens" on the company's home article and place orders for cordless and mobile telephones, spare parts for trains or (in Finland) vacuum cleaners and cleaner bags. Siemens's automation and drives division, to take one example, generates some 30% of its sales online. Almost all its sales should be online by 2005.

The fourth part of the strategy is to change the company's "value chain". Some of this is administrative. For instance, 30,000 job applications a year are now handled online. The business travel of all European employees and most in the Americas (who together make up almost 90% of the company total) is now supposed to be booked over the Internet. For the most part, it is. Unlike some American companies, Siemens has not had to resort to fining those who do not book online.

However, there is more to this than paperless administration. The idea is to make sure that the chain—going from customers, through Siemens, and then on to its suppliers—is as smooth as possible. Hitherto, different bits of Siemens have developed their own e-businesses, from websites to proprietary EDI and ERP systems, more or less independently. Links in the demand chain have been snaggled by the need to deal with several different information systems. "Before e-business," explains Mr Goller, "it was almost impossible to connect all these different systems in order to get information to flow from your customer to your supplier."

The shift to becoming an e-conglomerate should also expand the number of potential customers and suppliers. EDI, explains Mr Goller, has been useful mainly to big companies. In principle, anyone with Internet access, whether they are big or small, ought to be able to trade with Siemens.

Look at the airport, says Mr Goller, pointing outside his window. Several of Siemens's business units could sell something to such a customer. That, he says, is a big advantage of the company's wide range of activities. But he adds: "I don't think that in the future such a customer will tolerate four or five different views about Siemens. They want one view of our capabilities." Even if a customer is buying things from several different Siemens divisions, it should deal directly with only one, which should act as a sort of lead manager within the company. Inside Siemens, the customer should be identified by only one code.

The hard part

In all, Mr von Pierer expects to cut costs by 2% in the short run and by 3–5% in the "medium term". Of the four elements of his strategy, he expects e-procurement to yield the quickest returns. However, they will also be the easiest. "If you want to transform a company to an e-business company," he told analysts in February, "the problem is not so much e-procurement and the face to the customer. All this can be done rather fast. What is truly difficult is to reorganise all the internal processes. That is what we see as our main task and where the main positive results will come from."

Working out this "truly difficult" part is Mr Goller's job. The key, he says, is to marry the present fragmented array of company-wide information systems together, using a "corporate approach". That means agreeing on (and occasionally imposing) some standards across the Siemens empire, and not allowing semi-autonomous kingdoms to go their own way. So deals have been signed with two American software companies: i2 Technologies, which will provide a supply-chain software platform, and Commerce One, which is supplying software on the purchasing side of Siemens's business.

For those who believe that the Internet is best exploited by letting a thousand flowers bloom, all this may come as a surprise. In turning itself into an e-company, the sprawling Siemens empire will become more centralised, not less. So, far from empowering local managers, the Internet increases the authority of those at the centre. Yet this makes perfect sense. If you think that the various parts of Siemens belong under one roof, they surely ought to speak the same e-language, to share information and to sell things in partnership, rather than tripping over each other's feet. And if organisational changes are going to be pushed through, they have to be decided at the top.

Mr Goller says that he has been encouraged by the willingness of executive and second-tier management to accept the necessity of change. There is much more openness to change, he says, than there was in the past.

The Internet ought, therefore, to make Siemens a more cohesive, less unwieldy conglomerate. Yet is this the only or the best use of the new technology? Economic theory could point in a completely different direction.

A prime reason why economic activity is organised within firms rather than in open markets is the cost of communication.

The costlier it is to process and transmit information, the more it makes sense to do things in firms; the cheaper communication becomes, the more efficient (relatively) markets will be. Because the Internet and other inventions have cut the cost of communication so much, firms ought to be able to do less in-house and to outsource more. In 1999 General Motors, a by-word for vertical integration, spun off Delphi Automotive Systems, one of its supply divisions, for instance.

So should the advent of the Internet have prompted Siemens to sell more businesses, or even to break itself up? Arguably, yes. The Internet may make a conglomerate cheaper to run; but it could also make other forms of organisation cheaper still.

CASE QUESTIONS

Question 1 Why is Siemens spending €1 billion ($860 m) in a bid to turn itself into an e-company? What benefits does it seek to obtain?

Question 2 Do you belief that the return from an IT investment is far bigger in companies that are also prepared to change work practices, strategies and the products and services they sell? How do Investment in IT and "organizational" investment complement each other?

Question 3 What are the four elements of Mr von Pierer's plan? In your opinion, what are the biggest challenges facing Siemens? You may find it useful to get an update of the Siemens organization by visiting its web site, www.siemens.com.

MINI CASE STUDY I
E-strategy brief: Seven-Eleven – Over the counter e-commerce, The Economist, 24 May 2001
© *The Economist Newspaper Limited, London*

How to blend e-commerce with traditional retailing

Just as the Internet penetrated different countries at different speeds and in different ways, so its impact on traditional companies, the subjects of this series of case studies, has varied from one part of the world to another. Consider Seven-Eleven, a convenience-store operator, which this year snatched the title of biggest retailer in Japan from Daiei, a troubled supermarket giant.

Seven-Eleven's e-strategy is built mainly around proprietary systems. For the most part, it has used the Internet to talk to its retail customers, not to run its business. Yet few companies in Japan have been more admired for their use of electronic communications.

Unlike Daiei, and many other retailers, Seven-Eleven has managed to overcome a stuttering economy and spiralling deflation to raise sales and profits by 4% and 15% in the year to the end of February. Its pre-tax profits last year were more than double those of Fast Retailing, a clothing outlet that holds the second spot.

One reason for Seven-Eleven's sparkling performance is its cautious management. Other Japanese convenience stores, such as Lawson and FamilyMart, the second- and third-biggest, expanded recklessly over the past decade. They have recently announced the closure of hundreds of stores. In contrast, Toshifumi Suzuki, Seven-Eleven's chairman, says that he would stop opening new stores if sales at existing ones declined sharply. His caution is reflected in Seven-Eleven's finances, which are largely debt-free.

Yet solid management is not the only contributor to Seven-Eleven's success. The chain's other distinction lies in its deft use of electronics. It pioneered many techniques for using the Internet that are still ahead of the curve.

Seven-Eleven Japan was set up in 1973. By the mid-1980s it had already replaced old-fashioned cash registers with point-of-sale (POS) systems that monitor customer purchases. By 1992, it had overhauled its information-technology systems four times.

But the biggest overhaul of all took place in 1995. With hindsight, the timing looks bad: that was the year when the Internet wave was beginning to swell in the United States but had barely begun to touch Japan's shores. The new system that Seven-Eleven installed was therefore based on proprietary technology—albeit state-of-the-art—rather than on the still barely tested open structure of the Internet.

Convenience online

Back in those days—and indeed, even now—it would have been hard to build on the back of the Internet alone a system that satisfied all Seven-Eleven's complex demands. It wanted an easy-to-use multimedia system with pictures and sound, since most workers are part-timers with scant computer skills. It also wanted a system that could quickly repair itself if something went wrong.

Then the chain needed a network to speed up the transmission of orders, ideas and feedback. It wanted all the companies in its supply chain to use one common system, and it wanted a system that could be easily updated to take advantage of technological advances. Then it wanted the system to run for at least 15 years.

Such connectedness—hooking up suppliers, stores, staff and even banks—is the sort of thing that most retailers can still only dream of, even with the Internet around to reduce the cost and the complexity. What made Seven-Eleven's task more daunting was that the system had to serve some 6,000 stores (the figure is now more than 8,500 and growing) scattered across Japan.

It built the system itself, creating the hardware with NEC, a consumer-electronics company. Coming up with the right software was harder, and it eventually asked Microsoft, America's software giant, to help it build a tailor-made Windows-based system.

By 1996 the software was being installed in some 61,000 computers at Seven-Eleven's stores, head office and vendor firms. By 1998, the overhaul, which cost ¥60 billion ($490m), was complete. The new system replaced the ragbag of systems used before. A pipeline to Microsoft's offices in Seattle provided instant support. The software back-up constantly monitored and automatically rebooted the system when it crashed, and alerted local maintenance firms if such errors occurred more than twice.

All Seven-Eleven stores now have a satellite dish. Cheaper than using ground cables, this is often the only option for shops in rural areas. And in earthquake-prone Japan, the satellite dish provides an extra layer of safety on top of two sets of telephone lines, and separate mainframes in Tokyo and Osaka.

Win–win–win–win

Seven-Eleven's new technology gave it four advantages. The first was in monitoring customer needs, which were changing as deregulation made shoppers more demanding. "We believed that the nature of competition was changing. Instead of pushing products on to customers, companies were being pulled by customer needs. In this environment, the battleground was at the stores themselves—the interface between businesses and customers," says Makoto Usui, who heads the information-systems department at Seven-Eleven.

Second, Seven-Eleven uses sales data and software to improve quality control, pricing and product development. Thanks to its systems, the company can collect sales information from all its stores three times a day, and analyse it in roughly 20 minutes.

This has helped it rapidly to discern which goods or packaging appeal to customers. "Seven-Eleven's merchandising and product-development capabilities are formidable. Its ability to sense new trends and churn out high-quality items is far superior to other operators," says Michael Jacobs, an analyst at Dresdner Kleinwort Wasserstein, an investment bank. Now Seven-Eleven is using these skills to increase its own-brand products, which have higher profit margins.

Third, technology has helped to predict daily trends. As customers become more fickle, product cycles are shortening. Fashions in boxed lunches, riceballs and sandwiches, which make up almost half of a convenience store's daily sales, are especially short-term. Most last about seven weeks, but they can be even shorter.

Seven-Eleven says it can keep abreast of these partly by keeping an eye on the weather. Five reports a day arrive electronically at its stores from hundreds of private weather centres, each covering a radius of 20km (13 miles). This is useful in Japan, where temperatures between towns 40km apart can vary by as much as 5°C. The reports also compare today's temperature with yesterday's. "The same 10°C can feel very different depending on whether it was 1°C or 20°C the day before. This is critical for predicting food purchases," points out Mr Usui.

Finally, Seven-Eleven's electronic investment has also improved the efficiency of its supply chain. Orders flow quickly. Those sent in by 10am, for delivery after 4pm, are electronically processed in less than seven minutes. They are sent to 230 distribution centres that work exclusively for Seven-Eleven. Truck drivers carry cards with bar codes that are scanned into store computers when they arrive with a delivery. If a driver is often late, the operator will review his route and might add another truck to lighten the load. Seven-Eleven folk boast that their trucks run even more punctually than Japan's on-time buses.

In the same way, Seven-Eleven also helps vendors and manufacturers to control their inventories. It uses its database to instruct them on all sorts of small details, such as what sauce to put into its ready-made noodles in order to maximise sales.

As well as the system that links together its supply chain, Seven-Eleven has worked hard to use technology to improve communications and training. Multimedia tools have helped to train store attendants, always a difficult task for a business with lots of stores and part-time workers. Technology has also provided a way for store workers to keep in touch. That is important in a business which runs round the clock, with stores manned by a dozen or so workers, some of whom never see each other.

What about the Internet?

If Seven-Eleven had built its new system three or four years later, would it have based it around the Internet? The company says that, even if it were developing a similar system today, it would not necessarily use the Internet for all its operations. It prefers the security of a proprietary network. And some of the advantages of an Internet-based network for American and European companies are less apparent in a Japanese context, where supplier relationships tend to be deeper and more stable. Seven-Eleven sees no virtue in allowing new Japanese suppliers to put in bids over the Internet.

It is, however, hedging its bets by studying how international rivals such as Wal-Mart use the Internet for global product procurement. And it will watch closely what happens at Lawson, which together with Mitsubishi Corporation, the biggest trading house, is building a replica of Seven-Eleven's system based on the Internet.

Seven-Eleven is already using the Internet to lower its annual overhead costs of around ¥70 billion. It plans to install an e-commerce software package offered by the Japanese arm of Ariba, an American e-procurement company, to bulk-buy goods and services such as office equipment and insurance policies for its employees.

The big question is whether Seven-Eleven can integrate the Internet into its other operations. In the past, it has been clever at finding new ways to use its technology. Back in 1987, after installing bar-code recognition systems, Seven-Eleven turned its stores into payment points for utility bills. Almost 15 years later, the move (which required only a small incremental investment in software) has given Seven-Eleven 3% of a massive market that includes big rivals such as banks and post offices.

Now the company has increased its customer traffic by turning shops into payment and pick-up points for Internet shoppers. This was a clever move in a country in which people are still wary of using credit cards over the Internet, preferring instead to pay cash at a store. Most customers at e-Shopping!Books, an online bookseller, pick up and pay for their purchases at a Seven-Eleven store. Indeed, says Seven-Eleven, some 75% of Internet shoppers pick up their purchases from bricks-and-mortar stores.

Thanks in part to such tactics, Seven-Eleven's stores now sell almost 50% more on average every day than those of its closest rival. Whether its latest projects will be as successful has yet to be seen. Its Internet site, 7dream.com, was launched last July with seven other companies, including NEC and Nomura Research Institute. The site offers a wide range of goods and services, including books, CDs, concert tickets and travel.

But the site's lack of focus could hurt its ability to develop specific online brands, argues Mr Jacobs. The company has already said that the heavy costs it will incur to build up 7dream.com's content mean that its consolidated pre-tax profits will not grow in the current financial year.

Seven-Eleven has also had problems with its branchless bank: IY Bank, which opened in May. The bank, officially owned by its parent company, the Ito-Yokado supermarket chain, had a struggle to win approval from the authorities (it was the first non-bank to apply for a banking licence). It is also expected to have a tough time meeting the strict profit targets set out by the Financial Services Agency.

When it comes to running such online businesses, Seven-Eleven seems likely to have just as much difficulty as others have done: lots of costs, few customers. For the convenience store, as for other businesses, the real savings are likely to come from deploying the Internet as a management tool. It already knows how to cut costs by replacing paper with electronic delivery: it has trimmed ¥300m a year over the past decade by becoming a "paperless" business. Now it wants to save more.

To do this, however, it will have to answer two more big questions. First, can it integrate the Internet into its elaborate proprietary network? Seven-Eleven's managers think it can: indeed, they claim to have designed such potential for flexibility into the existing system. But an investment designed with a 15-year life may be a big psychological barrier to seeing the Internet's strengths.

Secondly, is Seven-Eleven willing to use technology to cut costs? The company says—as do many others—that human capital, augmented by technology, stands at the centre of its business. Like most Japanese companies, it insists it does not use technology to lower staff count. The point is to improve service, not cut staff.

However, only by using technology to expand markets or to reduce staff can a company earn back the cost of such an investment. So far, Seven-Eleven has found ingenious ways to expand its markets. If that were to stop, it might find it needed less human capital than it has now.

CASE QUESTIONS

Question 1 How did Seven-Eleven, a convenience-store operator, snatch the title of biggest retailer in Japan from Daiei? What were the four advantages provided by Seven-Eleven's new technology?

Question 2 How was Seven-Eleven able to increase customer traffic? Why were customers unwilling to pay for goods over the Internet? What are the implications to the e-business strategist?

MINI CASE STUDY II
Changing the Face of Enterprise Resource Planning, by Duncan Gourley, Principal Consultant, Management Consulting Services, PricewaterhouseCoopers www.pwcglobal.com, 18 June 2001

In the new millennium several business trends are transforming the traditional realm of enterprise resource planning (ERP) systems which provide integrated software for the management of internal business operations – from sales, purchasing and manufacturing through to finance and human resources. First, organisations are moving to a customer and demand-driven business system. Second, companies are setting up or expanding e-business systems to conduct business on the internet with their suppliers, customers and partners. And third, organisations are placing a greater emphasis on the integration of their computer systems so that they are operate together seamlessly and efficiently. This includes the integration of systems for supply chain management (SCM) which enables businesses to co-ordinate and optimise their logistics, manufacturing and distribution operations – from acquiring raw materials to scheduling production and delivering products to customers.

It also includes integrating the software applications for sales force automation (SFA) and customer relationship management (CRM) systems – which connect into a managed relationship, the various contacts a customer has with an organisation via marketing, product selection, sales, delivery, post-sale support etc. CRM systems thus enable businesses to identify the preferences and needs of their customers to focus their resources on enhancing customer retention. Organisations now require fully integrated software applications which work harmoniously together from their e-business sites and call centres through to these SCM, CRM and ERP systems and that enable their entire organisations to respond to quickly and effectively to events such as customer orders, inquiries or complaints. They want to have these trigger events – such as a customer placing an order – automatically generate a series of processes throughout the organisation, so that when a customer order is received it is automatically communicated to sales, purchasing, manufacturing, distribution, billing and customer service and the appropriate databases and data warehouses.

With customers linked to enterprises using the internet, business-to-business and business-to-customer systems are expected to respond directly to customer demand, whether for product information or actual product purchase and delivery. Furthermore, businesses want to be able to communicate in a consistent way with their networks of suppliers, partners and customers, and use the information gained in these exchanges in their planning and production applications. Until recently, ERP software applications have been very much focused on the core internal business functions of an organisation, such as finance, logistics, manufacturing and human resources. Now sellers or "vendors" of ERP system want to provide organisations with total business solutions and have their products act as the business information backbone.

To maintain their predominant position in the corporate applications market, the major ERP vendors have responded to the above trends in two main ways. First, they have redeveloped their products to web-enable them for both internal and external users, from simple web-interfaces through to e-procurement and e-marketplaces. Second, to overcome the perception their systems are too internally focused to be relevant in a customer-driven world, they have jumped into the SCM and CRM arenas to provide an expanded, external reach to their ERP back office systems. The ERP systems available today provide the breadth of applications and depth of functionality required to offer a comprehensive business solution to any organisation. What do these developments in the ERP applications market mean for organisations and their enterprise application strategy?

The ERP application suites available from the major vendors today, in many cases, will allow an organisation to source all corporate applications, from finance through SCM and CRM through to e-procurement and e-marketplaces, from a single vendor. This provides the organisation with significant benefits over sourcing applications from a variety of vendors:

- strong integration between all applications using pre-developed interfaces
- reduced risk during implementation
- system implementation is easier
- operational system management and maintenance is simplified
- single vendor relationship to manage
- consistent look and feel to applications

There is a downside to these benefits though:

- the functionality of an application from an ERP suite is often less than a "best of breed" equivalent application
- the organisation is locked into the vendor's strategy for product development that may not follow its requirements – especially for New Zealand (NZ) specific requirements when dealing with a global vendor
- specialist applications offered as part of the ERP application suite – such as e-procurement, e-market, CRM, SCM – are often too expensive for NZ organisations to implement

From an enterprise application strategy point of view, using a single ERP vendor's application suite for all the organisation's enterprise applications offers significant benefits, provided that the scale and functionality of the applications matches its requirements. But often in New Zealand, organisations find that ERP vendors' core applications for finance, logistics, manufacturing and human resources provide a good fit to their organisation's requirements; while the ERP vendors' applications to extend functionality into the CRM, SCM and e-business arenas are often too expensive or do not sufficiently meet the organisations requirements.

An important and rapidly developing area of corporate application technology is enterprise application integration (EAI) middleware – software that helps integrate different applications, particularly ERP to SCM or CRM and ERP to the internet. These "middleware" products offer a solution to allow organisations to integrate their core ERP applications with CRM, SCM and e-business applications from other vendors, and they are now an important component of an organisation's enterprise application strategy. Even with special middleware, however, linking diverse applications into a single system is a complex and difficult task, but one that should become easier in the future as middleware products mature, and emerging integration standards are widely adopted by the enterprise application software industry.

Although yet to be fully realised, the middleware products offer organisations the ability to build their enterprise applications architecture around "best of breed" applications, utilising the applications that provide the best fit to the organisation's requirements and integrating them into a seamless virtual system. This "best of breed" approach is especially relevant to New Zealand organisations as they look to integrate specialist CRM, SCM and e-business applications into their core ERP applications. This gives them freedom of choice in terms of their enterprise application strategy and avoids them being locked in to a single software vendor's product strategy.

CASE QUESTIONS

Question 1 How do ERP systems enhance core internal processes? With regards to the weaknesses of traditional ERP systems, how have ERP vendors responded to the Internet?

Question 2 How do middleware products help organizations link diverse applications into a single system?

REFERENCES

Alba, J., J. Lynch, B. Weitz, C. Janiszewski, R. Lutz, A. Sawyer and S. Wood (1997) Interactive home shopping: consumer, retailer and manufacturer incentives to participate in electronic marketplaces, *Journal of Marketing*, vol. 61, no. 3, pp. 38–54.

Andersen Consulting (2000), *Cracking the Value Code*, www.ac.com.

Bakos, J.Y. (1997) Reducing buyer search cost: implications for electronic marketplaces, *Management Science*, vol. 43, no. 12, pp. 1676–1692.

Burnett J. and M. McCollough (1994) Assessing the characteristics of the non-store shopper, *International Review of Retail, Distribution and Consumer Research*, vol. 4, no. 4, pp. 443–463.

Casillas, J., P. Crocker Jr, F. Fehrenbach, K. Haug and B. Straley (2000) *Disruptive Technologies: Strategic Advantage and Thriving in Uncertainty*, Kellogg TechVenture 2000 Anthology, Kellogg School of Management.

Chaffey, D. (2002) *E-business and e-commerce Management*, Pearson Education, Harlow.

Chou, D.C. (2000) A guide to the Internet revolution in banking, *Information System Management*, vol. 17, no. 2, pp. 51–8.

Christensen, C. (1997) *The Innovator's Dilemma. When New Technologies Cause Great Firms to Fail.* Harvard Business School Press, Boston, MA.

Dadomo, S. and B. Soars (1999) *A Guide to E-Commerce: Business to Consumer*, IGD Business Publications, London.

De Kare-Silver, M. (2000) *E-Shock 2000 – The Electronic Shopping Revolution: Strategies for Retailers and Manufacturers*, Macmillan Business, London.

El.Pub (2000) *Comparison Shopping on the Web*, http://inf2.pira.co.uk/top002.htm#comp.

Enders, A. and T. Jelassi (2000) The converging business models of Internet and bricks-and-mortar retailers, *European Management Journal*, vol. 18, no. 5, pp. 542–550.

Evans, P.B. and T.S. Wurster (1997) Strategy and the new economy of information, *Harvard Business Review*, vol. 75, no. 5, pp. 71–82.

Fornell, C. (1992) A national customer satisfaction barometer: the Swedish experience, *Journal of Marketing*, vol. 56, January, pp. 6–21.

Furash, E.E. (1999) Internet strategy: why banks may be getting it wrong – and how to get it right, *Journal of Retail Banking Services*, vol. 21, no. 2, pp. 37–43.

Gehrt, K., L. Yale and D. Lawson (1996) The convenience of catalog shopping: is there more to it than time?, *Journal of Direct Marketing*, vol. 10, no. 4, pp. 19–28.

Graham, P. (2001) *Putting e-business to Work*, IBM mid market business, www.ibm.com/e-business.

Greenfield Online (1999) *Shopping 2000: A digital consumer study*, www.greenfieldcentral.com/research_findings/Shopping%202000/shopping_2000.htm.

Hagel, J., T. Hewlin and T. Hutchings (1997) Retail banking: caught in a web?, *The McKinsey Quarterly*, no. 2, pp. 42–55.

Hagel, J. and M. Singer (1999) *Net Worth: Shaping Markets When Customers Make the Rules*, Harvard Business School Press, Boston, MA.

Herbst, A.F. (2001) e-finance: promises kept, promises unfulfilled and implications for policy and research, *Global Finance Journal*, vol. 12, no. 2, pp. 205–215.

Hofman, D., T. Novak and P. Chatterjee (1997) Commercial scenarios for the Web: opportunities and challenges, *Journal of Computer-Mediated Communication*, vol. 1, no. 3, www.ascusc.org/jcmc/vol1/issue3/hoffman.html.

Hoque, F. (2000) *e-Enterprise Business Models, Architecture and Components*, Cambridge University Press, Cambridge.

Jayawardhena, C. and P. Foley (2000) Changes in the banking sector – the case of internet banking in the UK, *Internet Research: Electronic Networking Applications and Policy*, vol. 10, no. 1, pp. 19–30.

Kalakota, R. and M. Robinson (2001) *e-business: Roadmap for Success*, Addison Wesley Longman, Reading, MA.

Lafferty Group (2001) www.lafferty.com/products/internet_ratings.asp.

Li, H, C. Kuo and M. Russel (1999) The impact of perceived channel utilities, shopping orientations, and demographics on the consumer's online buying behaviour, *Journal of Computer-Mediated Communication*, vol. 5, no. 2, www.ascusc.org/jcmc/vol.5/issue2/hairong.html.

Llewellyn, D.T. (1997) Banking in the 21st century: the transformation of an industry, *Bulletine Economique et Financier*, vol. 11, no. 49, pp. 5–27.

Lund, V. (2000) *Assessing the Impact of E-business on European Retail Financial Services*, IBM Business Strategy.

McKnight, L.W. and J. Boroumand (2000) Pricing Internet services: after flat rate, *Telecommunications Policy*, vol. 24, pp. 565–590.

Mackie-Mason, J.K. and V.R. Hal, (1997) *Economic FAQs about the Internet*, Internet Economics, L.W. McKnight and J.P. Bailey (eds), MIT Press, Cambridge, MA, pp. 27–62.

Martinez, P. (2000) *Models Made "e": What business are you in?*, Centers for IBM e-business innovation, IBM Global Services, USA

Mason, R. (2000) Simple competitive Internet pricing, *European Economic Review*, vol. 44, no. 4–6, pp. 1045–1056.

Methlie, L.B. and H. Nysveen (1999) Loyalty of on-line bank customers, *Journal of Information Technology*, vol. 14, pp. 375–386.

O'Connor, G. and B. O'Keefe (1996) *Viewing the Web as a Marketplace*, www.december.com/cmc/mag/1996/jun/ocodrive.html.

Odlyzko, A. (1997) *A Modest Proposal for Preventing Internet Congestion*, AT&T Labs, Research Mimeo.

——— (2001) Internet pricing and the history of communications, *Computer Networks*, vol. 36, pp. 493–517.

Online Finance Europe (2000) J.P. Morgan, September.

Pennathur, A.K. (2001) Clicks and bricks; e-risk management for banks in the age of the Internet, *Journal of Banking and Finance*, vol. 25, no. 11, pp. 210–223.

Rappa, M. (2000) *Managing the Digital Enterprise: Business Models*, ecommerce.ncsu.edu/topics/models/models.html.

Rasch, S. and A. Linter (2001) *The Multichannel Consumer: The Need to Integrate Online and Offline Channels in Europe*, Boston Consulting Group, July.

Rozanski, H. and G. Bollman (2001) The great portal payoff, matching internet marketing to consumer behaviour, *eINSIGHTS*, Booz Allen & Hamilton, www.strategy-business.com/enews/021601/02-16-01_eInsight,pdf.

Salste, T. (1996) *The Internet as a Mode of Non-Store Shopping*, www.aivosto.com/vbq5/study.html.

Seybold, P. (2000) *How to change your e-business model(s): Morphing your e-business on the fly*, Patricia Seybold Group, Customer.com, Strategic Planning Service.

Shenker, S., D. Clark, D. Estrin and S. Herzog (1996) Pricing in computer networks: Reshaping the research agenda. *ACM Computer Communication Review*, pp. 19–43.

Stabell, C.B. and Ø.D. Fjeldstad (1998) Configuring value for competitive advantage: on chains, shops, and network, *Strategic Management Journal*, vol. 19, pp. 413–437.

Swaminathan, V., E. Lepkowska-White and B. Rao (1999) Browsers or buyers in cyberspace? An investigation of factors influencing electronic exchange, *Journal of Computer-Mediated Communication*, vol. 5, no. 1, www.ascusc.org/jcmc/vol5/issue2/oldswaminathan.htm.

Timmers, P. (2000) *Electronic Commerce: Strategies and Models for Business-to-Business Trading*, Wiley, Chichester.

Turban, E., J. Lee, D. King and H. Chung (2000) *Electronic Commerce: A Managerial Perspective*, Prentice Hall, Upper Saddle River, NJ.

Vernon, M. (2000) Cherry-pickers move online: traditional banks are coming under increasing pressure from internet-savvy newcomers, *Financial Times, Understanding CRM*, 16 March 2000.

Wallace, D. (1995) Shopping online: a sticky business, *Advertising Age*, vol. 20, 10 April.

Zott, C., R. Amit and J. Donlevy (2000) Strategies for value creation in e-commerce: best practice in Europe, *European Management Journal*, vol. 18, no. 5, pp. 463–475.

CHAPTER 6
E-ORGANIZATIONAL DIMENSIONS

LEARNING OUTCOMES

When you have read and worked through this chapter, you will be able to:

- Appreciate the various approaches to organizational design
- Appreciate the importance of the seven e-organizational dimensions
- Understand the organizational challenges in the Internet era
- Understand the concept of e-business infrastructure
- Understand the information system function chain
- Appreciate the complexity of measuring e-business performance

INTRODUCTION

As electronic marketplaces and e-businesses proliferate, there is a need to examine this phenomenon closely. There is now growing evidence that e-business is different enough to warrant an in-depth examination of traditional organization design (Wang, 2000). In summary two types of structures have emerged, the first being an extension of the 'bricks-and mortar' company, installing an e-business ('clicks-and-mortar') division, subsidiary or spin-off. The second is an enterprise initiated as an e-business company (dot.com), without previous organizational links to a traditional 'bricks-and-mortar' organization.

Both clicks-and-mortar and dot.com companies require organizational redesign, recalibration and even restructuring of salient dimensions. In addition to issues relating to the development of new business models for such firms, there is also the question of the applicability of traditional organizational dimensions to e-business. This chapter reviews five organization design theories and then considers the e-organizational dimensions. The importance of e-business infrastructure is examined and the chapter ends with a discussion about measuring e-business performance.

ORGANIZATION DESIGN

Wang (2000) is of the opinion that e-business should be viewed less as a phenomenon of purely online business and more as a challenge of organization redesign. There are five major organization design theories that are well recognized in the organizational theory field and have established empirical records of application within various types of organizations. They are:

- Coherence design
- Five-track approach
- Process approach
- Self-design
- Sociotechnical system

Key Term...

Coherence design

The coherence design approach focuses on the alignment of the strategy, task, structure, reward systems and people processes

Key Term...

Five-track approach

The five-track organization design model is based on the premise that each organization has five leverage points: firm's culture, the managers' skills for problem solving, team-building approaches, strategy analysis and the reward system

Key Term...

Self-design

The theory asserts that managers have an ongoing capability to conduct redesign activities, and that the organization can make a teacher out of the learner

Coherence design

The **coherence design** school proposed an information-processing model for organization design (Galbraith, 1977). As it names implies, the coherence design approach focuses on the alignment of the strategy, task, structure, reward systems and people processes (Galbraith and Lawler, 1993). The organization redesign begins with the examination of strategic shift, task redefinition, cultural and political change, anticipated growth or problems, and change in people.

This conceptual model seeks to integrate many of the different contingency approaches. The ensuing stages include the generation of design criteria, generation and evaluation of grouping alternatives, generation and evaluation of structural linking alternatives, impact analysis, and refinements for final designs (Mowshowitz, 1997). According to the coherence design approach, the fundamental function of organizational arrangements is to process information. A set of organization arrangements collects and channels information to individuals and groups in support of the tasks. The key to fit is to match the information-processing capacities of organization design to the information-movement or processing requirements of the work. Nonetheless, the model of information processing capacity is difficult to define and the theory does not provide useful principles of network design for e-businesses.

Five-track approach

The **five-track** organization design model (Kilmann, 1985) is based on the premise that, each organization has five leverage points that can affect morale and performance: the firm's culture; the managers' skills for problem solving; team-building approaches; strategy analysis; and the reward system. The five leverage points are not meant to be exhaustive, as there are other leverage points such as replacing personnel or job redesign, but they tend to provide quick fixes rather than strategic solutions for the organization. The model also suggests five stages of planned change that constitute the practice behind the five tracks: initiating the problems; diagnosing the problems; scheduling the tracks and deriving solutions; implementing the tracks; and evaluating the results.

The five-track approach design school uses a design technology known as multivariate analysis, participation and structure (MAPS) (Kilmann, 1977), which can be applied for the strategy structure track. By utilizing the MAPS methodology, all organization members can define problems and create solutions so that the organization can find the most advantageous match between people and tasks. The five-track theory provides a robust framework for organizational change, as it emphasizes a planned change process. However, the lack of specific examples relating to the roles of network design and task design reduces the value of the approach for e-businesses.

Self-design

Self-design theory focuses on the internal learning of the organization. The theory asserts that managers have an ongoing capability to conduct redesign activities, and that the organization can make a teacher out of the learner (Weick, 1977). Self-design activities are performed by organizational members themselves. In practice, for a large organizational design project, a representative design team is formed that includes various stakeholders in the design process is formed. The self-design approach relies on managers identifying the strategies and opportunities for the organization, and planning and implementing their own strategy change projects. It is anticipated that the new design enables the organization to achieve high performance. The success of the implementation depends on the organization investing in the training of organizational members so that they develop practical skills in diagnosis, assessment and innovation (Mohrman and Cummings, 1989). Obviously, in a new economy environment, there is little evidence to use as a guideline about task design and network design. Moreover, in an e-business context initial team building could, at best, be challenging.

Process approach

The **process approach** (Mackenzie, 1991) adopts the view of the organization as a set of processes. Given the number and complexity of business processes, understanding the processes and operations of the organization is the pivotal concern for the organization design team. The task of organization design is actually to identify the salient processes that need to exist throughout the organization in order to achieve enhanced: efficiency, productivity and adaptability.

The process approach provides a mechanism for ongoing adaptation of the organization to the changing environment by defining and tracking the changes. The ABCE model can be used to implement change. The conceptual schema postulates that organizations and individuals can be represented by four elements: A – goals and strategies, B – organization technology which translates C – goals and strategies into practice, results and effectiveness; and E – their environments. The performance of the organization depends on the consistency or congruence among these elements of the organization (Mackenzie, 1991).

An organization audit and analysis tool can be used to perform a strategic assessment to identify organizational problems. The methodology involves the stages of organizational auditing, organizational design and implementation, and ends with an all-embracing assessment of the new design (Mackenzie, 1986).

As in the previous approaches, there is a paucity of evidence about the relationship between organizational logic and architecture. The theory fails to address an integral concept of network design, work-team building and a regulation and reward system.

Sociotechnical system

Sociotechnical system theory is one of the classical organization design theories (Pasmore, 1988). The three determinants of organizations according to sociotechnical system theory are the social system, the technical system and the climate. The social system consists of the people, their relationships and organizational arrangement. The technical system consists of the tools, techniques and knowledge in the organization. The climate of the organization is dependent on issues such as supervision, rewards, measurements and training.

According to the theory, the organization must design its social and technological systems so that they fit the demands of each other and the environment (Pasmore, 1988). The sociotechnical system provides a useful framework for organization design in the e-business context as the aspiration is to optimize IT and self-directed work group teams.

The five organization design schools present a variety of frameworks for use when dealing with organizational design components in an e-business. E-business strategy and environment are speculated to be two salient inputs influencing organizational design. Once these two factors are determined, technology, people, decision systems, human resource systems, structure and organizational values and norms must then be designed to facilitate the performance of the organization (Wang, 2000). Nonetheless, these frameworks have not been rigorously tested in an e-business environment and the challenge is for academics in partnership with practitioners to identify the salient e-organizational dimensions.

Key Term...

Process approach
The process approach provides a mechanism for ongoing adaptation of the organization to the changing environment by defining and tracking the changes

Key Term...

Sociotechnical system
The three determinants of organizations according to sociotechnical system theory are the social system, technical system and climate

E-ORGANIZATIONAL DIMENSIONS

In the new economy, where markets are changing rapidly, there are ample opportunities to position on the basis of creativity. As organizations embrace the Internet, one of the burning issues management faces is that of getting people to work differently in organizations that are changing shape. E-business organizations need to have a broad range of competencies. The original notion of how to create a new-economy business was being quick to market, prior to surveying the competitive landscape. In an attempt to evaluate the speed with which a range of B2C, B2B and infrastructure providers came to market and their success, the study by Bates, Rizvi, Tewari and Vardhan (2001) provides practitioners with some valuable observations. They quickly noted that moving fast without a solid business plan and without obtaining the appropriate resources rarely paid off. Being quick only gave an advantage to 10 per cent of the Internet companies studied. Moving at 'e-speed' without full marketing knowledge can sometimes be justified if three conditions are in place: lasting barriers to entry; large market potential; and manageable hazards (Bates *et al.*, 2001).

ILLUSTRATIVE EXAMPLE I
Scottish Enterprise E-Business Priorities, www.scottish-enterprise.com/business

---

The Scottish Enterprise, the government-funded economic development agency in Scotland, has demonstrated the importance of creating an appropriate climate for the diffusion of e-business with emphasis on some of the e-organizational dimensions. E-business is about making companies more competitive. It provides competitive advantage by increasing efficiency and effectiveness through, for example, increased market share; cost reductions; improved customer service; improved flexibility; and the creation of new opportunities.

In *A Smart, Successful Scotland* the Scottish Executive sets out their ambitions for the Enterprise Networks. The report recognises the importance of e-business in helping companies and the economy of Scotland to grow. The levers it identifies as key to 'More e-business' are based on *Connecting Scotland*, which was published in June 2000 and set out a framework for developing Scotland as an e-economy. *Connecting Scotland* was developed as a strategic framework for Scotland. Its preparation drew contributions from over 300 people and organizations across Scotland and the work was led by a Steering Group that was representative of the Scottish business, education and public sectors.

In line with *A Smart, Successful Scotland* and *Connecting Scotland*, Scottish Enterprise has an integrated strategy:

"To accelerate the competitive capability of Scottish organizations and individuals through the development and use of e-business applications".

We have concentrated our investment on a number of key areas where we have influence, where we can take measured risk, and where a real impact can be made on Scotland's competitiveness and productivity. We have embarked on a series of initiatives directly related to the Themes of *Connecting Scotland*:

- Accelerating Uptake **We have mounted a range of Network initiatives to raise awareness and lock e-business into our organizational development activities;**
- Accelerating Supplier Development **We were engaged with the software and e-business supply industry before the publication of *Connecting Scotland*. Since then, we have enhanced the scope and depth of our work;**

- Creating the Right Environment **A competitive infrastructure is vital for success and we have developed an ambitious telecoms project to enable Scottish enterprises to compete with the world;**
- Skills & Knowledge for the Future **We have developed a number of programmes to develop ICT (Information and Communication Technologies) skills in SMEs, and supported training initiatives aimed at promoting the availability of technical skills.**
- Promotion **In addition to the four Themes set out in** *Connecting Scotland*, **and underpinning them all, we have an extensive programme to promote e-business and to project the strengths of Scotland as an e-economy nationally and internationally.**

Against this background, SE chooses annual strategic priorities relevant to one or more of the *Connecting Scotland* Themes. For 2002–3, we have elected to focus on:

- **Awareness & Engagement**
- **Telecoms**
- **M-business**
- **E-learning.**

With an eye on tomorrow, we have sought to anticipate the next generation of change and believe that looking to e-learning and to m-business will bring key competitive advantage to Scotland.

A central tenet of this book is that organizations operating in the new economy must align themselves internally with the demands that the dynamic environment imposes on strategic behaviour. A good example of this is that, despite making a significant investment in their e-business strategies and IT, some managers remain unclear about how to adapt their organization. Advances in technology, which create the opportunities for new forms of arranging work, such as collapsing boundaries between supplier, customers and the competition, make it imperative for management to identify the key attributes and processes required for competitive advantage. In one of the first studies to examine the influence of management diversity and creativity on the assessment of opportunities for e-business organizations, Gundry and Kickul (2001) made some important contributions to the literature.

In the study by Gundry and Kickul managerial creativity was enhanced by the functional differences of the top management team. Those CEOs who were able to draw on the diversity of perspectives present within their top management team and who encouraged openness and creative exploration were able more successfully to consider and identify new e-business opportunities. In addition, it was observed that effective opportunity assessment has a mediating effect on the interaction of diversity and managerial creativity, which facilitate the formation of external and internal organizational relationships. In conclusion, Gundry and Kickul state that top management must have the ability to identify and assess multiple emerging opportunities in order to achieve the necessary high growth.

However, the development of new products/services is a form of internal development that can be viewed as a competence in its own right. The expansion of new products/services increases risk. In traditional markets even those organizations that specialize in innovation do not always get it right. In an e-business environment the costs of innovation are higher as, in addition to capital cost, sometimes firms invest considerable time and resources in developing a breakthrough product/service, only to have an imitator reap the benefits.

The Internet offers ample opportunities, yet the promise is often difficult to realize. While much has been written about the disintermediation of value chains, little has been written about the impacts on traditional organizational forms. Success depends upon the ability to align, link and manage all critical business elements. According to Neilson, Pasternack and Viscio (2000), the e-business organization is no longer a single corporate entity, but rather an extended network consisting of a streamlined global core, market-focused business units and shared support services. The evolution to e-organization takes place along seven key dimensions (Neilson, Pasternack and Viscio, 2000):

- Organizational structure
- Leadership
- People and culture
- Alignment
- Knowledge
- Alliances
- Governance

Organizational structure

The strategy–structure debate is one of the central tenets of strategic management. Since Chandler's seminal study in 1962, there has been debate over the temporal sequence and relative importance of strategy and structure. Chandler was of the opinion that structure follows strategy, because the firm acts as a control mechanism for the desired strategy. Alternatively, several organizational theorists have suggested that there is a significant effect from strategy to structure (e.g. Fredrickson, 1986). Others (e.g. Mintzberg, 1990) see neither strategy nor structure taking precedence.

In the new economy it would be desirable to know the financial impact of e-business strategy and structure changes in various marketplaces. Given the lacuna in existing knowledge relating to e-business transformation, it is perhaps necessary to consider previous models and frameworks developed in the traditional economy. As they entered the 1990s, organizations were sceptical about the pay-off from IT expenditure. In an attempt to provide guidelines for deriving benefits from IT investment, a framework of IT-enabled business transformation was advocated by Venkatraman (1994). His five levels of IT-induced reconfiguration model provide a useful model for assessing the relationship between the degree of business transformation and the range of potential benefits (see Figure 6.1). Venkatraman's premise was that IT potential benefits are directly related to the degree of change of organizational routines.

Neilson, Pasternack and Viscio (2000) state that instead of a bureaucratic, hierarchical structure, organizations should form more flexible, decentralized team- and alliance-based organizations that allow employees to react to market shifts. This form of enterprise is built around a global core, shared services business units and market-facing units.

When embarking on an e-business transformation project, the organization needs to be prepared to replace traditional bureaucratic, hierarchical structures with flexible, decentralized, team- and alliance-based structures. If the e-business transformation is successful then employees are able to respond instantaneously to threats and opportunities. Traditional support functions such as accounting and human resources can be managed as shared serv-

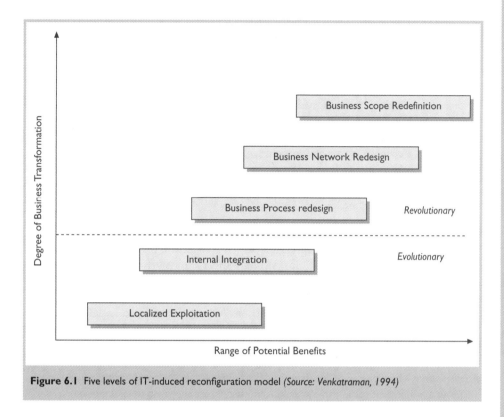

Figure 6.1 Five levels of IT-induced reconfiguration model *(Source: Venkatraman, 1994)*

ices. The shared services function can collect fees by selling services to the global core or other business units. Adopting a shared-services model allows frees managers from developing and maintaining the e-business infrastructure and lets them concentrate on revenue-earning activities.

Leadership

According to Neilson, Pasternack and Viscio (2000), the old role of the CEO becomes irrelevant in a dot.com. The responsibility for setting agendas and change becomes the responsibility of all employees. Everyone is a leader with collective responsibility for growth and success. Unfortunately, this model of cascading leadership is sometimes seen as a luxury. Organizations wrestle with institutional barriers that hinder the transformation to this type of organizational model.

Citrin and Neff (2000) asked top executives from more than 55 companies at different stages of Internet deployment the question 'what specifically should an individual keep in mind as he or she seeks to lead the organization?'. They identified six augmented qualities of leadership in the digital economy:

- *Obsessing about the customer* – organizations must focus on creating customer winning, as no revenue can be derived without a customer.
- *Building a flat cross-functional organization* – the command and control style of the traditional economy has given way to organizational flexibility. Employees need to work across functional disciplines to ensure that they have the information that they need and the authority to make decisions.
- *Managing via business model* – in the digital economy the strategy development must be more fluid than in the traditional economy. Organizations are more integrated than traditionally.

Instead of managing via a detailed annual strategic planning process, the best digital leaders manager via a business model.

- *Evangelizing and generating positive buzz* – as the profits are hard to come by in the new economy, business leaders must be able to communicate effectively with the media, institutional investors, analysts and a range of other stakeholders. The ability to generate confidence is paramount, as the market capitalization remains in excess of discounted cash flows from the business.
- *Encouraging risk-taking for real* – now that barriers to entry are low and the rewards for success can be high, a continuous flow of new approaches needs to be created to remain ahead.
- *Rolling up the sleeves and working hard* – in a traditional large organization the bulk of the CEO's time is spent working through others, whereas, during the early stage of an Internet start-up that organizational structure is much flatter and the hours worked tend to be longer.

People and culture

Hofstede's (1980) pioneering research was aimed at detecting the structural elements of culture and particularly those that most strongly affect known behaviour in the work situations of organizations and institutions. In perhaps one of the most extensive cross-cultural surveys ever conducted, Hofstede collected data about 'values' from over 100,000 employees of IBM Corporation in more than 50 countries. Subsequent statistical analysis and reasoning revealed four underlying societal value dimensions, which Hofstede labelled **Individualism, Masculinity, Power Distance** and **Uncertainty Avoidance**:

- *Individualism* – how people define themselves and their relationships with others. Individualism implies a loosely knit social framework in which people are supposed to take care of themselves and of their immediate families only, while its opposite, collectivism, is characterized by a tight social framework in which people are interested in the wellbeing of a wider group with a more extended network of support and loyalty.
- *Masculinity* – how society is characterized by assertiveness (masculinity) versus nurturance (femininity). More masculine societies place greater value on achievement, tasks, money, performance and purposefulness, whereas more feminine ones emphasize quality of life, interpersonal relationships and concern for the vulnerable.
- *Power distance* – how society and its individual members tolerate an unequal distribution of power in organizations and in society as a whole. Cultures with high power distance have power and influence concentrated in the hands of a few rather than distributed throughout the population.
- *Uncertainty avoidance* – how people in a culture are made nervous by situations they perceive as being unstructured, unclear or unpredictable. In these cultures, such situations are avoided by maintaining strict codes of behaviour and a belief in absolute truths.

Given Hofstede's work, it is surprising that there is a belief that technology is culturally neutral and that the underlying process of technology adoption is uniform across countries, once basic economic and political conditions are met. Moreover, it has been observed that many projects involving almost similar information technologies in different countries falter because their design is not sufficiently tailored to the country's history and industrial traditions. Specifically, 'problems arise that cannot be attributed to the lack of technology development in a particular country, but rather to the cultural differences between designers of the technology and its recipients' (Hasan and Ditsa, 1999, p. 5).

The velocity of e-business will put people strategies and corporate culture to the test. IT has taken over routine tasks and administrative duties previously performed by employees. This will expand the demand for skilled employees throughout the organization. Employers must

Key Term...

Individualism
How people define themselves and their relationships with others

Key Term...

Masculinity/femininity
How society is characterized by assertiveness (masculinity) versus nurturance (femininity)

Key Term...

Power distance
How society and its individual members tolerate an unequal distribution of power in organizations and in society as a whole

Key Term...

Uncertainty avoidance
How people in a culture are made nervous by situations they perceive as being unstructured, unclear or unpredictable

widen the culture of the organization culture to support the new ways of doing business. Areas worthy of attention include innovation, change management and leadership through shared values.

Alignment

With the threat of disintermediation it is imperative that organizations extract the maximum value from their operations; achieving 70 or 80 per cent of their potential may not be sufficient. Firms must be efficient at each point in their value chain. To generate the maximum value, innovation must flow through the entire depth and breadth of the business. This can be achieved by alignment. The shared sense of direction allows synergistic effects. In aligned organizations, objectives are clear, with action plans containing defined roles and responsibilities and the performance measurement system ensuring that rewards are fairly distributed. Aligned firms are prevalent in Internet start-ups, with employees possessing the incentive to drive the business forward towards the strategic objectives.

Knowledge

The highly competitive external landscape has generated the need for e-organizations to share knowledge. Despite the fact that there is no commonly agreed definition of knowledge management, companies, governments, institutions and organizations are becoming increasingly interested in the topic (Malhotra, 2000). In regulated markets, protection is a driver that does not necessarily promote knowledge sharing or efficiency. Some CEOs may decide to watch the movement towards knowledge management from the sidelines, but evidence suggests that this form of intellectual capital can be a driver of wealth generation. For example, the CEO of Hewlett Packard, Lew Platt, has articulated the motivation for most by saying 'If HP knew what HP knows, we would be three times as profitable'. Bearing in mind the financial performance of dot.coms, Lew Platt's statement should not be ignored. However, it cannot be over-emphasized that there is more to knowledge than sheer data. It is what you do with the information, how you package and distribute it.

However, a recent McKinsey study by Hauschild, Licht and Stein (2001) which included a survey of 40 companies in Europe, Japan and the USA, showed that many managers were of the view that knowledge management begins and ends with building sophisticated IT systems. More pertinent was the fact that successful organizations understand that knowledge management and IT are not tantamount. Successful knowledge-management practices are not one-off projects, but long-term projects that embrace the entire company and complement the strategic decision-making.

Alliances

As a result of the Internet accelerating and intensifying the need for organizations to address strategic weaknesses, strategic alliances are a favourable way of strategy development. Moreover, competitive boundaries are becoming blurred with 'the death of the distance', so that formerly disparate products, markets and geographical regions are now potential competitors. This now places organizations so that they are exposed to co-operative strategies.

Alliances can take a variety of legal and cultural forms. In the e-business environment strategic alliances of all forms have become increasingly common. Alliances provide the opportunity for e-business firms to acquire additional competencies quickly. In addition, alliances can provide certain benefits through reducing risk in terms of lower investment cost, which allows all parties to be more experimental. Senior management does not have limitless resources to act more quickly and smartly. Successful firms will have to build and deploy the critical capabilities that can be leveraged to enhance shareholder value. Alliances are a quick way to secure immediate access to differentiating capabilities. Members of the alliance are able to extend their business operations by making use of internal and external capabilities.

In a review of existing systems offering collaborative services, Bafoutsou and Mentzas (2002) concluded that collaborative work based on information sharing is becoming a necessity. E-collaboration leverages the connective powers of the Internet to co-ordinate the efforts of two or more companies. Using e-collaborative capabilities, alliance members (suppliers, franchisees and customers) can operate as a single business entity. They can make joint decisions and focus on adding value for their customers. If the barriers between alliance members can be reduced with enhanced interactions and transactions among them, this will reduce costs and strengthen relationships.

Governance

The Internet has evolved through spontaneity without an overall controlling authority. Matters have not been helped by the pace of technological developments, which make the Internet increasingly difficult for governments to regulate. There is an opinion that governments are driven by the material and ideological interests of politicians and bureaucrats and by special interest groups that can reward them. An alternative view is that some commercial organizations are seeking competitive advantage via the Internet by being a monopoly, which has invoked government action. Conflict between the proponents and opponents of governmental regulation of the Internet have led some to think that meddling is likely to be wealth destructive and counter-productive (Brady, 2000).

The area of governance covers three areas: governance of the organization by the board of directors, governance of intracompany alliances and governance of intercompany entities. The traditional top-down, internally focused governance structure of the past has now changed to a more fluid model that encompasses both internal and external scrutiny. The role of the board of directors should move from a passive guardianship role to that of an active supporter. The advent of shared services, where support functions operate as autonomous business units, has created the need for a shared-services board. All parties are represented to ensure alignment of shared-services policies with strategic objectives. The increased use of alliances has created the need for formal intercompany governance processes. These processes can, in themselves, be a key differentiator among alliances as they seek to enhance shareholder value.

ILLUSTRATIVE EXAMPLE II
People—not technology, From Towers Perrin, Management Consultants, Canadian Manager, Summer 2000, vol. 25, no. 2, pp. 26–27

THE BIGGEST CONCERN FOR COMPANIES TACKLING E-BUSINESS
The next two years are going to bring unprecedented change to the way work is organized within large companies around the world, according to a Towers Perrin survey on the impact of the Internet on **organizations**. The changes go far beyond technology, and will dramatically shift **organizations' structure** and operations, affecting both people and processes.

"The drivers of the first wave of the **e-business** revolution have been largely dot.coms and start-ups," said Simon Ashbourne, a Principal in Towers Perrin's Strategy and

Organization Practice. "Large traditional businesses are still better characterized as 'not-coms'. These companies have been scrambling to gain greater technology literacy and to develop **e-business** strategies. Many have pilots or nascent *e-business* ventures now in place."

"However, in the second wave, these large companies will be very significant drivers of the future of **e-business**, as they start implementing their strategies. These companies have tremendous assets and resources, and will have a major impact as they 'get serious' about **e-business**."

Overwhelmingly, **organizations** are determined to avoid being 'not.coms' according to the findings. While **e-commerce** represents only four percent of sales today, participants expect this to quadruple in the next two years and one fifth expect it to become almost half their **business**.

The survey found that the most prominent reasons companies pursue **e-commerce** strategies are centred on customers and markets, with the top two reasons cited as being increasing brand equity and deepening customer relationships. It is not surprising then that fully two-thirds of respondents foresee significant or dramatic changes in the next years in their management **structure**, shifting to a more customer-based **structure**. 'Many of the trends of recent years, such as increasing organizational flexibility, and more cross-functional team-work with less hierarchical **structures**, start to take on critical urgency in the new economy,' said Ashbourne.

One third of survey participants are based in Canada, and the findings for this group reinforce the fact that Canadian companies tend to be more cautious than their U.S. counterparts in joining the "internetworked" economy. Canadian participants have, for the most part, made fewer changes so far in response to the Internet, and fewer Canadian respondents see "dramatic change" ahead. They're less concerned overall about the "burning issues" than most U.S. respondents, and express less concern about getting their workforces **e-literate** and helping their employees understand their **e-business** strategies. "Canadians still seem to have a 'wait-and-see' attitude," said Ashbourne. "But if they don't pay attention, they could be missing significant opportunities."

One positive note from a Canadian perspective is the widely anticipated importance, and great shortage, of generalist management talent. Given the smaller scale of the marketplace, Canadian businesses are often unable to allocate a multi-functional team to resolve a particular challenge – relying instead on an individual capable of wearing many hats. This ability to work across functions and disciplines will be highly valued in the market and Canadian management talent will have access to tremendous opportunities. "We interviewed several start-ups as part of this research," explained Ashbourne. "One of the U.S. dot.coms said that they hire smart generalists . . . and they don't know what they'll need to do until they start."

Despite all the investment to date in strategy development and new technology, implementing **e-business** effectively remains a challenge. Respondents say that their **organizations** have made relatively modest changes to date in how they manage their **business** as a result of the internet. While technology itself creates huge opportunities for growth, survey respondents say that their current **organizations** hold them back from realizing its potential.

The biggest challenges focus on "people" and "**organization structure** and design". Issues such as recruiting, retaining and re-educating employees, traditionally the concern of the HR department, have leapt into the executive suite. For example, 59 percent of respondents believe that their current culture is a barrier to getting things done, and 74 percent admit that their current **structures** inhibit the speed of decisionmaking. Participants also said that *e*-commerce strategies are often poorly articulated and poorly communicated through the company. An overwhelming majority (87%) agreed that employees lack the skills and capabilities to make **e-commerce** happen. At the same time, traditional training and people development approaches are seen as inadequate. What emerges is a consensus that the shortage of talent challenge is at least as critical as the shortage of time challenge.

"What I found disturbing," said Ashbourne, "is that when we looked at those companies with more than two years experience in **e-business**, we found that they experienced the same issues as those just starting out. Companies plunging into the world of **e-commerce**, and pushing their people beyond their limits just to get their operations up and running more or less reliably. This may be a sustainable model for two dozen 22 year olds. But it's simply not a sustainable model for larger **organizations**. Despite – or perhaps because of – the need to manage at the speed of *e*, executives need to apply some discipline and order to their **organization** design. Speed cannot simply become anarchy. Employees certainly need to buy into a vision and a strategy . . . but they also need to understand their roles and accountabilities."

The survey also examined the **structure** of **e-commerce**, and found that most companies generally intend to hold their **e-commerce** groups within their main **business**, at least for the next two years. This is counter to conventional wisdom, which argues that big companies should spin-off their **e-business** units.

Not surprisingly, respondents anticipate a huge increase in the velocity of change across their entire **business** model. The changes go far beyond the 'business as usual' adjustments that have marked the recent past, and affect strategy, processes, people, **organization** design and equally important, communication and culture.

These findings are some of the highlights of the Towers Perrin Internetworked **Organization** Survey of more than 300 companies, worldwide, which were surveyed between December 1999 and January 2000. The majority of respondents were from the United States, Canada, and Europe. Thirty-five percent were in **organizations** with more than 5,000 employees. Over half responded to an on-line questionnaire. Their main businesses are financial services (28 percent), physical goods (32 percent), electronic/digital goods (7 percent), or other services (34 percent).

Nineteen percent of respondents' **organizations** had offered services over the Internet for more than two years, 38 percent had been offering services for less than six months and 43 percent had been offering services for between six and 24 months.

Towers Perrin is a global management consulting firm which helps **organizations** implement their **business** strategies through innovative, cost-effective solutions to managing people, performance and risk. Towers Perrin has more than 8,000 people in 78 offices around the world, including 5 in Canada.

E-BUSINESS INFRASTRUCTURE

Given the rapid advancement of the Internet, IT is now a critical business driver that must be well managed, tightly aligned and highly efficient. The Internet euphoria is now slowing down with organizations placing emphasis on getting their e-business infrastructure to cope with the unpredictable levels of traffic and competing applications. Organizations sometimes find themselves locked into proprietary systems, which prevents them easily adapting and adopting new e-business technologies. In these instances managing e-business infrastructure becomes problematic as IT managers attempt to juggle complex, unplanned and interlinked but non-integrated systems. Moreover, the preponderance of e-business, new distribution channels, mergers and acquisitions, and new forms of competition have added to these challenges. If management wish to control their e-business infrastructure, they need to consider both the technology and applications infrastructures. The technology infrastructure consists of the hardware elements, while the applications infrastructure consists mainly of the software elements. An e-business infrastructure should address four criteria: scalability, availability, security and manageability:

- *Scalability* – the ability to handle more users doing more things, which consists of two dimensions, vertical and horizontal. Vertical scalability can occur when a company replaces one server with a much larger one. Horizontal scaling refers to the ability to add more servers, more instances of the application, to accommodate increasing amounts of traffic. An automatic load balancer is required to spread the traffic across the servers.
- *Availability* – operating in an e-business environment involves being available 24/7, as any downtime can mean lost business, lower levels of productivity and unhappy customers. Therefore, availability, which is usually described in terms of the amount of downtime a company can tolerate, is critical for organizational success.
- *Security* – e-business security today typically takes the form of secure systems. There are several parties to a transaction and these can include: purchaser, merchant, certification authority, traditional banks and virtual banks. Fraud can entail transaction or credit-card details stolen in transit, customer credit-card details stolen from a merchant's system, or misrepresentation of merchant or customer. As a control mechanism, password-based authentication and authorization can be used to ensure privacy and confidentiality. Checks can also be made for integrity of message and non-repudiability of sender. Approaches to enhancing security entail digital certificates and digital signatures, and incorporate public key infrastructure and certificate authorities.
- *Manageability* – goes beyond application management and website performance by considering monitoring system and network management. Various tools are being introduced to address the various aspects of e-business management and system-performance measurement. Manageability addresses system and network management as well as application management and website performance monitoring.

The Information System Function Chain

A five level model entitled the Information System Function Chain has been proposed by Kampas (2000). Kampas asserts that the five levels, together with their 12 elements, are the fundamental building blocks that constitute every information system – past, present and future. It is anticipated that by using the proposed systemic approach as a conceptual framework, the role and implications of all current and future IT developments can be much more easily assimilated and assessed.

- *Level I – Storage/Physical.* The kernel of all information systems is rooted in the physical world of atoms and electrons, although higher-level applications are broken down into bits. Higher-level functions can ultimately be affected by operational failures, such as system crashes and power outages. This implies that magnetic storage is a critical activity.
- *Level II – Processing.* The computer processor is the heart of the information system. Rapid advances in processing power have had huge enabling effects on the ability to accomplish expanded functions at higher levels in a broad range of areas. These include speech recognition, video conferencing, molecular design, animation and artificial intelligence.
- *Level III – Infrastructure.* As previously discussed, the infrastructure is the critical central function of every system. It provides the essential control and connectivity that binds the various elements together into a unified, well regulated system. The categories of infrastructure include: human interface, the control system and external interfaces.
- *Level IV – Application/Content.* The actual work of an information system is accomplished in the

last stratums, Levels IV and V. The application software operates on either data or media of some form to produce an output, which can include editing text, executing a transaction, simulating a product or process, or controlling a device.

■ *Level V – Intelligence.* IT developments have led to systems being used to augment intrinsic human capabilities. This function of intelligence is one of the last frontiers. Even today, computers, which include reasoning, inference, learning and creativity, remain limited in what they can do. Nevertheless, enhanced processing power will enable increasing computer-based capabilities over time, but not quickly.

Infrastructure Resource Management

In an attempt to address the above concerns, a concept, known as **Infrastructure Resource Management (IRM)**, has emerged to address the increasing need to manage enterprise-wide changes effectively while maintaining control over the total cost of ownership to ensure that IT infrastructure serves to enhance the bottom line rather than merely increase costs. The ability to achieve the desired return on technology investment is highly desirable, but, as an organization's strategic capabilities broaden and develop, so does the complexity of business. While managing a traditional bricks-and-mortar business with a basic Web presence is relatively low-risk, the impact of full-blown e-commerce and other e-business initiatives can be substantial. In addition, the proliferation of merger and acquisition activity increases the need for the IT portfolio to be well managed. As organizations have now heeded the lessons from the first wave, infrastructure resource management is fast becoming a critical component of e-business management.

Kriebel (2000) uses the four Cs of asset management to help identify the salient activities for effective IT asset management. The four distinct data categories are: the Characteristics (hardware data); Configuration (software information); Contracts (service and warranty information); and Costs (financial data) of the entire IT assets. The technical and financial data comprising the four Cs allows organizations to understand fully the nature of their organizations' technology resources – from requisition to disposal of the asset. These capabilities rely on a supportive, carefully aligned and well-managed e-business infrastructure, plus solid coordination of on-site activities. Although deploying such a comprehensive solution can be a daunting proposition, the results can be dramatic. The IRM process is not a one-size-fits-all proposition, but most technology consultants will follow a three-step approach (Ming, 2001):

■ *Evaluation* – includes an assessment of an organization's current infrastructure and total cost of operations.
■ *Design* – involves the identification of the resource management needs of the organization and provides strategic design for its IRM solution.
■ *Implementation* – deals with arranging the in-house or out-tasked resource management initiatives.

MEASURING E-BUSINESS PERFORMANCE

Improving business performance has been one of the central tenets of management and remains fundamental to organizational success (Neely, 1999). Despite the evanescent view that managers can manage solely with accounting-based indicators, strict financial outcomes remain the dominant measures utilized. During the last decade, an increasing number of scholars and practitioners have expressed disquiet with traditional quantitative performance measures that tend to focus on conventional financial post hoc indicators (e.g. Fitzgerald and Moon, 1996; Wright, 1998; Buckmaster, 2000).

The multiplicity of management processes required in an e-business organization suggests that the identification of salient measures is of paramount importance. In the new economy, where business is conducted digitally, performance management involves measuring both IT and business processes. From a management perspective, healthy Web servers and high levels of bandwidth are insufficient to ensure e-business success. E-businesses also need to make sure that the data that end users are receiving are the data they want (Liebmann, 2001).

As the reliance upon traditionally based performance indicators has been highlighted as inadequate for new economy, the search for suitable metrics to measure e-business performance has increased. Nevertheless, very few companies use even some of the most basic yardsticks of Internet-based measurement metrics such as:

- *Site awareness* – ratio of number of site visitors to total Internet users
- *Site attractiveness* – ratio of number of visitors seeking information to number of site visitors
- *Promotional effectiveness* – ratio of number of visitors initiating dialogue to number seeking information
- *Purchase effectiveness* – ratio of number of visitors placing orders to number initiating dialogue
- *Loyalty effectiveness* – ratio of number of repeat customers to total number of customers ordering

Cyberspace traffic measurement needs to go beyond the use of these types of stand-alone and complementary ratios (albeit very useful) and attempt to measure a myriad of new measures. In an attempt to identify what managers in e-businesses should be measuring, Adams, Kapashi, Neely and Marr (2000) sought the views of senior managers from more than 70 bricks-and-mortar, clicks-and-mortar and dot.com businesses. Adams *et al.* used the performance prism (Figure 6.2) as the performance measurement framework, as in

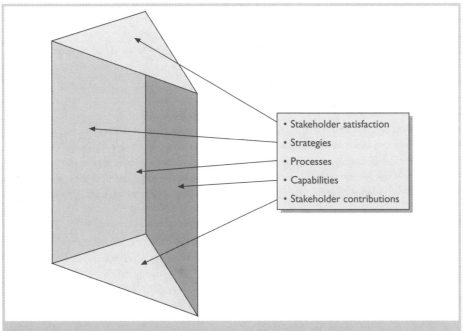

- Stakeholder satisfaction
- Strategies
- Processes
- Capabilities
- Stakeholder contributions

Figure 6.2 The five facets of the performance prism *(Source: Adams et al., 2000)*

their opinion it provides a number of real advantages over the balanced scorecard of Kaplan and Norton (1996). According to Adams *et al.*, the performance prism helps managers answer five key questions that lead to appropriate measures for e-business performance:

- Who are the key stakeholders and what do they want and need?
- What strategies do we have to put in place to satisfy the wants and needs of those key stakeholders?
- What critical processes do we require if we are to execute these strategies?
- What capabilities do we need in order to operate and enhance these processes?
- What contributions do we require from our stakeholders if we are to maintain and develop these capabilities?

The most significant finding was the fact that 96 per cent of bricks-and-mortar, 96 per cent of clicks-and-mortar and 100 per cent of dot.coms stated that they wanted to improve their e-business measurement framework. Dot.coms felt more confident with their measures than traditional businesses or clicks-and-mortar organizations. Customer satisfaction was viewed as important, with 100 per cent of those surveyed either measuring customer satisfaction or stating that they should measure it. As stated in an earlier discussion on e-CRM in Chapter 2, having satisfied customers is not enough; it is more important to consider customer loyalty and profitability. New measures were sought for supplier satisfaction and for the effectiveness of demand-generation processes. However, the demand for new measures needs to be balanced with resources such as availability of data, availability of technology, capital and the frequency of organizational change.

SUMMARY

This chapter has drawn attention to the fact that e-business organizations are faced with a dynamic environment that requires flexibility and structural abilities to react rapidly to the turbulence of market changes. It is anticipated that the literature on organizational design theory can be used to help managers establish the crucial role that structural dimensions play in migration to e-business. As researchers accumulate empirical knowledge in the context of e-business, managers will hopefully gain the knowledge to address the unique attributes of e-business.

Organizational design

Wang (2000) is of the opinion that e-business should be viewed less as a phenomenon of purely online business and more as a challenge of organization redesign. There are five major organizational design theories (coherence design, five-track approach, process approach, self-design and sociotechnical system) that are well recognized in the organizational theory field and have established empirical records of application within various types of organizations.

E-organizational dimensions

According to Neilson, Pasternack and Viscio (2000), the e-business organization is no longer a single corporate entity, but rather an extended network consisting of a streamlined global core, market-focused business units and shared support services. The evolution to e-organization takes place along seven key dimensions (Neilson, Pasternack and Viscio, 2000) – organizational structure, leadership, people and culture, coherence, knowledge, alliances, and governance.

E-business infrastructure

The Internet euphoria is now slowing down, with organizations placing emphasis on getting their e-business infrastructure to cope with the unpredictable levels of traffic and competing applications. If management wish to control their e-business infrastructure, they need to consider both the technology and applications infrastructures. The technology infrastructure consists of the hardware elements, while the applications infrastructure consists mainly of the software elements. An e-business infrastructure should address four criteria: scalability, availability, security and manageability.

Measuring e-business performance

The multiplicity of management processes required in an e-business organization suggests that the identification of salient measures is of paramount importance. In the new economy, where business is conducted digitally, performance management involves measuring both IT and business processes. From a management perspective, healthy Web servers and high levels of bandwidth are insufficient to ensure e-business success. E-businesses also need to make sure that the data that end users are receiving are the data they want (Liebmann, 2001).

DISCUSSION QUESTIONS

1. How does the Internet impact traditional organizational forms?

2. What does the term e-business infrastructure mean? Why is it some important to e-business organizations?

3. In your opinion, what are the salient e-business performance metrics? How do they differ from metrics used to measure traditional organizations?

ASSESSMENT QUESTIONS

1. According to Wang (2000), 'there is now growing evidence that e-business is different enough to warrant an in-depth examination of traditional organization design.' Do you agree with this proposition? What evidence do you have to support your point of view?

2. Using any one of the seven key e-organizational dimensions of Neilson, Pasternack and Viscio (2000), you are required to critique how the selected dimension has been affected by e-business.

3. It has been argued that the sole use of traditional measures is inadequate for the new economy. You are required to state your views on the relative strengths and weaknesses of this proposition.

GROUP ASSIGNMENT QUESTIONS

1. Why is an understanding of organization design helpful to the e-business manager? Which theory of organization design do you believe is most useful to the e-business strategist? You should give appropriate examples to illustrate your views.

2. Moving at 'e-speed' without full marketing knowledge can sometimes be justified if three conditions are in place: lasting barriers to entry, large market potential and manageable hazards (Bates *et al.*, 2001). Using any industry to illustrate your answer, critically evaluate this statement.

3. According to Neilson, Pasternack and Viscio (2000), the e-business organization is no longer a single corporate entity, but rather an extended network consisting of a streamlined global core, market-focused business units and shared support services. What are the implications of this statement and what are your views about this proposition?

MAIN CASE STUDY
The People's Company, by Robert D. Hof, Business Week e-biz, 3 December 2000

eBay is run like a democracy, with customers playing a major role. But will that relationship become a casualty of the auction site's success?

It seemed like a boffo idea to the brass at the Internet auction site eBay Inc.: By referring losing bidders to similar auctions by other eBay sellers, they'd keep bidders coming back. Within minutes of the program's debut in early June, though, all hell broke loose. Hundreds of angry sellers jammed eBay's online discussion boards, furious that their bidders were being siphoned away. One veteran seller of stamps and postcards, Bob Miller, auctioned a rare eBay jacket as an excuse to post a long screed slamming 'eBay's new policy of screwing the folks who built them.'

Even among the 7 million ongoing auctions, this one quickly caught the attention of Chief Executive Margaret C. Whitman and founder Pierre Omidyar. Within a week, they met with Miller in eBay's suburban Salt Lake City office near Miller's home. As they listened for 45 minutes, Whitman took four pages of notes. Two days later, they promised to switch course.

E-mails would first recommend the same seller's other auctions, or the seller could simply opt out. 'No other large corporation listens nearly as well as they do,' says Miller, who's now happily running several thousand auctions on eBay.

Good times and bad

Meet the People's Company. Like a democracy, it can be a noisy and unruly place, where citizens sometimes think the folks in charge are numbskulls. But the people's passion prevails at eBay because the people are firmly in charge. Its customers—the 38 million buyers and sellers who trade on its site—wield the kind of influence over the online auction site that most consumers and businesses could never dream of exerting on conventional companies.

Oh, sure, eBay has a delicious business model that doesn't require carrying any inventory. And, yes, it's growing like a weed and minting juicy profits because bargain hunters, in good times and bad, flock to the auction site. But the real secret of eBay's unlikely success is this: It's a master at harnessing the awesome communications power of the Net—not just to let its customers sound off directly in the ears of the big brass, but to track their every movement so new products and services are tailored to just what customers want. Remember that famous tagline, 'When E.F. Hutton speaks, people listen'? At eBay, it's the other way around: When people speak, eBay listens.

One month in late 1998, for instance, eBay managers noticed an uptick in listings in various miscellaneous categories, such as die-cast cars—suddenly, people were selling *real* cars. Now, eBay's the country's biggest car dealer, with $1 billion in sales of cars and car parts this year. In January, shortly after an eBay seller suggested speeding up auctions for impatient bidders, eBay debuted a Buy It Now feature that lets bidders end an auction at a set price. Now, 40% of listings use it, attracting more mainstream buyers and helping close auctions nearly a day faster on average than a year ago.

All in one

In essence, customers are eBay's de facto product-development team, sales and marketing force, merchandising department, and security detail—all rolled into one. It's not just that they have catapulted eBay, in just three short years, from a funky little online garage sale full of Beanie Babies and attic trash into a global marketplace for almost anything, from a $1 baseball card to a $4.9 million Gulfstream jet. eBay's customers also take it upon themselves to tell the world about eBay through word of mouth. They crowd eBay's online discussion boards, posting 100,000 messages a week to share tips, point out glitches, and lobby for changes. eBay's customers even police the site by rating each other, keeping fraud minimal.

By using the Net to tap into the talent and imagination of its customers, eBay has multiplied the brainpower of its executives by millions. Imagine a retailer trying to do this: It would have to interview every single person leaving every store, post a list of what each thought of the shopping experience, then ask them to write up a merchandising plan and call suppliers to arrange deliveries—and oh, by the way, could they keep an eye out for shoplifters? That's what eBay's customers voluntarily do each day. Says Whitman: 'It is far better to have an army of a million than a command-and-control system.'

The success of this let-'em-loose-and-listen strategy holds some potent lessons for Corporate America. By staying in close touch with customers, eBay can reinvent itself every day, since it knows precisely what its clientele wants. The trick is to keep up with what buyers and sellers want. 'We've had to constantly change how we run,' says Chief Operating Officer Brian Swette. 'We start from the principle that if there's noise, you better listen.'

And, because it set a firm corporate goal from the start—to create 'global economic democracy'—it has managed to maintain focus even while growing at a crazy clip. First-time eBay buyers are often shocked at the intensely personal service they get from eBay merchants, from handwritten thank-you notes to free shipping. It's an example of how building a strong brand depends more on understanding that each and every transaction can create a personal, one-on-one relationship that will endure. Says eBay board member Howard Schultz, CEO of Starbucks Corp.: 'The imprinting of the eBay brand was not based on 30-second ads, but the relationship with the users.'

That's why neither the September 11 tragedy nor the recession has put a pall on eBay's prospects. Despite losing about $5 million in revenues from a drop in activity following the terror attacks, eBay beat third-quarter estimates. Sales rose 71%, to

$194.4 million, surpassing expectations by 3%. It earned an $18 million profit, 15% above analysts' forecasts. eBay even raised its fourth-quarter sales forecast by 5%, to $200 million or more. Analysts now expect 2001 sales to jump at least 70%, to $736 million. Next year looks just as promising. Analysts figure sales will rise 40%, to $1 billion, and profit will be up 56%, to $150 million. Rivals are in awe: 'These guys have done a killer job,' admits Amazon.com Inc. Chief Financial Officer Warren C. Jenson.

Smarts, moxie

Now, eBay appears poised to buck what looks to be a gloomy holiday season for almost every retailer, online and off. That's largely thanks to the smarts and the moxie of its customers, who—unlike big retailers—can switch gears instantly on what they sell or buy and at what price. This year, for instance, sales of discount products, from overstocked PCs to excess toasters and bedsheets, have rocketed. As the economy worsens, more and more corporations, from IBM to Walt Disney to Sears Roebuck, are turning to eBay as a place to unload mounting inventory. 'The mix of products on the site changes by the minute as our highly entrepreneurial community of users adapts their own buying and selling strategies to trends in the economy,' says Whitman.

eBay aims to press that advantage hard this season. It has just kicked off its first-ever holiday TV-ad campaign, which aims to show how shoppers can find almost anything on eBay. Produced by AOL Time Warner Inc., for which eBay is the exclusive auction partner, the ads also promote how easy it is for AOL members to find the perfect gift on eBay. eBay also is sending out catalogs in newspapers nationwide on Dec. 2 and opening a 'Great Gifts' shop on its site, highlighting auctions of everything from gold necklaces to digital cameras.

For all its nonstop success, though, eBay faces a lot of challenges. Its $60 stock price represents a nosebleed 2002 price-to-earnings ratio of 82, more than double Microsoft's premium ratio of 31. The tiniest slip—or even, say, a few more anthrax-laden packages—could whack billions off its value overnight and limit the expansion opportunities that have in turn buoyed the stock.

Indeed, eBay is increasingly a victim of its own success. As Whitman moves to make eBay more of a clean, well-lighted place that attracts greater numbers of mainstream merchants and shoppers, she has riled existing customers who don't want more rules—or more rivals. These moves also pit eBay much more directly against bigger and more consumer-savvy behemoths. AOL Time Warner, Microsoft, Amazon, and Yahoo! are all trying to create online malls where people can buy just about anything from anyone.

Momentum

Still, eBay has the Big Mo' right now, thanks to the groundwork laid way back on Labor Day weekend in 1995, when Omidyar unveiled a bare-bones site called Auction Web. Even then, the programmer and entrepreneur had much more in mind than simply helping his girlfriend trade Pez dispensers. He aimed to create a Nasdaq-like market for a wide range of goods, but with a twist. 'I wanted to give the power of the market back to individuals, not just large corporations,' says Omidyar. 'It was letting the users take responsibility for building the community—even the building of the Web site.'

For instance, he would answer e-mails from buyers and sellers during the day, then rewrite the site's software that night to incorporate their suggestions, from fixing software bugs to creating new product categories. Says e-commerce expert John Hagel III, chief strategy officer with e-business incubator 12 Entrepreneuring Inc.: 'It really helped give people a sense of ownership and participation.' Likewise, Omidyar set up an online bulletin board for customers, whose volunteered help kept early support costs almost nil—and cemented their loyalty.

Omidyar's biggest breakthrough was the Feedback Forum, a rating system that allows buyers and sellers to grade each transaction positive, negative, or neutral. Amazingly, it works. More than 99% of feedbacks are positive (sample comment: 'Great Bidder! AAAAA+++++ Highly Recommended!'). And eBay's rate of fraud remains below 0.01%. By contrast, credit card fraud runs at nine times that rate. And positive ratings, which translate to more sales, keep people from straying to other sites. Says Dwayne Rogers, who sells vintage fruit crate labels on eBay from his home in Chico, Calif.: 'They just don't have any competition.'

Stringent rules

But as eBay grew from a small town into a city, urban problems erupted, such as contraband goods. Since early 1998, eBay has used more stringent rules to crack down on crime, and banned sales of firearms. Indeed, eBay has increasingly realized that, like government in a democracy, it can't leave absolutely everything to the people. Says Jeff Jordan, senior vice-president in charge of eBay's U.S. operations: 'You can't govern a metropolis the same way you governed Mayberry.'

eBay's key public-works project: its computer network. Until last year, it was plagued with outages—including one in June, 1999, when eBay was completely shut down for 22 hours thanks to software problems and no backup systems. Former Gateway Inc. Chief Information Officer Maynard Webb, who joined as president of eBay's technology unit, has upgraded systems so eBay's site is down less than 42 minutes a month despite much higher traffic. Credit that partly to Whitman, who dived into the technology despite her lack of experience in it. Still, eBay's customers had a big part, too. Shortly after Webb joined, he recalls, eBay's discussion boards twice lit up with user complaints about site glitches. His techies claimed nothing was amiss—and both times were proved wrong. 'They catch things we don't,' Webb says of eBay's customers. 'The community actually moves faster than we do.'

Sometimes, so do rivals. Yahoo and Amazon beat eBay on such features as online bill payment and uploading of product photos. Shmuel Gniwisch, CEO of online jewelry seller Ice.com, says Yahoo early on provided services more tailored to helping commercial companies. eBay admits it sometimes doesn't have the resources to do everything all its customers want—and, on occasion, just forgets to listen. Says Brian T. Burke, senior manager of community support: 'Sometimes we're kind of slow.' As befits a corporate democracy, eBay's biggest challenges are political. Features good for buyers, such as those e-mail auction referrals, can hurt sellers. Lately, sellers are especially peeved at eBay's promotion of large commercial companies such as Disney, which rates a special area in the Disneyana category. Says David Steiner, an eBay seller who's also president of the online auction watchdog site AuctionBytes.com: 'The general consensus of veteran sellers is that they've forsaken the people who built them in favor of corporate sellers.' eBay argues that commercial sellers lend credibility to their categories, drawing more buyers to all the sellers—a point many merchants concede.

Too big?

Yet others think eBay isn't listening as well as it once did to its core individual and small-business merchants. 'They've gotten too big for their britches,' fumes Ron Saxton, an Apple Creek (Ohio) seller of die-cast cars. eBay didn't consult its customers when it launched its Auction for America campaign a week after the September 11 attacks, aiming to raise $100 million in 100 days for victims. And eBay's insistence that sellers use its billing system, rather than let them accept checks or use a more popular rival system called PayPal, rubbed many the wrong way. That may partly explain why the charity drive has raised less than $6 million halfway through—despite donations such as Jay Leno's celebrity-signed Harley-Davidson motorcycle, which sold for $360,200.

Few complaining sellers, however, stop or even reduce selling on eBay, or go anywhere else. Partly, that's because eBay commands more than 80% of the online person-to-person auction market. 'The only way I'm leaving eBay is kicking and screaming,' says longtime eBay collectibles seller Tina DeBarge. Sure, eBay's relationship with its customers can be messy, says eBay board member Scott Cook, chairman of financial software maker Intuit Inc., 'but in the same way that democracy is messy compared with the straightforwardness of a dictatorship.'

It doesn't hurt that Whitman, despite her traditional top-down marketing background at Disney, FTD.com, and Stride Rite, became a convert to the eBay way shortly after she joined as CEO in early 1998. Indeed, she's a top seller among the company's 2,500 employees, with a positive feedback rating in the hundreds. In May, she auctioned some $35,000 worth of furnishings in her ski condo in Colorado to understand the selling experience—and immediately required fellow execs to sell on eBay so they, too, can detect problems firsthand.

It's no surprise, then, that as eBay grew beyond its ability to address individual user concerns, Whitman has pushed it to devise a constant stream of new ways to tap the expertise of its customers en masse. Naturally, eBay harnesses the special qualities of the Internet to gather intelligence much deeper than most brick-and-mortar businesses can obtain. For instance, before eBay revamped its bread-and-butter collectibles categories earlier this year to make products easier to find, it first e-mailed 1.2 million customers asking them to check out the proposed structure. Of the 10,000 who responded, 95% of them had suggestions, and many were used.

Changes

Some of its most effective ways of getting user input, though, don't depend on the Net. Since early 1999, eBay has convened Voice of the Customer groups, flying in a new group of about 10 sellers and buyers from around the country to its San Jose (Calif.) headquarters every few months. Execs grill them on issues and ask for their views on new features and policies. 'Some of the things we discussed led to changes,' such as improving eBay's feedback policies, says Voices participant George Hawkins, who sells antiques and collectibles on eBay from Duncan, B.C.

The result: fewer problems with new features and policies, and fewer big blowups. Even when something does go wrong, eBay uses all that input to shift gears quickly. In the past three months, in fact, Whitman says eBay has deliberately started budgeting an extra 10% to new projects so it has the resources in place to make a quick turn. 'They can essentially negotiate with 50,000 users at once and make it work,' says Munjal Shah, CEO of the auction services firm Andale Inc.

Most of all, eBay simply watches—very carefully. Virtually all of its fastest-growing new categories, such as autos, grew out of its noticing seller activity and giving it a shove at the right moment. After noticing random car sales, eBay created a separate site called eBay Motors in 1999, with special features such as vehicle inspections and shipping. This year, eBay expects to gross some $1 billion worth of autos and parts—many of them sold by dealers. 'It's the way of the future,' says Bradley Bonifacius, Internet manager at Dean Stallings Ford Inc. of Oak Ridge, Tenn., which has sold 50 cars on eBay in the past year.

New territory

Most intriguing, customers have been pushing eBay to move its e-commerce system outside the borders of its own Web site. Ritz Interactive, the online unit of Ritz Camera, for instance, is using the technology to run eBay auctions on its own site. Says Ritz CEO Fred H. Lerner: 'eBay has very, very aggressive plans to create an e-commerce platform.' Indeed, eBay is encouraging others to build software applications based on eBay technology—much as Microsoft does with its Windows operating system. A flourishing ecosystem of companies could enrich eBay's marketplace by providing support services such as listing tools, escrow, and bill payment. Essentially, says S.G. Cowen Securities Corp. analyst Scott Reamer, eBay aims to become the operating system for e-commerce: the preeminent place for people and businesses to sell online.

It's exciting new territory—and dangerous, too. For starters, a raft of rivals from Yahoo and AOL to Microsoft and Amazon aim to be the biggest places for e-commerce, too, and some are making fast progress. But there's a bigger question: Can eBay's values survive such grand ambitions? After all, trying to be the Microsoft of e-commerce doesn't sound, well, very eBaysian—which may be why Whitman frowns and demurs when people describe eBay's goal in such stark terms.

For his part, Omidyar frets that the growing participation of large commercial sellers could dilute eBay's unique culture. 'If we lose that, we've pretty much lost everything,' he says. eBay's people power made building a business a breeze compared with everything conventional companies must do. Keeping in touch with all those millions of customers from here on out won't be so easy.

CASE QUESTIONS

Question 1 What are the attractive features of the eBay business model? How does eBay incorporate customers into their product development team?

Question 2 How does eBay keep track of developments in the marketplace? Use some examples to illustrate your answer?

Question 3 AuctionBytes.com: 'The general consensus of veteran sellers is that they've forsaken the people who built them in favor of corporate sellers.' eBay argues that commercial sellers lend credibility to their categories, drawing more buyers to all the sellers – a point many merchants concede. Do you think that eBay is pursuing the correct strategy regarding corporate sellers?

MINI CASE STUDY 1,
Creative Industries Mapping Document 2001,
www.culture.gov.uk/creative/mapp_advertising.htm

Some of the salient features of the *Creative Industries Mapping Document* 2001 are as follows:

Impact of e-commerce/Internet/technology on advertising

The Internet and e-technology have had three distinct impacts on the advertising industry
(i) traditional advertising using new advertising space (online/new media);
(ii) new 'dot coms' using traditional ad media (print/TV/radio); and
(iii) the creation of new media agencies.

New advertising space

Spend on online advertising is a growth area. Internet marketing budgets rose from 1.5% of total marketing expenditure in the second quarter of 2000 to 2.5% in the third quarter. Other areas opening up to advertisers include interactive television, WAP technology, free phone calls in exchange for short advertising messages, and virtual signage. The fragmentation of the market created by new media provides the ability to target niche markets economically and with improved accountability.

The provision of flat monthly fee Internet access without call charges in the UK is likely to increase the number of people online and time spent online. This may impact on patterns and attitudes towards browsing the Internet and may transform it into a leisure activity, akin to watching TV, rather than as at present, a means of a planned business or leisure transaction. The take-up of the Internet as a leisure medium will make it a more attractive display advertising medium that may erode spend on traditional advertising and media.

New dot com clients

Internet start-ups represent a lucrative market for the advertising sector. There is extreme pressure on start-ups to differentiate themselves in the somewhat amorphous virtual marketplace that requires clear brand value and development, and large amounts of initial capital are spent on traditional advertising in awareness campaigns. Internet service providers spent £57 million in advertising in 1999, a fourfold increase from 1997.

New media agencies

In 2000 the Top 50 new media agencies declared income of £168 million, up from £63 million in 1998 and forecast to rise to £370 million by 2003. E-commerce is also an opportunity for UK firms to serve a global market. Many new media agencies have emerged but are likely to be swallowed up by large advertising conglomerates wishing to strengthen their new media competencies.

Convergence

Interactivity increasingly blurs the line between advertising and direct marketing. It is estimated that 17% of television adverts already carry a website address and 90% of press advertising now includes response coupons, Internet addresses, freephone numbers, etc. to encourage direct response.

While the opportunities for growth are significant in new technology, as in-house resources and knowledge of electronic media grows, it may represent a threat to agencies. As technology and creativity become more closely linked, suppliers to the industry may also represent competitors, for example digital printers offering design services directly to their customers. These issues challenge the sector to explain that new media is a creative issue rather than an IT issue.

Digital media has also altered the capital requirements of the industry. The primary resource of advertising agencies has traditionally been people, but investment in technology is on the increase, which may place pressure on SMEs who do not have the resources of the major players.

CASE QUESTIONS

Question 1 Outline how the Internet and e-technology have affected the advertising industry?

Question 2 Do you feel that Internet start-ups represent a lucrative market for the advertising sector?

MINI CASE STUDY II
Online Education: Lessons from Auntie, The Economist, 13 June 2002
© *The Economist Newspaper Limited, London*

The BBC wants to move into online education. The private sector is not happy

While talk in the commercial media world these days is all about bankruptcies and job losses, the sweet sound of expansion is still humming at the BBC. This year, it has launched three new digital television channels, a clutch of digital radio stations, a new Internet search engine and a rebranded interactive-TV service. Its latest push is into online education.

The BBC submitted an application to launch a new 'digital curriculum service' to the government last month. It wants to supply schools with free online educational materials, based on the curriculum for 5–16-year-olds, in subjects ranging from English and maths to the Welsh language and 'Citizenship'. It plans to spend £150m of licence-fee money on developing the service. The idea is that, as schools become increasingly linked to fast Internet connections, they will be able to offer pupils the chance to learn at their own speed by sitting at a computer terminal and having their lessons online. As with all new services it dreams up, the BBC needs government permission to branch out into this.

Naturally, the educational publishers are livid. While the use of online materials by schools is still fairly limited, this is chiefly because Britain has so few broadband Internet connections and so the experience of online learning is still clunky. But this will change. Already, there are some 2,000 commercial titles of software and digital content available for the English national curriculum alone. Once high-speed connections are in place, online learning could become a lucrative market.

Unless, that is, the BBC tramples over it. 'It's going to grossly distort the market,' says Dominic Savage, head of the Digital Learning Alliance, which represents both the small software companies and the big publishers, such as Granada Learning, Reed Elsevier and Pearson, which owns half of *The Economist*. Lots of smaller companies, claims Mr Savage, could go under if the BBC gets its way. The Alliance has written to Tessa Jowell, the culture minister, to ask her to throw out the request.

Mindful of this objection, the BBC stresses that it will contract out half its content production. It insists that its service will be 'distinctive', which is its usual excuse for launching a product that the market already provides. And it says that it intends to supply only half the total market, presumably leaving the more obscure subjects to others.

In an attempt to satisfy the commercial publishers, the government now says that it will provide state schools with 'electronic learning credits', worth £50m in the school year 2002–03, which they can use to buy content from the private sector if they wish. The publishers dismiss this as trifling: they claim that it would take more than three times that sum to stimulate any serious competition to the BBC. Moreover, why would a school that could get the BBC lessons free bother to fill out the forms to use their credits to buy commercial products instead?

The bigger question is why the BBC, which is supposed to be a public-service broadcaster, wants to stride off into online education in the first place. It argues that education has been part of its 'mission' since the 1920s: online learning is simply a natural extension of this. But, with no sign of market failure, it is hard to suppress the sense that this is less an exercise in public service than in corporate expansionism.

CASE QUESTIONS

Question 1 Why does the BBC wish to move into online education? What are the potential benefits to schools, school children and parents?

Question 2 What is the purpose of the Digital Learning Alliance (DLA)? Why are the members of the DLA concerned about the BBC's proposed strategy?

REFERENCES

Adams, C., N. Kapashi, A. Neely and B. Marr, (2000) *Managing with Measures: Measuring eBusiness Performance*, Accenture and Cranfield School of Management.

Bafoutsou, G. and G. Mentzas, (2002) Review and functional classification of collaborative systems, *International Journal of Information Management*, vol. 22, no. 4, pp. 281–305.

Bates, M., S.S.H. Rizvi, P. Tewari and D. Vardhan (2001) How fast is too fast?, *The McKinsey Quarterly*, Vol. 3, pp. 52–61.

Brady, G. L. (2000) The Internet, growth and governance, *Economic Affairs*, vol. 20, no. 1, pp. 13–20.

Buckmaster, N. (2000) The performance measurement panacea, *Accounting Forum*, vol. 24, no. 3, pp. 264–277.

Chandler, A.D. (1962) *Strategy and Structure: Chapters in the History of the American Industrial Enterprise*, MIT Press, Cambridge, MA.

Citrin, J.N., and J. Neff (2000) Digital leadership, *Strategy and Business*, Booz Allen Hamilton First Quarter, pp. 41–50.

Fitzgerald, L. and P. Moon (1996) *Performance Measurement in Service Industries: Making it Work*, CIMA, London.

Fredrickson, J.W. (1986) The strategic decision process and organizational structure, *Academy of Management Journal*, vol. 11, pp. 280–297.

Galbraith, J.R. (1977) *Organization Design*, Addison-Wesley, Reading, MA.

Galbraith, J. R. and E.E. Lawler III (1993) *Organizing for the Future: The New Logic for Managing Complex Organizations*, Jossey-Bass, San Francisco, CA.

Gundry, L. K. and J. Kickul (2001) Breaking through boundaries for organizational innovation: new managerial roles and practices in e-commerce firms, *Journal of Management*, vol. 27, no. 3, pp. 347–361.

Hasan, H. and G. Ditsa (1999) The impact of culture on the adoption of IT: an interpretive study, *Journal of Global Information Management*, vol. 7, no. 1, pp. 5–15.

Hauschild, S., T. Licht and W. Stein (2001) Creating a knowledge culture, *McKinsey Quarterly*, pp. 74–81.

Hofstede, G. (1980) *Culture's Consequences: International Differences in Work Related Values*, Sage, Beverly Hills, CA.

Kampas, P. (2000) Road map to the e-revolution, *Information Systems Management Journal*, Spring, pp. 8–22.

Kaplan, R.S. and D.P. Norton (1996) Using the balanced scorecard as a strategic management system, *Harvard Business Review*, vol. 74, no. 1, pp. 78–92.

Kilmann, R.H. (1977) *Social Systems Design: Normative Theory and the MAPS Design Technology*, Elsevier North-Holland, New York.

——(1985) *Beyond the Quick Fix: Managing Five Tracks to Organizational Success*, Jossey-Bass, San Francisco, CA.

Kriebel, N. (2000) *IT Asset Management Part 1: Asset Management Product Differentiation Makes Concept Vague to End Users*, Giga Information Group Cambridge, MA, www.gig.web.com.

Liebmann, L. (2001) Defining e-business performance, *Communication News*, February, Nokamis, FL, February.

Mackenzie, L.D. (1986) *Organization Design: The Organization Audit and Analysis Technology*, Ablex, Norwood, NJ.

——(1991) *The Organization Hologram: The Effective Management of Organizational Change*, Kluwer Academic Publishers, Boston, MA.

Malhotra, Y. (2000) Knowledge management for e-business performance: Advancing information strategy to Internet time, *Information Strategy: The Executive's Journal*, vol. 16, no. 4, pp. 5–16.

Ming, C.T. (2001) *A Holistic Approach to Management of the e-business Infrastructure*, IBM Malaysia, News, www.ibm.com/news/my/2001090902.html.

Mintzberg, H. (1990) The design school: Reconsidering the basic premises of strategic management, *Strategic Management Journal*, vol. 11, pp. 171–195.

Mohrman, S.A. and T.G. Cummings (1989) *Self-designing Organizations: Learning How to Create High Performance*, Addison-Wesley, Reading, MA.

Mowshowitz, A. (1997) On the theory of virtual organization, *Systems Research and Behavioral Science*, vol. 14, no. 6, pp. 373–384.

Neely, A. (1999) The performance measurement revolution: why now and what next? *International Journal of Operations & Production Management*, vol. 19, no. 2, pp. 205–228.

Neilson, G.L., B.A. Pasternack and A.J. Viscio (2000) Up the (E)organization! A seven-dimensional model for the centerless enterprise, *Strategy and Business*, Booz Allen & Hamilton, First Quarter.

Pasmore, W.A. (1988) *Designing Effective Organizations: The Sociotechnical Systems Perspective*, Wiley, New York.

Venkatraman, N. (1994) IT-enabled business transformation: From automation to business scope redefinition, *Sloan Management Review*, Winter, pp. 73–87.

Wang, S. (2000) Managing the organizational aspects of electronic commerce, *Human Systems Management*, vol. 19, no. 1, pp. 49–59.

Weick, K.E. (1977) Organization design: organizations as self-designing systems, *Organizational Dynamics* vol. 6, no. 2, pp. 31–46.

Wright, G. (1998) Perspectives on performance measurement conflicts in service businesses, *Journal of General Management*, vol. 23, no. 4, pp. 35–50.

CHAPTER 7
LEVERAGING THE WEB FOR MARKETING

LEARNING OUTCOMES

When you have read and worked through this chapter, you will be able to:

■ Appreciate the business enhancements made possible by the Internet
■ Understand the salient issues of Web marketing
■ Appreciate the concept of Web usability
■ Understand the importance of content management
■ Understand how to leverage the Web for competitive advantage

INTRODUCTION

The Internet has not only opened up new opportunities for marketers; it has also changed the skills they need to succeed. The companies that succeed will touch customers directly and individually with a combination of responsive processes, customer-focused organizations and fresh skills (Aufreiter, Ouillet and Scott, 2001). In Chapter 2 we explored the relationships between organizations and their customers and considered relationship marketing and customer relationship management. In this chapter we review the features of online marketing. A framework for Web marketing is used to illustrate the different options available in terms of product type and delivery mode. Web usability and content management are used to illustrate how to design and maintain effective websites. Reputation-building activities are mentioned as one of the key determinants of competitive advantage for Internet firms.

BUSINESS ENHANCEMENTS

Not long ago the expense of developing and implementing a website together with the complex procedures and esoteric protocols put Web presence beyond the reach of small firms. Now with the size and popularity of the Internet, businesses of all sizes have access to reap the benefits of online activity. From a marketing perspective, marketing offline is different to marketing online. The emergence of e-business has led to a rethink of conventional marketing practices and strategies (Nour and Fadlalla, 2000).

The following section considers the decisions that need to be made, once a business decides that it wishes to use the Internet as a marketing tool. The first decision is to decide what type of Internet use is best for the business. Wilson and Abel (2002) summarize the various uses of the Internet as a marketing tool and these are illustrated in Table 7.1. A business is faced with two types of enhancements: business (communication, market research and brand building) and revenue (e-commerce and e-organization).

Communication

Good-quality communication is a prerequisite for any business in the new economy. The level of communication is dependent upon the nature of the issue. For example, it is still

Business Enhancement	Revenue Enhancement

Communication
   Email
   Usenet groups
   Listserv groups
	E-commerce
	   Interactive website

Market research
   Search for secondary data
   Gather primary data
	E-organization
	   Majority of revenue generated from Internet
	   Full integration of order taking

Brand building Build a website	
(Source: Wilson and Abel, 2002)	

Table 7.1 Use of the Internet as a marketing tool

normal to conduct face-to-face meetings during the early stages of a new business relationship, whereas email is fast becoming the preferred way of communicating with suppliers, employees and customers.

As mentioned in Chapter 1, Usenet and listserv groups allow discussion among people who share common interest. Usenet groups communicate via a world-wide distributed discussion system, which consists of a set of newsgroups with names that are classified hierarchically by subject. Members of these newsgroups can use computers with appropriate software to send articles or messages, which are posted for viewing by other members. These articles are then broadcast to other interconnected computer systems via a wide variety of networks. In an attempt to control content some newsgroups are 'moderated'; in these instances, the articles are first sent to a named moderator for approval, before appearing in the newsgroup.

It is now much easier to participate in newsgroups, because of innovative services such as those provided by Google (www.google.com), which since 11 December 2001 has provided a 20-year Usenet Archive. This fully integrated service offered by Google Groups (www.groups.google.com) now offers access to more than 700 million messages dating back to 1981. This is by far the most complete collection of Usenet articles ever assembled and is a most fascinating first-hand historical account.

Listserv is similar to Usenet, but tends to operate more professionally. The listserv is a communication tool that offers its members the opportunity to post suggestions or questions to a large number of people at the same time. Questions or information that a user wishes to share to the listserv can be distributed to all members on that list. Each listserv decides upon predetermined topics and discussions and welcomes submissions from members. Submissions are then read to ascertain those that are acceptable.

Each listserv has two different addresses, the list address and listserv. The former is the address you use to submit a query or to share knowledge with the entire group. This is known as 'sending mail to the list'. The listserv address is the address that users send commands to, such as subscribing and unsubscribing.

Market research

The Internet provides the researcher with an array of quality information and some organizations have exploited the opportunity. CyberAtlas (cyberatlas.internet.com) and Forrester Research (www.forrester.com) are two high-profile organizations that provide useful information about the Internet.

CyberAtlas is a useful Web marketer's guide to online facts and produces readers with valuable statistics and Web marketing information, enabling them to understand their business environment and make more informed business decisions. CyberAtlas gathers online research from the best data resources to provide a complete review of the latest surveys and technologies available. Since its inception in 1996, CyberAtlas has amassed numerous awards from reputable Web sites. The site was acquired in August 1998 by internet.com. Forrester Research identifies and analyzes emerging trends in technology and their impact on business. It provides companies with rigorous research, practical ideas and objective guidance to help them thrive on technology change. Since its inception in 1983, it has also won numerous awards. In addition to written research and primary research data, Forrester clients also rely on its Events and Strategic Services, including advisory programmes.

The provision of secondary data enables organizations to acquire information to help them grow the business and find out valuable information about competitors and new markets.

For example, the UK government (www.ukonlineforbusiness.gov.uk) has a website that aims to help UK firms exploit the benefits of the Internet. Operating in partnership with industry, the voluntary sector, trades unions and consumer groups, the goal is to help make the UK one of the world's leading knowledge economies. UK online seeks to make the UK the best place in the world for doing business online. Therefore, a primary objective is to encourage businesses to migrate towards e-business. To help entrepreneurs to go online, the website is organized into two main sections, which offer business advice and business benefits.

Business advice is provided to show how and where to get help from a network of UK online business advisers. To enhance understanding of e-business, a range of free publications, e-business packs and briefings is available. This stimulates interest, while business benefits are highlighted through the inclusion of real-life examples drawn from comparable UK firms. In addition, more than 100 case studies, organized by business sector, can be used to provide to determine good practice.

Brand building

One of the foremost differences between B2B marketing and B2C marketing is that of branding. Attempting to reach 10 to 20 distributors is a much different proposition to reaching a few million consumers. Branding is an important issue in both B2B and B2C environments and costs significant sums of money. In the 2001 Interbrand (www.interbrand.com) survey of the world's most valuable brands, AOL (www.AOL.com) and Yahoo (www.Yahoo.com) were ranked 58th and 59th respectively. According to Interbrand calculations AOL has a brand value of $4,495m, which represents 2 per cent of the market capitalization of the company. Yahoo had a brand value of $4,378m, which represents 39 per cent of market capitalization. Interestingly, in the corresponding 2000 Interbrand survey, Yahoo reported a 258 per cent increase in brand value ($1,761m to $6,300m), while in the 2001 survey there was a decline by 31 per cent ($6,300m to $4,378m).

Organizations that already have an established brand have an advantage, as they may be able to participate in the market without giving up too much share (Cunningham, 2001).

Branding Issue	B2B	B2C
Influence consumers	Somewhat important	Very important
Influence business partners	Very important	Less important
Investor relations	Important	Important
Press relations	Very important in market segment	Important in demographic segment
Consistent image across all media	Important	Very important
(Source: Cunningham, 2001)		

Table 7.2 Branding issues and their importance to the firm

Established organizations will have to spend money on the brand transition, but they can use the Internet as a hybrid marketing vehicle tool, not as the primary distribution channel.

The cost of building the brand will tend to be greater in B2C firms, as the necessity to influence consumers is salient. Cunningham (2001) illustrates the key branding issues and their importance, which are shown in Table 7.2. Even when the firm gets an online presence, this is not the end of the story. Attention must be given to the three dimensions of profit, growth and control. Too much emphasis on growth without adequate management controls is a recipe for disaster. Firms can spend large chunks of their capital on managing their websites and on online advertising, but there are increased inherent risks in activities that they do not control. For example, these can include: online reviews and newsgroups that help formulate perception.

E-commerce

It is widely acknowledged that e-commerce entails more than simply creating a Web presence. Firms need to consider moving along the evolution path from an information focus to being market oriented with a primary aim to treat individual customers individually. Being **customer centric** means developing a customer experience that each customer values. E-commerce presents an excellent opportunity for organizations to get to know their customers – who they are and their buying patterns. Organizations need an integrated e-business strategy that supports customers from the moment they visit the website, through to fulfilment, support and promotion of new products and services.

Within organizations there is a need to develop behavioural and change management skills so that a cross-functional e-business team plays an effective role. Knowing the customer is crucial, so managers should use any opportunity to analyse, define, profile and update repositories of customer information. If the management team is able to develop and implement techniques that could measure true customer acquisition costs, focus on the most profitable customer, extend customer life spans, and identify and respond to behavioural changes, this would enhance shareholder value.

E-organization

Despite the turbulent stock markets, there are still significant Internet opportunities to gain a competitive advantage on the basis of creativity. However, as an organization embraces the Internet and the organization changes shape, managers must get themselves and employees used to working differently. E-business organizations need to have a broad range of competencies.

Chapter 6 focused on the importance of understanding the organization, using the seven e-organizational dimensions postulated by Neilson, Pasternack and Viscio (2000). The seven e-organizational dimensions of Organizational Structure, Leadership, People and Culture, Coherence, Knowledge, Alliances, and Governance lead to websites that have the following features:

- Significant percentage of revenue is generated over the Internet.
- Salient business processes are conducted online.
- The store is open 24/7 to a global audience.
- Organizational structure has changed from a traditional hierarchical to a centre-less structure.

Organizational flexibility and the ability to execute changes quickly are crucial to achieving competitive advantage.

FRAMEWORK FOR WEB MARKETING

The multi-layed nexus of various telecommunications and information technologies provides another direct marketing tool to the marketer. Figure 7.1 illustrates the diverse toolbox of **direct marketing** strategies, which enables the firm to reach the consumer and business markets. According to Joseph, Cook and Javalgi (2001) the Internet represents arguably the most versatile direct marketing tool for creating a borderless world (see Figure 7.2). Nevertheless, there is a multitude of Internet tools and technologies available to firms to market their products on the Internet. If firms wish to achieve their goals, then the decision about what Internet technologies to use, in what marketing function and for which type of product remains unanswered for many firms (Nour and Fadlalla, 2000).

Given the paucity of new conceptual frameworks for Web-based marketing strategies, research by Nour and Fadlalla (2000) is timely. The proposed classification model for virtual markets is based on the two principal categories of product type (goods and services) and delivery mode (terrestrial or digital).

The product type of goods or services is self explanatory, whereas the delivery mode relates to how the product is transferred to the buyer. This can take two forms. The first is terrestrial delivery, meaning that the product can be physically transmitted through such means as air, sea or ground transportation. The second, digital delivery, relates to transfer of a digitized product via the Internet. Overall, this provides the e-marketer with four classes of products:

- Pure (or soft) services – where the seller offers services to the consumer, without a transfer of physical goods.
- Hard services – buyers need to be physically present at the point where service is rendered.
- Digitized products – includes software and digital multimedia.
- Basic goods – tangible physical goods.

Using Kotler's (1989) four functions of marketing (i) promotion, (ii) selling, (iii) delivery and (iv) support, Nour and Fadlalla (2000) present a framework for Internet tool selection strategies to support marketing functions in specific virtual markets. Supporting the Nour and Fadlalla (2000) framework is a plethora of Web tools and technologies. These tools can be broadly classified as Web-based and non-Web-based. Internet technologies may also be classified as information search and retrieval, communications and modelling technologies.

Key Term...

Direct marketing
Relates to the advertisements of products and services directly to consumers by mail, telephone, magazine, Internet, radio or television

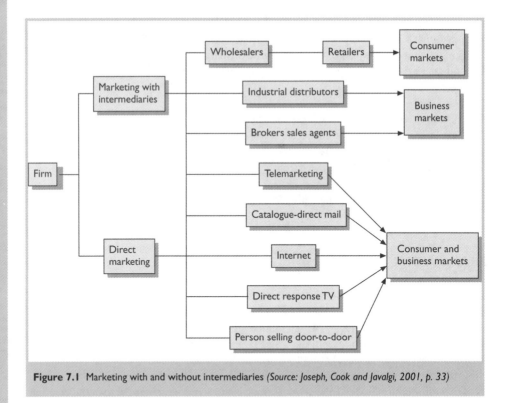

Figure 7.1 Marketing with and without intermediaries *(Source: Joseph, Cook and Javalgi, 2001, p. 33)*

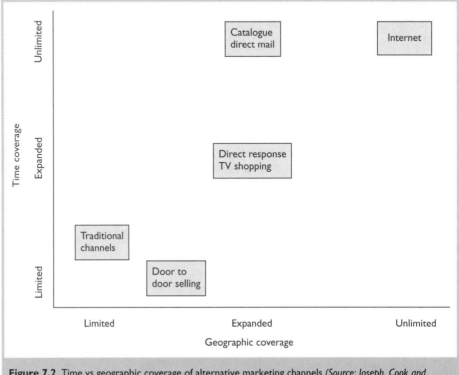

Figure 7.2 Time vs geographic coverage of alternative marketing channels *(Source: Joseph, Cook and Javalgi, 2001, p. 33)*

Web-based technologies for promotion strategies

Many Internet-based firms are using significant resources to acquire a new customers. If an e-tailer is selling high-ticket, high-margin items or if it can be sure of a steady stream of loyal customers, then customer acquisition costs are not a problem and make economic sense. However, in some instances, they are suicidal, as the average customer acquisition cost is higher than the average lifetime value of the customers.

Understanding how to make a consumer aware of the product and convince them to buy the product is something that must be continually addressed. Making consumers aware and ensuring that they make the correct buying decision can be managed to some extent by using a variety of techniques that can include advertising, publicity, demonstration and try-outs.

Web-based technologies for selling strategies

Although the need to sell online goes without saying, this is precisely the problem with many organizations. The supply chain starts with the sourcing of the product for sales, pricing, order acceptance and accepting payment. Hypertext links can be used to guide consumers through the product offering via the website. Alternatively, a search engine can be used to identify specific products quickly. HTML ordering forms can be used to capture ordering information.

Web-based technologies for delivery strategies

In spite of the fact that the promotion and delivery strategies are core activities, it is surprising how many organizations devote limited time and resources to understanding and designing delivery strategies. During the first wave of e-business, those products that could be digitized were ideally suited to be delivered through cyber space. Physical products could only be delivered through terrestrial means. Some services are not delivered terrestrially, but require the buyer to be physically present to receive the service, such as going to the dentist.

Web-based technologies for customer support strategies

Good service now means extending the value chain beyond the mere exchange of goods. Digitally enabled merchandising (DEM) and Electronic tele-services (ETS) can be enhanced by reducing the risk of ownership. To reduce this uncertainty, which can affect the purchasing decision, the seller could offer a warranty that guarantees the product to be free from defects. If any defects are found within the warranty period of time, the seller will fix or replace the item or even refund the price. Web-based support can utilize hypertext links and email to facilitate interaction between buyer and seller.

Intelligent agents and the search for market intelligence

The sheer magnitude of information available through the Internet, which at first can be a major strength, is at the same time one of its major weaknesses. The information available to the consumer is vast, with the information that is being sought probably available somewhere. Often, however, only parts of it can be retrieved, or sometimes nothing can be found at all. These inquiries for information are being confronted with information overkill. There are many different kinds of software agents, ranging from Interface agents to Retrieval agents. For example, Copernic Shopper Plus (www.copernic.com) enables automated searches and email notification. Consumers can automatically search for the product they require and will be notified by email when the product becomes available or reaches the target price.

WEB USABILITY

Jakob Nielsen coined the term '**Web usability**', which he describes as the degree to which websites have been designed with the needs of users in mind – as distinct from those of the designer or the site owner. Nielsen's (2000) main priority is the creation of fast down-loading pages. According to Nielsen, Web designers must bear in mind that 'speed must be the overriding design criterion', on the basis that people simply will not wait. Ten seconds would appear to be the average maximum. Web page size should be kept below 35 Kbytes, with the maxim 'Remove graphic; increase traffic. It's that simple'.

Page design

As a rule of thumb, the content on a Web page should account for 50 per cent to 80 per cent of a page's design. Navigation should be kept below 20 per cent of the space for destination pages. A Web page should be likened to a piece of real estate, with various parts of the screen carrying different values. Whitespace, that is, unused screen real estate is not necessarily useless. Too much content that is overly compact will not be easy on the eye. White space can be used as a border, instead of a line, as it will download faster.

Interestingly, Nielsen encourages well-annotated outbound links, on the basis that each pointer towards useful information adds quality to your site. Despite the strong temptation, it is no good attempting to link everybody to your home page. While you would naturally prefer every visitor to explore your site in full, it is better not to frustrate users who have been referred on the promise of something specific.

Content design

Researchers have shown that reading from computer screens is about 25 per cent slower than from paper. Neilsen, therefore, suggests three main guidelines for writing for the Web, which include:

- Be succinct – use no more than 50 per cent of the text that you would use for a print publication.
- Write for scannability – break text up into short paragraphs, subheadings and bulleted lists.
- Use hypertext – split up long information into multiple pages.

Overall, writing for the Web is about brevity, content chunking (short paragraphs) and accuracy on the basis that content is king. As Neilsen puts it, we should 'write for scannability'. Page titles are a source of micro content and need to be a pearl of clarity. Designers get 40 to 60 characters to explain the website, so unless the title is clear, users may never open it. The rapid development of technology will lessen the value of what Neilsen has to say about the use of audio, video, animation and even 3D effects.

Site design

According to Neilsen, site design is more challenging and also more important than page design. Neilsen argues extreme functionality over aesthetic form with a home page offering three features:

- Directory of the site's main content areas (navigation).
- Summary of the most important news or promotions.
- Search feature.

The most prominent feature on the home page should be the name of the company or the site. The most expensive piece of real estate on the screen is the top left-hand corner. The site

Principle	Action
1. Motivate	Design your site to meet specific user needs and goals. Use motivators to draw different user 'personae' into specific parts of your site
2. User task flow	Who are your users? What are their tasks and online environment? For a site to be usable, page flow must match workflow
3. Architecture – it's 80 per cent of usability	Build an efficient navigational structure. Remember – if they can't find it in three clicks, they're gone
4. Affordance means obvious	Make controls understandable. Avoid confusion between emblems, banners, and buttons
5. Replicate	Why reinvent the wheel? Use ergonomically designed templates for the most common 8–12 pages
6. Usability test along the way	Test early in design using low-fidelity prototypes. Don't wait until the end when it's too late
7. Know the technology limitations	Identify and optimize for target browsers and user hardware. Test HTML, JavaScript, etc. for compatibility
8. Know user tolerances	Users are impatient. Design for a 2–10 second maximum download. Reuse header graphics so they can load from cache. Avoid excessive scrolling
9. Multimedia – be discriminating	Good animation attracts attention to specific information, then stops. Too much movement distracts, slowing reading and comprehension
10. Use a stats package	Monitor traffic through your site. Which pages pique user interest? Which pages make users leave? Adjust your site accordingly
(Source: www.humanfactors.com/library/10tips.asp)	

Table 7.3 Ten usability principles to guide you through the Web design maze

name should be repeated on all pages, as not all users enter from the home page. Deep-linking enables other sites to point users to the exact spot on the screen that is of interest to them. Due to the number of web pages, users need to know: where they are; where they have been; and where they can go. Table 7.3 gives a suggested top ten usability principles.

CONTENT MANAGEMENT

Once the decision has been made to go online, the road to content management begins. One of the discerning facts about Web-based marketing is that while every company with a website has to become a publisher to some degree, few are equipped for the job (Harrington, 2001). If not refreshed, content gets out of date and gets clogged up with irrelevant material, which will mean that visitor numbers will fall. In addition, websites need to offer some form of personalization to consumers, so that different groups derive specific benefits from the content.

A content management system (CMS) is a system used to manage the content of a website. CMS have emerged as the standard method of dealing with complex authoring, management, updating and distribution problems associated with websites.

ILLUSTRATIVE EXAMPLE I

Toyota (GB) PLC relies on Documentum Enterprise Content Management solution as foundation for dealer system, website and showroom system, 21 February 2002
http://www.documentum.co.uk

SYSTEM REAPS RETURN ON INVESTMENT WITH SIGNIFICANT EFFICIENCY GAINS AND ACCELERATED TIME-TO-MARKET LONDON, UK

Documentum, the leading enterprise content management provider, today announced that Toyota (GB) PLC has launched an enterprise-wide Retail Asset Management System based on Documentum's ECM Platform. The system, which enables Toyota to provide accurate and up-to-date product information to dealers and customers throughout the United Kingdom, is already producing return on investment through significant efficiency gains and accelerated time-to-market.

Prior to implementing Documentum's enterprise content management system, Toyota (GB) PLC's computer systems automated the distribution of wholesale information to Toyota (GB) PLC's independent dealers – but not retail information. Toyota needed a system that could integrate all its disparate enterprise data and deliver to its employees, dealers and customers in an easily accessible and secure way.

E-business integrator Latitude360, a division of RWD Technologies (Nasdaq: RWDT), integrated Documentum's enterprise content management platform into Toyota (GB) PLC's key systems—developing a central information repository of business-critical databases containing model data, vehicle images and inventory, available accessories and dealership information. By deleting the need for manual updates and by eliminating data duplication, Toyota streamlined the sales process and increased customer satisfaction.

According to Andrew Singer, finance and systems director for Toyota (GB) PLC: 'By managing and manipulating content in a central repository, we are able to increase efficiency and accelerate time-to-market. Now, when we launch new vehicles and the associated promotions, we can make information instantly available on our web site—while simultaneously issuing confidential pricing and other valuable data to our dealers. With immediate access to information, images, editorial, customer profiles and inventory, we are confident we'll increase customer, employee and dealer satisfaction '

'Documentum, Latitude360 and Toyota worked together to ensure that Toyota maximised the benefits of their enterprise content management system,' said Matt Shanahan, VP International Operations, Documentum. 'By ensuring that employees, distributors, customers and partners have access to vehicle information according to user profiles, Toyota (GB) PLC is able increase efficiency and accelerate time-to-market.'

The CMS usually consists of two elements: the content management application (CMA) and the content delivery application (CDA). The CMA element allows the author, who may not know how to use HTML, to manage the creation, modification and removal of content from a website without needing the involvement of the webmaster. The CDA element uses and compiles the necessary information to update the website. Most CMS include Web-based publishing, format management, revision control, indexing, and search and retrieval. CMS systems at the top end of the market include: Broadvision (www.broadvision.com), Vignette (www.vignette.com) and Interwoven (www.interwoven.com).

Web-based publishing features allow the author to use a set of templates approved by the webmaster, as well as wizards and other tools to create/modify website content. Format management features allow documents, including legacy electronic documents and scanned hard-copy documents, to be formatted into HTML or **Portable Document Format** (PDF). Checks can be made for unauthorized changes by revision controls, which identify changes made by individuals. A useful feature of CMS is the ability to enable users to search for data using keywords, which the CMS system retrieves.

CMS systems can also be used for one-to-one marketing, where the organization can harmonize the content and advertising to specific user characteristics using information provided by the user or gathered previously by the site. For example, if you visit a search engine and search for 'roller skates', the advertising banners will advertise businesses that sell roller skates instead of businesses that sell book products.

However, as stated by Harrington (2001),

> 'The moral of the (CMS) story for organizations seems to be that CM is a pool that you shouldn't paddle in, unless you have a compelling, strategic reason for your dip. And if you do decide to take the plunge, be prepared to reach deeply into the corporate purse to fund your swim.'

LEVERAGING THE WEB FOR COMPETITIVE ADVANTAGE

In one of the first attempts to identify value drivers that impact the performance of Internet firms, Kotha, Rajgopal and Rindova (2001) postulated that reputation-building activities may be one of the key determinants of competitive success for Internet firms. Kotha *et al.* suggest that, in comparison with traditional markets, there is greater need to build reputation in an e-marketplace. Reputation building is made easier by the lower cost of information acquisition and greater information exchange among stakeholders, whereas factors such as lower entry barriers, competitive clutter and lower consumer awareness about existing products and services are likely to impede the process.

As suggested repeatedly throughout this book, acquiring new customers and increasing market share is one of the most important goals for any firm. In the era of the Internet and World Wide Web, researchers have sought to identify good practice in online marketing. The following sections highlight some of the pivotal areas.

After studying the topic of online marketing for more than seven years, Hoffman and Novak (2000) note the success of music retailer CDnow. They concluded that advertising strategies should link payment to advertising performance and not merely exposure. Also building numerous alliances with associate websites is both economically and effective.

CDnow is a powerful online music brand that was one of the first to develop a truly multifaceted, integrated customer acquisition strategy that reflects a sophisticated understanding of the economics of leveraging the web. The company's BuyWeb programme was the first application of what has come to be known as 'affiliate' or 'associate' marketing programmes. Customers are acquired via its Cosmic Music Network, which allows unsigned artists to put up a Web page at the CDnow site. In addition, the company uses radio, television and print advertising, online advertising, strategic partnerships, word of mouth, free links, and public relations. Interestingly, CDnow is seeing a drop in its pure CPM (cost per thousand people who would see an advertisement) buys, despite the sophistication of its

ILLUSTRATIVE EXAMPLE II
*Coast and Country Holidays, Pembrokeshire – http://www.opportunitywales.co.uk
Reproduced with permission from Opportunity Wales and eCommerce Innovation
Centre, Cardiff University*

THE BUSINESS

Liz Davies and Rachel Thomas founded Coast and Country Holidays (CCH) in 1990. The business specialises in letting holiday cottages in West and North Wales. In the summer of 1999 it was decided that the business should seriously consider the use of eCommerce and, in particular the Internet and a web site, as a way of promoting the business. With supporting help from Pembrokeshire Business Initiative (PBI), plans were made to evaluate this potential, with the development of their first web site and an overall budget of £5000.

USE OF E-COMMERCE

The web site was officially launched in February 2000, with the aim of replicating the quality and success of their paper brochure online. CCH are very much a people-orientated business, with most of the sales of cottage holidays being finalised over the 'phone. So how could the company offer a web site as an alternative to a traditional glossy brochure, yet somehow retain that human contact that was so important to the selling of holidays?

BENEFITS AND ISSUES

Developing a successful web site was not without problems, and finding a good Web designer who not only understood the needs of the company, but who would also keep to agreed dates and deliverables, was a major issue. The case study describes CCH's experience of eCommerce and illustrates the importance of Web marketing in achieving success.

In the first year of operation CCH has found the Internet to be a far more cost effective means of marketing than their traditional channels, and their target number of annual web site bookings was achieved within weeks of the launch. CCH have learnt much from their exposure to eCommerce and feel the following are the key issues that they would bring to the attention of anyone entering this arena for the first time:

- Carefully evaluate previous work of a Web developer, and their ability and willingness to provide ongoing support – talk to previous customers;
- All plans and contracts with a Web developer must be in writing before any work is commenced;
- Domain name ownership – make sure they are registered in your business name;
- Copyright issues of the developed web site;
- Web hosting – chose an ISP with large bandwidth and high availability rates.

"I would have never believed a year ago that I would become such a fan of the Internet"

The last year has seen a significant change in the way that CCH operates, due primarily to their use of their new web site. Their £5,000 experiment with a new marketing medium has turned out to be an unqualified success, with nearly £300,000 of online bookings in the first year. This has not been achieved without many sleepless nights and, at times, during the development phase, there were occasions when doubt existed as to whether it was all worth while.

Coast and Country Holidays can be found at www.welsh-cottages.co.uk.

marketing strategy. This trend is likely to affect firms that are overly Web based and high-lights the problem of trying to select the best marketing strategy (Hoffman and Novak, 2000).

The development of the Internet as a communication and transaction channel enables firms to make one-on-one marketing and relationship marketing a reality. However, according to Willcocks and Plant (2001) the B2C organization must address several pertinent questions:

- What do the Internet and its associated technologies mean for our business, our competitive strategy and our information-systems strategy?
- What former imperatives need to be considered to build a sustainable Internet business?
- How do we leverage the speed, access, connectivity and economy created by Web technologies to extend our business vision?
- How do we organize to execute our business-Internet strategy?

Willcocks and Plant identified the following characteristics of B2C e-business leading companies:

- Regard the Internet as a cornerstone of a network centric business era.
- Distinguish the role of information and technology .
- Competition, opportunities and customer expectations evolve rapidly.
- Learn quickly and have the capacity to shift focus.
- Inform e-business processes with critical business thinking.
- See the Web as part of a larger strategic investment in e-business.

THE INTERNET'S IMPACT ON MARKETING

In a special issue of the *Journal of Business Research* (Biswas and Krishnan, 2003), the articles published sought to collectively offer a rich set of insights for managerial practice and for further research related to Internet adoption and the success and failure of Internet businesses.

Biswas and Krishnan provide a useful roadmap for understanding the impact of the Internet on marketing. Their valuation creation model is built upon three paths.

- The Internet allows companies to create value through one-to-one marketing.
- The Internet allows cost-effective integration of electronic trading into a company's core business.
- The Internet allows sellers to learn more about their best customers, one customer at a time, and provide customised service.

Contributors to the special issue of the *Journal of Business Research* examined various aspects of value creation. The research can be segmented as either macro or micro perspectives.

Macro perspective
Organizational issue
Sharma and Sheth (2003) are of the opinion that organizations need to change from 'supplier perspective' to 'customer perspective'. Starting with the customer, organizations must identify those customer segments that are attractive, which may involve redesigning organizational structures and processes. This theme has been picked up by Grewar, Iyer and Levy

(2003), who stress the need to understand how various functional and organizational issues impact the integration of traditional bricks and mortar with the Internet.

Strategic alliances

In addition to dealing with the intraorganizational issues, firms need to deal with interorganizational issues (Chatterjee, 2003). According to Chatterjee strategic alliances will enhance the product/service offering, gaining channel access, gaining access to a partner's customer base and gaining access to technology and marketing services.

First mover advantages

Biswas (2003) asserts that consumers will experience higher switching costs due to higher perceived risks and information overload. Despite the links between first mover advantage and success being tenuous, this area remains ripe for future longitudinal research.

Privacy issues at the societal level

Langenderfer and Cook (2003) advocate quasi-public regulation at the federal level, as the increasing volume of detailed personal information has not kept pace with privacy regulation. It is suggested that, whatever the actual legal requirements, companies must undertake appropriate measures to protect data privacy in order to attract new online consumers.

Micro perspectives

Typologies of e-shoppers

Rohm and Swaminathan (2003) introduce a four-group typology of online grocery shoppers. The convenience shopper group is primarily attracted to the overall convenience of online shopping. The variety seeker group finds the variety of retail alternatives, product types and brands appealing. The balanced buyer group appears to be attracted to all the benefits of online shopping, but with less intensity on each dimension when compared with convenience and variety groups. The final group, namely the store-oriented shopper, is motivated by the desire for immediate possession of goods and social interaction.

Perception of risk

Bhatnagar and Ghose (2003) argue that consumers are more concerned with the downside risk than with gains. Security of sensitive information remains a problem for consumers who wish to transact online. Garbarino and Strahilevitz (2002) suggest that women perceive a higher level of risk in online purchasing than do men.

Heuristics used in the search process

Thakor, Borsuk-Shtevi and Kalamas (2003) argue that being included in a bookmark becomes important for Internet companies as consumers are overwhelmed by the amount of information they find on the Web. The use of bookmarks shortens the search process and therefore enhances visitors to a website. Greater understanding of the heuristics that guide online decision-making should be the focus of future research.

Web design

Rosen and Puriton (2003) state that Web designers should integrate minimalism, appeal, access, fast loading and distinctiveness into their websites in order to be more effective. Dailey (2003) finds that restrictive navigational cues act as barriers that threaten consumers' control over Web navigation, which, in turn, arouses psychological reactance and leads to negative consequences for the online marketer.

It is anticipated that future e-business related research will begin to explore some of the issues raised above and that the macro and micro perspectives will be contextualized, so that they can be implemented in a variety of e-business organizations.

SUMMARY

In Chapter 2 we explored the relationships between organizations and their customers and considered relationship marketing and customer relationship management. In this chapter we have reviewed the features of online marketing. A framework for Web marketing is used to illustrate the different options available in terms of product type and delivery mode. Web usability and content management are used to illustrate how to design and maintain effective websites.

Business enhancements

Now, with the size and popularity of the Internet, businesses of all sizes have access to reap the benefits of online activity. From a marketing perspective, marketing offline is different to marketing online. A business is faced with two types of enhancements: business (communication, market research and brand building) and revenue (e-commerce and e-organization).

Framework for Web marketing

The multi-layed nexus of various telecommunications and information technologies provides another direct marketing tool to the marketer. If firms wish to achieve their goals, then the decision about what Internet technologies to use, in what marketing function and for which type of product remains unanswered for many firms (Nour and Fadlalla, 2000). Given the paucity of new conceptual frameworks for Web-based marketing strategies, research by Nour and Fadlalla (2000) is timely.

Web usability

Jakob Nielsen coined the term ' Web usability', which he describes as the degree to which websites have been designed with the needs of users in mind – as distinct from those of the designer or the site owner. Nielsen's (2000) main priority is the creation of fast downloading pages. According to Nielsen, Web designers must bear in mind that 'speed must be the overriding design criterion', on the basis that people simply will not wait. Ten seconds would appear to be the average maximum. Web page size should be kept below 35 Kbytes, with the maxim 'Remove graphic; increase traffic. It's that simple'.

Content management

A content management system (CMS) is a system used to manage the content of a website. Most CMS include Web-based publishing, format management, revision control, indexing, and search and retrieval. CMS systems at the top end of the market include: Broadvision (www.broadvision.com), Vignette (www.vignette.com) and Interwoven (www.interwoven.com).

Leveraging the Web for competitive advantage

In one of the first attempts to identify value drivers that impact the performance of Internet firms, Kotha, Rajgopal and Rindova (2001) postulated that reputation building activities may be one of the key determinants of competitive success for Internet firms. Reputation building is made easier by the lower cost of information acquisition and greater information exchange among stakeholders, whereas factors such as lower entry barriers, competitive clutter and lower consumer awareness about existing products and services are likely to impede the process.

The Internet's impact on marketing

Biswas and Krishnan (2003) provide a useful roadmap for understanding the impact of the Internet on marketing through three dimensions. First, the Internet allows companies to create value through one-to-one marketing. Second, the Internet allows cost-effective integration of electronic trading into a company's core business. Third, the Internet allows sellers to learn more about their best customers, one customer at a time, and provide customized service.

DISCUSSION QUESTIONS

1. Summarize the reasons why communication is important on the Internet?

2. What do you believe makes the difference between successful and unsuccessful website?

3. From a marketing perspective what are the key factors of creating value online?

ASSESSMENT QUESTIONS

1. According to Nour and Fadlalla (2002) 'e-business has led to a rethink of conventional marketing practices and strategies'. Do you agree with this proposition? What evidence do you have to support your point of view?

2. With emphasis on branding, why is it important for the marketer to understand the difference between B2B and B2C marketing? Using any appropriate organization of your choice, you are required to illustrate your answer.

3. Find an example of a website that you feel demonstrates best practice Web usability as explained by Jakob Nielsen. You are required to state in your views the relative strengths of this website.

GROUP ASSIGNMENT QUESTIONS

1. One of the discerning facts about Web-based marketing is that while every company with a website has to become a publisher to some degree, few are equipped for the job (Harrington, 2001).

With emphasis on the role of content management systems, what can websites do to enhance the degree of personalization to consumers, so that different groups derived some benefits from the available content? You are required to illustrate your views with relevant examples.

2. What do you believe is the strategic significance of the Internet as a marketing tool? You may find the paper by Joseph, Cook and Javalgi (2001) useful during your deliberations.

3. The emergence of e-business has led to a rethink of conventional marketing practices and strategies (Nour and Fadlalla, 2000). What are the implications of this statement and what are your views about this proposition? You are required to illustrate your views with relevant examples.

MAIN CASE STUDY
Web smart companies, by Andy Reinhardt, Business Week e-biz, 1 October 2001

Tesco bets small – and wins big
Britain's top supermarket chain was slammed for its go-slow approach to selling goods over the Net. Now it's the world's largest online grocer

'But oh, ho, ho, who's got the last laugh now?' – Ira Gershwin, 1936

John Browett, CEO of British online grocer Tesco.com, isn't smug enough to amble around the company's headquarters singing the old Gershwin tune. But few would begrudge him if he did. Assailed by analysts during the peak of the dot-com boom for its go-slow approach to selling groceries over the Internet, Britain's No. 1 supermarket chain has watched one rival after another put up the white flag. Now, Tesco.com has assumed the mantle of the world's largest and most successful online grocer. 'We've been a bit lucky,' says Browett, 'but we've also been right.'

Tesco's big bet was to bet small. In 1996, when the Web was exploding and online groceries seemed like a brilliant idea, Tesco PLC dipped its toe ever-so-gently into the water, outfitting a single store in Osterley, England, to accept orders by phone, fax, and a crude Web site. The idea was to test whether customers would buy groceries without shopping in conventional supermarkets. Equally important, Tesco had to figure out whether it made more sense to pick those groceries off the shelves of its stores or build separate warehouses to fill online orders.

By March, 1998, the company had proved there was sufficient demand and that picking from stores worked. But it had to keep tweaking the process to get the economics right. It wasn't until September, 1999, that it rolled service out to 100 stores.

They get it
Now, Tesco.com is firing on all cylinders. It has expanded to 250 outlets – more than a third of the chain's 690 British stores – enabling it to deliver to 91 per cent of Britain's population. The business is on track to turn in revenues this year of more than $450 million and boasts a respectable net operating margin from groceries of around 5%, or more than $22 million, analysts estimate. Last year, the dot-com unit lost $13 million due to the cost of expanding into new businesses such as CDs and videos, but it was profitable on groceries. "They were the only company in the world to really get it," says retail analyst David V. McCarthy of Schroder Salomon Smith Barney.

What Tesco got was that selling groceries over the Net was going to be small potatoes for the foreseeable future. After all, the chain is expected to book sales this year of $30 billion, making its online operation a mere 1.5 per cent of revenues. So instead of spending a fortune to build distribution warehouses outfitted with fancy technology, Tesco chose a decidedly low-tech approach. Fewer than two dozen employees are needed to pull products off the shelves in each store and schlep them in vans to customers in the neighborhood. It's kind of like an electronic version of the 1950s delivery boy.

Today, Tesco.com handles more than 3.7 million orders per year – and half of its online customers weren't previous Tesco patrons. Now, the company is building on that foundation to expand into other businesses, such as baby products and wine by the case. "We've got a chance to become the leading 'last mile' delivery service in Britain, because we're taking it very incrementally," Browett says.

Out on a limb

That's a lesson that failed dot-coms likely wish they had learned. Many Net startups were undone by focusing so much energy on growth that they never knew whether their business models worked until they hit the wall. Says Browett, who at 37 could easily be mistaken for the head of a Web upstart: "You can't make a run for revenues and then work out the cost structure later." Despite that timeless logic, e-commerce gurus from McKinsey & Co. and Andersen Consulting (now Accenture Ltd.) questioned Tesco in 1999 for not building warehouses, prompting the company to recheck its math to make sure it wasn't heading down the wrong path. "We were clearly out on a limb when the hype was at its peak," Browett says.

Staying the course proved even sweeter for Tesco after the ignominious failure of Webvan Group Inc. The Foster City (Calif.) startup, one of the most richly funded in history, went bankrupt in July. It burned through $1.2 billion in two years trying to establish a purely Web-based grocer in the U.S. Webvan's strategy was vintage dot-com: It shot for the moon, aiming to build two dozen automated warehouses around the country, costing up to $35 million apiece, that were supposed to cut 40 per cent off the labor expense of handling groceries. Each was meant to serve a 60-mile radius encompassing millions of potential customers. But after building only three warehouses – in Oakland, Calif., Atlanta, and Chicago – the numbers got worse and worse.

Webvan's Waterloo: Customer demand wasn't high enough to operate the facilities at anywhere near their capacity, so fixed costs swamped revenues. "The first 10,000 customers were easy to find – San Franciscans sitting on the edge of their couches waiting for Web groceries," says analyst Ken Cassar of Internet researcher Jupiter Media Metrix Inc. "But the rest of the country isn't the same." He and other analysts figure Webvan lost $5 to $30 on an operating basis for every order it delivered. When you crank in depreciation, marketing, and other overhead, the loss jumps to a staggering $132 per order.

Growing competition

By contrast, Tesco's decision to pick groceries out of existing supermarkets kept startup costs low. The company spent just $58 million over four years to launch its online grocery operation, and has since laid out $29 million more to expand into nonfood items. The wisdom of that tortoise-vs.-hare approach has been validated by a host of other companies. "Now that the high-cost wacko Internet business model turns out to have been a disaster, Tesco's store-based picking is the direction everybody's going," says analyst Andrew P. Wolf of BB&T Capital Markets in Richmond, Va.

The prime example: In June, Safeway Inc., the No. 3 supermarket chain in the U.S., said that it would partner with Tesco to deliver groceries to online customers. The British chain is investing $22 million for a 35% stake in GroceryWorks, a money-losing Net startup half owned by Safeway. The companies already have shuttered three GroceryWorks warehouses in Texas. They plan to begin rolling out the Tesco.com system this fall or early next year in a handful of Safeway's 1,500 U.S. stores. "We liked Tesco's track record," says Safeway spokeswoman Debra Lambert. "They understand how to combine technology with bricks and mortar."

That's not to say there aren't drawbacks to Tesco's approach. Orders are automatically routed from a data-processing facility in Dundee, Scotland, to the nearest store, so customers are limited to buying only what's available there. If it happens to be one of Tesco's smaller outlets, they may have only 20,000 items to choose from, vs. 40,000 at larger stores. Analysts worry, too, that the Tesco.com model won't "scale up" when the business gets bigger. Although its fixed costs are low, Tesco.com has relatively high variable costs because more orders require more labor for picking and delivery. As a result, Tesco.com won't likely be able to reap the economies of scale that Webvan expected from its warehouses – meaning it may never become much more profitable than it is today.

On top of that, Tesco will face growing competition. Despite Browett's claim that the secret of Tesco's success lies in painstakingly tested and refined processes, some analysts think competitors can fairly easily copy or improve upon them. For instance, archrival J Sainsbury PLC, the *grande dame* of British supermarkets, is belatedly rolling out delivery service at 36 of its stores but will also operate warehouses near London and Manchester. "We think picking centers are the way to go in the long run," says Sainsbury spokesman Matt Samuel, "but we're using stores to get to market faster."

Hybrid approach

None of this worries Browett. He thinks Tesco.com can hit $4.35 billion in sales – about 10 times today's levels – before running out of headroom in its stores. The biggest concern: Aisles could get clogged with pickers, interfering with everyday shoppers. But long before reaching that point, Browett says, Tesco.com likely will embrace a hybrid approach, using warehouses in dense regions and store-picking for rural customers. As for selection, he says, even Tesco's smallest markets can offer more items than Webvan's warehouses did because human pickers can grab a single jar of capers or sate sauce from a shelf, while Webvan stocked goods by the palette, limiting each warehouse to about 15,000 products.

What really riles Browett, though, is the notion that rivals will have an easy time catching up. "This looks simple on the surface, but the detail underlying it has turned out to be very, very hard," he says. That's where Tesco's by-the-numbers management has proven to be an invaluable asset. Founded in the 1920s by immigrant businessman Jack Cohen, for decades the company played scrappy second fiddle to Sainsbury's. The turning point came seven years ago, when Tesco marketing execs won an internal power struggle with the traditionally dominant purchasing managers. That resulted in the elevation of then-marketing head Terry Leahy to his current role as CEO of Tesco PLC.

From that point, says Richard Hyman, a principal at British retail consultancy Verdict Research Ltd., Tesco has obsessively focused on satisfying customer demand. By the late 1990s, it surged past Sainsbury's in sales and market share, despite its less upscale image. "We think Tesco is the best retailer in Britain, period," Hyman says. In recent years, it has expanded into Central Europe and Asia, where it now gets 12.5 per cent of sales, and has opened catalog and financial-services units.

Slow start

But the dot-com operation may be Tesco's most unlikely triumph. Launched as a skunkworks project with six mid-level managers reporting directly to Leahy, Tesco.com got off to an inauspicious start. For two-and-a-half years – an eternity in Internet time – the unit's managers tinkered with the formula. 'We went down some blind alleys and back,' admits Tesco.com Chief Operating Officer Carolyn Bradley.

After rejecting phone and fax orders as too expensive and error-prone, Tesco settled three years ago on a system that lets customers place orders only over the Web. But the process of picking products off the shelf was punishingly inefficient. In the supermarket business, where margins are thinner than a slice of prosciutto, a few pennies per item can make the difference between profit and loss. And the one thing Tesco wasn't willing to do, Bradley says, was to lose money on its dot-com operation.

When the company retrenched in 1998, it came up with a nifty solution. Rather than having pickers traverse the entire store filling orders for individual customers, each supermarket is divided into six zones – groceries, produce, bakery, chilled foods, frozen foods, and "secure" products such as liquor and cigarettes. Each picker, outfitted with a rolling cart, scours a single zone retrieving products for six customers at a time. To save valuable seconds and improve accuracy, each item is scanned at the moment it's picked. Then, customer shipments are assembled in the back room and stacked in vans for delivery. Tesco.com typically fills two to three waves of orders per day, which allows customers to buy as late as noon and receive a delivery by 10 that night.

Quick picks

It's not just the process but also judicious use of technology that lets Tesco.com keep expenses to a minimum. Each picking cart, for instance, is topped with a wireless touch-pad computer that plans the optimal route through the store and tells pickers what to grab, one item at a time. That lets them average just 30 seconds per item, so a typical order of 64 items can be filled in 32 minutes, at a cost of about $8.50, including labor and depreciation, say analysts. Despite Tesco's efficiencies, that's still pretty steep – some 7% of the average $123 order.

The company makes up the difference in several ways. First, it saves about 3 per cent of the order value by not using checkout clerks, Jupiter figures. The real saving grace is that online orders tend to have higher gross margins – more than 30%, vs. Tesco's typical 25 per cent, Schroder Salomon Smith Barney analysis shows. That's because online shoppers are more affluent and buy more profitable products, such as organic vegetables, quality meats, and private-label packaged goods. "Our success is dependent on the fact that Tesco.com's margins tend to be higher," concedes Marketing Vice-President Tim Mason, though the company wouldn't provide figures or comment on analyst estimates.

There's another surprising factor that has spelled the difference between success and failure for Tesco. When the company rolled out Web shopping, it bucked conventional wisdom and imposed a £5 ($7.25) delivery fee per order, an amount it figured the market could bear. By contrast, Webvan offered free delivery for orders over $50, which ended up costing it millions in unrecovered expenses. Tesco.com insists customers are willing to pay for service – and the quadrupling of its orders over the past year seems to bear that out.

Customer Krista Levey, 27, an executive assistant at Arthur Andersen who buys from Tesco.com about once a month, says the fee 'is nothing' compared to the convenience of not having to lug home cases of bottled water on the London Underground.

Delivering the goods

Charging for delivery proved to be a masterstroke. First, it largely covers the cost of the vans and drivers who blanket the country. Tesco.com takes in about $27 million per year from the fees, close to the estimated $34 million cost of deliveries, figures Booz, Allen & Hamilton Inc. analyst Timothy Laseter. Imposing a fee also boosts the likelihood that customers will be at home during the two-hour window for their deliveries, since they have to pay again for redelivery. That's a big win for Tesco, given that returning merchandise to the store and restocking it could savage margins.

Even more important, the delivery fee has helped raise the typical order size because customers want to get their money's worth. So the average purchase from Tesco.com is three times a typical $35 supermarket transaction, a vital contributor to the online operation's solid gross margins. Eliminating the fee in an effort to stoke demand "would take away the incentive to spend up," says Schroder's McCarthy. And indeed, Tesco.com has no interest in boosting sales if the result is a loss on operations.

Instant legitimacy

Truth be told, Tesco.com also enjoys advantages Webvan never could have recreated even with another $1 billion in funding. By being a part of the Tesco empire, it can piggyback on the parent company's advertising, branding, and customer database. As one of the best-known and most trusted names in Britain, Tesco confers instant legitimacy on its dot-com unit. Plus, the online operation gets free ads in Tesco's quarterly mailing to its 10 million affinity-card holders and has linked its Web site to store databases so customers can easily reorder products they've previously purchased online or in a supermarket. On top of that, having pickers in Tesco stores provides constant publicity for the Web service – a benefit Webvan could never enjoy because it had no retail presence.

Tangible and intangible advantages such as these have prompted some analysts to question whether Tesco.com would turn a profit if it were a stand-alone business. ABN Amro's Mark Wasilewski, for one, thinks the parent may not be charging its dot-com unit enough in-store costs – depreciation, utilities, marketing, and so on – as a way of making Tesco.com's books look better. Browett dismisses the charge. "There's no point in fooling yourself," he says. Every unit, whether Tesco's financial-services arm or its dot-com operation, has to carry its own weight, he insists.

Besides, he adds, the criticism entirely misses the point: Tesco isn't trying to create a stand-alone business. Tesco.com is merely an additional sales channel that lets the company boost revenues and push more products through its system. As long as it's not leaking red ink, it's a net gain.

Next stop, Korea

So what's next for Tesco.com? Analysts are confident it will keep expanding its business in Britain. By 2004, predicts Wasilewski, it will hit $2.2 billion in revenues – still just 7.5 per cent of Tesco's total – and generate net profits of $181 million. Tesco also has announced the first international expansion of its dot-com business, other than the Safeway deal: By the first quarter of 2002, it aims to launch online shopping in South Korea, where it operates seven supermarkets, with 11 more on the way. Tesco chose South Korea because it has the highest residential penetration of broadband Net connections in the world, offering fertile opportunity for online shopping.

Meanwhile, at home, Tesco.com is rolling out new services such as its baby center and wine club. These offer not just commerce but also chat areas and simple content – information about, say, infant development or top French vintages. With innovations such as these, Browett may soon start singing the old Gershwin song out loud.

CASE QUESTIONS

Question 1 What were the key issues in Tesco.com assuming the mantle of the world's largest and most successful online grocer? How did this contrast with Webvan Group's Inc. business model?

Question 2 What strategies have Tesco.com utilized to maintain its margins in a sector where margins are notoriously low?

Question 3 Do you feel that Tesco.com business model is sustainable? What are the opportunities available to Tesco.com and how will competitors respond?

MINI CASE STUDY I

Is Amazon out of it depth?, by Robert D. Hof and Diane Brady, Business Week e-biz, 6 August 2001

The online emporium has broadened its wares from books to items like blenders and lawn furniture. The risk: brand dilution

Bill Fowler is well aware of Amazon.com's key dilemma. As the Web site adds product offerings, such as outdoor grills and camcorders, to its original books business, the longtime Amazon.com customer wonders if it's going too far afield. 'They're trying too hard to become the Wal-Mart of the Internet,' says Fowler, an advertising-agency art director in Huntsville, Ala. 'I don't think people want that.'

Or do they? Despite his reservations, Fowler has bought merchandise ranging from a digital camera to toys from the e-tailer. And as Amazon prepares to add even more products, such as personal computers, he figures he'll go along: 'Sooner or later, I'll be buying all kinds of things at Amazon.'

While Amazon hopes its more than 30 million customers will follow suit, the eventual outcome remains far from certain for the company that once billed itself as 'Earth's Biggest Bookstore.' 'Amazon has a brand image as a purveyor of books and CDs,' says David Schehr, a research director at market watcher Gartner Group Inc. Yet the pioneering e-tailer, under intense pressure to make its huge investments pay off, is rapidly expanding into everything from toys to tableware as it attempts to achieve a promised operating profit by the year end.

Virgin territory

The problem: The expanding range of goods may confuse both longtime customers and new ones – something that might potentially dilute its brand, which still ranks above those of Shell, Heineken, and Federal Express. 'If you want to be everything for everybody, it's hard to build a brand like that,' says Jan Tindemann, global director for brand valuation at the consultancy Interbrand. That's just one reason the value of Amazon's brand fell 31 per cent to $3.1 billion this year, after more than tripling in 2000 to $4.5 billion, according to Interbrand. While there is ample precedent – from General Electric to Virgin – for a brand being stretched into a broad range of categories, Amazon's expansion has worked to make its business model less certain because the new products on which its growth depends carry lower profit margins, according to Interbrand's analysis.

Not surprisingly, Amazon.com Chief Executive Jeffrey P. Bezos sees his company's brand doing 'better than ever.' Bezos' goal is for Amazon to represent more than limitless selection – he also wants it to provide customers with a focused, satisfying, and personalized way to shop. Says Bezos: 'We've created what we think is recognized as the best shopping experience online.' His acknowledged model: Virgin, whose brand successfully encompasses everything from airlines to soft drinks.

Bezos' expansive goal isn't completely wishful thinking. Amazon has sold more than $500 million worth of electronics, kitchen gear, and tools in the past year. More recently, by forming alliances with bricks-and-mortar retailers like Toys 'R' Us, it has managed to add products at minimal cost.

The primary focus

But investors aren't yet convinced. Over July, 2001, Amazon fluctuated from as low as $11 to around $17 – way below its peak of $106 in December, 1999. That makes maintaining its brand an even more critical goal than it is for other technology companies: By Interbrand's reckoning, Amazon's brand equity represents much more of the company's overall value than at many other technology companies – more than half its $6 billion market capitalization. By contrast, AOL's brand is relatively less important, says Tindemann, because it has a more stable revenue base of subscriptions and can reach those subscribers directly.

Of course, Bezos doesn't have to be told that. More than anyone, he realizes that time is tight for expanding the reach of Amazon's brand. 'Brands are like quick-drying cement,' he says. And Amazon's, while impressive in its value, is rapidly setting.

CASE QUESTIONS

Question 1 Why has Amazon.com had to broaden its product range?

Question 2 Do you feel that the strategy of providing customers with a focused satisfying and personalized way to shop will dilute the Amazon brand? In your opinion how will this affect shareholder value?

MINI CASE STUDY II
WSJ.com completes web site overhaul, by Julia King, Computerworld, www.computerworld.com, 8 February 2002

While other have companies cut back sharply on their Web site spending, *The Wall Street Journal* has just completed a two-year, $28 million overhaul of its WSJ.com site.
The revamped WSJ.com relies heavily on personalization technology to boost advertising revenue and expand paid reader services.

A key goal of the rebuilt site, which was launched two weeks ago, is to attract higher-value, repeat customers by letting them more easily customize their home pages with columns, stock quotes and other regular WSJ.com features.

Studies by Web-based market researcher Fulcrum Analytics (formerly Cyber Dialogue Inc.) in New York and others show that customers are more apt to frequently visit Web sites they can customize. Users who personalize such sites also more frequently subscribe to paid sites, use online bill payment services and promote products via e-mail to their friends, all of which make them an advertiser's dream.

'If every person looks at one more page – even in a bad advertising climate – the number of pages you deliver grows pretty quickly, and since you charge advertisers by ad impression, you increase your revenue pretty quickly,' said Neil Budde, *WSJ.com*'s publisher. 'You don't have to move the gauge too far or change the percentages too much before getting a substantial return on investment.'

Budde wouldn't disclose *WSJ.com*'s target ROI or payback period for the Web project. Currently, the site has 626,000 subscribers who pay $59 per year for the online service.

Rebuilding *WSJ.com* entailed switching out a patchwork of homegrown systems that had been cobbled together during the past six years. They were replaced by Austin,

Texas-based Vignette Corp.'s content management and publishing software, which is powered by IBM Web servers running Big Blue's proprietary version of Apache, said Ken Ficara, director of product operations and a project manager at *WSJ.com*.

Simplicity was key to designing the new Web site's personalization capabilities, Ficara said.

'In focus groups, we found out that the easier we made things, the more apt people were to use them,' he said. 'But it's the *Journal*, so we had felt like we had to do things as sophisticated as possible.'

Now subscribers personalize content with the click of a single button on the *WSJ.com* home page. Before, they had to go to a separate setup center, where Boolean search engines and other complex tools could be found.

That simplicity is the value customers receive in exchange for providing personal data to *WSJ.com*, said Kevin Mabley, an analyst at Fulcrum Analytics.

'From data mining and modeling work, we know that a customer who personalizes a Web site is a higher-value customer, but it works only as long as there is a value exchange. At *WSJ.com*, you type in stock [symbols], and you get the stock quotes you're interested in,' Mabley said.

'We see a lot of companies get that wrong,' he added. 'They ask for a lot of wrong information, like household statistics, that are not related to the user's experience. It becomes a Trojan horse for other marketing methods.'

Budde said that because the Vignette publishing system is database-driven, WSJ.com can reuse and repackage content in the database to quickly and cheaply spin off additional revenue-generating products and services, such as customized newsletters.

CASE QUESTIONS

Question 1 Why did WSJ.com rebuild its website? Do you feel that the $28 million overhaul will be money well spent?

Question 2 'If every person looks at one more page – even in a bad advertising climate – the number of pages you deliver grows pretty quickly, and since you charge advertisers by ad impression, you increase your revenue pretty quickly,' said Neil Budde, *WSJ.com*'s publisher. Do you agree with this assertion?

REFERENCES

Aufreiter, N., P.-Y.Ouillet and M.-K. Scott (2001) Marketing Rules, *Harvard Business Review*, vol. 79, no. 2, pp. 30–31.

Bhatnagar, A. and S. Ghose, (2003) A latent class segmentation analysis of e-shoppers, *Journal of Business Research*, forthcoming.

Biswas, D. (2003) Economics of information in the web economy: towards a new theory, *Journal of Business Research*, forthcoming.

Biswas, A. and R. Krishnan (2003) The Internet's impact on marketing introduction to the JBR special issue on 'marketing on the web – behavioural, strategy and practices and public policy', *Journal of Business Research*, forthcoming.

Chatterjee, P. (2003) Interfirm alliances in online retailing, *Journal of Business Research*, forthcoming.

Cunningham, M.J. (2001) B2B: *How to Build a profitable E-commerce Strategy*, FT.Com, Pearson Education Limited, London.

Dailey, L. (2003) Navigational web atmospherics, exploring the influence of restrictive navigation cues, *Journal of Business Research*, forthcoming.

Garbarino, E. and M. Strahilevitz, (2003) Gender differences in the perceived risk of buying online and the effects of receiving a site recommendation from a friend, *Journal of Business Research*, forthcoming.

Grewal, D., R.G. Iyer and M. Levy (2003) Internet retailing enablers, limiters, and market consequences, *Journal of Business Research*, forthcoming.

Harrington, A. (2001) The road to content management, *Management Consultancy*, March, pp. 9–12.

Hoffman, D.L. and T.P. Novak (2000) How to acquire customers on the web, *Harvard Business Review*, vol. 78, no. 3, pp. 179–188.

Joseph, W.B., R.W. Cook and R.G. Javalgi (2001) Marketing of the web: how executives feel, what businesses do, *Business Horizon*, vol. 44, no. 4, July–August, pp. 32–40.

Kotler, P. (1984) *Marketing Management: Analysis, Planning and Control*, 5th edn, Prentice-Hall, Englewood Clifs, NJ.

Kotha, S., S. Rajgopal and V. Rindova (2001) Reputation building and performance: An empirical analysis of the top-50 pure Internet firms, *European Management Journal*, vol. 19, no. 6, pp. 571–586.

Langenderfer, and J. D.L. Cook (2003) Oh, what a tangled web we weave: the state of privacy protection in the information economy and recommendations for governance, *Journal of Business Research*, forthcoming.

Neilsen, J. (2000) *Designing Web Usability*, New Riders Publishing, Indianapolis, IN.

Neilson, G.L., B.A. Pasternack and A.J. Viscio (2000) Up the (E)organization! A seven-dimensional model for the centerless enterprise, *Strategy and Business*, Booz Allen & Hamilton, First Quarter.

Nour, M.A. and A. Fadlalla (2000) A framework for web marketing strategies, *Information Systems Management*, Spring, pp. 41–50.

Rohm, A.J. and V. Swaminathan (2003) A typology of online shoppers based on shopping motivators, *Journal of Business Research*, forthcoming.

Rosen, D.E . and E. Puritan (2003) Website design: viewing the web as a cognitive landscape, *Journal of Business Research*, forthcoming.

Sharma, A. and J.N. Sheth (2003) Web-based marketing: the coming revolution in marketing thought and strategy, *Journal of Business Research*, forthcoming.

Thakor, M.V., W. Borsuk-Shtevi and E. Kalamas (2003) Hotlists and web browsing behaviour – an empirical investigation, *Journal of Business Research*, forthcoming

Willcocks, L.P. and R. Plant (2001) Pathways to e-business leadership: getting from bricks to clicks, *MIT Sloan Management Review*, Spring, pp. 50–59.

Wilson, S.G. and I. Abel (2002) So you want to get involved in e-commerce, *Industrial Marketing Management*, vol. 31, pp. 85–94.

CHAPTER 8

FINANCIAL APPRAISAL OF E-BUSINESS ORGANIZATIONS

By Paul Phillips and Alastair Day

LEARNING OUTCOMES

When you have read and worked through this chapter, you will be able to:

■ **Understand the complexity of valuing e-business companies**

■ **Understand how to apply a range of financial techniques to value dot.coms**

■ **Appreciate some of the cash-based and newer financial valuation techniques**

■ **Appreciate the psychological climate that makes it possible for investors to purchase Internet stocks**

INTRODUCTION

The explosive growth of the Internet and associated e-businesses in the last decade has created a wave of 'new economy' companies, which have sought to capitalize on the opportunities the Internet offers for managing information processes and opening up new markets. Nevertheless, the meteoric rise of the dot.coms in 1998 to 2000 has been followed by a dramatic fall in share values and a realignment of opinion about the long-term prospects for the sector.

The rise and fall of the sector brings into question 'traditional' methods of valuing companies when applied to a volatile sector of business. There is no doubt that the Internet has had a profound effect on new and old business. However, many companies were brought to the market at an early stage in their development and proceeded to gain valuations in excess of traditional companies. Alternatively, companies were purchased that possessed little in the way of revenue. For example, Excite@Home purchased BlueMountain.com for $780m in 1999 without revenues or profits. The major component was 9.2 million monthly visitors to the site and therefore the 'value' lay in prospects for the future.

Some commentators have spoken of a new bubble (Perkins and Perkins, 1999), where sales and earnings growth rates implied by 1999 prices were 'unparalleled in financial history'. This is on a par with the South Sea Bubble in the UK in 1720 or Tulipmania in Holland between 1633 and 1637. Recent events have shown such stocks to be overvalued as the price of **NASDAQ** stocks in the US or **Techmark** in the UK have fallen dramatically and private investors have withdrawn from the market.

In the light of the above, the purpose in this chapter is to review different valuation techniques to provide a comparison of different methods and to discuss the advantages and disadvantages of different methods with reference to two e-business companies.

Key Term...

NASDAQ (www.nasdaq.com)
The acronym original stood for National Association of Securities Dealers Automated Quotations. NASDAQ has quickly matured far beyond its original quote-service roots, evolving into what it is today – a major world stock market

Key Term...

Techmark UK (www.londonstock exchange.com/tech mark/)
This is an international market for innovative technology companies and has established itself as a leading global market for shares in businesses at the cutting edge of technological innovation

---

ILLUSTRATIVE EXAMPLE I
AOL Time Warner posts £54bn loss, by David Teather, The Guardian, 25 April 2002

AOL Time Warner, the largest media group in the world, yesterday warned that core earnings this year would be lower than previous forecasts as it reported losses of $54.2bn (£37bn) for the first quarter, the largest in corporate history.

The lower guidance followed a downward revision in January on revenues for 2002. The company is blaming continued weakness in the advertising market. Earnings in the coming year would be between 5% and 9% instead of the 8% to 12% previously forecast.

The unprecedented loss, which had been flagged earlier this year, was due to a massive $54bn write down in the value of Time Warner since America Online acquired the business in January 2000. The deal was struck at the peak of the dotcom bubble.

AOL Time Warner businesses include film making, CNN, Madonna's record label and the British magazines operation IPC.

Shares in the group have been under pressure in the past 12 months, largely because of investor concerns over stalling advertising and subscriber growth at the core AOL internet business. The shares have fallen by 40% since January.

The figures included a strong performance in the movies business, which scored huge worldwide hits with the Lord of the Rings and Harry Potter films. The Time Warner cable division also put in a robust performance but AOL and the music business proved a drag on earnings.

'Online advertising is a disappointment,' said Dick Parsons, who succeeds Gerald Levin as chief executive next month. He said the company expects AOL online advertising sales to be between $1.8bn and $2.2bn this year, down from $2.7bn in 2001.

The AOL internet business recorded core earnings of $433m in the first quarter, down from $507m last time.

'Overall, except for online advertising, the performance of our businesses remains at least as strong as we expected when we provided out earlier outlook and we anticipate that they will collectively drive growth this year,' Mr Parsons. 'The weakness of the internet advertising business is still a challenge however and we have taken decisive steps to address it.'

The group's chief operating officer, Bob Pittman, was dispatched to run the ailing AOL internet business two weeks ago.

Revenues at group level rose by 4% to $9.8bn over the same period in 2001, slightly higher than analysts had anticipated. Within that number, advertising fell by 13%.

Valuing companies is not an exact science and different individuals and organizations have an array of ideas about the value of assets or growth prospects. This is more pronounced in the case of new and untested businesses. Companies are worth whatever investors are prepared to pay. Valuations in e-business vary for different purposes as with traditional companies, for example:

- Annual report where the accounting value is reported to stakeholders
- Take-over and acquisition where the value normally includes a premium for control
- **Initial public offering**
- Merger with another concern in the same sector
- Trade sale to a third party

- Bankruptcy and liquidation where the business is not considered a 'going concern'

This chapter reviews the application of valuation methodologies to assigning a value to e-business companies. E-business companies include a wide range of organizations. However, they display these common characteristics:

- They gain a significant amount of their revenues through the Internet.
- Rapid growth using investor funds to fuel product development, brand creation and advertising.
- Low fixed-assets requirement.
- Preponderance of knowledge and process as key value drivers.

There are a number of phases in development of an online business and its ability to successfully compete with existing organizations. To be successful, an e-business organization must offer real advantages against traditional players and integrate all operations as in the last phase below. The phases are:

- *Presence* – static information on a website, with little ability for any interaction beyond e-mail or company background.
- *Business* – the company is 'e-enabled' when it starts to conduct business electronically. Customers can browse its website and place orders, but there is not yet a true integration of customers, suppliers and partners.
- *Integrated online business* – a company has effectively integrated the customer-facing front-end of its website with back-end systems linked to essential suppliers and third parties.
- *Integrated e-business* – seamless integration of partners, suppliers and customers into its online operations. The company concentrates on core competencies and outsources all non-essential e-business functions, from manufacturing to logistics.

This chapter on valuing e-business companies is divided into the following sections:

- Background information on the two example companies, lastminute.com and QXL ricardo plc
- Traditional methods:
  - *Accounting value* – the shareholders fund
  - *Adjusted accounting value* – accounting value with adjustments for undervalued or overvalued assets
  - *Dividends* – the value of the dividends over time
  - *Market pricing* – stock market methods using share prices and earnings per share
- Alternative methods such as free cash flow, options, subscriber levels, traffic conversion or composite techniques
- Psychological factors in valuation
- Conclusions

The next section introduces the two example companies and illustrates important financial information.

BACKGROUND TO LASTMINUTE.COM AND QXL RICARDO PLC

Lastminute.com

Lastminute.com (LM) is an Internet business that provides Web-based shopping opportunities of perishable goods and, as its name suggests, acts as an online clearinghouse. The original UK web site was launched in October 1998 and its French, German and Swedish services were launched in the last quarter of 1999.

LM does not take inventory risk on the products that it offers but instead charges a commission to suppliers for allowing them to use its marketing channel. Its relationships include organizations such as British Airways, British Midland, Virgin Atlantic, Bass, Starwood, Apollo SFX, English National Ballet, The Royal Albert Hall, Conran Restaurants and One for the Road. In order to offer its service across non-PC-based Internet platforms, LM also has relationships with providers such as Cable and Wireless Communications, Telewest, BT Cellnet, Orange, AvantGo and Psion.

In August 2000, LM acquired the online travel company in France, Degriftour, for £27m in cash and £32m in shares. This has added 250 000 French customers to the group and has increased pro forma revenues to £64m. In June 2000, LM had 2.1m registered subscribers across its own European sites and net cash balances (before the acquisition of Degriftour) of £117m.

In December 2000, LM announced its full year result to September. Registered subscribers were 2.8m, 312 000 items had been sold, revenues for the year were £3.7m and operating losses before goodwill and exceptional items were £42.9m. The company had net cash of £104m at the period end, before paying for the acquisition of Degriftour.

By the quarter ending December 2000, total transaction value had risen to £20.2m, and registered users to 2.9m. Net cash at December was £71m and this was deemed by directors to be sufficient to enable the company to reach full profitability.

| lastminute.com | | Units £'000 |
Item £'000	Sep–99	Sep–00
Sales	195.0	3,740.0
Cost of Goods Sold	(18.0)	(401.0)
Gross Margin	177.0	3,339.0
Depreciation Manufacturer	–	–
Amortization/Other	–	–
Sales, General & Administration Overheads	(4 744.0)	(42 823.0)
Net Operating Profit (NOP)	(4 567.0)	(39 484.0)
Interest Expense	(1.0)	(41.0)
Interest Income	68.0	3 770.0
Other Financial Income	(40.0)	–
Profit after Financial Items	(4 540.0)	(35 748.0)
Exceptional Expense–	0.0	
Profit before Tax	(4 540.0)	(35 748.0)
Tax	–	–
Net Profit after Tax (NPAT)	(4 540.0)	(35 748.0)
Minority Interest	–	–
Dividends	–	–
Retained Profit for the Year	(4 540.0)	(35 748.0)

Table 8.1 lastminute.com income statement

lastminute.com Assets £'000	Sep-99	Units £'000 Sep-00
Cash and Deposits	4319.0	103688.0
Marketable Securities	–	–
Trade Receivables (Debtors)	743.0	10543.0
Inventory	1.0	52.0
Sundry Current Assets	–	–
Current Assets	5063.0	114283.0
Land and Buildings	–	
Plant and Machinery	403.0	13972.0
Depreciation	–	–
Net Property, Plant and Equipment	403.0	13972.0
Other Investments	–	(39.0)
Intangibles/Goodwill	–	58636.0
Non Current and Fixed Assets	403.0	72569.0
Total Assets	5466.0	186852.0

Liabilities £'000	Sep-99	Sep-00
Short Term Bank Loans	70.0	–
Trade Creditors (Receivables)	852.0	10250.0
Other Creditors	1196.0	2119.0
Other Current Liabilities	171.0	25932.0
Current Liabilities	2289.0.	38301.0
Long Term Bank Loans	–	6031.0
Long Term Liabilities	–	6031.0
Tax/Deferred Taxation/Provisions	614.0	1410.0
Long Term Liabilities and Provisions	614.0	7441.0
Ordinary Shares (Common Stock)	3.0	114625.0
Profit and Loss and Other Reserves	2560.0	26485.0
Shareholders' Funds	2563.0	141110.0
Total Liabilities and Equity	5466.0	186852.0

Table 8.2 lastminute.com balance sheet

The income statement (Table 8.1) shows a high rate of growth matched by a ten-fold increase in administrative expenses. The interest income is derived from the remaining deposits of cash from the initial public offering.

The balance sheet (Table 8.2) reveals little in the way of borrowings: the liabilities relate to deferred consideration on the acquisition of Degriftour and this is matched by an intangible asset as goodwill. The largest investment is in IT, communications equipment and fixtures to enable the high growth rate and build the customer base. With the increase in sales, debtors have risen from £0.7m to £10.5m.

The reserves of £26m are made up of a merger and other reserves of £66m and retained earnings of minus £40m.

lastminute.com Item £'000	Sep-99	Units £'000 Sep-00
Net Operating Profit (NOP)	(4 567.0)	(39 484.0)
Depreciation/Amortization	–	–
Earnings before Interest, Tax, Depreciation and Amortization (EBITDA)	(4 567.0)	(39 484.0)
Operating Items (+)/– Current Assets (+)/– Current Liabilities	(744.0) 2 219.0	(9 851.0) 36 082.0
Net Operating Cash Flow (NOCF)	(3 092.0)	(13 253.0)
Returns on Investment and Servicing of Finance Interest Received Interest Paid Dividends	68.0 (1.0) –	3 777.0 (41.0) –
Net Outflow from Investments & Servicing of Finance	67.0	3 736.0
Taxation Taxes Paid Deferred Tax	– 614.0	– 796.0
Net Cash Outflow for Taxation	614.0	796.0
Investing Activities Exp. on Property, Plant and Equipment Exp. on Investments, Assets & Intangibles Marketable Securities	(403.0) (40.0) –	(13 569.0) (58 597.0) –
Net Outflow for Capital Exp. and Financial Investment	(443.0)	(72 166.0)
Exceptional and Minority items Exceptional Income and Expense	–	0.0
Net Outflow from Exceptional and Minority Items	–	0.0
Reconciliation Reconciliation Figure	7 100.0	59 673.0
Total Cash (Outflow)/Inflow before Financing	4 246.0	(21 214.0)
Financing Share Capital and Reserves Short Term Debt and Provisions Long Term Debt and Provisions	3.0 7.0 –	114 622.0 (70.0) 6 031.0
Net Inflow (Outflow) from Financing	73.0	120 583.0
Increase/(Decrease) in Cash	4 319.0	99 369.0
Reconciliation of Net Cash Flow to Bank Cash	4 3190.0	99 369.0

Table 8.3 lastminute.com cash flow

The cash flow statement (Table 8.3) demonstrates the 'cash burn' on building the lastminute.com brand with **EBITDA** falling from minus £4,567,000 to £38,484,000. The effect of the acquisition is listed in current liabilities and expenditure on investments. The cash flow is balanced by the increase in share capital from the initial public offering leaving a net increase in cash of £99,369,000.

QXL ricardo plc

QXL ricardo runs a series of on-line sites and conducts consumer-to-consumer and business-to-consumer online auctions across a wide range of products in the UK, Germany, France, Italy, Belgium, Netherlands and Spain. Acquisitions have been made in Norway, Denmark, Sweden, Finland, Switzerland and Poland. In 2000, QXL ricardo added to its presence in the German market by acquiring ricardo.de AG and in Scandinavia with bidlet AB. As the newer sites are integrated, QXL ricardo will allow its users to buy and sell goods cross-border as its technology platform is multi-lingual and multi-currency. This is seen as an important advantage with the launch of Euro notes and coins in 2002.

QXL ricardo's technology and systems allow consumers and its merchant partners to upload details and images of their product offerings after registering and allow consumers to make online bids for items. Bids can be left open for a predetermined length of time and, once a sale is closed, the parties involved agree a method of goods delivery. QXL ricardo has also launched an evening delivery and escrow service to offer added convenience and security to its members.

QXL ricardo charges a fee on success from its buyers and is introducing suppliers' listing fees on the consumer-to-consumer auctions that are conducted on its site. QXL ricardo also generates revenues from the profit on auctioning goods it buys itself and through commissions by allowing its merchant partners to sell their goods.

In the year to March 2000, the gross auction value of goods sold over the QXL ricardo sites was £20m and the number of items listed for auction was 5.4m. Total members were

QXL Ricardo plc		Units £'000
Item £'000	Sep-99	Sep-00
Sales	2 545.0	6 8920
Cost of Goods Sold	(2 340.0)	(6 151.0)
Gross Margin	205.0	741.0
Depreciation Manufacturer	–	–
Amortization/Other	–	–
Sales, General & Administration Overheads	(2 309.0)	(78 297.0)
Net Operating Profit (NOP)	(2 104.0)	(77 556.0)
Interest Expense	(7.0)	(13.0)
Interest Income	59.0	1 777.0
Other Financial Income	–	–
Profit after Financial Items	(2 052.0)	(75 792.0)
Exceptional Expense	–	–
Profit before Tax	(2 052.0)	(75 792.0)
Tax	–	–
Net Profit after Tax (NPAT)	(2 052.0)	(75 792.0)
Monthy Interest	–	–
Dividends	(343.0)	(2 112.0)
Retained Profit for the Year	(2 395.0)	(77 904.0)

Table 8.4 QXL income statement

550 000 and revenues were £7m (+170 per cent). QXL ricardo made an operating loss of £32.8m before exceptional items and had net cash of £77m. The acquisitions of Ricardo.de and bidlet.se after the year-end trebled the total registered users to around 1.5m.

At the interim stage, gross auction value was £20m, the company had 1.4m members and revenues were £6m. At the same time, QXL ricardo announced the issue of a convertible bond to raise an additional £15m and access to a further £15m of facilities.

The gross margin in the income statement (Table 8.4) represents the difference between commission paid and received. As in the case of LM, administrative expenses have risen, in this case from £2.3m to £78m. There is also a dividend payout despite the scale of the losses.

QXL Ricardo plc			Units £'000
Assets	£'000	Sep–99	Sep–00
Cash and Deposits		6 557.0	77 662.0
Marketable Securities		–	
Trade Receivables (Debtors)		437.0	6 374.0
Sundry Current Assets		–	–
Current Assets		7 351.0	84 437.0
Land and Buildings		–	–
Plant and Machinery		181.0	7 233.0
Depreciation		–	–
Net Property, Plant and Equipment		181.0	7 233.0
Other Investments		–	–
Intangibles/Goodwill		–	435.0
Non Current and Fixed Assets		181.0	7 668.0
Total Assets		7 532.0	92 105.0

Liabilities	£'000	Sep–99	Jan–00
Short Term Bank Loans		933.0	9 731.0
Trade Creditors (Receivables)		–	–
Other Creditors –		–	
Other Current Liabilities		–	–
Current Liabilities		933.0	9 731.0
Long Term Bank Loans		–	337.0
Long Term Liabilities		–	337.0
Tax/Deferred Taxation/Provisions		–	11 557.0
Long Term Liabilities and Provisions		–	11 894.0
Ordinary Shares (Common Stock)		–8 792.0	127 949.0
Profit and Loss and Other Reserves		(2 193.0)	(57 469.0)
Shareholders' Funds		6 599.0	70 480.0
Total Liabilities and Equity		7 532.0	92 105.0

Table 8.5 QXL balance sheet

| IXL Ricardo plc | | | Units £'000 |
Item £'000		Sep–99	Sep–00
Net Operating Profit (NOP)		(2 104.0)	(77 556.0)
Depreciation/Amortization		–	–
Earnings before Interest, Tax, Depreciation and Amortization (EBITDA)		(2 104.0)	(77 556.0)
Operating Items			
(+)/– Current Assets		(794.0)	(5 981.0)
(+)/– Current Liabilities		–	–
Net Operating Cash Flow (NOCF)		(2 898.0)	(83 537.0)
Returns on Investment and Servicing of Finance			
Interest Received		59.0	1 777.0
Interest Paid		(7.0)	(13.0)
Dividends		(343.0)	(2 112.0)
Net Outflow from Investments & Servicing of Finance		(291.0)	(348.0)
Taxation			
Taxes Paid		–	–
Deferred Tax		–	11 557.0
Net Cash Outflow for Taxation		–	11 557.0
Investing Activities			
Exp. on Property, Plant and Equipment		(181.0)	(7 052.0)
Exp. on Investments, Assets & Intangibles		–	(435.0)
Marketable Securities		–	–
Net Outflow for Capital Exp. and Financial Investment		(181.0)	(7 487.0)
Exceptional and Minority Items			
Exceptional Income and Expense		–	–
Net Outflow from Exceptional and Minority Items		–	–
Reconciliation			
Reconciliation Figure		202.0	22 628.0
Total Cash (Outflow)/Inflow before Financing		(3 168.0)	(57 187.0)
Financing			
Share Capital and Reserves		8 792.0	119 157.0
Short Term Debt and Provisions		933.0	8 798.0
Long Term Debt and Provisions		–	337.0
Net Inflow/(Outflow) from Financing		9 725.0	128 292.0
Increase/(Decrease) in Cash		6 557.8	71 105.0
Reconciliation of Net Cash Flow to Bank Cash		6 557.0	71 105.0

Table 8.6 QXL cash flow

The balance sheet (Table 8.5) and cash flow statement (Table 8.6) show the cash received from the sale of shares. The net worth of £70 million is derived from a share capital of £127m and retained losses of £57m. There is an investment in equipment and fittings rather than 'old-fashioned' assets such as real estate. The cash outflow before financing was £57m and there is £77m in cash at the year-end. Therefore, QXL must start to make profits or gain further capital or loan injections.

Overall, the companies possess these similarities:

- Rapid growth in excess of one hundred per cent
- Large injection of funds from shareholders
- Negligible traditional borrowings
- Investment in equipment and facilities rather than real assets

TRADITIONAL METHODS

This section reviews 'traditional' methods of valuing companies and demonstrates how difficult it can be to apply these techniques to e-business companies.

Accounts

The accounting net worth of a company is shown by the shareholders' funds, which represents the trial balance at the accounting period end. This is equivalent to the net assets of the company.

The accounting value of a business is based on:

- Accounting conventions such as accruals and matching methods
- Accounting standards such as the treatments of goodwill on acquisition or the capitalization of finance leases
- Requirements of local and international stock markets

On this basis, the accounting value of LM is £141m (with 100 537 ordinary shares) and QXL £70m (with 288 548 ordinary shares) and the value per share is 140 pence for LM and 24 pence for QXL. Notwithstanding discussion of how accounting standards and conventions have been applied, this approach does not recognize the 'cash burn' in the companies and the fact that neither company possesses a positive cash flow. In addition, the balance sheet omits several sources of potential value that are discussed in the next section.

Adjusted accounting value

Annual accounts pose important problems for valuation purposes on all companies and may not provide a fair market value for these reasons:

- Differing accounting standards, conventions and standards in different countries and continents
- Differing approaches where certain countries, such as Germany, allow a more conservative approach to recognizing profits
- Creative accounting and changing accounting methods
- Leasing and other off-balance-sheet financing instruments
- Inventory accounting methods and write-offs

- Depreciation methods and periods
- Goodwill and merger accounting
- Intangibles such as brands, patents, software or research and development capitalization
- Exclusion of knowledge, brands and the value of proprietary systems

Internet companies are concerned with the economic rather than legal ownership of assets and the companies may have substantial operating or 'services' leases, which are not shown as borrowings. Nevertheless, there could be a contractual commitment to pay rentals in the medium term.

The accounting net worth depends on the above factors and one method is to adjust the accounting values for perceived extra value. In this example, the value of the IT and fixtures is divided by two to provide an alternative value. In a receivership, it is unlikely that the systems would be valued at book value as computer and communications equipment historically depreciates sharply. When Boo.com went into receivership in 2000, the proprietary system was sold for only £400,000, but cost many times this figure to develop. As for brands, companies are spending heavily to build up a brand and, while companies such as Amazon are well known, this has not yet been translated into accounting profits.

On this basis, the accounting value of LM is £134m and QXL £67m and the value per share is 133 pence for LM and 23 pence for QXL. Criticisms of this method include:

- It is based on replacement cost of assets.
- It divulges no information about the future and the organization's future earning power.
- Ignores the value of information, non-financial capital
- It ignores the ability of management to make strategic decisions that affect the company's prospects.
- E-business companies spend little on traditional assets and much is expended in customer acquisition. This cannot be capitalized like real estate and so the high growth rate leads to increasing losses.

Dividends

Companies can also be viewed as a stream of dividends. This method values these payments using the **Gordon's growth model**. The formula is:

$$P_{\text{I}} = \frac{D_{\text{I}}}{E(R_{\text{I}}) - g}$$

where D_{I} is the dividend for the next period, i.e. $D_0 \times (1 + g)$, $E(R_{\text{I}})$ is the desired return and g is the implied growth:

$$g = \frac{\text{Cost of equity} - \text{dividend yield}}{1 + \text{dividend yield}}$$

Since the companies are new and unprofitable, it is difficult to apply a perpetuity model, in which it is essentially assumed that dividends will grow at a constant rate. In addition, these models are very sensitive to changes in the growth rate and a wide variation of values could be derived.

Key Term...

Gordon's growth model

This dividend valuation model is equal to the dividend yield plus the expected growth rate in dividends

Dividend methods suffer from three important failings:

- Policy on dividends can change, especially on take-over.
- The area of signalling theory states that management often signals its intentions using dividends and prospects. Often a company will retain dividends at a particular level in order to bolster a share price.
- There is no examination of future prospects in terms of earnings or growth.

Stock market

Stock-market methods using share prices, earnings per share, **price/earnings per share (P/E)** and price/sales ratios can be applied to overcome some of the disadvantages of accounting or dividend-based methods and can be helpful in valuing mature businesses. They are:

- Understood by the market and the analysts and available in the *Financial Times* and financial press each day.
- Simplistic and easy to calculate on a basic calculator without the need for calculations of time value of money or discounted cash flow.

The formulae are:

P/E = Market price per share / Earnings per share
Market price per share = P/E ratio × Earnings per share

The same result can be obtained if the share price is multiplied by the number of shares or if the earnings are multiplied by the P/E ratio. The disadvantage of applying the method to e-business companies is negative earnings. The P/E ratio has no meaning and there are no earnings per share.

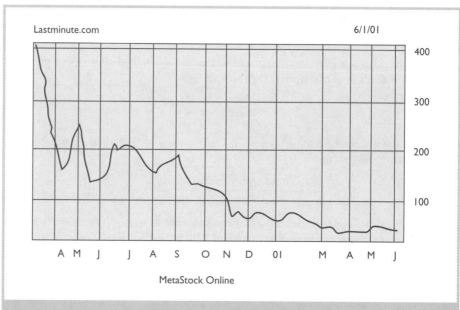

Figure 8.1 lastminute share price (*Reproduced with permission of Reuters plc*)

<div class="sidebar">

Key Term...

Price earnings P/E ratio

P/E ratio is a valuation ratio of a company's current share price to its earnings per share

</div>

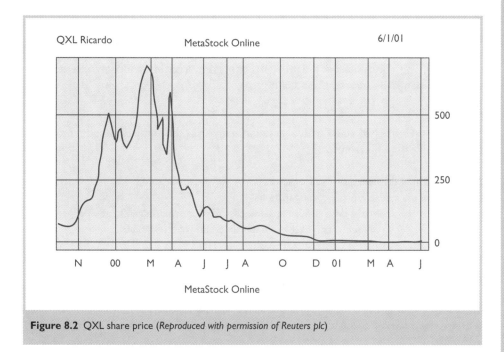

Figure 8.2 QXL share price (*Reproduced with permission of Reuters plc*)

At the time of writing, i.e. the period end, the market capitalization of LM was £197m and the share price was £1.31; the market capitalization of QXL was £130m and the share price was £0.45.

The share prices (Figures 8.1 and 8.2) were volatile over the period from April 2000 to June 2001. Investors placed money in technology stocks. This was followed by steep falls in the latter half of 2000 as the 'bubble' burst and therefore it is difficult to assess *true* or *intrinsic* value.

This stock market method suffers from weaknesses such as:

■ A high P/E denotes a share with growth prospects, but this is also dependent on general market sentiment for the sector and the market.
■ The method is not based on time value of money concepts or *real* future prospects.
■ The method is based on the accounting model rather than on cash flow.
■ Companies invest now for returns in future periods and this is not included in the method. One criticism of UK and US stock markets is usually their 'short-termism' and their reaction to sentiment.
■ Companies may issue shares at any time and optimism may overvalue shares and stock-market sectors. This is certainly the case with technology shares.

FREE-CASH-FLOW METHOD

The 'traditional' methods above can be criticized, since they do not take account of the organization's earning ability and they are based on accounting methods or market sentiment. Free-cash-flow methods examine the company and its potential prospects closely by computing a present value of forecast future cash flows. This method forces the user to focus on real cash flows and prospects rather than on accounting information and is linked to theories of enhancing and maximizing shareholder value (Rappaport, 1998).

The essential idea is that stakeholders, such as management, should be concerned with value management. The value of the corporation is represented by the discounted value of its free cash flows since cash is felt to be the only meaningful measure of investment return that is valid. This solves most of the problems of historic accounting models, international accounting standards and creative accounting.

Method

The process (Figure 8.3) starts with a strategic analysis of the company and its prospects over a suitable time horizon:

- Examination of the macro or exterior environment for the organization.
- Analysis of the industry, products and markets.
- Forecast of the important drivers, such as sales, cost of goods sold, administration expenses, debt and working requirements. These are the main determinants of value.

This information can then be used to produce forecast accounting statements and a cash flow. The methodology is:

- Forecast operating cash flows and prepare related financial statements.
- Determine a suitable discount rate (cost of capital using a weighted average cost of capital formula).
- Determine a suitable residual value (continuing value using an EV/EBITDA multiple or Gordon's Growth Model).
- Calculate the present value of the two items above at the weighted average cost of capital.
- Add cash and cash equivalents and subtract debt; the resulting figure is the equity value.
- Interpret and test the results of calculations and assumptions using sensitivity analysis.

The model produced can be compared with the results of other methods with tables and charts. This means that comparisons of the future projections with the historic data using trend-lines can be made, in order to review critically all assumptions and inputs. Changes can then be made or the complexity of the model increased to include other variables.

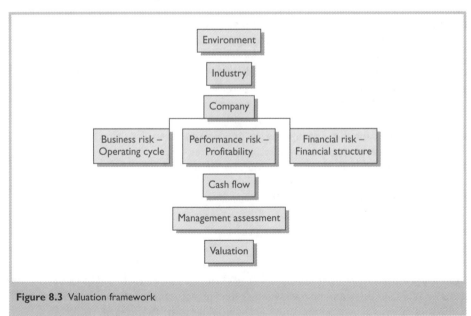

Figure 8.3 Valuation framework

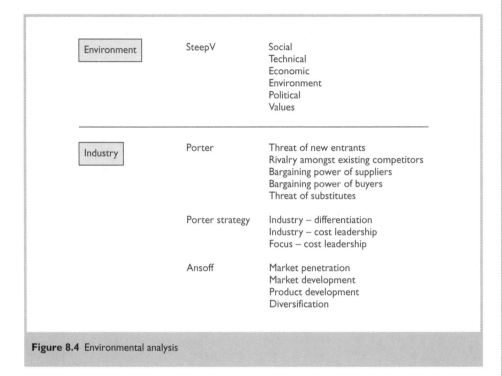

Environment	SteepV	Social
		Technical
		Economic
		Environment
		Political
		Values

Industry	Porter	Threat of new entrants
		Rivalry amongst existing competitors
		Bargaining power of suppliers
		Bargaining power of buyers
		Threat of substitutes
	Porter strategy	Industry – differentiation
		Industry – cost leadership
		Focus – cost leadership
	Ansoff	Market penetration
		Market development
		Product development
		Diversification

Figure 8.4 Environmental analysis

Strategic analysis

An environmental analysis (Figure 8.4) reviews the impact of exterior influences, over which the company normally has little control, on the company's likely success. E-business companies are vulnerable to technology shifts and changes in consumer tastes, since they are trying to build businesses that challenge traditional organizations. The past five years have seen sustained economic growth and this has presented favourable conditions for consumer demand. This is very different to the period at the beginning of the 1990s, which were typified by recession.

E-business companies are often grouped together as a homogeneous group. However, they follow different business models. Both QXL and LM are trying to build barriers around their business using technology and brands in order to build 'competitive advantage'. The costs are mainly allocated to the income statement; hence the increased losses in the last 12-month period related to substantial advertising budgets. Figure 8.5 illustrates Porter's (1985) Five Forces, which leads LM and QXL to a focused strategy.

Forecast inputs

Analysis of the environment and the industry leads to a review of the company and its prospects. In particular, e-business companies spend large amounts of cash attracting customers and therefore the forecast needs to include some assessment of future customer spending. Value can be gained or lost from:

- Average revenue per customer
- Advertising revenue
- Total number of customers
- Margin or contribution per customer
- Cost of acquiring each new customer

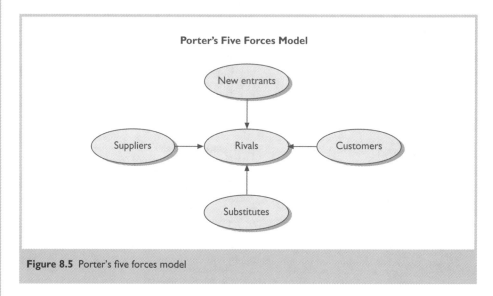

Figure 8.5 Porter's five forces model

- Number of customers who visit the site and fail to purchase any goods
- Customer churn rate (number of customers lost each year)

Table 8.7 shows one method of using 'drivers' to forecast a balance sheet and using cash or short-term debt as the balancing item.

The key drivers are:

- Sales growth (per cent)
- Cost of goods sold (per cent)
- Depreciation rate (per cent)
- Administrative expenses (per cent)
- Interest cost (per cent)
- Effective tax rate (per cent)
- Dividend payout ratio (per cent)
- Fixed assets requirement (£)
- Debtor days
- Inventory days
- Creditor days
- Long term debt (£)
- Share capital (£)

Cost of capital

The **cost of capital** needs to reflect systematic risk and therefore the **weighted average cost of capital (WACC)** is calculated as the merged cost of capital. The cost of equity is calculated using the **Capital Asset Pricing Model**:

$$E(R_i) = R_f + \beta_i[E(R_m) - R_f]$$

where $E(R_i)$ is the expected return on share i, $R_f =$ is the risk-free rate, $E(R_m)$ is the expected return on the market and β_i is the beta of share i. The beta input is based on a historic debt equity ratio and therefore the beta is ungeared and then re-geared for the forecast debt/equity ratio. The formulae for unleveraging and leveraging are:

Key Term...

Cost of capital

This depends on the capital components of: ordinary shares, preference shares, bonds and retained earnings

---

Key Term...

Weighted average cost of capital (WACC)

WACC is dependent upon the capital structure. By taking a weighted average, the cost that the company has to pay for every pound it borrows can be determined

---

Key Term...

Capital asset price model (CAPM)

CAPM looks at risk and rates of return and compares them to the overall stock market. The basic premise is that most investors want to avoid risk but those who do take risks expect to be rewarded

---

Item	Description
Income statement	
Sales	Calculate using sales growth
Costs of goods sold	Calculate using gross profit margin
Depreciation	Use Depreciation/Average fixed assets ratio
Net operating profit (NOP)	
Interest paid on debt	Use interest % on average debt
Interest earned on cash	Simplify and use above figure
Exceptional items	Include actual from forecast
Profit before tax	Sum
Taxes	Use tax payout ratio
Profit after tax	Sum
Dividends	Use dividend payout ratio
Retained earnings	
Balance sheet	
Cash & marketable securities	
Current assets	Use debtor days based on sales
Fixed assets	Add CAPEX to fixed assets
At cost	
Depreciation	Add P&L depreciation to balance
Net fixed assets	
Intangibles	Input if relevant
Total assets	
Current liabilities	Use creditor days based on goods sold
Tax	
Debt	Add new long term debt
Stock	Add Equity increase or decrease
Accumulated retained earnings	Add retained earnings to balance
Total liabilities and equity	

Table 8.7 Using 'drivers' to forecast a balance sheet and using cash or short-term debt as the balancing item

$$\beta_u = \frac{\beta_l}{1 + (1 - \text{Tax})\left(\dfrac{\text{Debt}}{\text{Equity}}\right)}$$

$$\beta_l = \left[1 + (1 - \text{Tax})\left(\dfrac{\text{Debt}}{\text{Equity}}\right)\right](\beta_u)$$

There are input cells in the model above for the forecast debt equity ratio, the tax rate and the cost of debt. The formula is:

$$\text{Cost of debt} = \text{Cost of debt} \times (1 - \text{Tax rate})$$

With this information, the WACC can be computed as the weighted cost of each category of funds and the free cash flows discounted at this rate.

Terminal value

The enterprise must have a value at the end of the forecast period, which could introduce a range of values from break-up to a going concern. Great care needs to be taken in the method and inputs since the terminal value often forms more than 50 per cent of the overall computed enterprise value. This makes any model very sensitive to small changes. Terminal value can be calculated using a variety of methods: in this example, it is calculated using an EV/EBITA multiple variable from the inputs section. This is simply multiplied by the final EBITA.

An alternative would be the Gordon's growth model used to calculate a value in perpetuity. Since this model is sensitive, it is usual to use a nil or low growth figure:

$$\text{Value in perpetuity} = (\text{Final cash} \times (1 + \text{Growth rate}))/(\text{WACC} - \text{Growth rate})$$

Present value

The terminal value is discounted back over the five-year period. The present values of cash flows and the terminal value are added to form the enterprise value, which is the sum of the market value of debt and the market value of equity. Adjustments are then made to subtract the debt and add cash and cash equivalents. The result is the equity value. This process could be summarized as:

- Calculate valuation-free cash flows for a defined time horizon.
- $A=$ Discount at cost of capital.
- Calculate terminal cash flow by using an EV/EBITDA multiple or the perpetuity model, e.g. [Final cash flow $\times$ (1 + Growth)] / (Cost of capital − Growth).
- $B =$ Terminal cash flow discounted at cost of capital.
- Add $A + B =$ Enterprise value.
- Add cash + deposits and marketable securities.
- Subtract debt and minority interests.

Comparison

The comparisons (Tables 8.8 and 8.9, Figures 8.6 and 8.7) summarize the results from each of the methods with both actual and per share values.

	Equity Valuation	Per Share	Variance	%
Accounts Net Worth	141,110	1.40	0.09	7.1%
Adjusted Accounting Value	134,202	1.33	0.02	1.9%
P/E Valuation at a P/E of 0	197,155	1.96	0.65	49.7%
Dividend Growth Model	0	0.00	(1.31)	(100.0%)
Free Cash Flow Model	110,209	1.10	(0.21)	(16.3%)
Current Market Value	197,155	1.31	0.00	−

Table 8.8 Comparison for lastminute.com (units £000). The number of ordinary shares is 100 537

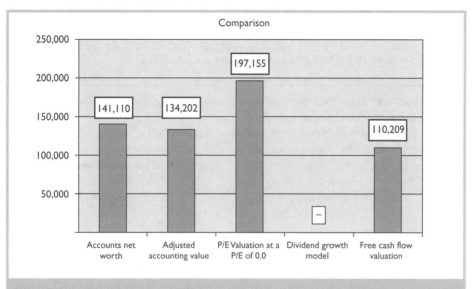

Figure 8.6 Bar-chart representation of the comparison for lastminute.com (units £'000)

	Equity Valuation	Per Share	Variance	%
Accounts Net Worth	70,480	0.24	(0.21)	(45.7%)
Adjusted Accounting Value	66,864	0.23	(0.22)	(48.5%)
P/E Valuation at a P/E of 0.0	129,847	0.45	–	0.0%
Dividend Growth Model	0	0.00	(0.45)	(100.0%)
Free Cash Flow Valuation	64,679	0.22	(0.23)	(50.2%)
Current Market Value	129,847	0.45	–	–

Table 8.9 Comparison for QXL ricardo (units £000)

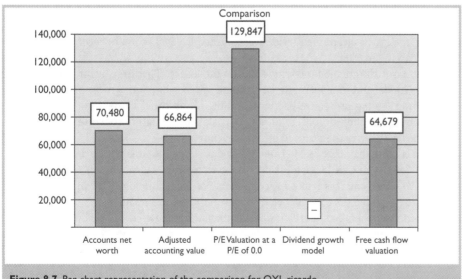

Figure 8.7 Bar-chart representation of the comparison for QXL ricardo

---

ILLUSTRATIVE EXAMPLE II
*Extracted from After boom and bust, it's boom again for dot.coms, by Nigel Cope,
The Independent, http://news.independent.co.uk, 27 July 2002*

Online business' talent for survival puts profitability within grasp as bricks-and-mortar firms watch share prices dive

After another week of turbulent stock markets, a casual observer might believe that the internet generation had long since slipped away. The dot.com entrepreneurs who started the boom in 1999 and rode its wave into the spring of 2000 must surely be struggling. Mustn't they?

Well, actually, no. Sure, many high-profile names such as boo.com, boxman and Clickmango have long gone. But many others are not only surviving but prospering.

The best-performing share on the UK stock market this year is, wait for it, Lastminute.com. The online travel business, founded by Martha Lane Fox and Brent Hoberman, has seen its shares treble this year. It has pulled off four acquisitions in the past three months and is aiming for revenues of £1bn a year.

It is not alone. Ebookers, an online flights specialist, has seen its shares rise 80 per cent this year, making it one of the top 10 performing stocks. And Sportingbet, an internet betting service, now has a stock market value of £125m after capitalising on one of the Web's fastest-growing areas. It had revenues of £1bn last year and it even made money, with profits of £5m.

As one former internet analyst said yesterday: 'It was the first sector to head down and, for the ones who survived, it is one of the first to come back up. If you want safety, hide in the internet. What an irony that is.'

It is important not to overstate the success of this small group of companies. For every Lastminute, there is a QXL, the online auction house that was worth a fortune in the boom but which is virtually worthless now. For every Martha Lane Fox there are countless other twentysomethings whose dreams of entrepreneurial greatness have turned to nothing. But the internet is still here and still growing. Specialist websites such as friendsreunited.com, which puts school and college friends back in touch, have grown exponentially and show how powerful a medium the internet can be.

It is the same story in the United States. The Big Daddies of the internet scene, such as Amazon.com and eBay, have proved remarkably robust. A runaway success such as Napster, the music swapping service, was quashed by legal action by record companies rather than the market.

What has distinguished the winners from the losers? The three factors are money, business model and management. Lastminute raised more than £100m from its flotation, giving it a big protective barrier when the tough times came. Less well-funded operations found they simply could not cut costs fast enough to conserve their capital when the City money men turned off the cash supplies.

But it is more than that, as Ms Lane Fox said yesterday. 'Our service is an online service. It is not just an offline business put on the web. Brent's ideas couldn't have worked without the Web and it is really a very good use of the technology. Our brand name is also very strong and does exactly what it says on the box,' she said.

As for those that failed: 'Partly it was just the natural life cycle of new businesses, 80 per cent of which fail anyway. But a lot didn't have very good sites or the technology didn't work very well.'

ADJUSTED FREE CASH FLOW

Copeland *et al.* (2000) suggested a modified approach to valuing Internet companies by generating scenarios of values and then assigning probabilities to them. This is an extension of the free-cash-flow approach outlined in the previous section. Since the losses of e-business companies have appeared to increase in line with value, they argue that short-term methods are meaningless; however, they put forward discounted cash flow techniques as the most logical approach. This is supported by Desmet *et al.* (2000) and Higson and Briginshaw (2000).

These authors suggest constructing a series of probability-weighted scenarios or using the Monte Carlo approach to simulation. The latter technique involves setting distributions for the variables, distribution shape (e.g. normal, triangular, uniform) and volatility, such as sales growth, and then running many simulations to produce output of the range of possible outcomes.

There is, of course, a great deal of uncertainty in any forecast and one could argue that the assigned probabilities are subjective. However, the modelling is a framework for outlining the possibilities such as market size and penetration. Table 8.10 applies this technique in simple form to LM. There are three scenarios of growth rates, which result in three equity values. The valuation is then multiplied by its assigned probability and the results added together. The share price is 1.19 and this compares with a current value of 1.31.

This approach allows 'stress testing' of the growth assumptions in the free-cash-flow models. This does allow valuations of volatile companies. Given the uncertainty in the sector, it is likely that there will be consolidation (e.g. LM's acquisition of Degriftour in France in August 2000) and failures such as the high profile of Boo.com.

The method could be expanded into a risk model involving Monte Carlo simulation using industry standards such as @RISK from Palisade Corporation (www.palisade.com) or Crystal Ball from Decisioneering (www.decisioneering.com). This involves setting distributions rather than single points for the inputs, running the model through a large number of simulations and then outputting the answer as a distribution. Typically, the products provide a mean, median and mode together with percentile statistics and standard deviations. The charts can be specified as histograms and cumulative probability distributions. Depending on the distribution of the inputs, it is likely that such modelling would reveal the volatility and sensitivity of the models and the result. Nevertheless, it is necessary to run a number of scenarios to test the assumptions underpinning the analysis.

OTHER METHODS

There are a number of other methods and approaches that have been used in e-business valuation. Some investment banks use discounted cash flow (DCF) models to establish a benchmark for comparison. However, DCF analysis proves difficult, since, as shown, e-business companies rarely have sufficient cash-flow history to predict future growth rates accurately. In addition, DCF also fails to take into account potential or underutilized assets, such as management expertise, flexibility and strategic partnerships, that do not directly contribute to the cash flow of the company. Techniques may need to incorporate more factors than cash flow alone.

Probability-Based Value:

Probability	30.00%	50.00%	20.00%
Equity Value	110 209.21	177 177.13	286 997.58
Amount	33 062.76	86 588.57	57 399.52
Total Equity Value	179 050.84		
Value per share (150 500 shares)	1.19		
Current Share Price	1.31		
Variance	(0.12)		
Percentage	(9.18%)		

	Scenario 1	Scenario 2	Scenario 3
Results:			
Depreciation/NBV of Fixed Assets	10.0%	10.0%	10.0%
Fixed Assets % of Sales	5.0%	5.0%	5.0%
Depreciation % of Fixed Assets	12.0%	12.0%	12.0%
Working Capital % of Sales	10.0%	10.0%	10.0%
Tax-rate	30.0%	30.0%	30.0%
Cost-of-Debt	10.0%	10.0%	10.0%
Risk-Free-Rate	5.0%	5.0%	5.0%
Risk-Premium	6.0%	6.0%	6.0%
Share-Beta	2.00	2.00	2.00
Forecast–Debt–Equity–Ratio	5.00%	5.00%	5.00%
EV–EBITDA–multiple	15.0	15.0	15.0
Growth–Model-rate	1.0%	1.0%	1.0%
Sales Growth Year 1	(90.0%)	(105.0%)	(110.0%)
Sales Growth Year 2	(110.0%)	(60.0%)	(70.0%)
Sales Growth Year 3	(20.0%)	(50.0%)	(60.0%)
Sales Growth Year 4	(20.0%)	(40.0%)	(50.0%)
Sales Growth Year 5	(20.0%)	(30.0%)	(40.0%)
Results:			
TV	11 785.0	68 265.0	167.001
TV Per cent	84.4%	84.4%	87.5%
Cash Flows	2 178.0	12 666.0	23 750.0
Cashflow Per cent	15.6%	15.6%	12.5%
Enterprise Value	13 962.0	80 930.0	190 751.0
Equity Value	110 209.0	177 177.0	286 998.0
Share Price	0.73	1.18	1.91
Variance	(0.58)	(0.13)	0.60

Table 8.10 Scenarios

Real options

The core rule of the traditional management teams used to be 'accountability to the business plan'. Unfortunately, high-technology start-up businesses face a range of shifting opportunities that simply cannot be researched or predicted. Flexibility and the ability to respond may increase the chance of success.

Borison (2000) applies options theory to valuing Internet companies as an extension to its use in investment appraisal. **Real options** are the equivalent of options in derivatives and include factors such as flexibility and management response. Traditional investment appraisal and free-cash-flow valuation use a forecast set of cash flows as if they are fixed.

Borison (2000) and Copeland *et al.* (2000) argue that the real world is more complex and management decisions have an influence on the underlying risky asset. The value of a company can change rapidly as management respond to new information, which can change the probability of achieving a certain level of cash flow. The method assumes that the company is composed of a series of projects that produce discrete cash flows. The option value is therefore the difference between the value of the company based on current information and a value that incorporates flexibility. The value has value since it can be exercised at the discretion of the management.

The approach is mathematically complex and involves these stages:

1 Deriving a simple free cash-flow-model without flexibility
2 Modelling uncertainty using event trees
3 Incorporating managerial flexibility in a decision tree
4 Calculating the value of the option as the difference between the decision tree and the initial free-cash-flow valuation

Decisions that may need to incorporated in a model could be:

- Abandoning projects or products
- Deferring market entry or product development
- Expanding investments or contracts
- Shortening investments or contracts
- Increasing or reducing the size of investments

Features

At the height of the 'dot.com' boom, many other methods were suggested that are not really methods, but were suggested in order to justify some of the valuations at initial public offering. These included some of the following features:

- Size
- Traffic conversion rates
- Peer group comparison
- Killer applications
- Stategic partnerships
- Management expertise

Size

Value based on subscriber/user/customer numbers since traffic is the lifeblood of the e-business market. It is the determinant of advertising rates, revenue streams and ultimately profits. The LM December 2000 report confirms that the company is in top position in the UK for traffic as defined by NetValue. Since the company has invested heavily in building brands, one would expect to see increased traffic through the site. The figures for LM in December 2000 are given in Table 8.11.

	31/12/00	31/12/99	Growth
Registered subscribers	2 860 736.0	571 687.0	5.0×
Customers since inception	234 549.0	28 687.0	8.2×
Cumulative items sold	160 819.0	39 683.0	4.1×

Table 8.11 LM traffic figures

Traffic conversion rates

While the number of visitors is a useful yardstick, the key is to convert these visits into unique users, who in the end will generate revenue and profit. Conversion rates have become one of the most valuable ways to access the strength of an e-business brand. Tesco-direct, the online retailer, for example, has a high conversion rate per user in excess of 50 per cent. Although its site does not attract vast numbers of visits, Tesco has created a very loyal unique user group, the members of which regularly convert their visits into e-business revenue. Conversely, LM confirms in its recent report that its conversion rate has risen from 5.5 to 8.9 per cent.

This analysis can be extended to the concept of lifetime value (LV) of a customer. The LV of a customer is the present value of all future profits that the company can generate from that customer. It is similar to DCF with the modification that customer retention (loyalty) is built into the calculation:

$$\text{LV} = \text{Annual gross margin per customer} \times \text{Margin multiple}$$
$$\text{Margin multiple} = 1 / (1 + \text{Discount rate} - \text{Retention rate})$$

Peer group comparison

When trying to establish a current valuation by comparison with a peer group it becomes very important to look at all the leading public and private brand names in the sector. These act as a benchmark in terms of potential revenues, margin and cash flow and the size of the overall market. This is usually difficult in the case of e-business companies, which may be creating new markets where the demand is yet untried.

Relative valuation is the value of the company based on the pricing of comparable companies relative to earnings, cash flows, book value or revenues. Illiquid markets for opportunities, together with lots of very different companies, make these companies very difficult to compare. There is no uniformity of knowledge, while there are many new ideas and rapidly changing markets, resulting in divergent views.

When a sector becomes 'flavour of the month', demand exceeds supply and this drives up all comparable valuations. The fear of being left behind and the herd mentality are reinforced by momentum investors who have recently chased the companies to ultimately unsustainable price levels.

'Killer applications'

One of the most important factors in the long run success of an e-business company is the invention of 'killer applications' that address potentially huge, inefficient and fragmented markets. Examples of existing 'killer applications' are word processing for the PC, voice communications in transit for cellular telephones, and address book and calendar management for personal digital assistants (PDAs). Both LM and QXL are creating new demand, which could have significant valuation potential.

Strategic partnerships

Strategic partnerships are important in gaining critical mass and credibility. Getting large well-known companies to endorse directly or indirectly through use or co-branding of a company's site is often essential. Technology and service partnerships that add value to the core market proposition will become increasingly important as the market matures. LM states in recent accounts that it has 9200 supplier relationships, and this number is growing quickly.

Management expertise

The most underestimated and most difficult success criterion to achieve for an Internet company is assembling an experienced management team capable of executing the vision. Management teams used to be judged on business skill and record of accomplishment. However, management depth is a prerequisite for implementing a solid business plan.

The above features lead towards a composite approach, which takes into account the failings of standard price/earnings ratios and includes:

- Cash-flow or free-cash-flow approach
- Examinations of various scenarios through modelling
- Critical examination of the client business model and its flexibility
- Review of the potential market size and likely growth
- Power of the brand, knowledge and intangibles, together with their potential leverage into value
- Assessment of the ability of management

PSYCHOLOGICAL FACTORS IN VALUATIONS

The psychological climate can quickly change from hot to cold over Internet stocks. We are no longer in an environment where dot.coms with revenues of only a fifth of that of bricks and mortar could have market capitalization four times that of their brick-and-click competitor. Notwithstanding the fact that market values can be complex and volatile, the number of market manias of the past – the South Sea Bubble, Dutch tulip frenzy – is worrying. The need for new metrics is obvious, given the way the traditional analytical techniques have been thrown away by the investment community. According to the editorial of the *Journal of Psychology & Financial Market* (2000), the old psychology behind 'new metrics' that we have experiencing in recent years is not just a financial phenomenon, but a psychological one. This observation has significant implications for shareholders. These include:

- *Peer pressure* – if the price of a share rises sharply, investors believe that there must be something good to justify the higher rating. Although the reasoning is circuitous, this has been the bedrock of decision-making of many investors.
- *E-tailers' saga* – at the height of the dot.com boom, one yard stick used was to measure every customer that had purchased anything from the e-tailer and then assign unrealistic growth rates. The issue of one-time purchases was conveniently ignored. Dot.coms purchased other dot.coms with the goal of increasing customer lists, which in turn would boost share price. In addition, acquisition costs were capitalized and the revenues from the acquired firm fed through to the bottom line.
- *Psychological roots of a mania* – researchers are at an embryonic stage in the study of the effects of psychology on investor decision-making. Cognitive psychology tells us that people use simplifying strategies (heuristics) in an attempt to manage large amounts of information. However, when it comes to using statistics, the use of heuristics leads investors into major errors. Psychological influences on statistical recall tend to distort the normally useful heuristical processes.
- *Availability bias* – despite the errors in available heuristics leading to investors losing money, lessons would appear not to have been learnt. For example, at the height of the dot.com, the average IPO closed 120 per cent above the issue price from the first day of trading for the first

three months of 2000. The fact that large gains were both recent and salient made investors ignore research evidence. These gains were achieved despite academic studies showing that IPOs have proved to be poor investments. Moreover, when IPOs fell nearly 50 per cent, the same heuristic flaw may help explain why even the experts were so willing to ignore their valuation tools.

- *Representativeness* – Another major heuristic relates to what Tversk and Kahneman (1971) call the 'Law of Small Numbers'. According to Tverk and Kahneman, researchers systematically overstate findings taken from small samples. In statistics findings from large samples are normally more representative than findings from small samples. In other words, the smaller the sample or the shorter the record, the more likely the findings are to have resulted from chance, which will prove unreliable if extended beyond the sample.

- *Anchoring* – the third major heuristic is called anchoring. In this instance, investors use the present value of a share as a reference point, when their evaluation may be anchored too narrowly. For example, if a share trades between £5 and £7 and there is debate whether £5 or £7 is the proper value, in reality the universe of discourse in which these values are anchored may be too narrow. It ignores the possibility that the true share price may be £1 or £11.

- *Hindsight bias* – the fourth statistical problem relates to the fact that with hindsight it is easy to tell whether shares were fairly priced or wildly overvalued. In the frenetic environment of the stock markets, judgement is much more difficult. Knowing whether shares will continue to move upwards or that they have reached their zenith has proved problematic.

- *Social reality* – social psychology helps explain how experts react to sudden changes in stock markets. Social reality refers to how a group of people receives reality and how the group's perceptions influence insight. In the stock markets individual experts have to justify their views against those of their peers in conditions of turbulence.

The above issues certainly suggest that in the area of valuation much more research is required, so that investors gain a better understanding of the stock markets.

SUMMARY

This chapter has reviewed the application of traditional methods to valuing e-business companies and demonstrated that these methods do not result in meaningful figures. The cash-flow-based methods with some extra modelling for likely scenarios appear to offer one way of modelling the uncertainty and volatility inherent in e-business operations. Since this approach is also partially subjective in assigning probabilities to particular market states, a more composite methodology is required, which takes into account the management, market conditions, flexibility and knowledge.

Lastminute.com and QXL ricardo plc have been used as illustrative examples to show how dot.com financial performance can be assessed using various financial techniques. Income, balance sheet and cash flow statements were produced to perform ratio analysis. When the two companies were compared they displayed the following similarities:

- Rapid growth in excess of one hundred per cent
- Large injection of funds from shareholders
- Negligible traditional borrowings
- Investment in equipment and facilities rather than *real* assets

Valuing organizations with no profits and negative cash flows has been the thrust of this chapter. Matters are further complicated by the fact that analysts still need to place value on dot.coms after the decline in global stock markets. Koller (2001) suggests that experts need to generate new insights into the potential value of Internet opportunities. Koller believes the following issues are critical:

- Cash flow is king.
- Spotting the value creators.
- Spotting how the company will generate revenue.
- Calculating the average return on capital once the industry matures.
- Determining the size of the relevant market.

In addition, it must not be forgotten that if a company has a competitive advantage due to the management, technology, brand or first-mover advantage, this may be not be sustainable in the medium term. Moreover, the advances in technology innovation and the difficulty of predicting consumer demand will ensure that the volatility and risk remain imperative variables during the decision-making process. The area of psychology and financial markets presents an interesting area of research as experts attempt to understand their own behaviour during the rise and fall of stock markets. Overall, the individual shareholder is looking for the establishment of new metrics that will justify the current valuation of a favoured company.

DISCUSSION QUESTIONS

1. How should the financial analyst value an e-business organization? What are the problems of valuing an e-business organization when it is generating negative cash flow?

2. Which valuation methodology would you use to value an e-business?

3. Based on the material presented in this chapter, how would you assess the performance of Lastminute.com and QXL Ricardo plc?

ASSESSMENT QUESTIONS

1. Critically discuss how an e-business that is unprofitable can maintain a high market value. On what basis would you attempt to justify the share price?

2. Do you believe that the share price of e-businesses as quoted in the stock markets is a good proxy for business performance in the long term?

3. How important do you feel are the concept of psychological factors in valuation? Which heuristics should be the most important to the shareholder?

GROUP ASSIGNMENT QUESTIONS

1. Using the latest annual reports of Lastminute.com and QXL Ricardo plc you are required to briefly update the financial analysis performed on the two companies in this chapter.

2. Choose any Internet organization of your choice and critically evaluate its financial performance over a three-year period. What lessons could be learned? What are the salient implications of your findings in terms of e-business strategy?

3. Using an organization of your choice that has raised a significant amount of money through an initial public offering (IPO), explain, discuss and analyse how successful the organization has been post IPO.

MAIN CASE STUDY
The future of e-business, by Timothy J. Mullaney, Business Week Special Report, 13 May 2002

Break out the black ink
Profitable dot-coms? Being in the right business helps

One of the lingering effects of the dot-com bust is that the phrase 'profitable Internet company' has become a sniggering joke. In this sadder-but-wiser era, it's the ultimate oxymoron. Even CEOs of Internet companies can't resist getting in their digs. When asked how many Net companies are making money, Srivats Sampath, the boss of profitable online software maker McAfee.com Corp., quips: 'About four?' Fortunately for his stockholders, Sampath is better at running his company than he is at sizing up the performance of his e-business peers.

This is the Net's pretty little secret: By our count, 52 Net companies were profitable last quarter, and analysts project that at least four more will clear the bar by yearend. There are two ways of putting the numbers into context. Of the 456 Internet companies that went public since 1994, 11% are profitable. If you look at just the 208 public Net companies that are still in business and were not acquired, a full 25% make money. If you count companies that profit on a pro forma basis—before noncash charges, that is—another 30 or so are in the black. The market 'has weeded out bad companies very quickly. And the rest have reduced their operating losses dramatically,' says Greg Kyle, CEO of market researcher Pegasus Research International, and a longtime bear on Net stocks.

Profits are coming in from all over. The big winners are e-travel and e-finance — headlined, respectively, by Expedia and Priceline and by IndyMac and Schwab. But almost every Web sector has at least a couple of profitable public companies. Here's a surprise: Health services company WebMD Corp., once branded a loser, is making money before noncash accounting charges. And forget the notion that mixing the Internet with physical stores is the only way to make money online: Virtually all the profitable Web companies are selling information-based products rather than items that require shipping. So they don't need bricks to go with their clicks.

Nor do dot-coms rely any longer on pro forma accounting to show profits. Indeed, the oft-criticized gap between net income under generally accepted accounting principles and Web companies' pro forma results has never been smaller. Why? Lower stock prices mean noncash stock option payments take a smaller bite out of earnings. Also, companies can now write off merger-related goodwill in a single stroke, rather than taking write-offs every quarter for years. That boosts the quality of earnings at companies such as e-tailer Amazon.com Inc. Its stock compensation costs fell from $11 million in 2001's first quarter to $3 million in the quarter ended Mar. 31. Goodwill amortization fell from $51 million to $2 million. Analysts now say Amazon will break even for the year—not in pro forma earnings but by conservative accounting principles.

Indeed, our rules for sizing up the profit picture are conservative in a number of ways. We don't count profitable startups that were acquired, such as travel agency Travelocity.com Inc. Nor do we count businesses that have become profitable since being bought out, such as online dating site Match.com. We also don't count private companies such as search company Google Inc., which claims to be profitable.

The education of the first wave of Web companies is hardly over. But their performance so far works out to a C average on our report card—an average that should rise over the next two years. Here are our grades for eight of the Net economy's biggest sectors:

Travel
A

The valedictorian so far. The three remaining public companies are profitable—Expedia, Hotels.com, and Priceline. Travelocity was profitable when it merged with Sabre Inc. in April.

The reason Web travel agencies make money is simple: Travel reservations are just data, which can be shipped easily over the Net. And the interactive nature of the medium lets customers do more research on vacation options online than they can do with brochures.

Even the ever-slimming commissions agencies collect on airline tickets are tidily profitable once online agencies get big enough. And now they are. Leading agency Expedia Inc. got $123 million in travel commissions last year, up 107%, but the cost of processing those reservations rose just 57%, to $53.4 million. What's more, smart online agencies have protected themselves against falling commissions by moving into the tour-packaging business.

Finance
A−

Ten public companies are profitable—with up to five more due to be profitable by yearend. Online brokers are in the black, despite slow trading volume. Now, online mortgage, tax-prep, and banking companies are joining them.

E-finance has the same advantages as online travel: a bottomless ability to crunch numbers and compare products, and no boxes to ship. Online brokers such as E*Trade Group Inc. and Charles Schwab & Co. began making money first—and still do, despite trading declines that have prompted consolidation.

The Web's impact on financial services is hard to miss. Productivity gains already are beating bullish forecasts, and established companies are responding. No. 1 mortgage lender Washington Mutual Inc. issued $60 billion in loans on the Web last year. Online brokers forced incumbents such as Merrill Lynch & Co. to slash commissions. And market researcher Gartner Group Inc. says 25 million Americans will pay bills online this year.

Media and advertising
B−

Eight of the 50 that went public are profitable. The ad slump hurts, but online media is still a $7 billion business. AOL Time Warner Inc. is the Goliath, while specialty sites such as job site Monster.com make money, too.

It's easy to snark about Web advertising. Boosters promised hypercatchy ads that would be targeted at precisely the right customers. Moreover, they said consumers' behavior could be predicted by tracking what Web pages they visited. That hasn't happened. Still, profits have arrived for companies that handle advertising innovatively—such as Overture Services Inc.'s paid-search engine. Bottom line: Advertising is a cyclical business, online advertising included. Web advertising may not become more effective than other media soon, but it can support a number of companies with even a modest recovery.

Retail
C+

Five of the 40 that went public are profitable, including 1-800-Flowers.com Inc. and teen site Alloy Inc. Amazon.com should join the group with a good Christmas. About a dozen of the public e-tailers failed.

Funny, but there was no recession in online retailing last year. Sales rose 13% last Christmas, to $10 billion, compared with a 2% gain in total shopping. The gorilla: Amazon, whose Christmas and first quarter beat expectations. The one to watch: Ticketmaster, which books about 35% of its ticket sales online—and operates the Match.com dating site and the CitySearch hometown activities sites. Ticketmaster is looking for more Net acquisitions.

Exchanges
C

EBay is one of only two exchange companies to make money. Still, corporate-auction site FreeMarkets Inc. and hospital supply exchange Neoforma Inc. are making progress

Online exchanges were supposed to transform business by squeezing inefficiencies from business-to-business deals and putting buyers and sellers in direct contact with one another. And they were supposed to do it by, say, Tuesday. Oops! Still, three years after they debuted with much fanfare, enough is happening that exchanges aren't a total fizzle.

EBay has been the benchmark for profitable online companies. Its magic is that it collects fees on transactions without ever holding inventory. Other companies are now proving that eBay was not a fluke. Online bond exchange eSpeed Inc. made $7.8 million in the fourth quarter. ESpeed's success was especially poignant: The Web spin-off of Cantor Fitzgerald LP saw its automated bond-trading system help the parent company keep going after the World Trade Center attack killed 658 Cantor and eSpeed employees.

Software
C

Only 14 out of about 150 companies are profitable. The money makers are Intuit Inc. and McAfee.com, which deliver software over the Web mostly to consumers. Startups that target corporations, including Commerce One Inc., have had problems.

This sector has gotten whipped much harder by the corporate spending slump than by the dot-com bust—although both hurt. It was investment delays by big companies that crimped companies such as Commerce One, Ariba, and i2 Technologies, which were about as big a trio of Internet rock stars as anyone could be in 1999. BroadVision Inc. and Art Technology Group Inc. are scrambling to make themselves more enterprise-friendly and less focused on e-commerce. It could be a tough road.

Access/Infrastructure
D+

Seven companies out of 80 are profitable. Startups bet big that companies would outsource major computing applications to others. Those bets haven't paid off.

Remember back in April, 2000, when venture-capital incubator Safeguard Scientifics Inc. rattled Web stocks by saying it would invest only in 'infrastructure' companies? Bad plan. Infrastructure is among the Web's toughest businesses. The reason: A glut of companies wanted either to sell Internet access or convince corporations to hire someone to run their computing applications and deliver them via the Web. The profitable ones are mainly companies that provide services corporations can't easily provide for themselves. Example: WebEx Communications Inc., a seller of Web-conferencing services. An uptick will come only when businesses decide to risk handing their operations over to outsiders in exchange for fewer headaches.

Consulting
F

Only 3 of the 14 public companies make money—Modem Media, Razorfish, and Inforte. Consultants such as Scient Inc. got hammered when corporations lost interest in e-commerce.

Of all the mind-bending Web moments, one of the most recent came when left-for-dead Razorfish reported a first-quarter profit of $2.5 million. The Web consulting industry was one of the first Net businesses to make money. One pioneer, Sapient Corp., reported net income every year from 1997 to 2000. But the whole sector crashed in 2000 because the e-commerce boom led them all to expand their staffs too fast—then the bust left them with sky-high expenses. And don't look for lots of comeback stories. The business that's around now comes from bigger companies that are the customers of giants such as Electronic Data Systems Corp. and IBM.

Amazon, Priceline.com Inc., and their dot-com brethren may never again be as sexy as they once were, but they're shaping up to be far sounder companies. If this profit-making trend continues, we may have to coin a new name for them: the com-back kids.

CASE QUESTIONS

Question 1 Why do you believe that e-travel and e-finance organizations, who were awarded an A and A− respectively, have been able to deliver profits?

Question 2 Why did the consulting profession perform so poorly? What are the salient lessons learned for employers and employees working in the consulting profession?

Question 3 Are you surprised that eBay is one of only two exchange companies to make money. Why do you think exchange companies have been unable to formulate and implement a profitable e-business model?

MINI CASE STUDY 1

Ebookers signs up for London listing, by Julia Snoddy, www.mediaguardian.co.uk, 13 March 2001

Ebookers.com, the online travel firm, yesterday announced it is to list its shares on the London Stock Exchange, shrugging off the turmoil in the hi-tech sector.

The London-based firm, already listed on Frankfurt's Neuer Markt and the NASDAQ, also confirmed that it aims to move into profit by 2002.

Navneet Bali, Ebookers' chief financial officer, said the company was seeking a London listing to give it access to future funding from UK-based investors, even though it is not raising any new money at the moment. Despite the negative sentiment about online companies, it had decided to stick to its plans rather than waiting for a market recovery.

'The move brings us closer to our investor base in our largest market,' Ebookers said. 'It is expected to allow us access to institutional funds that could not previously buy Ebookers.com stock.'

Mr Bali emphasised that the firm, which raised $45m from European institutional investors last July and has $50m in the bank, has enough cash to take it into profitability.

'We are not raising new money.' said Mr Bali. 'It is just a technical listing that allows our ordinary shares to be traded.' Ebookers hopes London trading in its stock will begin before the end of March. It has no plans to change its listings on NASDAQ and the Neuer Markt at present.

The news came as the company reported a fourfold increase in fourth quarter sales to $36m (£24.5m), up from $9m for the same period in 1999. Full year sales reached $123.5m, up from $23m in 1999, with registered users increasing from 740,000 at the end of the third quarter to 850,000 at the end of 2000.

Ebookers said its pre-tax loss, excluding stock compensation, was $40m – compared to $7m in 1999.

Chief executive Dinesh Dhamija said: 'Losses have gone up so much because we spent a lot more on sales and marketing in the first half of last year.'

Mr Bali said sales and marketing costs would continue to be reduced. As a percentage of sales, they fell from 34% in the first quarter of 2000 to 17% in the fourth quarter.

'Since mid-1999 we've grown tremendously, and obviously we've had to invest a lot in technology as well as sales and marketing to build a brand,' Mr Bali said. 'All that is behind us now.'

Analysts were yesterday positive about Ebookers' results.

'They seem on target to be profitable at the end of 2001 or the start of 2002, and revenues were pretty good for an online business', one analyst said.

However, the analyst was sceptical about the interest the firm could expect to receive from institutional investors because of the relatively small size of the business.

Mr Dhamija also admitted yesterday that Ebookers, which has expanded into 11 countries including Spain, Switzerland and Ireland, is on the hunt for acquisitions.

'We want to go into Italy and into the business side of travel,' he said. 'I would also like to acquire larger leisure companies in Germany and France.' Shares in the company have plunged in line with the rest of the technology sector – from a high of 44 euros in March they fell yesterday by 0.27 euros to 3.33 euros.

CASE QUESTIONS

Question 1 Why is e-booker.com seeking a listing on the London Stock Exchange?

Question 2 Since the London Stock Exchange listing in April 2001, has Ebookers.com been trading successfully? You may find it useful to gather additional information from www.hoovers.co.uk.

MINI CASE STUDY 11
7 Lessons learned from the dot-com fallout, by Alex Gutzman, Internet News, www.internetnews.com, 17 April 2001

Layoffs have plagued the Internet industry. First came the initial waves of dot-com failures. The dot-com consultancies weren't far behind, as they too began laying off employees.

Surely, amid the rubble that was the Internet bubble, there must be some lessons we can all learn. Some of these are so obvious it's almost too embarrassing to list them. But since (presumably) smart people parted with their money, I'm going to go ahead list them anyway.

1. There is no substitute for business experience.

Genius is close, but few true geniuses do very well in business, so genius is an inferior criterion for investment. Most venture capitalists that gave millions of dollars to twenty-somethings were simply gambling that only a small fraction would pay off.

2. The Web is not (and doesn't have to be) the most economical way to shop.

Neither B2C nor B2B commerce is exclusively about offering the lowest price. That's okay, though, because the most desirable customers aren't the most price conscious customers. In fact, some customers aren't price conscious at all. The perception of abundant inventory doesn't drive all shoppers to price bots.

Catalog suppliers like Eddie Bauer have done well precisely because they have not tried to compete on price. Offer service and convenience, and you will attract customers who won't click away even when you charge a US$3 per order handling fee (such as Eddie Bauer does).

3. Free is an unsustainable business model.

I'm inclined to add a 'duh!' to the end of the previous sentence, but I still hear from readers who are trying to make a go of offering something for free now, only to start adding fees at some future date.

It reminds me of an old episode of 'The Twilight Zone'. A stranger arrives at a woman's door and hands her a box with a big button on it. He tells her that if she presses the button, she'll get a large sum of money and someone she's never met will die. After looking at the box for a several days, she presses the button, and right away the doorbell rings. It's the stranger with her money. She asks where he's taking the box, and he replies, 'Don't worry. I'll give it to someone you've never met.'

When you open your doors and offer something for free, you're sounding the death knell for that company (storage provider, ISP, or some other interchangeable service) that has been in business for six months, giving their own services away, and has recently decided to charge. On the other hand, you're only six months away from having to start charging for your services, and consequently being put out of business by someone else's free service.

4. E-everything is about time and money.

For some the savings will be time, for others it will be money. For few parties will it be both (directly). For e-business, long-term relationships matter most.

5. Standardization is good.

Even if the Internet disappeared tomorrow, we'd still have XML. XML permits business applications and even businesses to communicate with each other in a standard (non-proprietary) way.

The standardization that you want to avoid is any standardization decided by someone other than the market. Who should really be surprised that standardization is good? Isn't this why we have patents? Every company would move toward the ideal model on its own if we didn't give proprietary ownership of the ideal model to the patent owner (for some limited period of time).

6. Spend marketing money wisely.

marchFIRST filed for bankruptcy last week. I knew they were some type of dot-com services company because their frequent television commercials (and I don't watch three hours of television a week) told me nothing about them. Quirky and mysterious is not great branding for a consulting firm.

Also, unless your product or service is targeted to a general audience, don't advertise during 'ER'. Television commercials for dot-coms seem to be more about executive egos than about driving traffic and selling products.

7. The Web is a channel.

The Internet is not really a sector of the economy, the way that consumer goods and energy are sectors. The Internet is more like accounting. It's a part of every company, with some companies making it all they do, but only to the degree that they can help companies with their own execution of this specialized task.

Actually, NASDAQ (and my portfolio) aside, the dot-com meltdowns weren't necessarily a bad thing. Most industries take years to mature. The Internet industry is maturing at the speed of ... well, the Internet. Those of us who need to take action today ignore these lessons at our own peril.

This article has been reprinted from ECommerce Guide.com, a sister site to asia.internet.com.

CASE QUESTIONS

Question 1 What do you believe are the most important lessons learned from the dot.com fall out?

Question 2 According to Gutzman in this case study, 'the Internet is not really a sector of the economy, the way that consumer goods and energy are sectors. The

Internet is more like accounting. It's a part of every company, with some companies making it all they do, but only to the degree that they can help companies with their own execution of this specialized task . . .' Do you agree with this assertion?

REFERENCES

Borison A (2000) *Market Value in the New Millennium*, PricewaterhouseCoopers, www.ebusiness.pwcglobal.com.

Copeland, T., T. Koller and J. Murrin (2000) *Valuation, Measuring and Managing the Value of Companies*, 3rd edn., Wiley, Chichester and New York.

Desmet, D., T. Francis, A. Hu, T.M. Koller and G.A. Reidel (2000) Valuing dot.coms, *The McKinsey Quarterly*, no. 1, pp. 148–157.

Higson, C. and J. Briginshaw (2000) Valuing Internet businesses, *Business Strategy Review*, vol. 11, no. 1, pp 10–20.

Journal of Psychology & Financial Market, (2000) Editorial: The old psychology behind 'new metrics', vol. 1, no. 3/4, pp. 158–160.

Koller, T. (2001) Valuing dot.coms after the fall, *McKinsey Quarterly*, special issue 2, vol. 1, no. 3/4, pp. 158–160.

Perkins, M. and A. Perkins (1999) *The Internet Bubble*, HarperCollins, New York.

Porter, M. (1985), *Competitive Advantage*, Free Press, New York.

PricewaterhouseCoopers (PwC) (2000), *Valuing technology stocks*, www.pwcglobal.com.

Rappaport, A. (1998), *Creating Shareholder Value*, Free Press, New York.

Tversky, A. and D. Kahneman (1971) Belief in the law of small numbers. *Psychological Bulletin*, vol. 76, no. 1, pp. 105–110.

CHAPTER 9
ONLINE RESOURCES AND THEIR DEPLOYMENT

LEARNING OUTCOMES

When you have read and worked through this chapter, you will be able to:
- Appreciate the problems of the Internet
- Appreciate some of the major meta-search engines
- Appreciate some of the major subject directories
- Understand how to perform Boolean searching on the Internet
- Identify some best-practice Web searching techniques
- Appreciate the value of shopping bots
- Understand the problems of the Invisible Web
- Appreciate some useful business websites

INTRODUCTION

The Internet with excess of three billion documents provides a vast array of information to the user. The Internet can affect commercial and non-commercial organizations and continues to do so. It seems pertinent that researchers and students should be able to find information and transfer this visual knowledge to applied knowledge. However, locating the Web documents that you want can be easy or seem impossibly difficult.

In this chapter we review some of the resources available on the Internet. The focus of the discussion is to provide an overview of the salient features of some of the academic and practical services available to users. The problems of haphazardly trying to locate information are examined. A selection of meta-search engines are used to illustrate how they can assist the online researcher. The systematic features of subject directories are highlighted. Some practical aspects of Boolean Web searching and best-practice Web searching are used to assist readers locate specific items of information. The benefits of shopping bots are discussed and the chapter concludes with a discussion about the Invisible Web.

THE PROBLEM

Matters are complicated by the fact that, given the size of the Internet, surfing the net is now a haphazard way to explore the Internet. Nevertheless, when the Internet is used effectively, significant benefits can be derived. Unfortunately, the Internet is not indexed in any standard vocabulary, unlike the system used by the British Library (www.bl.uk), which is the national library of the United Kingdom. The vision of the British Library is to make the world's intellectual, scientific and cultural heritage accessible and to bring the collections of the British Library to everyone's virtual bookshelf – at work, school, college and home. The British Library receives a copy of every publication produced in the UK and Ireland and the collection currently includes more than 150 million items, in over 400 languages. More than three million new items are incorporated into the collection every year.

In contrast, when you are 'surfing the Web' you are not searching a single source directly. The Internet is the totality of the many Web pages that reside on servers all over the world, which makes it impossible for a single computer to find or go to all Web pages directly. To access information you need to use one of the many search tools that are available. To gather information, the user is merely searching the search tool's database or collection of Web sites, which is still a relatively small subset of the World Wide Web. Hypertext links and URLs are used to guide the user through the Web. By clicking on these links, the user is able to retrieve documents, images and sounds from servers around the world.

If users are familiar with catalogues, search engines and search sites, two benefits are achievable:

- Search tools can help users find out information about competitors.
- Collectively, Web search systems will enable users to determine how to list or register their website on the Internet, so that their organization is visible online.

Synergistic search systems (meta-search engines)

As previously explained, search engines do not really search the World Wide Web. Each search performed by a user searches a database of the full text of Web pages selected from the billions of Web pages residing on servers. Search-engine databases are selected and built by computer robot programs called spiders. Although it is said that they 'crawl' the Web in their hunt for pages to include, in truth they stay in one place. They find the pages for potential inclusion by following the links in the pages they already have in their database. After spiders find pages, they pass them on to another computer program for 'indexing'. This program identifies the text, links and other content in the page and stores it in the search-engine database's files so that the database can be searched by keyword and whatever more advanced approaches are offered, and the page will be found if your search matches its content.

The distinctions between catalogues (a company like yahoo.com was one of the earliest Internet catalogues) and search engines are now fuzzy, as some websites now combine the catalogues and a search-engine system. Others provide access to many catalogues and/or search engines from one website. These synergistic or meta-search websites can save a lot of time by searching only in one place and sparing the need to use and learn several separate search engines. The **meta-search engine** requires the user to submit keywords in its search box, and the system transmits the search simultaneously to several individual search engines and their databases of Web pages. Moments later the user receives the results from all the search engines queried. However, it must be borne in mind that meta-search engines do not own a database of Web pages; they send search terms to the databases maintained for other search engines.

Key Term...

Meta-search engines
These enable users to search simultaneously to several individual search engines and their Web pages

SOME META-SEARCH ENGINES

Google, WiseNut, AllTheWeb and Alta Vista

The better meta-search engines allow the user to use a variety of Web media to perform searches. In addition to Web pages, some meta-search engines can search news articles and for pictures. A variety of video formats and audio files in MP3 format can be investigated and some engines can also locate FTP files on other computers.

Google (www.google.com)

Google's complex, automated methods make its results extremely robust. Although Google does run relevant advertisements above and next to results, it does not sell placement within the results themselves (i.e. no one can buy a higher PageRank). Google speed is attributed to its unique combination of advanced hardware and software, which coupled with its search algorithm and thousands of networked low-cost PC's, creates a super-fast search engine.

Google's search engine is distinguished from its competitors by its ranking algorithm, which is based on how many other pages link to each page, along with other factors like the proximity of search keywords or phrases in the documents. It uses not only the number of other pages that link to a page, but also the importance of the other links (measured by the links to each of them). At the heart of the system is PageRank™, which is a system for ranking Web pages developed by Google's founders Larry Page and Sergey Brin.

PageRank relies on the uniquely democratic nature of the Web by using linkages among structures as an indicator of an individual page's value. For example, Google interprets a link from page X to page Y as a vote, by page X, for page Y. But, in addition to Google using the sheer volume of votes, or links a page receives, it also analyses the page that casts the vote. Votes cast by pages that are themselves 'important' weigh more heavily and help to make other pages 'important'. Thus, important, high-quality sites receive a higher PageRank, which Google remembers each time it conducts a search. These important pages need to be matched with a user's query. Google, therefore, combines PageRank with sophisticated text-matching techniques to find pages that are both important and relevant to your search. Google does not merely record the number of times a term appears on a Web page, but examines all attributes of the page's content (and the content of the pages linking to it) to determine if it's a good match for the user's query.

AllTheWeb (www.AllTheWeb.com)

This meta-search engine was initially launched in April 1999, as a vehicle to demonstrate Fast technology to prospective portal partners. Currently, AllTheWeb Web searching is performed using the FAST Search software technology to build indices and perform queries. Its advanced search allows users to formulate very complex search strategies. The FAST web crawler is used and AllTheWeb is now one of the world's largest, fastest and most comprehensive search engines, offering the following benefits:

- Highly relevant results.
- The world's freshest index.
- Unified search where Web pages, files and multimedia content are all available in one place.
- Intelligent Search Tips that will help you find just what you're looking for.
- Other advanced features including language detection, duplicate filtering, offensive content reduction, site collapsing, etc.

Alta Vista (www.altavista.com)

Since 1995, AltaVista has sought to provide Web enthusiasts with a broad range of Internet search services and, through its technology, deliver relevant and useful information faster. AltaVista is now one the Internet's premier search engines that integrate technology and services to deliver relevant results.

AltaVista uses a ranking algorithm to determine the order in which matching documents are returned on the results page. Each document gets a grade based on how many of the search terms it contains, where the words are located in the document, and how close they are to each other. Intentionally and unnecessarily repeating a word on a Web page is known as spamming and has a negative effect on a website's ranking. To overcome spamming, AltaVista uses special software to detect spamming and the offending site is prevented from appearing in the index. Alta Vista is now a fairly large search engine with full Boolean logic capability in its Advanced Search. It offers two levels of searching – simple and advanced.

WiseNut (www.wisenut.com)

Launched in September 2001, WiseNut has quickly become one of the fastest, smartest and most comprehensive new search engines on the market. WiseNut is an advanced search technology company founded by Yeogirl Yun, the former CTO and co-founder of mySimon. WiseNut's mission is to become the leading provider of advanced technology and services in the Internet search market.

The company's technology has been heralded for its ability to deliver exact results every time. WiseNut has also designed several new products including WiseVote, a revolutionary new way for users to customize search results and for portals to generate new revenue.

WiseNut uses an algorithm similar to Google's PageRank to compute relevance, examining the web's link structure and popularity of pages to help determine the best results for your query. WiseNut has several additional added-value features such as the ability to automatically categorize results into 'wiseguides' that are semantically related to the words in the user's query. WiseNut lists the exact number of pages on a website that it has determined are relevant to the query. Similar to Google's cached pages, WiseNut offers a feature called 'Sneak-a-Peek' that enables the user to get a preview of a Web page without leaving the WiseNut's result page.

SOME SUBJECT DIRECTORIES

Key Term...

Subject directories
These types of directories are particularly useful for specifying websites on a variety of topics

Librarians' Index, Infomine, Academic Info, About

General **subject directories** are extremely useful for identifying specific websites on a variety of topics. For the academic or student there is a rich collection of Web pages, databases, links to full-text publications, organizations selected primarily for academic research at the undergraduate level and above.

Librarians' Index (www.lii.org)

Librarians' Index (LII) originated in 1990 as reference librarian Ms Carole Leita's Gopher bookmark file. It then migrated to the Berkeley Public Library's Web Server in 1993 as the Berkeley Public Library Index to the Internet. In late 1996, Ms Leita began working with Mr Roy Tennant at the Digital Library SunSITE to add a search engine to LII and develop a virtual workspace to facilitate team-based record creation and maintenance. In March 1997, the Berkeley Public Library Index to the Internet was moved to the Berkeley SunSITE and was renamed the Librarians' Index to the Internet.

The Librarians' Index has the motto: 'Information You Can Trust'. LII is a searchable, annotated subject directory of more than 9000 Internet resources selected and evaluated by librarians for their usefulness to users of public libraries. LII is used by both librarians and the general public as a reliable and efficient guide to Internet resources.

Infomine (infomine.ucr.edu)

Infomine contains over 23 000 links with substantive databases, electronic journals, guides

---

ILLUSTRATIVE EXAMPLE I
WebWise – www.bbc.co.uk/webwise

A good website which provides useful information can be found at BBC webwise (www.bbc.co.uk/webwise/)

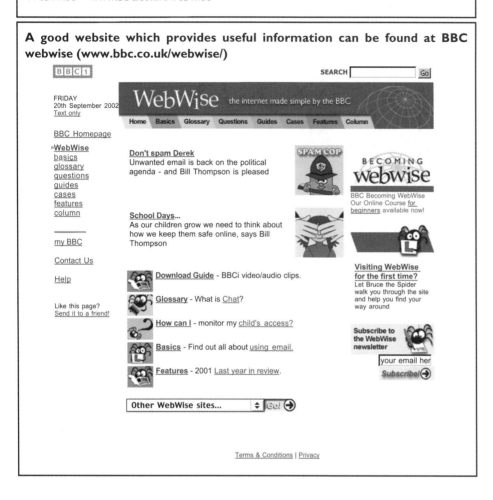

---

to the Internet for most disciplines, textbooks and conference proceedings are among the many types of resources included. Infomine is a Web resource featuring well organized access to important university-level research and educational tools on the Internet. A virtual library, Infomine is notable for its collection of annotated and indexed links. Infomine began in January 1994 as a project of the Library of the University of California, Riverside. It was one of the first Web-based, academic virtual libraries as well as one of the first to develop a system combining the advantages of the hypertext and multimedia capabilities of the Web with those of the organizational and retrieval functions of a database manager. It now includes focused, automatic Internet crawling and text extraction functions.

Academic Info (www.academicinfo.net)
Academic Info went online in 1998 and started life as an independent Internet subject directory owned by Mr Michael Madin and maintained with the assistance of a quality group of subject specialists. In the spring of 2000 Michael left the University of Washington Gallagher Law Library to focus solely on Academic Info. In 2002 Academic Info became a registered non-profit organization of the state of Washington. Academic Info is now ad free and relies on donations to remain online.

The mission statement of Academic Info states that it aims to be the premier educational gateway to online high-school, college and research-level Internet resources. Academic Info seeks to be the 'white pages' to the academic community.

About.com (www.about.com)

In February 1997, Mr Scott Kurnit and his team launched The Mining Company. The company quickly grew in size and scale and in 1999 the company was renamed About, to reflect its breadth of content, services and ease of use. Today, About is visited by one in five online users each month.

About markets itself as the Human Internet, where real people help users gather information from the Web. The About network consists of hundreds of Guide sites, which are organized into 23 channels. These sites cover more than 50,000 subjects with over one million links to the best resources on the Web and one of the fastest-growing archives of high-quality original content.

Each site in the network is run by a professional Guide, who is carefully screened and trained by About. Guides build a comprehensive environment around each of their specific topics, including the best new content, relevant links, How-To's, Forums and answers to just about any question. The insight and perspective that Guides bring to each area of interest is what makes the About experience enjoyable and interactive.

BOOLEAN SEARCHING ON THE INTERNET

Key Term...

Boolean logic
Boolean logic consists of three logical operators – OR, AND, NOT

Given the increasing nature of the Internet, users who are looking for specific information may have to perform a search according to the rules of computer database searching. Cohen (2002) provides a useful introduction for performing Boolean searching on the Internet. This form of researching can be executed using the principles of **Boolean logic**. For illustration purposes the Boolean logic operators OR, AND and NOT are used to show how to perform basic Web searches.

OR – e-commerce OR e-business

Query: I would like information about e-commerce.

This search will retrieve records in which at least one of the search terms is present. We are searching on the terms e-commerce and also e-business since documents containing either of these words might be relevant.

This is illustrated in Figure 9.1 by:

- The shaded circle with the word e-commerce representing all the records that contain the word 'e-commerce'
- The shaded circle with the word e-business representing all the records that contain the word 'e-business'
- The shaded overlap area representing all the records that contain both 'e-commerce' and 'e-business'

OR logic is most commonly used to search for synonymous terms or concepts. An example of how OR logic works is given in Table 9.1.

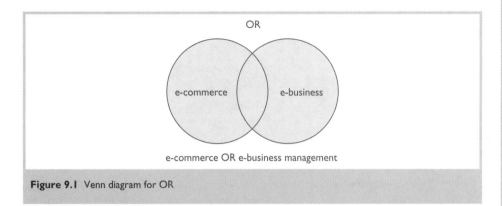

Figure 9.1 Venn diagram for OR

Search Terms	Results
e-commerce	3 630 000
e-business	3 130 000
e-commerce OR	
e-business	4 480 000

Table 9.1 How OR logic works

OR logic collates the results to retrieve all the unique records containing one term, the other or both.

The more terms or concepts we combine in a search with OR logic, the more records we will retrieve; see Table 9.2.

Search Terms	Results
e-commerce	3 630 000
e-business	3 130 000
e-commerce OR	
e-business	4 480 000
e-commerce OR e-business OR Internet	6 630 000

Table 9.2 Using more terms in a search with OR logic

AND – strategy AND performance

Query: I'm interested in the relationship between strategy and performance.

In this search, we retrieve records in which BOTH of the search terms are present. This is illustrated in Figure 9.2 by the shaded area overlapping the two circles representing all the records that contain both the word 'strategy' and the word 'performance'. Notice that we do not retrieve any records with only 'strategy' or only 'performance'. Table 9.3 gives an example of how AND logic works.

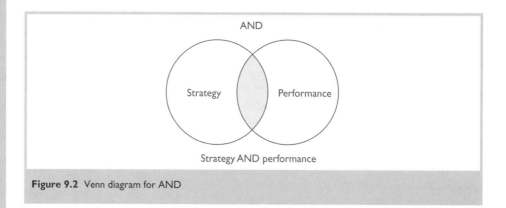

Figure 9.2 Venn diagram for AND

Search Terms	Results
Strategy	12 900 000
Performance	32 000 000
Strategy AND performance	2 290 000

Table 9.3 How AND logic works

The more terms or concepts we combine in a search with AND logic, the fewer records we will retrieve; see Table 9.4.

Search Terms	Results
Strategy	12 900 000
Performance	32 000 000
Strategy AND performance	2 290 000
Strategy AND performance AND business	1 720 000

Table 9.4 Using more terms in a search with AND logic

NOT – hotels NOT restaurants

Query: I want to see information about hotels, but I want to avoid seeing anything about restaurants.

In this search, we retrieve records in which *only one* of the terms is present. This is illustrated in Figure 9.3 by the shaded area with the word hotels representing all the records containing the word 'hotels'. No records are retrieved in which the word 'restaurant' appears, even if the word 'hotels' appears there too. Table 9.5 gives an example of how NOT logic works.

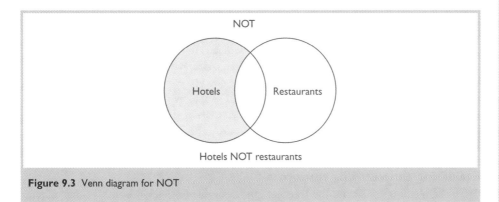

Figure 9.3 Venn diagram for NOT

Search Terms	Results
Hotels	22 700 000
Restaurants	9 350 000
Hotels NOT restaurants	1 420 000

Table 9.5 How NOT logic works

It must also be borne in mind that when you use an Internet search engine, the use of Boolean logic may be manifested in three distinct ways:

- Full Boolean logic with the use of the logical operators – many search engines offer the option to do full Boolean searching requiring the use of the Boolean logical operators.
- Implied Boolean logic with keyword searching – keyword searching refers to a search type in which you enter terms representing the concepts you wish to retrieve. Boolean operators are not used.
- Predetermined language in a user fill-in template – some search engines offer a search template that allows the user to choose the Boolean operator from a menu. Often the logical operator is expressed with substitute language rather than with the operator itself.

BEST-PRACTICE WEB SEARCHING

Ackermann and Hartman (2000) have proposed a useful guideline, which can be used for a broad range of searches ranging from the simplest to the most complex. Obviously, the more complex the search the greater the need to follow a strategy, particularly when using a search engine for the first time. An unsophisticated search strategy can help you get used to a search engine's features and how they are expressed in the search query. Best practice cited by Ackermann and Hartman (2000) includes:

1. Identify the important concepts of your search.
2. Choose the keywords that describe these concepts.
3. Determine whether there are synonyms, related terms or other variations of the keywords that should be included.
4. Determine which search features may apply, i.e. truncation, proximity operators, Boolean operators, etc.

275

5 Choose a search engine.
6 Read the search instructions on the search engine's home page. Look for sections entitled help, advanced search, frequently asked questions, etc.
7 Create a search expression, using syntax, which is appropriate for the search engine.
8 Evaluate the results. Were they relevant to your query?
9 Modify your search if needed. Go back to steps 2–4 and revise your query accordingly.
10 Try the same search in a different search engine, following steps 5–9 above.

This is taken from www1.mwc.edu.

Evaluating and verifying resources

Given the plethora of data on the Internet, it is desirable to check the authenticity, usefulness and appropriateness of the information retrieved and gathered during searching. The following section provides some of the salient points that the user should consider.

Who is the author or institution?
- If the author is a person, does the resource give biographical information?
- If the author is an institution, is there information provided about it?
- Have you seen the author's or institution's name cited in other sources or bibliographies?
- The URL can give clues to the authority of a source. A tilde (~) in the URL usually indicates that it is a personal page rather than part of an institutional Web site.

How current is the information?
- Is there a date on the Web page that indicates when the page was placed on the Web?
- Is it clear when the page was last updated?

Is some of the information obviously out-of-date?
- Does the page creator mention how frequently the material is updated?

Who is the audience?
- Is the Web page intended for the general public, scholars, practitioners, children, etc.? Is this clearly stated?
- Does the Web page meet the needs of its stated audience?

Is the content accurate and objective?
- Are there political, ideological, cultural, religious, or institutional biases?
- Is the content intended to be a brief overview of the information or an in-depth analysis?
- If the information is opinion, is this clearly stated?
- If there is information copied from other sources, is this acknowledged? Are there footnotes if necessary?

What is the purpose of the information?
- Is the purpose of the information to inform, explain, persuade, market a product or advocate a cause?
- Is the purpose clearly stated?
- Does the resource fulfill the stated purpose?

This is taken from www1.mwc.edu.

ILLUSTRATIVE EXAMPLE II
Clearlybusiness: Business Information Online, www.clearlybusiness.com

---

Clearlybusiness.com aims to increase the survival and growth prospects of small businesses freeing up owner managers from the day to day bureaucracy involved in running a business, and giving them access to the kinds of information, cost and efficiency benefits that have previously only been available to larger companies in the UK

Clearlybusiness won the UK's 'Best Business Portal', as voted in the Internet Business Awards 2001.

Backed by Barclays and Freeserve, clearlybusiness already has helped over 130,000 users set up and grow their own small businesses.

Registering with clearlybusiness is free and will make sure you have full access to the wealth of practical information, business tools and services available on the site. All of which have been designed to help you increase the survival and growth prospects of your business.

From free access to expert business advice, free market research data on your industry sector to financial management tools and sales and marketing tips for a budget, clearlybusiness will help give your business a better chance of success.

See some of our most popular articles and services below:

* *Clearlybookkeeping*, the integrated financial management tool to help improve your cash flow, bookkeeping and understanding of your finances.
* *5 step marketing and planning guide* – our step by step plan to the getting the basics right, from understanding your market potential to knowing and beating the competition.
* *The basics of your funding option* – understand the different options you have to finance your business and find out what is right for your business, from Business Angels to how to approach the bank.
* *Tips to avoid the common legal pitfalls* – get to know what your obligations are, from Health and safety to writing your first commercial contract.
* *Preparing and planning for the web* – understand what it takes to be successful on the web, from design to making sure you appear at the top of the search engine.

SHOPPING BOTS

A recent phenomenon of Internet shopping has been the emergence of comparison shopping agents as a powerful tool for the consumer. **Shopping agents** are sometimes called bots (bot is short for robot) and describes a software programme given a specific task to locate and compare products. Shopping bots have been a useful innovation and reduce some of the anxieties associated with shopping for specific products online (Rowley, 2000). Bots can perform all kinds of ingenious tasks on the Internet, such as taking a query, searching for information, monitoring sites and alerting people when those sites have changed. For example, a shopping bot will search the Web for the products specified by the user and display on screen a list of merchants with the best deals.

According to Price-Guide (www.price-guide.co.uk), a UK shopping bot, there are various features that distinguish this site from competitors:

Key Term...

Shopping agents
Sometimes called bots (short for robot), these are software programs given a specific task to locate and compare products

- They maintain the largest database of comparative prices of computer components and consumer electronics available anywhere in the UK. Other shopping guides tend to offer somewhere between 3000 and 100 000 price comparisons, but this database offers well in excess of a quarter of a million price comparisons from 250 retailers.
- While most shopping guides solely use 'robots' to download information from vendors' web sites, Price-Guide also gathers information from magazine ads, catalogues and price lists forwarded by vendors, as well as from other publicly available sources. This saves having to page through countless PC magazines and Web sites for the best prices!
- All the prices are thoroughly examined, manually captured and indexed prior to entry, thus avoiding the type of problems associated with 'dumping' downloaded data from Web sites directly onto Web pages. This involves changing product descriptions into the site's preferred format, adding unique identifier codes and synchronizing price and availability information with suppliers' databases.
- While other shopping guides rely solely on search strings to identify products (which often return many unwanted products), Price-Guide's directories allow users to search by specific categories. This is especially useful when users are uncertain which search string to use. It could be likened to Yahoo, which is a search directory rather than a search engine.

About.com provides a useful website that provides examples of a directory of Bots and Intelligent Agents, organized by subject, with a section spotlighting 'the Best of the Bots.' MySimon (www.mySimon.com) is a leading intelligent bot, which uses a variety of algorithms to mimic human shopping behaviour. A wholly owned subsidary of CNET Networks, mySimon is a free site designed to help users shop for millions of products at more than 2000 online stores. It scans the stores' products and prices through patent-pending Virtual Learning Agent software, which sends 'intelligent agents' across the Web to collect information.

THE INVISIBLE WEB

While there are some types of Web pages and links that are excluded from most search engines by policy, others are excluded because search engine spiders cannot access them. These latter Web pages are referred to as the **Invisible Web**, i.e. what you do not see in search-engine results. Search engines are well aware of the Invisible Web, but limitations in time and money could make it unfeasible to index all dynamic page possibilities. While the usefulness of meta-search engines and directories, which have been pre-indexed by humans according to some intelligent classification scheme has been highlighted, it must be borne in mind that the Invisible Web (sometimes referred to as Deep Web) is estimated to be more than 500 times larger than what traditional search engines can index (Bergman, 2001). Table 9.6 provides some interesting facts about the Invisible Web. Sending spiders to crawl through billions of Web pages is resource intensive, so many search engines do not look at each page at a Web site. Known as 'depth of crawl', most search engines are aware of this problem and are using innovative products to increase the number of pages they index.

As previously mentioned, search engines send out an automated 'spider' or 'crawler' to visit Web pages, read the information on the page and then follow links to other pages within the site. The information identified is sent to the index or catalogue, which is searched when the user types in key words at the search engine. These spiders generally return every month or two to find new material.

Key Findings
Public information on the Deep Web is currently 400 to 550 times larger than the commonly defined World Wide Web
The Deep Web contains 7500 terabytes of information compared to 19 terabytes of information in the surface Web
The Deep Web contains nearly 550 billion individual documents compared to the one billion of the surface Web
More than 200 000 Deep Web sites presently exist
Sixty of the largest Deep Web sites collectively contain about 750 terabytes of information – sufficient by themselves to exceed the size of the surface Web 40 times
On average, Deep Web sites receive 50 per cent greater monthly traffic than surface sites and are more highly linked to than surface sites; however, the typical (median) Deep Web site is not well known to the Internet-searching public
The deep Web is the largest growing category of new information on the Internet
Deep Web sites tend to be narrower, with deeper content, than conventional surface sites
Total quality content of the Deep Web is 1000 to 2000 times greater than that of the surface Web
Deep Web content is highly relevant to every information need, market and domain
More than half of the Deep Web content resides in topic-specific databases
A full 95 per cent of the Deep Web is publicly accessible information – not subject to fees or subscriptions

Table 9.6 Some facts about the Invisible Web (*Source: BrightPlanet – www.brightplanet.com – has quantified the size and relevancy of the Deep Web in a study based on data collected between 13 and 30 March 2000*)

Authors Chris Sherman and Gary Price, who are two leading Invisible Web experts have a mission of trying to save users time and aggravation and help them succeed in their information quest. They introduce users to top sites and sources and offer tips, techniques, and analysis that will let you pull needles out of haystacks every time. According to Price and Sherman (2001), exploring the Invisible Web isn't really that difficult if you're willing to invest some time and get caught up in the excitement of the hunt. They outline seven strategies that will help users get started on their own journey of exploration of the Web's hidden content:

1 Adopt the Mindset of a Hunter.
2 Use Search Engines.
3 Datamine Your Bookmark Collection.
4 Use the Net's 'Baker Street Irregulars'.
5 Use Invisible Web Pathfinders.
6 Use Offline Finding Aids.
7 Create Your Own 'Monitoring Service'.

Heller (2001) also offers some useful tips for navigating through the Invisible Web:

■ Use more than one search engine. Since each search engine, meta-search engine and directory uses different methodologies, tapping more than one for your search can help yield better results.

279

■ Use some of the specific, topic-focused search engines listed in the Invisible Web resources table.

■ Use quotes when looking for exactly worded phrases, especially if the words themselves are very common. For example, using "publishing house" will return more relevant results using quotes than not.

■ For more precise results, instead of using AND between words, consider using your search engine's variant of the proximity operator NEAR. For example, a search for 'system NEAR administrator' will usually return more relevant results than 'system AND administrator'.

SUMMARY

The problem

The Internet with excess of three billion documents provides a vast array of information to the user. The Internet can affect commercial and non-commercial organizations and continues to do so. It seems pertinent that researchers and students should be able to find information and transfer this visual knowledge to applied knowledge. However, finding the Web documents that you want can be easy or seem impossibly difficult.

Meta-search engines

The better meta-search engines allow the user to use a variety of Web media to perform searches. In addition to Web pages, some meta-search engines can search for news articles and for pictures.

Some subject directories

General subject directories are extremely useful for identifying specific Web sites on a variety of topics. For the academic or student there is a rich collection of Web pages, databases, links to full-text publications and organizations selected primarily for academic research at the undergraduate level and above.

Boolean searching on the Internet

Many search engines offer the option to do full Boolean searching requiring the use of the Boolean logical operators – AND, OR, NOT.

Best-practice Web searching

Given the plethora of data on the Internet, it is desirable to obtain information quickly and the authenticity, usefulness and appropriateness of the information retrieved and gathered during searching is paramount.

The Invisible Web

While there are some types of Web pages and links that are excluded from most search engines by policy, others are excluded because search engine spiders cannot access them.

SOME USEFUL WEBSITES

Corporate information

Hemscott (www.hemscott.com)
Hemscott is one of the leading providers of UK company information. Using their extensive data sources, they have developed 'Company Guru' an online company research tool for business professionals.

Company Annual Reports On line™ (Carol – http://www.carol.co.uk/)
Carol is a corporate online service offering one point access to company annual accounts online and provides a range of investor information.

Hoover's Online (www.hoovers.com/uk/)
Provides coverage of more than 65 000 companies worldwide. The Hoover's hallmark Company Capsules include company descriptions, key competitor and officer information, as well as financials on more than 17 000 public, private and international companies, including the entire FTSE 100 and FTSE 250.

The Public Register's Annual Report Service (PRARS – www.prars.com/web50/top50list.html)
PRARS is one of America's largest annual report service and provides a listing of the top 50 financial websites as indicated by its users.

Sources of useful e-business research material

Brint (www.brint.com)
Brint is one of the Premier Business and Technology Portal and Global Community Network for e-business, information, technology and knowledge management, and is widely recommended.

CIO (www.cio.com)
Focusing on the growing influence of the chief information officer, this website provides use e-business material.

IBM (www.ibm.com)
IBM was one of the first to use the term e-business, so this website provides vast array of information the e-business researcher.

Accenture (www.accenture.com)
Accenture (formerly Andersen Consulting) is one the world's leading management and technology services organization.

Cap Gemini Ernst & Young (www.cgey.com)
Cap Gemini Ernst & Young is one of the largest management and IT consulting firms in the world and combines the resources of Gemini Consulting, Cap Gemini IT Services, Ernst & Young LLP and Ernst & Young Consulting Services.

PricewaterhouseCoopers (www.pwcglobal.com)
PWC is one of the world's largest professional firms and was created by the merger of two firms – Price Waterhouse and Coopers & Lybrand – each with historical roots going back some 150 years.

Deloitte Consulting (www.dc.com)
Deloitte Consulting is one of the world's leading consulting firms, helping clients to translate leading ideas and technologies into sustainable competitive and strategic advantage.

Strategy firms
- T. Kearney (www.atkearney.com)
- Bain & Co. (Www.bain.com)
- Booz Allen & Hamilton (www.bah.com)

- Boston Consulting Group (www.bcg.com)
- LEK (www.lek.com)
- McKinsey & Co. (www.mckinsey.com)
- Mercer Management Consulting (www.mercermc.com)

DISCUSSION QUESTIONS

1. Why is it important for users to be familiar with catalogues, search engines and search sites?

2. How do subject directories help the student?

3. What are the important features of best-practice Web searching?

ASSESSMENT QUESTIONS

1. What do you believe are the major problems users face when using the Internet to locate specific information? What steps can be taken to improve the effectiveness of online searching?

2. Using any appropriate key word of your choice, you are required to compare and contrast the performance of any three meta-search engines. From your selection, which meta-search engine do you believe is best?

3. You are required to use any shopping bot of your choice to locate the best deal for any item of consumer electronics of your choice. Products identified by the shopping bot should be compared. In your opinion did you get a cheaper price and/or better value for money?

GROUP ASSIGNMENT QUESTIONS

1. Using any appropriate website(s) that provide annual reports, press articles and relevant Internet material, write a short report that performs a competitive analysis of any two organizations of your choice that are operating in the same industry.

2. Using evidence to support your views, how well do Internet subject directories satisfy the needs of the business user? How does the research need of the undergraduate or postgraduate student differ from that of the practitioner? You are required to support your answer with relevant examples.

3. Using any country of your choice, you are required to identify the 10 largest organizations within your selected country in terms of market capitalization. You may find it easier to restrict your selection to organizations that trade on a listed stock exchange, e.g. FTSE, NASDAQ.

MAIN CASE STUDY

Freshness issue and complexities with Web search engines, by Greg Notess,
Information Today, www.onlinemag.net, November 2001

The Web is aging. We can find plenty of Web pages that are more than several years old, and many more that contain out-of-date information. At the same time, the Web is ever-new. Every day, if not more rapidly, new Web pages and new data appear, providing up-to-date content and breaking news. And no algorithm can predict perfectly which pages will have new content today and which will remain static into perpetuity.

Pity the poor search engines. They crawl this seething, bubbling maelstrom we call the Web, indexing the text from hundreds of millions of pages, all of which can change at a moment's notice. For the past few years, most search engines claimed to refresh their entire database once a month or so. Yet, older records in their databases showed that the refresh rate was often more than claimed rate.

Some users still think that when they enter a query into a search engine's search box, that it goes out and searches the existing Web rather than an older database built from crawling the Web over some range of dates in the past. Given the technology used by the search engines, the Web search engines will always provide searchers with the ability to search a picture of the Web past. While much of that snapshot will still exist on the Web of today, other portions will be dead, changed, or inaccessible.

Understanding the currentness (or freshness) patterns of the search engines' databases helps the searcher to better understand the results and what might not be found. Several recent search engine initiatives are changing the freshness of their databases, but the impact on searchers varies.

Importance of freshness

Why is the freshness of the search engine important? Certainly, many Web sites have posted content on pages that do not change, may never be updated, and may always stay in the same location at the exact same URL. It might be surprising to know exactly how many pages are like this. For these kinds of pages, a single crawl of their content should be sufficient.

Yet, plenty of other Web sites make significant changes to their site content on a frequent basis. New pages are added. Old pages are moved to new URLs. New content is added to old pages. New sites spring up while others disappear. The longer the time lag since the search engine crawled, the less of this kind of content that will be searchable. In addition, older content that was crawled the last time and is no longer available will be found by the search engine, but it will result in dead links, pages that no longer match, or other errors.

Consequently, the fresher the search engine database, the fewer errors, misdirections, and dead pages will be included in the results. And there will be more new pages, updated sites, and revised content that will be searchable and retrievable. For most searches, and for most searchers, the fresher and more up-to-date search engines will provide better and more useful results.

Paid inclusion impact

One way in which the search engines are beginning to address the issue of freshness is in their paid inclusion programs. For many years, Webmasters of large sites have observed that when the search engine spiders visit their sites, they do not crawl every available page. The search engines would train their spiders to be sure first to find new sites and unindexed domains rather than crawling every single page on just one site. However, this becomes frustrating for Web sites who would like to have all of their pages indexed and accessible via the search engines.

For several search engines, that are also certainly seeking to become profitable companies, their recent introduction of paid inclusion programs helps both the bottom line and the freshness and completeness of content in their databases. At AltaVista, Inktomi, and Fast, Web sites can pay a fee to be sure that all the pages on their site are indexed and that they are reindexed more frequently. In some cases, all the pages are refreshed every one or two days, while others who pay for inclusion programs have even more frequent updates for some pages, and still others can have a longer refresh period. The difference is that the Web site can determine the rate to match the changes in content.

It is important to note that the participation in a paid inclusion program does not affect the ranking of the pages by the search engine; it just makes sure that they are included and are recrawled more frequently.

More frequent updates

Another approach to improve the freshness of their databases is being undertaken at Google and Fast, and perhaps shortly at AltaVista as well. These search engines are developing automated ways of identifying sites with frequently changing content. Once this subgroup has been identified, the search engines can train their spiders to visit those sites on more frequent, even daily, intervals. News sites, especially ones that offer today's news, are obvious examples and beneficiaries of this kind of approach.

Google is indexing some of these sites on a daily basis. Fast announced a nine-day refresh period on a portion of its database that includes such sites. However, even these improvements and well-intentioned efforts fail to truly keep current. Many news sites change and update content so frequently that the search engines will still always have an older version indexed than the one currently on view at the site.

For example, even with daily indexing, Google's cached copy of several news sites is still several days old, while Fast's varied at about a week. Either way, today's content is not indexed and available until it has moved off the front page. Thus, use of a specialty news search engine is still far more effective for searching news on the Web.

Measuring freshness

Aside from news sites, there are still plenty of reasons to hope for a greater indexing frequency from the search engines. To get some sense of the frequency of search engine updates, I ran a brief comparison of how the search engines indexed 12 sites that change on a daily basis and reflect the current date in their title. By comparing the title displayed by the search engine to the date the test was run, this test gave some sense of the time lag of each search engine.

The comparison was run on August 13, 2001. On any other day, including today, the results would likely be quite different, so this is just one snapshot in time of the lag time of the search engines. Only Fast, Google, and Inktomi even found all 12 of the sites, and many had duplicate entries for one or more of the sample sites. Google actually had 43 separate URLs for a major media site. All the URLs were redirected to the exact same location, but the dates reported on those 43 ranged from June 22 to August 11.

Results

Running this comparison demonstrated the problems with maintaining a fresh index. All the pages used for the study should have had the August 13 date. Instead, the oldest results found, by search engine, are as follows:

February:	Wisenut, Northern Light
March:	Teoma, Excite, AltaVista, MSN, HotBot
June:	Google
July:	Fast

By contrast, the most recent page dates were:

May 15:	Teoma
May 22:	Excite
July 4:	AltaVista
July 21:	Northern Light
July 23:	Wisenut
July 31:	Fast
August 4:	HotBot
August 7:	MSN
August 12:	Google

However, Google's August 12 hit was from a site in India, so it would probably have been August 11 if it had been in a North American time zone. These results show decent freshness for Google, Inktomi (used by MSN and HotBot), and Fast, but each only had a few results from that recent. While the oldest and most recent dates give some sense of the range, a rough median gives a better sense of the general date of their database:

AltaVista:	Early April
Teoma:	Early May
Excite:	May 20–22
Northern Light:	May–July
Wisenut:	Mid-June
Google:	Early July
MSN:	Mid-July
HotBot:	Mid-Late July
Fast:	Late July

Such results show the wide range of dates, with some very old content. While the freshest search engine is likely to change over time and from day to day, these findings reinforce the advice to use more than one search engine, especially when trying to find recent information.

The downside of freshness

The search engines may be getting better at keeping their databases more current, but there are times when a fresher database is not necessarily better. This is especially true at Google, with its cached copies of pages that show what the page contained when it was crawled. If you are looking for an older copy of a page and Google just updated the cached copy yesterday, you will not have access to an older version. If the site was alive last week, and Google has checked several times since then and found that it has been unavailable, will the cache continue to have the old version or will it just be purged?

Yet, in most cases, more attention to getting their databases as up-to-date as possible and frequently refreshed will just make it easier for searcher and Webmaster alike. Several search engines have major initiatives underway to improve their freshness. In the meantime, freshness will vary, depending on the day and time, which cluster of the search engine's computers your search hits, and the specific pages that have matching information. Just remember that search engines provide a searchable picture of the Web of the past. And maybe, it will soon become the more recent past.

CASE QUESTIONS

Question 1 In your opinion why is freshness so important? Are they any disadvantages to freshness?

Question 2 What does the term 'paid inclusion programs' mean? How does this benefit search engines?

Question 3 What are the implications of the results obtained by Greg Notess? Which search engines performed the best in the tests?

MINI CASE 1
Are best buys really unbiased?, by Steve Mathieson, The Guardian,
www.guardian.co.uk/online, 11 January 2001

Prices on comparison shopping sites cannot be taken as gospel – and some only list retailers prepared to pay a fee for that final click-through
Comparing is natural, asserts a recent advert for comparison shopping website Kelkoo.com. It shows one child smugly clutching a huge Christmas parcel with another bawling at the size of his more modest gift. But users of such sites cannot assume they are getting accurate, unbiased information.

Comparison shopping sites should be a boon for those wanting to buy online. Sites such as the UK's ShopSmart.com, French rival Kelkoo and recently-launched EasyValue.com (part of the UK group that owns airline EasyJet) ask you what you want to buy, then checks its price at several online retailers.

They then present you with a list of shops, their prices and delivery charges for the item, and in some cases information on delivery times and an overall store rating. ShopSmart, which according to web ratings agency MMXI Europe received 490,000 unique visitors last October, also offers reviews of items such as CDs. You can then click straight through to your chosen shop, saving much mouse-work.

It seems a great idea: but buyer, beware. Both ShopSmart and Kelkoo charge retailers a referral fee for that final click-through. No one will reveal the exact value, but Alexander Broich, UK managing director of online book and music retailer Bol.com, describes it as "more than pennies, but below a pound". Broich says he's happy to pay this fee, because someone who has chosen Bol from the list is ready to buy. This makes it a more efficient way of snaring paying customers than blanket advertising, he adds.

Indirectly, the fees charged by the comparison engines are paid by customers. Of course that can be said of all kinds of advertising, and retailers do not charge comparison site users more than those who come straight to their website. But the fees do lead some retailers to reject the comparison sites. "We try to avoid them like the plague," says Steve Bennett, chief executive of technology and music retailer Jungle.com.

But he adds: "You can't stop them coming to your site." Both ShopSmart and Kelkoo list Jungle products. When questioned on this, Kelkoo admitted it was listing Jungle for free, in the hope of cutting a deal with the Midlands-based retailer this year. ShopSmart said it does collect fees from Jungle, although Jungle insists its deal with the comparison site has lapsed.

Regardless of exceptions, the fees mean retailers with the keenest prices may well not be in the comparison list. And results differ widely. A search of these three comparison sites for two recently-released CDs produced no fewer than five different "cheapest" prices. When asked to search for U2's All That You Can't Leave Behind, ShopSmart and Kelkoo both identified 101CD.com as the cheapest retailer, at £9.99 including postage. EasyValue concluded that CDShop.com was the cheapest, at £10.75 inclusive.

These are not bad savings when compared with high street prices of £12.99 or £13.99. But an observant user of Kelkoo's site might notice a small advert for retailer CD-Wow.com, selling titles including the U2 album for £8.99 inclusive.

"In some situations, we may not always have them in the comparison engine, but may build them up through other promotions," says Brad Monaghan, UK head of commercial operations for Kelkoo, when asked why CD-Wow can advertise, but not get listed in comparisons. Monaghan says Kelkoo restricts its comparisons to retailers that have passed standards involving security of transactions and product guarantees – as well as a willingness to pay its fees, of course. ShopSmart has a similar set of standards, and says it is aiming to cut the number of retailers it uses.

Both have removed retailers after receiving complaints. EasyValue says it would in principle. There is something in this idea of quality control: CD-Wow delivered the £8.99 U2 album on the Wednesday morning after a Friday night order, but it came from Hong Kong – and lacked a bonus track available to UK shoppers. To be fair, CD-Wow did respond promptly to a complaint, offering a full refund with a UK return address.

The three comparison sites came up with three different answers when searching for the Beatles' Christmas cash-in compilation, 1. Kelkoo said the lowest price was from Amazon.co.uk, at £11.47 including delivery – but Amazon's actual total price is £11.73. ShopSmart recommended 101CD at £10.99, and EasyValue thought that CDShop was the cheapest at £10.75. This time, EasyValue got its prices right, but it had incorrectly priced the U2 album from 101CD at £10.99 – meaning price-conscious customers would have missed the best bargain and paid 76p more than they needed.

The difference may not be much, but what's the point of comparing if the prices used are wrong? Both Kelkoo and EasyValue were thrown by postage and packing charges. Lyndon Hearn, head of technology for Kelkoo UK, passed the query to the firm's team of checkers in Grenoble, and a few hours later called back with the answer: Amazon.co.uk's list of delivery prices does not include VAT, hence the 26p discrepancy. "It just highlights the problems we have on the internet," says Hearn, who corrected the glitch as a result of Online's query.

The problem stems from one of the ways used by Kelkoo to gather prices. It prefers to collect the entire price-list including delivery charges once a day, either through the retailer sending a file, or by Kelkoo reading a specially-formatted web page on the retailer's site. "If the merchant has got some time for us and we've got a strong deal, we do it that way," says Hearn.

But with Amazon, Kelkoo uses software that browses its website as if it were a customer gathering prices. This can lead to mistakes or no data if Amazon changes the format of web pages, or as in this case where the rules for charging are wrongly programmed by Kelkoo. EasyValue's mistake, which the firm says it is correcting, came from a similar assumption: its systems were set to assume 101CD charged £1 postage on all items. In fact, as a special offer, the U2 album was free of delivery charges.

Normally, EasyValue relies on software which scans the web pages of retailers – which Kelkoo has found the less accurate way of gathering price information. On the plus side, EasyValue does not try to insist that retailers in its comparison site pay referral fees. "The other [comparison sites] tend to be walled gardens, as they only offer those with whom they have an agreement," says James Rothnie, director of corporate affairs for EasyGroup.

EasyValue plans to make money by providing enhanced listings to those willing to pay fees, rather like bold-type entries in a telephone directory. EasyGroup, run by internet enthusiast Stelios Haji-Ioannou, has been famous for reducing prices at its airline EasyJet partly by taking three-quarters of bookings through the web. The group's recently-launched car rental business EasyRentacar only takes bookings online.

In both cases, prices are reduced by cutting out travel agents, who charge commission, and even telephone operators, who cost more for each transaction than a computer. So why is EasyValue trying to make money from putting a layer back between the customer and the retailer?

Rothnie says that sometimes customers need advice. This doesn't apply to booking a short flight within Europe, which is why EasyJet doesn't deal with travel agents. "But if you're travelling to Australia and staying in hotels, then travel agents can provide value, although they charge money [through commissions]," he says. Automated shopping should have a great future, according to Ian Lynch, a director of analyst firm Butler. He says shopping software agents, sometimes known as robots or bots, will negotiate with similarly computerised sellers to strike the best deals, having been pre-programmed by their users.

"What's going to make them more interesting is when they have game theory built in, so you can release a bot into an auction to act on your behalf," says Lynch. A simple example can be seen on auction site QXL.com, where sellers enter both a start price and a secret reserve, below which an item will not be sold. Buyers can enter a secret maximum bid. If another buyer bids for an item, the first buyer's shopping robot matches the bid automatically, up to the maximum. Jungle's Steve Bennett has an alternative vision, of comparison shopping sites acting like consumer champions. "If they were more professional, placed test orders, and rated retailers' abilities, then we would be very interested," he says, adding that price is usually just one factor when customers choose a shop. Lynch believes sites charging referral fees will need to think again: "We don't think that's a sustainable business model," he says.

However, he admits the current generation is better than nothing. "As long as you don't expect them to be 100% accurate, they are a useful aid." The problem is that the advice of a comparison shopping site today may not be worth the pixels it is displayed on. EasyValue's fee-free approach looks like the way forward, but customers need to remember that automated processes for gathering information from retailer websites are fallible.

CASE QUESTIONS

Question 1 What are the benefits of shopping bots? Why should users be careful when using some shopping bots?

Question 2 It is said that, indirectly, the fees charged by the comparison engines are paid by customers. In your opinion does this differ from traditional forms of advertising? Why do some retailers reject comparison sites?

MINI CASE STUDY II
Indexing Deep Web Content, by Paul Bruemmer, www.promotionbase.com/article/669

As the World Wide Web morphs from a limited database of text documents into a much wider collection of files (including PDF, Excel, Power Point, audio, images and many other formats), it's important to know more about indexing deep Web content.

Until recently, most search engines indexed only the surface Web – those pages easily found and spidered by traditional search engines. But now the focus is shifting to the deep Web (AKA the invisible Web), which consists of a vast depository of underlying content in dynamic databases – databases that remained untapped due to the limitations of Web crawling technology.

What's the difference between the surface and deep Web? It's both qualitative and quantitative. Qualitatively, the deep Web includes images, sounds, presentations, and many types of media that are invisible to search engine spiders. Quantitatively, the deep Web has been estimated to be about 500 times larger than the surface Web, but this figure may be misleading.

How deep?

A BrightPlanet study conducted in March 2000 estimated that public information in the deep Web is about 500 times larger than that in the World Wide Web, and contains "billions of high-quality documents in about 350,000 specialty databases hidden from the view of standard search engines." However, Quigo CEO Yaron Galai feels some of these documents may not be relevant for indexation. "Although the BrightPlanet study is probably academically correct, our estimate is that the useful deep Web is two to three times the size of the surface Web," said Galai. "For example, sites like Barnes & Noble can generate millions of variations of the same page (due to personalization systems, price changes, etc.). While each variation on the Harry Potter page can be considered a unique page, Quigo normalizes these variations, indexing only one relevant Harry Potter page."

As the value of its content has heightened the importance of the deep Web, we've seen technological advances that have enabled search engines to access these hidden resources. This has resulted in the indexing of more than 100,000 large dynamic sites, which have proven extremely helpful for researchers, businesspeople, academics, and consumers.

Framed site visibility

Many search engines can't crawl URL that contain the characters "?" and "&", which are used to separate common gateway interface (CGI) variables; however, Google and Inktomi began to index framed sites recently, and others will follow.

In the meantime, technicians can get around this dilemma by creating static versions of the site's dynamic pages for search engine crawlers. But this solution takes time, and it's a lot of work, requiring continuous maintenance. A better strategy is to rewrite your dynamic URLs in a syntax that search engines can crawl. For more info, see Spider Food's Dynamic Web Page Optimization.

Dynamic site indexing

A number of search engines now index dynamic content:

- Last November, FAST relaunched its crawler technology, which indexes all kinds of dynamic content.
- Google indexes dynamic content and supports hundreds of file formats, including PDF, RTF, PostScript, Word, Excel, and PowerPoint.
- Inktomi indexes dynamic content, but only goes a few pages deep within each site, though a paid partnership programme with Inktomi allows more pages to be indexed.
- AltaVista also indexes dynamic content. Basic Submit is free and Express Inclusion requires a fee. However, AltaVista doesn't like to index pages that change often because by the time these pages are indexed, the content is no longer fresh.

Paid inclusion programmes

Premium services for indexing dynamic sites include those of AltaVista, Inktomi and FAST, to name a few. Note that generally these services do not influence you site's position or rank in the way PPC engines do.

AltaVista's Trusted Feed service is ideal for the submission of Web pages that have proven difficult to crawl. It allows businesses to submit 500 or more URLs via an eXtensible Markup Language (XML) feed directly into the AltaVista index. Partners receive detailed performance reports for each URL submitted, to help calculate your return on investment (ROI).

Inktomi also has a premium inclusion programme that indexes framed and dynamic pages, and allows partners to determine which pages to include in the database.

FAST AllTheWeb's paid-inclusion PartnerSite service guarantees entry in the engine's databases for a per-URL fee (through partners such as Lycos). This service includes a 24-hour refresh and distribution to all FAST's customers.

The above programmes operate on a pay-per-click (PPC) model, and compete directly with Overture and other PPC programmes. Note that such paid services require close tracking and monitoring to ascertain the best ROI.

Deep web search tools

There are a number of products and services that enhance deep Web searching, including BrightPlanet, Intelliseek's Invisible Web, ProFusion, Quigo, C|Net's Search.com, and Vivisimo. At present, Quigo is the only one with the capability to retrieve, normalize and index documents in an offline crawling process. The others focus on expanding the meta-search engine concept, enabling users to submit queries to thousands of sites (rather than the dozen or so through regular meta-search engines).

CASE QUESTIONS

Question 1 In your opinion what is the difference between the surface and deep Web? What are the problems in trying to determine the size of the deep Web?

Question 2 Why is it important to index the deep Web? How can users locate information on the deep Web?

REFERENCES

Ackermann, E. and K. Hartman (2000) *The Information Specialist's Guide to Searching and Researching on the Internet & the World Wide Web.* ABF Content, www1.mwc.edu/~ernie/presentations/syllabus99/index.html.

Bergman, M.K. (2001) The Deep Web: Surfacing hidden value, *The Journal of Electronic Publishing*, August, 7(1), www.press.umich.edu/jep/07-01/.

Cohen, L. (2002) *Boolean Searching on the Internet*, http://library.albany.edu/internet/boolean.html.

Heller, G. (2001) How to uncover mysteries of the Invisible Web, *Employee Benefit News*, vol. 15, no. 5, pp. 51–53.

Price, G. and C. Sherman (2001) Exploring the Invisible Web, *Online*, July/August, vol. 25, no. 4, pp. 32–34.

Rowley, J. (2000) Shopping bots: intelligent shopper or virtual department store?, *International Journal of Retail & Distribution Management*, vol. 28, no. 7, pp. 297–306.

CHAPTER 10
VIRTUAL MARKETSPACE

LEARNING OUTCOMES

When you have read and worked through this chapter, you will be able to:
- ■ **Appreciate the opportunities provided by the virtual marketspace**
- ■ **Appreciate the theoretical and practical aspects of the virtual organization**
- ■ **Understand the concept of virtual teams**
- ■ **Appreciate the importance of trust when working virtually**

INTRODUCTION

The growth of the Internet has created opportunities for organizations to design new forms of arranging work, such as collapsing boundaries between supplier, customers and the internal organization. The highly turbulent environment makes it imperative for management to identify the key attributes and processes required for competitive advantage. This book has considered e-business strategy as the main driving force behind organizational transformation. The ability to perform transactions in the virtual marketspace has been one of the central themes throughout the book.

In Chapter 1 the focus was on the Internet as a business driver, Chapter 2 considered the online transaction process from the supplier to the customer. Chapter 5 examined business models, and organizational aspects were considered in Chapter 6. Marketing issues have been considered in Chapter 7 with Financial issues in Chapter 8. This chapter seeks to aggregate some of the issues already discussed in the book, by considering the implications of virtuality. Organizations possessing an e-business operation have had to radically transform organizational processes. To obtain sustainable competitive advantage, it is necessary to identify the key facets of the intra- and inter-organizational aspects of virtual organizations. This chapter seeks to contribute to the theoretical and practical understandings of virtual organizations with emphasis on virtual marketspace, virtual teams and trust.

VIRTUAL MARKETSPACE

The importance of virtual marketspace or cybermarkets has spread from society to society (Venkatesh, 1998). This diffusion of online activity has been illustrated in Chapter 1, with the Internet Industry Almanac stating that the number of Internet users surpassed 530m in 2001 and will continue to grow strongly in the next five years. This growth will be fuelled by online developments in Asia, Latin America and parts of Europe. Moreover, by the end of 2005 the number of worldwide Internet users will double to 1.12bn with increasing numbers of Internet users using wireless devices such as Web-enabled cell phones and PDAs to go online.

Businesses hoping to expand their activities onto the Internet are currently re-engineering or refining their products and services in order to take advantage of the new opportunities, as well as face the new challenges. Nevertheless, despite the Internet providing alternative

Key Term...

ICDT model
The ICDT model (see Figure 10.1) is a systematic approach to the analysis and classification of salient business-related Internet strategies

Key Term...

Netoffer model
The NetOffer model developed through case study analysis has made a worthy contribution to the development of Internet offerings. The NetOffer model consists of two elements: customer participation and communication

channels for exchanging information, communicating, distributing different types of products and services and initiating formal business transactions, managers need help when classifying their product/service offerings. The following sections consider two frameworks that have made a contribution to the literature, the **ICDT model** (Angehrn, 1997) and **NetOffer model** (Gronroos, Heinonen, Isoniemi and Lindholm, 2000).

Information, Communication, Distribution and Transaction (ICDT) model

Ideally a firm's activities in a majority of virtual marketspaces should be aimed at increasing overall profitability, which can be achieved either:

- By increasing revenues:
  - broadening the customer base (by acquiring new customers)
  - increasing the average spend by customers (through enhancing product/service offerings)
  - increasing the number of customer transactions (by enhancing re-purchase convenience)

- Or by decreasing costs:
  - reducing new service/product development costs
  - improving marketing effectiveness
  - improving inventory management
  - reducing process costs

The ICDT model (see Figure 10.1) proposes a systematic approach to the analysis and classification of salient business-related Internet strategies. The ICDT Model is generic and has been used to diagnose the Internet 'maturity' strategies of sectors, such as banking (Angehrn & Meyer 1997). It serves as a framework for segmenting the virtual marketspace into four distinct areas: virtual information space, virtual communication space; virtual distribution space; and virtual transaction space.

Virtual information space (VIS)
The virtual information space was the dominant development during the first phase of the Internet, as it provides an opportunity to obtain visibility on the Internet. Economic agents can exploit the information space and get prospective customers to convert their interest into action. It offers a variety of channels but remains a one-way communication channel.

Virtual communication space (VCS)
The virtual communication space is the quadrant that has attracted the least attention of companies. VCS provides new opportunities in which economic agents can interact. Organizations can exchange information with the various stakeholders in their business, their suppliers, customers and business partners. However, unlike the information provision activity in the information space, communication is now a two-way medium.

Virtual distribution space (VDS)
The virtual distribution space is the channel that provides the medium for the distribution of goods and services. As with the traditional postal service, there are limitations on what can be delivered. Those goods and services that can be digitized and that possess high information content, such as digitized media (e.g. books, music, software) and non-physical services (e.g. consulting, technical support, education, financial services) are best suited.

Virtual transaction space (VTS)
The virtual transaction space provides a conduit for economic agents to exchange formal

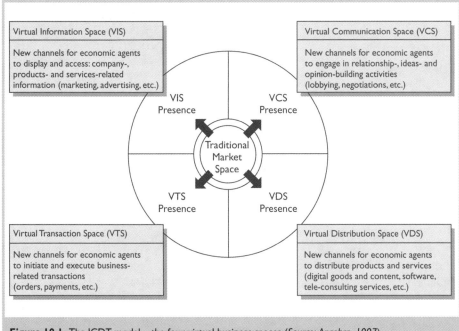

Figure 10.1 The ICDT model – the four virtual business spaces (*Source: Angehrn, 1997*)

business transactions, which can include taking orders, sending invoices and receiving payment. A good analogy is financial stock exchanges, where goods and services are not physically transferred, but orders, commitments, invoices and payments are exchanged in the virtual marketspace.

NetOffer model

Building on the Grongross Augmented Service Offering model (Grongross, 1990), the NetOffer Internet model (see Figure 10.2) was postulated as being a useful framework for virtual marketspace (Gronroos *et al.*, 2000). The NetOffer model, developed through case study analysis, has made a worthy contribution to the development of Internet offerings. Gronroos *et al.* (2000) sought not only merely to test hypotheses but to develop a richer understanding about Internet offerings. They concluded that Internet offerings (goods or services) are processes that should lead to an outcome. Hence, the quality of an Internet offering is dependent on the perceived quality of the process of using the Internet as a purchasing and/or consumption instrument, as well as on the perceived quality of the outcome. Therefore, regardless of whether the organization offering is a service or good, buying in a virtual marketspace should be characterized as service consumption, splitting into two dimensions, process quality and outcome quality.

The NetOffer model consists of two elements: customer participation and communication. Customer participation relates to the skills, knowledge and interest of customers at the user interface. The user interface is important as accessibility and interaction elements merge into a communication element, which can only be facilitated through a well-functioning interface between the user and the computer. This element allows customers to communicate with the organization. By improving communications, the functional/process quality of the Internet offering (the how factor) is enhanced and the customer is able to perceive the technical/outcome quality of what is offered (the what factor).

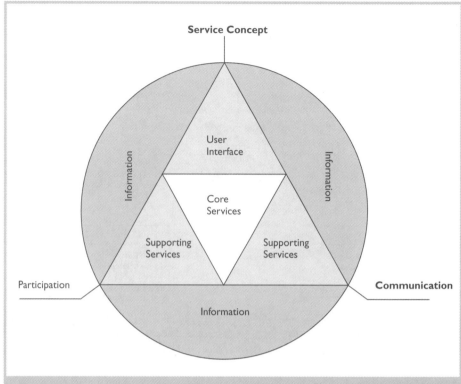

Figure 10.2 The NetOffer model for the virtual marketspace (*Source: Gronross, Helnonen, Isoniemi and Lindholm, 2000*)

VIRTUAL ORGANIZATION

The use of interorganizational systems, such as electronic data interchange and Internet-based extranets, enable new types of collaborative alliances between separate trading partners. These present additional B2C and B2B opportunities and successful adoption of these interorganizational systems will become a competitive necessity. Understanding how to best leverage the benefits from these IT-enabled alliances may mean the difference between industry dominance and industry exit.

As organizations take advantage of the networked economy, **virtual organizations** have been advocated during the last decade as a new paradigm of organization design. Organizational members can be separated by geographic boundaries or they can work in close proximity, but complex projects require collaboration and working across boundaries (Larsen and McInerney, 2002). Virtual organizations can be used in a variety of settings to enhance the efficiency and effectiveness of systems and to motivate managers and participants to reflect on organizational goals (Khalil and Wang, 2002).

The term 'virtual organization' was first coined by Mowshowitz (1986) and became a buzzword during the 1990s. Larsen and McInerney (2002) cite the definition of virtual organization advocated by Bultje and van Wijk (1998):

> "A virtual organisation is primarily characterised as being a network of independent, geographical dispersed organisations with a partial mission overlap. Within the

ILLUSTRATIVE EXAMPLE I
*Stitches in time, by Andrew Tanzer, Forbes Global, Forbes.com, 6 September, 1999
Reprinted by permission of FORBES Global Magazine © 2002 Forbes Global Inc.*

Leonard Rabinowitz runs Carole Little, a women's clothing outfit in Los Angeles. He had a problem. It was losing money and needed to shift more of its apparel manufacturing overseas to survive. But the company didn't have the resources to set up and manage a worldwide production network

"I can't afford to have somebody sitting in Mauritius making sure the colors are right and the factory is producing on time," Rabinowitz explains. "You can't do that when you're a $200 million company."

This year he made some radical moves. He shut Carole Little's Hong Kong buying office and outsourced 80% of purchasing and production management to Hong Kong's Li & Fung Ltd. Rabinowitz estimates that the move will save $4 million a year in costs and help return his privately held fashion firm to profit this year after four years of losses. He says, "Li & Fung was a godsend for me."

For him and for a lot of other American and European private-label merchandisers. Through its network of 45 offices in 31 countries, Li & Fung supplies apparel for every division of the company: kidswear for Gymboree, noncosmetic goods for Avon Products, home items for Bed Bath & Beyond, clothing for Abercrombie & Fitch and Reebok and consumer items for Warner Bros. retail shops.

In an age when the Internet is supposedly going to eliminate the middleman, here's a middleman, an old Asian trading company, that has made itself indispensable.

When Roger Markfield, president and chief merchandising officer of American Eagle Outfitters, joined the burgeoning Pittsburgh, Pennsylvania-based private-brand retailer in 1993, one of his first acts was to outsource supply-chain management to Li & Fung. Formerly at the Gap, he'd known the Hong Kong company's controlling shareholders, the Fung brothers, Victor and William, since 1977. "They're the most efficient trading merchants in the business," Markfield says. "They have the capability to do sourcing worldwide better than we can."

And the Fung brothers know how to turn a profit. Since Li & Fung Ltd. went public on the Hong Kong Stock Exchange in 1992, the trading house's earnings have compounded at 26% a year and the stock is up tenfold. Goldman, Sachs' Tristan Tian-Yu Chua estimates the company will earn $73 million after tax this year on revenues of $2.2 billion and achieve an eye-popping return on equity of 50%. Chua forecasts that earnings will double again from 1998 to 2001.

The Fung brothers effectively own about 48% of Li & Fung Ltd., mostly through their holding company, Li & Fung 1937, in which South Africa's Oppenheimer family has a 26% stake. Toss in Victor's holdings in Prudential Asia plus Li & Fung's private consumer-goods distribution and retail operations in Asia (which include Toys "R" Us and Circle K franchises) and the Fungs are easily billionaires.

Their grandfather, Fung Pak-liu, took some meager savings from his job teaching English to cofound the company in 1906. Li & Fung was an export trading company in Guangzhou, a city 120 miles northwest of Hong Kong, in the waning days of the Qing Dynasty. One of the first Chinese-owned trading houses, Li & Fung exported porcelain, fireworks, jade handicrafts and silk, mainly to the U.S. In 1937 the firm incorporated in Hong Kong—hence the holding company name—to take advantage of the British colony's oceangoing ships.

Then came World War II and, soon afterward, communism's bamboo curtain. China trade disappeared. Fortunately, Hong Kong was industrializing and becoming a competitive manufacturer of labor-intensive consumer goods.

"My father [Fung Hon-chu] reinvented the company to export what Hong Kong produced," explains William. "We lost China as the hinterland but gained 1.5 million refugees, who provided a labor pool." Li & Fung became a big exporter of garments, toys, wigs and plastic flowers.

Hon-chu gave his sons the best education money can buy. William, 50, graduated from Princeton and Harvard Business School; Victor, 53, earned two engineering degrees from MIT and a Ph.D. in business economics from Harvard. He also taught at Harvard Business School and became a U.S. citizen.

By the early 1970s the trading business was beginning to struggle, and Hon-chu called his boys home to help. Now Taiwan and Singapore were competing with Hong Kong. Li & Fung's broker role was being squeezed by both manufacturers and importers.

"My grandfather got a 15% commission basically because the buyers didn't speak Chinese and the sellers didn't speak English," recalls Victor, the listed company's nonexecutive chairman. "My father got 10%. We were getting 3% and all of our friends said, 'Why go into a sunset business?'"

So the Fung brothers set about remaking the company. First, they extended Li & Fung's buying network to Taiwan, Korea, China (open for business again) and Southeast Asia. "In many ways the Li & Fung story is the story of Hong Kong," explains Victor, who is also chairman of both Hong Kong's Trade Development Council and its Airport Authority. "Hong Kong has now become a real value-added nerve center offering services that support a manufacturing base which pervades the whole region."

Today Li & Fung buys from more than 2,000 factories around the world and supplies about 400 customers. Mexico, Honduras and Guatemala, for example, mostly serve the U.S.; Turkey, Egypt and Tunisia supply Europe. A fourth of Li & Fung's volume is in hard goods like toys, gift items and sporting goods, the balance in textiles and garments. One of Li & Fung's functions is to inspect factories in developing countries to ensure that they comply with rules in importing countries on environmental standards, child labor and prison labor.

But the Fung brothers aspired to more than just chasing the latest low-cost producer: China today, Bangladesh tomorrow. Explains William: "For labor-intensive consumer goods, where the technological barriers are low, there's always another country or factory that's going to be cheaper than you."

Victor: "We turned the whole thing into a concept of managing the supply chain. We orchestrate this great big network, from yarn to fabric to garments, moving to shipping and warehousing."

Li & Fung typically takes a product design, say, a toddler's outfit from Gymboree, and plans and manages global production and supply lines. This includes finding raw materials and fabrics, contracting production, conducting quality assurance and factory inspection, supervising the logistics of exporting, delivering on time and wading through the byzantine country-of-origin import quotas imposed by the U.S. and Europe.

Competitors? There are surprisingly few. The strong suit of William E. Connor & Associates, a closely held, American-owned, Hong Kong-based trading company, is large department store customers, such as Nordstrom and Dillard's, while Li & Fung focuses more on specialty store chains. Some private-label chains, such as the Gap (a former Li & Fung customer), take their buying back in-house when they grow to a certain scale.

For their efforts, the Fungs are rewarded with commissions of 5% to 8% on apparel and 7% to 12% on hard goods. Their spread is easily carved out of the wide-open spaces in the distribution channel: If a product costs $1 at the factory in Sri Lanka it will be

> priced at $4 or more by the time it reaches the retail shelf. The Fungs earn their keep with their skills at operations research, optimizing results such as price, quality and production lead time, subject to constraints like shipping costs and labor rates.
>
> Explains Victor: "I'm creating products that did not exist before, [for example] a product that is made from Korean yarn, Taiwanese dye and accessories from China, all sewn together in Thailand." Maybe an item is supplied from five different Thai factories. When it hits the retail shelf in the U.S., it must look as if it came from one factory.
>
> Li & Fung's brisk growth is driven by several trends in fashion and retailing. Private labels are proliferating, and retailing is becoming more global. Retailers are more disposed to contracting out their overseas buying, and they want to buy smaller batches of merchandise on a shorter cycle. That cuts end-of-season markdowns.
>
> Warner Bros. is setting up stores worldwide, so it is supplied globally through numerous Li & Fung offices. Reebok manages footwear production itself, while outsourcing its apparel line to Li & Fung; Avon handles cosmetics, but farms out giftware to Li & Fung. Speed is of the essence. When the Limited reorders a hot item, Li & Fung can arrange production and have it on the shelves in the U.S. within five weeks.
>
> Is the Internet going to put the Fungs out of a job? Doubtful. "The Internet is a storefront," says Victor Fung. "It can't orchestrate the whole supply chain." It also is no match for the Fung brothers' personal touch. Says American Eagle's Markfield, "They're gracious and warm, but very, very aggressive."

network, all partners provide their own core competencies and the co-operation is based on semi-stable relations. The products and services provided by a virtual organisation are dependent on innovation and are strongly customer-based *"*.

Virtual organizations have been widely debated within academic and popular communities, and some authors have created a variety of different terms and definitions to describe this new organizational paradigm, such as virtual company (Goldman, Nagel and Preiss, 1993), virtual enterprise (Hardwick, Spooner, Rando and Morris, 1996) and virtual factory (Upton and McAfee, 1996). All these authors identified ICT as a prerequisite, facilitator or even the core of the new emerging virtual organization paradigm (Franke, 2001). Interestingly, the virtual organization does not need to constitute organizational design in the traditional sense and can embrace a variety of new ways of working together (Kasper-Fuehrer, Ashkanasy and Neal, 2001).

Venkatraman and Henderson (1998) reject the notion that the virtual organization is a distinct structure (like functional, divisional, or matrix). Instead, they treat virtualness as a strategic characteristic applicable to every organization. They view virtualness as a strategy that reflects three distinct yet interdependent vectors:

- The customer interaction vector (virtual encounter) presents opportunities for B2C interactions. E-business allows customers to remotely experience products and services and actively participate in dynamic bespoke enhancement of products/services and online communities.
- The asset configuration vector (virtual sourcing) relates to the vertical integration in a business network, in sharp contrast to the vertically integrated model of the industrial economy. As discussed in Chapter 2 organizations using the Internet for B2B transactions can structure and manage a dynamic portfolio of relationships with customers.
- The knowledge leverage vector (virtual expertise) focuses on the provision of diverse sources

of knowledge within and across organizational boundaries. IT is an enabler that allows organizations to enhance the intellectual capital of the organization.

Jansen, Steenbakkers and Jagers (1999) indicate that, although there is a relationship between virtual organizations and e-Commerce, the relationship is not completely unequivocal. They assert that there are two reasons for the emergence of virtual organizations, these being an increasing need for flexibility and the need for greater efficiency. An organization may have a number of characteristics that can be used to assess its virtuality. These include:

- Boundary crossing
- Complementary core competencies/pooling of resources
- Sharing of knowledge
- Geographical dispersion
- Changing participants
- Participant equality
- Electronic communication

A virtual organization typically has minimal formal structure and is a practical grouping to address a particular business proposition. The focus of design can be on (intraorganizational) or between (interorganizational) issues. Another way of analysing the virtual organization is to ask to what extent do virtual organizations resemble traditional organizations? Previous researchers have argued that the difference is largely one of decentralization versus centralization, non-hierarchical versus hierarchical. Interestingly, Ahuja and Carley (1998) find this distinction misleading. They found evidence of both centralization and hierarchy in a virtual organization. Therefore, Ahuja and Carley (1998) speculate that the issue is not merely about centralization and/or hierarchy, but the identification of the optimal form for specific tasks.

Jansen, Steenbakkers and Jagers (1999) then contrast the two different types of virtual organizations – stable and dynamic, which are illustrated in Table 10.1. Interestingly Bultje and van Wijk (1998) identified four different sub-concepts of virtual and make the following distinctions:

- *Unreal, looking real* – the virtual organization has the appearance of a traditional company, but in reality this company does not exist, as it is only an amalgamation of independent network individuals.
- *Immaterial, supported by information and communication technology* – in this instance, the virtual shopping mall does not really exist, as it is only created by data.
- *Potentially present* – relates to the instance when the attribute of an organization does not exist, but has the possibility to exist.
- *Existing but changing* – the organizational unit exists, but the composition of partners is temporary.

Khalil and Wang (2002) assert that virtual organizations can be deployed in a range of organizational settings to enhance the efficiency and effectiveness of systems. Using IT, virtual organizations have replaced traditional, unitary forms with contractual relationships and provide management with maximum flexibility in response to market changes. The task of managing virtual organizations is called meta-management and, according to Khalil and Wang, meta-management provides a systematic approach to the exploitation of organizational resources. Meta-management has two major characteristics, when compared with traditional organizations. First, organizational goals must be explicit, with

	Stable VO	Dynamic VO
Duration of co-operation	Permanent	Temporary
Boundaries	Clearly defined	Vague/fluid
Based on opportunism	No	Yes
Based on ICT	Possible	Possible
Core partners	Obvious	No
(Source: Jansen, Steenbakkers and Jagers, 1999)		

Table 10.1 Some characteristics of stable and dynamic virtual organizations (VO)

intangible goals such as subjective loyalty to the community not being apt in a virtual organization. Second, the key task in meta-management is the preservation of temporary relationships. According to Khalil and Wang, the salient unique functions for meta-management functions are:

- New information technology adoption of IT is an important attribute of meta-management. Information filtering, knowledge acquisition and case matching are examples of organizational requirements in an e-commerce environment.
- Organizational learning is becoming an imperative, and the application of methodologies to generate and leverage knowledge faster and more effectively is becoming a promising new management practice.
- Co-ordination of sub-units of virtual organizations is becoming a major task of meta-management. In the absence of physical supervision, trust is often advocated as control component.
- Organizational redesign is necessary in organizations as some migrate towards virtuality. While this may not be such a problem if the virtual organization is new, organizational design in existing virtual organizations will be much more difficult.

The new economy thrives on networking, with technology providing the medium for rapid communication among those with common interests and individual users providing the stimulus growth. It is argued that the virtual organization is greater than the sum of its parts and this synergy presents a mutually beneficial opportunity for everyone. Therefore, some organizations prefer to focus on virtuality, rather than being formalized. Reasons cited include:

- The cost of a formal structure may be too high.
- In times of rapid change it may be necessary to develop transitory structures.
- Formal alliances may prove insuperable.
- Organizations need to transact beyond traditional boundaries.

Virtual team

The concept of the **virtual team** is not clearly defined and sometimes overlaps with the notion of the virtual organization. A virtual team can be seen essentially as a project- or task-focused group. The virtual team may be drawn from the same organization, (e.g. marketing manager and financial accountant) or from several different organizations, (e.g. when projects involve consultants or external assessors). Virtual teams can maintain relationships by using e-mail or teleconferencing and work by phone, fax or compressed video (Larsen and McInerney, 2002).

Key Term...

Virtual team
A temporary, culturally diverse, geographically dispersed, electronically communicating work group

301

ILLUSTRATIVE EXAMPLE II

Exostar strengthens global leadership position with addition of Rolls-Royce as fifth founding partner, 15 June 2001

Paris – Le Bourget (Hall 1 Stand E40) – Exostar, an independent, global eMarketplace for the $400 billion aerospace and defense industry, announced today at the Paris Air Show that Rolls-Royce has become the consortium's fifth founding partner

Rolls-Royce's significant financial investment in Exostar gives the company ownership parity with Exostar's four previously announced founding partners: BAE SYSTEMS, Boeing, Lockheed Martin, and Raytheon. "The addition of Rolls-Royce to Exostar's founding partners makes an already impressive consortium even stronger," said Exostar's Non executive Chairman, Paul Kaminski.

Rolls-Royce's decision to become a founding partner and governing investor follows an exhaustive competitive analysis of all major players in the aerospace and defense e-commerce industry and completion of a thorough due diligence process with Exostar.

Rolls-Royce Chief Executive John Rose stated, "Exostar will allow us to reduce material and procurement costs, shorten lead times and reduce our inventory. It will also enable us to collaborate more effectively with partners on designs for future projects. Exostar will allow design teams to hold shared, secure information which can receive input from around the world. This will allow us to bring ideas to life in the marketplace more quickly, enabling a rapid response to customer requirements."

Kaminski added, "The addition of Rolls-Royce enhances our value proposition to the common supplier base of all founding partners through system standardization and reduced reliance on manual data entry in a secure, reliable platform. Exostar's product and service offerings, backed by strong support among the founding partners, have enabled us to become the clear leader among aerospace and defense exchanges."

Another founding partner noted that the addition of Rolls-Royce to Exostar will further extend the consortium's reach outside North America. "We're delighted to welcome Rolls-Royce to the Exostar family," said Rod Leggetter, Group Procurement and IT Director of BAE SYSTEMS. "Having two of the leading European based aerospace companies on board will significantly strengthen Exostar's European presence. With this new partner comes a new supplier base and strategic focus, broadening Exostar's reach even further across the industry, providing a standard procurement and collaboration solution for over 40,000 suppliers."

Over the next two years, Exostar plans to connect over 250 procurement systems currently used by the five founding partners in 20 countries. Approximately 4,000 suppliers have been activated so far. Exostar already has implemented exchange interoperability with CommerceOne.Net and is in discussion with other industry exchanges.

Exostar, a global eMarketplace owned and operated as a separate company, represents the co-operative efforts of some of the world's largest aerospace and defense companies—BAE SYSTEMS, Boeing, Lockheed Martin Corp., Raytheon Co., and Rolls-Royce—its five founding members. Using a secure and open environment, Exostar provides Internet-based products and services that connect manufacturers, suppliers and customers of all sizes, around the world, for trade [using Commerce One technology], and collaboration [using PTC technology]. Rolls-Royce Corporation announced on the 13 February that a cross-functional team including Exostar, CommerceOne and EDS has brought over 180 suppliers online in under three months to transact business electronically through Exostar's SupplyPass product.

Documents being transmitted are electronic planning schedules, goods receipt reports and invoice documents.

The team membership may be relatively stable (e.g. an established finance team) or change on a regular basis (e.g. project teams). Jarvenpaa and Leidner (1998) define a global virtual team to be a temporary, culturally diverse, geographically dispersed, electronically communicating work group (Figure 10.3). One of the core characteristics of a virtual team is the ability to link the culturally diverse and globally spanning activities so that members that can think and act in alignment with the diversity of the external environment. Further distinctions can be made relating to physical proximity (i.e. the team could be co-located or could be geographically separated) and to different time zones.

Ahuja and Carley (1998) assert that, in addition to managing formal reporting relationships, it is important to monitor and manage communication structures. Moreover, managers should not always assume that non-hierarchical communication structures are necessarily more effective than hierarchical structures. Attention should be placed on aligning the communication structure to the task characteristics. When a virtual team has a rudimentary task, a hierarchical structure may be preferable, because hierarchies provide efficient and economical forms of communication.

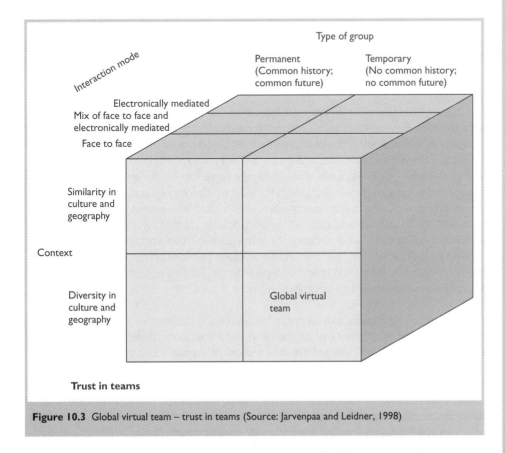

Figure 10.3 Global virtual team – trust in teams (Source: Jarvenpaa and Leidner, 1998)

When designing teams and their optimum structure for a particular task, it is not always easy to replicate the structure repeatedly. It must be borne in mind that designers should try to preserve organizational memory by retaining individuals who are at the centre of key information exchange networks.

Managers should monitor communication structures and design reward structures so that individuals acting as knowledge centres on specific topics can be retained and promoted. There should be a built-in reward structures that provide incentives for workers to exchange and share their expertise with other members of the organization. Furthermore, it is critical to develop members so that replacements are found as individuals are promoted, so that the communication structures can remain stable.

Interestingly, Ahuja and Carley (1998) found that objective performance was not influenced by task and structure fit. This could suggest that not all tasks are equally suitable for being performed in a virtual organization. Therefore, it is imperative that managers consider which tasks would benefit from a virtual environment prior to such an environment being launched. Tasks that need a high degree of expertise are competence-based, that require information and communication and that utilize distributed resources may be particularly suitable.

Trust

As discussed previously, the business world is rapidly changing and one of the crucial implications of the virtual organization is that an individual may work with other members in a team who they have never physically seen. Working virtually makes communication a complex issue and trust is seen as a linchpin of success. Jarvenpaa and Leidner (1998) argue that trust is most important in new and temporary organizations, as it acts as a substitute for the traditional mechanisms of control and co-ordination. This is supported by Luo (2002), who states that trust plays a crucial role in electronic markets that possess high uncertainty and lack of legal protection.

Jarvenpaa and Leidner (1998) interestingly asked the question whether trust can exist in global virtual teams. Factors such as shared social norms, repeated interactions and shared experiences as necessary elements to facilitate the development of trust have been cited by a variety of researchers (Bradach and Eccles, 1988; Lewis and Weigert, 1985; Mayer, Davis and Schoorman, 1995). Promotion of trust and co-operation in the anticipation of deeper relationships has also been highlighted (Powell, 1990). The expectation of future association is higher among group members who are co-located than among physically dispersed members. Co-location, or physical proximity, is said to reinforce social similarity, shared values and expectations and to increase the immediacy of threats from failing to meet commitments (Latane et al., 1995). In addition, face-to-face encounters are considered irreplaceable for both building trust and repairing a breakdown of trust (Nohria and Eccles, 1992; O'Hara-Devereaux and Johansen, 1994).

Some practical implications can be drawn from previous studies. For the manager of a virtual team, one of the factors that might contribute to smooth co-ordination early in the existence of the team is a clear definition of responsibilities, as a lack of accountability may lead to confusion and frustration. Providing guidelines on how often to communicate and, more importantly, inculcating a regular pattern of communication will increase the predictability and reduce the uncertainty of the team's co-ordination. Furthermore, ensuring that team members have a sense of complementary objectives and share in the overall aim of the team will help prevent the occurrence of desultory participation.

Key Term...

Trust
Trust is most important in new and temporary organizations, as it acts as a substitute for the traditional mechanisms of control and co-ordination

Trust Mechanism	Basis of Trust	Source of Trust	Solution to Privacy Concern	Example of E-business	Managerial Implications
Characteristic-based	Tied to person ascribed	Family, community, clan membership	Likely	Covisint, Boschtools.com, baby-center.com	Trust and brand loyalty is enhanced through e-community. B2B firms can enhance trust through strategic alliances
Process-based	Tied to repeated purchases or expected exchange	Reputation, brands, gift-giving	More likely	Dell.com, Honda.com Virtual Vineyard	Provision of free gifts and extra advice will enhance trust. B2B firms may use an exchange to enhance trust
Institutional-based	Tied to formal social structure	Signals/cues	Most likely		Institutional-based trust provides a useful infrastructure
Person/firm specific		Professional, firm associations		Verisign.com, Trust-E, BBB online	Online vendors should acquire institutional-based trust
Intermediary mechanism		Bureaucracy, banks, regulation		MoneySave.com, E-cash.com	Online intermediaries should acquire institutional-based trust

(Source: Luo, 2002)

Table 10.2 Trust-building mechanisms

Chapter 7 provided an overview on how organizations can gain and sustain online competitive advantage. However, despite projections that the online retailing market will continue to grow rapidly, with IDC (www.idc.com) predicting that by the end of 2002 more than 600m people worldwide will have access to the Web, security and privacy issues still remain a obstacle to success. Therefore, any theory that can provide some guidance as to how to identify salient obstacles to trust should be embraced by practitioners and academics. A framework (see Table 10.2) postulated by Luo (2002) provides a useful overview. Blending the theories from relationship marketing and social exchange theory, Luo (2002) identified three mechanisms that help increase customers' trust of e-commerce and decrease privacy concerns: characteristic-based (e.g. community); transaction (e.g. repeated purchases); and process-based (e.g. digital certificates).

SUMMARY

This chapter seeks to aggregate some of the issues already discussed in the book, by considering the implications of virtuality. Organizations possessing an e-business operation have had to radically transform organizational processes. To obtain sustainable competitive advantage, it is necessary to identify the key facets of the intra- and inter-organizational aspects of virtual organizations. This chapter seeks to contribute to the theoretical and practical understandings of virtual organizations with emphasis on virtual marketspace, virtual teams and trust.

Virtual marketspace

ICDT model

The ICDT model serves as a framework for segmenting the virtual marketspace into four distinct areas: virtual information space; virtual communication space; virtual distribution space; and virtual transaction space.

NetOffer model

Building on the Grongross Augmented Service Offering model (Grongross, 1990), the NetOffer Internet model was postulated as being a useful framework for virtual marketspace (Gronroos *et al.*, 2000). The NetOffer model consists of two elements: customer participation and communication.

Virtual organization

As organizations take advantage of the networked economy, virtual organizations have been advocated during the last decade as a new paradigm of organization design. Virtual organizations have been widely debated within academic and popular communities and some authors have created a variety of different terms and definitions to describe this new organizational paradigm, such as virtual company (Goldman and Nagel, 1993), virtual enterprise (Hardwick *et al.*, 1996) and virtual factory (Upton and McAfee, 1996).

Virtual team

The concept of the virtual team is not clearly defined and sometimes overlaps with the notion of the virtual organization. A virtual team can be seen essentially as a project- or task-focused group. Jarvenpaa and Leidner (1998) define a global virtual team to be a temporary, culturally diverse, geographically dispersed, electronically communicating work group.

Trust

The business world is rapidly changing and one of the crucial implications of the virtual organization is that individuals may work with other members in a team who they have never physically seen. Working virtually makes communication a complex issue and trust is seen as a linchpin of success. Jarvenpaa and Leidner (1998) argue that trust is most important in new and temporary organizations, as it acts as a substitute for the traditional mechanisms of control and co-ordination.

DISCUSSION QUESTIONS

1. What do you understand by the term virtual organization? You may find it useful to consider the variety of different approaches that are used to describe virtual organizations.

2. How does a virtual team maintain relationships across geographical boundaries? What are the problems of not maintaining face-to-face contact?

3. Businesses hoping to expand their revenues online are currently re-engineering or refining their products and services. How have the ICDT model (Angehrn, 1997) and the NetOffer model (Gronroos et al., 2000) helped the e-business strategist?

ASSESSMENT QUESTIONS

1. What do you believe are the main differences between traditional organizations and virtual organizations? What do you believe are the major reasons for the emergence of virtual organizations?

2. Why is it important to align the communication structure to task characteristics within virtual teams?

3. In your opinion why are communication and trust so crucial in virtual teams?

GROUP ASSIGNMENT QUESTIONS

1. You are required to outline how either the ICDT model (Angehrn, 1997) or the NetOffer model (Gronroos et al., 2000) can assist managers as they design new product/service offerings. You are required to illustrate your discussion with specific examples.

2. Lack of consumer trust has been cited by many analysts as an impediment to the continued growth of the e-business. What do you believe are the major issues consumers face when transacting online? What steps can be taken to enhance consumers' confidence?

3. The importance of virtual marketspace or cybermarkets has spread from society to society (Venkatesh, 1998). You are required to select any organization(s) of your choice to illustrate the emergence of a B2B virtual organization in any sector. You may find useful to look at the Li & Fung Ltd website (www.lifung.com).

Information technology will transform the company as we know it

It was only early last year that General Electric started to talk about its plan to digitise its entire business, but arguably the whole thing started much earlier, in the mid-1990s. That was when GE launched its "Six Sigma" initiative, the management method on which its redoubtable quest for perfection is based. It is no accident that this effort was first led by Gary Reiner, the company's chief information officer.

Six Sigma, in essence, is a way of creating a closed-loop system to make continuous improvements in business processes. First, you pick a goal, often customer-related, for instance the time you take to deliver a product, and measure how well you are doing against that goal—not on average, but in terms of variation. Then you try to change the business process in order to reduce that variation as much as possible. If you hit your goal 99.9997% of the time, you have achieved "six sigma", a statistical term describing the degree of variation. In Six-Sigma parlance, it means your "defects per million opportunities" are down to 3.4.

GE has trained tens of thousands of its managers in Six Sigma techniques, which now makes it much easier for the company to introduce real-time technology. It allows results to be measured easily, and business processes to be adjusted quickly to improve these results. In fact, most of the start-ups mentioned in this survey say that their products are designed for exactly this kind of closed-loop decision-making.

Not many firms will be as prepared as GE to go real-time. Many will have to adapt their culture and the way they do business. And, for better or worse, things are likely to get more quantitative, centralised and ever-changing. Until recently, the corporate spreadsheet—the IT guts of a firm—was shaped mostly by the organisation for which it was designed. Now it is the spreadsheet which in many ways will shape the organisation.

Once again, with more feeling

Not that re-engineering combined with IT is a new concept. In the 1990s, many firms went through a wrenching re-engineering experience, often in parallel with the equally difficult introduction of an enterprise resource planning (ERP) system. But these were one-off efforts usually limited to one company. Real-time technology should make it possible to re-engineer business processes on a continuous basis, and across the boundaries of many firms.

Both authors of the infamous 1993 bestseller "Re-engineering the Corporation", Michael Hammer and James Champy, have recently written new books. In "The Agenda" (Crown Business, 2001), Mr Hammer emphasises the need to "institutionalise a capacity for change". Mr Champy, now chairman of consulting at Perot Systems, in "X-Engineering the Corporation" (Warner Books, forthcoming) invokes the increasingly pressing need for "cross-organisational process change".

At this point, it is anybody's guess what a typical real-time enterprise will look like. Ray Lane, a partner with Kleiner Perkins Caufield & Byers, predicts that in the long run real-time technology will do away with all the features of a firm that were needed to assure information flow in an offline world: hierarchies, departmental boundaries, paper-shuffling employees. To the former number two at Oracle, this is a tempting prospect because it would empower top executives: they would no longer be isolated from their business by layers of bureaucracy.

Tibco's Vivek Ranadivé, for his part, already has a rather precise vision of what he calls the "event-driven" firm. If he is right, running a company will be rather like managing an IT system today: machines monitor the business, solve problems by themselves as far as possible and alert managers when something is amiss. Mr Ranadivé calls this "management by exception", and to some extent already practises it at Tibco: most of the firm's employees are equipped with a BlackBerry, a wireless device that can receive and send e-mail, so that they can be given warning of an "event" such as an unhappy customer.

The shape of things to come?
How real-time technology may change the nature of the company

Characteristic or practice	Contemporary company	Event-driven company
Business strategy	Long-term strategic plan guides actions	Medium- to long-term intent, but short-term planning horizon
Competitive posture	Study and understand your competition	Study and understand your customer
Management style	Consensus-oriented management	Entrepreneurial leadership, star system
Operational focus	Continuous monitoring to achieve quality	Quality is assumed, focus is on exceptional trends and events
Corporate culture	Egalitarian	Meritocratic
Recruiting	Hire team players	Team players are good, but prima donnas bring the greatest value
Implicit company/ employee contact	Promise of lifetime employment	Opportunity for lifetime employability
Employee career management	Company manages your career	Employee manages own career
Information technology	Database centric, passive, demand driven	Information centric, active, event driven
Partnership model	Formal or informal *keiretsu*	Shifting alliances and "co-op-etition"
Corporate anthem	Sousa march	Jazz improvisation

Source: "The Power of Now", by Vivek Ranadivé

Yet firms are not just paper- and people-based information systems, easily replaced by more efficient digital ones. Some aspects of non-computerised information systems that have developed over hundreds of years will be hard to digitise, not least because they are not always consciously understood, argues Ole Hanseth, the researcher at Oslo University, who is currently studying the way information about x-ray examinations is handled in a hospital. One example of such "hidden" data is the precise way a patient's chart is placed on a desk, which can indicate that the examination is over.

There are similar problems with another theory about the future of the firm: that information technology will slowly but surely deconstruct the company as we know it. According to this view, the fundamental building blocks of the economy will one day be "virtual firms", ever-changing networks of subcontractors and freelancers, managed by a core of people with a good idea. Eric Raymond, one of the intellectual leaders of the open-source software movement, even thinks that the future belongs to the "ex-corporation"—groups of people held together mainly by idealism or desire for self-expression and led by benevolent dictators, similar to today's open-source projects such as Linux.

Such predictions are often based on a one-sided interpretation of the ideas of Ronald Coase, a Nobel-prize-winning economist, says Phil Agre, a professor of information studies at the University of California at Los Angeles. True, he explains, technologies that speed up the flow of information bring down transaction costs, which should induce companies to do less themselves and outsource more. But Mr Coase also argued that the size of a firm is determined by organising costs, which technology tends to lower as well, so the real-time enterprise might end up being larger than its less nimble predecessors. And there are other forces that keep a firm together. Even the best information flow cannot replace old-fashioned trust and social bonds. Besides, a company might want to keep control of its supply chain to protect its brand and knowledge.

Yet better IT will certainly allow the economy to be reorganised in more efficient ways, giving rise to ever more specialised firms. For instance, if the underwriting department of an insurance company is delivered internally as a web service, it could easily be outsourced or, more likely, offered as a service to others. The electronics industry is at the forefront of this trend. Most big computer makers no longer build what they sell, but outsource production to huge, albeit lesser-known providers of manufacturing services such as Flextronics or Solectron.

Polarising force

The firm as an institution is thus pulled in two directions: to become smaller as well as bigger. Perhaps the economy will one day look like traffic patterns on the Internet. There are a dozen or so websites, mostly portals such as Yahoo! or AOL.com, that attract millions of visitors every day. Then there are millions of websites that are lucky if they get a dozen hits a week. And there is not much in the middle. Similarly, there could be a few dozen giant global concerns that offer more or less standardised services in manufacturing, finance or computer systems which millions of small firms will use.

Much easier to predict than what will happen to the firm is what will happen to contracts. Information technology makes monitoring much cheaper, says Hal Varian, an economics professor at the University of California at Berkeley. And just as good fences make good neighbours, he argues, good monitoring makes good contracts. His favourite example is video shops. Before 1998, they generally paid distributors a whopping $70 for each tape, which meant that they ordered only small numbers of even the most popular flicks. Now they pay a small charge of $3–8 up front and then hand over 40–60% of every rental fee. This has become possible because smart cash registers and network connections are now cheap enough for distributors to monitor sales.

In this instance everybody wins: video shops can afford to order many more copies of popular movies from Hollywood, and consumers do not have to wait for them. But the effect of new technology may not always please all concerned. Software such as Siebel's recently released employee-relationship management program allows companies to monitor their employees more effectively, which makes it easier for them to weed out their worst performers. Siebel fires the bottom 10% of its workforce every year.

More and better information will also change contracts with suppliers. Vivecon, a start-up founded by Blake Johnson, a Stanford business professor and former investment banker, has developed software that helps firms manage procurement contracts. For example, should they ask for fixed quantities and prices, or should they have flexible agreements? And what should be the penalty if they want to be released from their commitment?

The aim of the game is to structure agreements with suppliers in a way that lowers cost and risk. A manufacturer hoping to launch a new product for which demand is uncertain may not want to get locked into buying a large quantity of a critical component. It might commit itself to a smaller volume, with a guarantee that more will be available, and pay a bit more per unit.

Vivecon also helps firms to choose the right portfolio of these "structured contracts", along with long-term relationships with suppliers and spot-market purchases. Hewlett-Packard is already using the start-up's software and services to manage the procurement of some of its memory chips and electric power. And that is only the beginning, says Corey Billington, who runs HP's supply-chain services. To him, procurement will increasingly become like trading. Yet looking at Enron, the energy-trading giant which collapsed recently, that might not be such a good idea.

CASE QUESTIONS

Question 1 Why did General Electric use the 'Six Sigma' initiative prior to digitizing its entire business? What aspects of computerized information systems are hard to digitize?

Question 2 What general lessons have been learned from previous re-engineering efforts? How will real-time technology affect the features of a traditional organization?

Question 3 Tibco's Vivek Ranadivé postulates that running a company will be rather like managing an IT system today: machines monitor the business, solve problems by themselves as far as possible and alert managers when something is amiss. Do you agree with this assertion? You are required to support your answer with relevant examples.

MINI CASE STUDY I
What going virtual means for the hotel industry, by Tara A. Wenner, Andersen.com staff writer, www.hotelbenchmark.com, 12 May 2002

With so many businesses taking their operations online, it's no wonder analysts say e-procurement will quickly become a chief resource for many manufacturers and business owners. The hotel industry is no exception.
Known for its fragmented supply chains and inefficient distribution processes, the hotel industry would benefit from moving procurement and distribution online because of the potential to reduce infrastructure and transaction costs and improve efficiency and audit control.

Through various models, buyers are connected to suppliers and competitors are linked to potential partnerships, allowing the hotel industry to be better equipped to handle business needs.

According to an article by Elizabeth Ngonzi, a Hospitality consulting services manager at Andersen, digital marketplaces are breaking down trade barriers and offering access to hospitality companies of all sizes.

The article also includes estimates from Deutsche Bank, citing a US$60 billion domestic and $100 billion international market for hospitality e-procurement, including furniture, fixtures and equipment, renovation and construction, service contracts, operating supplies, and food and beverage. Cost savings from more efficient supply chain transactions are estimated at $3.5 billion to $4 billion in the United States and $7 billion globally.

The future of B2B commerce

E-procurement is quickly becoming an e-business necessity. Experts predict that businesses not using e-procurement measures after 2002 will encounter significant cost disadvantages.

"For a hotel management company, the benefits [of going online] could be huge," says Yael Nagler, a business consultant in Andersen's digital markets/e-procurement group. Nagler says management companies (typically managing more than one hotel and franchise) need to find ways to manage the purchasing and brand requirements for each hotel and franchise. An online system with "smart" catalogs that limit, control and/or manage the information that the owner can view will ensure that the property is making purchases within their standards.

On the supplier side, the cost of doing business will decrease, creating higher margins and lower prices for the buyers. If the supplier's customers were to place all orders online, the warehouses would only need to be staffed with people in charge of packing and shipping, which would be much cheaper than door-to-door sales and account management.

The cutting of costs at all ends is critical right now for the hotel industry, says Michael DiLeva, program director of electronic business-hospitality practice at Unisys, a company specializing in e-business solutions.

Unisys executives argue that within the next two years, 70 percent of all buying and selling will take place through electronic marketplaces, and the hotel industry is among the many that will benefit from its streamlined and cost-effective practices.

"The hotel industry is very fragmented in the decisions processes," explains DiLeva. "Many chains are just management groups ... a single hotel doesn't have the purchasing power like a 2,000 hotel chain."

DiLeva says that another problem for chain hotels owned and managed by different groups is that purchases like towels, pillows and bedding may not be "on brand" and consistent throughout the chain, which can lead to varying experiences for travelers.

If purchasing is done online, hotels can advocate brand standards and get a better product for a lower price because of aggregate purchasing power, DiLeva argues.

Many hotel chains have already caught on to the buzz surrounding e-procurement. On February 1, Marriott International, Inc. and Hyatt Corp. announced the launch of their independent company, Avendra. The new company provides the largest comprehensive procurement network in the North American market, estimated at $80 billion annually. Avendra will link purchasers and suppliers and provide hotel owners and operators with a portal that will integrate a full vertical supply chain.

Trends

Nagler points out many different business trends in the hotel industry, including:
- *Direct vs. indirect purchasing.* Currently, the majority of purchasing done online within the hotel industry is considered "direct spend." Hotels are able to afford direct-spend purchasing online because they keep some inventory in-house. Since the hotel industry does direct spend online, the opportunity for an e-procurement provider is increased.
- *Intranet and other online services streamlined.* Hotel companies are looking to incorporate efficiencies and functionality for a number of areas from the same engine. Nagler gives the example of hotels looking to make their online e-procurement provider also offer intranet services, like document posting and sharing.

- *FFE (furniture, fixtures and electronics)*. FFE and Hotel Design-Franchises are looking to put their concept and franchise development online. For example, if a management company wants to create a new Microtel hotel, company staffers could go to the Microtel web site and access a shopping list of items needed to build, open and operate a Microtel hotel. This would reduce the number of resources necessary from the franchise and would ensure brand standards are met.
- *Future Movement*. The industry is moving toward an "end to end" model which means all systems will be seamlessly integrated. For example, a restaurant's Point of Sales System (POS) will link the restaurant's reservations forecast to its kitchen inventory system to its purchasing engine, so the restaurant staff see their forecast for covers and can view their stock. If the stock is low, the inventory system triggers the purchasing system and generates a "smart" purchase order based on the number of covers forecasted, which would then wait for the approval of the manager to automatically place the order of goods.

From bricks and mortar to the Internet

At this year's annual UCLA Extension Hotel Investment Conference in Los Angeles, sponsored by Andersen, several industry insiders agreed there will definitely be more web players emerging, and the connection between the bricks and mortar and the online worlds will continue to increase.

So what does this mean for the future of the hotel industry?

According to the "eReal Estate: A Virtual Certainty" study conducted in 2000 by Andersen's Real Estate and Hospitality Services Group and the Rosen Consulting Group, the "Internet and e-business will have a mixed impact on the hospitality sector, from increased operating efficiencies and the expansion of potential markets, to dramatically stronger pricing pressure on room rates."

The study also found that Internet tools, such as comparative pricing tools, are being used with more frequency among travelers and corporate travel agents.

DiLeva says the combination of web-enablement and high-speed Internet access will allow the hotel industry to deliver services such as online reservations, room requests and even a virtual room tour that will create a better experience for the traveler.

The transformation to online services from more traditional means of advertising and business operations, say experts, will provide hotel owners and managers with more streamlined operations, resulting in fewer operational costs, better service offerings, happier patrons and more productive business relationships.

CASE QUESTIONS

Question 1 Given the nature of the hotel business, which in its simplest form is the letting of rooms to guests, in your opinion what does going virtual mean for the hotel industry?

Question 2 How will the Internet affect the major business trends in the hotel industry?

MINI CASE STUDY II

InternetWeek names Hilton Hotels Corporation 2001 e-business of the year, www.thetimesharebeat.com, 15 June 2002

Manhasset, NY & Beverly Hills, CA – InternetWeek has recognized Hilton Hotels Corporation as the 2001 E-Business of the Year, based on the results of the magazine's second annual InternetWeek 100 survey

Announced in the June 11, 2001, online and print issues, Hilton Hotels Corporation also secured the position of Recognized Leader in the Travel and Hospitality Industry for the second year in a row.

The InternetWeek 100, based on a performance-focused questionnaire of major U.S. companies conducted in February and March by InternetWeek Magazine, ranks the top 100 e-businesses in the U.S., across nine major industries that are driving their e-business initiatives to deliver new revenues, new customers and new opportunities.

More than 400 candidates were evaluated in several critical areas, including improved relationships with customers and suppliers, and the extent of involvement in electronic marketplaces.

Hilton Hotels Corporation was named the travel and hospitality industry winner – and the top e-business overall – because it has in the past year seen huge increases in the volume of online business booked through its brand websites, including Hilton, Doubletree, Embassy Suites, Hampton Inn and Red Lion Hotels & Inns, which booked more than $300 million total online business during 2000, double the previous year's," said Bob Violino, Managing Editor/Features for InternetWeek.

"Hilton Hotels has taken what it learned from early Internet efforts and applied those lessons to major effect. For relying on the power of e-business not only to boost sales and slash procurement costs, but also to entirely remake itself into a multibrand powerhouse, Hilton stands out as InternetWeek's E-Business of the Year," wrote Richard Karpinski, InternetWeek's Online Editor at Large in the June 11 InternetWeek issue.

Hilton's major accomplishments during the past year include an extensive website enhancement and redesign project that will integrate and improve Internet information and transaction services on a single platform for the company's family of nearly 1,900 hotels across North America.

"Hilton is honored to receive this year's top award from Internet Week. It represents our team's continued commitment to explore new technology opportunities and effectively develop a community of online resources and services that provide the greatest value and experience to our customers," said Bruce Rosenberg, senior vice president – eBusiness at Hilton Hotels Corporation. "We have and will continue our pioneering spirit in this arena to explore the dynamic power of e-business on all levels."

From a business-to-business perspective, Hilton has successfully developed and implemented its web-enabled, electronic procurement marketplace during the past year. An experienced procurement leader in the hospitality industry with more than 35 years of experience in the supply management field, Hilton's proprietary, real-time procurement network now links thousands of suppliers with more than 500 owned, managed and franchised hotels in the Hilton family of brands.

"Hilton's e-procurement marketplace has enterprise-wide connectivity and a consistent intuitive platform that everyone can use, thereby benefiting our entire portfolio of properties without the barriers typically associated with implementing technology at multiple sites across an enterprise," said Anthony Nieves, Hilton's senior vice president of purchasing and supply management. "The reduction in cycle time, improved accuracy and forecasting and the ability to aggregate our spend to realize economies of scale have greatly improved the way we do business and gives us the ability to operate our organisation much more cost-effectively, ultimately enhancing our value to our hotel guests."

Hilton's Information Technology team also has been working hard behind the scenes for internal customers – including back office technology initiatives that connect the company's corporate headquarters, worldwide sales and reservations offices and regional support centers with hotels in all 50 states, Canada and Mexico.

"Everything we do in our business can have an e-business implication. Whether it's our Internet site, a reservations call center, a meeting planner or a hotel, it is imperative that we are able to provide a consistent stream of information to every end user in our system," said Tim Harvey, chief information officer for Hilton Hotels Corporation. "I am proud of our endeavors during the past year to incorporate all of these channels with the ultimate goal of ensuring that we provide the right information at the right time to the right customer."

CASE QUESTIONS

Question 1 What do you understand by the term e-procurement? What are the opportunities available to hoteliers? How did Hilton Hotels exploit the benefits of the Internet?

Question 2 In addition to e-procurement, what additional benefits do you feel are available to a hotel company going online?

REFERENCES

Ahuja, M.K. and K.M. Carley (1998) Network structure in virtual organisation, *Journal of Computer-Mediated Communications*, special issue on Virtual organisations, vol. 3, no. 4, www.ascusc.org/jcmc.

Angehrn, A. (1997) Designing mature Internet business strategies: the ICDT model, *European Management Journal*, vol. 15, no. 4. pp. 361–369.

Angehrn, A. and J.F. Meyer (1997) Developing mature Internet strategies: Insights from the banking sector, *Information Systems Management*, vol. 14, no. 3, pp. 37–43.

Bultje, R. and J. van Wijk (1998) Taxonomy of virtual organisations, based on definitions, characteristics and typology, *VoNet: The Newsletter* vol. 2, no. 3, pp. 7–20, www.virtual-organisation.net.

Bradach, J.L. and R.G. Eccles (1989). Markets versus hierarchies: From ideal types to plural forms, *Annual Review of Sociology*, vol. 15, pp. 97–118.

Franke, U.J. (2001) The concept of virtual web organisations and its implications on changing market conditions, *Journal of Organizational Virtualness*, vol. 3, no. 4, pp. 43–64.

Goldman, S., R.S. Nagel and K. Preiss (1995) *Agile Competitors and Virtual Organisations: Strategies for Enriching the Customer*, Van Reinhold, New York.

Gronross, C. (1990) *Service Management and Marketing. Managing the Moments of Truth in Service Competition*, Lexington Books, Lexington, MA.

Gronross, C., F. Helnonen, K. Isoniemi and M. Lindholm (2000) The net offer model: a case example from the virtual marketspace, *Management Decision*, vol. 38, no. 4, pp. 243–252.

Hardwick, M., D. Spooner, T. Rando and K. Morris (1996) Sharing manufacturing information in virtual enterprises, *Communications of the ACM*, vol. 39, no. 2, pp. 46–54.

Jansen, W., W. Steenbakkers and H. Jagers (1999) Electronic commerce and virtual organisations, Proceedings of the Second International VoNet Workshop, Zurich, *Organisational Virtualness and Electronic Commerce*, vol. 1, no. 1. Special issue,

Jarvenpaa, S. and D.E. Leidner (1998) Communication and trust in global virtual teams, *Journal of Computer Mediated Communications*, Special Issue on Virtual organisations, vol. 3, no. 4, www.ascusc.org/jcmc.

Kasper-Fuehrer, E.C., N.M. Ashkanasy and M. Neal (2001) Communicating trustworthiness and building trust in interorganisational virtual organisations, *Journal of Management*, vol. 27, no. 3, pp. 235–254.

Khalil, O., and S. Wang (2002) Information technology enabled meta-management for virtual organisations, *International Journal of Production Economics*, vol. 75, pp. 127–134.

Larsen, K.R.T., and C.R. McInerney (2002) Preparing to work in the virtual organisation, *Information and Management*, vol. 39, pp. 445–456.

Latane, B., J.H. Liu, A. Nowak, M. Bonevento and L. Zheng (1995) Distance matters: Physical space and social impact. *Personality and Social Psychology Bulletin*, vol. 21, no. 8, pp. 795–805.

Lewis, J.D. and A. Weigert (1985) Trust as a social reality. *Social Forces*, vol. 63. no. 4, pp. 967–985.

Luo, A. (2002) Trust production and privacy concerns on the Internet; A framework based on relationship marketing and social exchange theory, *Industrial Marketing Management*, vol. 31, pp. 111–118.

Mayer, R.C., J.H. Davis and F.D. Schoorman (1995) An integrative model of organisational trust. *Academy of Management Review*, vol. 20, no. 3, pp. 709–734.

Mowshowitz, A. (1986) Social Dimensions of Office Automation, in M.C. Yovits (ed.), *Advances in Computers*, vol. 25, Academic Press, London.

Nohria, N. and R.G. Eccles (1992) Face-to-face: Making network organisations work, in N. Nohria and R.G. Eccles (eds), *Networks and Organisations*, pp. 288–308, Harvard Business School Press, Boston, MA.

O'Hara-Devereaux, M. and R. Johansen (1994) *Global work: Bridging Distance, Culture, and Time*, Jossey-Bass, San Francisco, CA.

Powell, W.W. (1990) Neither market nor hierarchy : Network forms of organisation, in B.M. Straw and L.L. Cummings (eds), *Research in Organizational Behavior*, JAI Press, Greenwich, CN, pp. 295–336.

Upton, D.M. and A. McAfee (1996) The real virtual factory, *Harvard Business Review*, vol. 74, no. 4, pp. 123–133.

Venatraman, N. and J.C. Henderson (1998) Real strategies for virtual organizing, *Sloan Management Review*, Fall, pp. 33–48.

Venkatesh, A. (1998) Cybermarketscapes and consumers' freedoms and identities, *European Journal of Marketing*, vol. 32, no. 7/8, pp. 664–676.

CHAPTER 11
CYBER RULES AND CHALLENGES

LEARNING OUTCOMES

When you have read and worked through this chapter, you will be able to:
- **Understand the difficulties of governance**
- **List and describe the basic crimes, fraud and deceit acts performed on the Internet**
- **Understand the value of contract validity and digital certification**
- **Describe the salient legal issues in: taxation, intellectual property rights, business model patents; and Internet domain names in e-commerce**
- **List and describe the major organizations involved in Internet governance**

INTRODUCTION

The rapid growth of e-business organizations, often with a paucity of tangible assets and lacking traditional management and internal controls, has led to many individuals and organizations looking for rules governing e-commerce (**cyber rules**). The Internet has created a gateway for new online opportunities, but once a computer is attached to the Internet, the risks of subterfuge increase because of the bewildering number of new entry points into business networks and technological changes. Put simply, data flowing through the Internet is now far more vulnerable to intrusion, theft and sabotage than in the traditional business environment.

Shinohara (2001) argues that the importance of cyber rules is intrinsically linked to the evolution of e-commerce. Brady (2000) asserts that the Internet has developed largely as a 'spontaneous order' without central co-ordination. Moreover, as e-business has become a universal phenomenon unrestricted by national boundaries, cyber rules must also be global (Shinohara, 2001).

For example, in recent years, businesses have seen a significant change in the nature of contractual relationships and the transmission of data (Lemmey, 2001). The increasing number of innovative features of ICT has led to contracts being virtual, with the contractual information being transferred to a database. Therefore, according to Grippo, Siegel, Warner and Smith (2001) it is imperative that proper and effective network security provides the following:

- *Accountability* – verification that an intended transaction actually took place
- *Confidentiality* – protection of confidential information from a third party
- *Integrity* – assurance that the information communicated is the same as the information received
- *Authority* – assurance that data or information is only sent to authorized individuals
- *Authenticity* – assurance that each party is genuine and does not misrepresent who they claim to be

Key Term...

Internet Governance

Rules created that affect the growth and development of the Internet, including the creation and activities of organizations that develop technical standards, set policies and otherwise influence the future of the Net

GOVERNANCE

A significant theme throughout this chapter will be the fact that the growth of e-business has been explosive and that **Internet governance** has lagged e-business in general. Rappa (2002) has postulated that there are two major issues relating to how the Internet itself, a technologically complex global communication network, can be managed so it can continue to grow. First, the multitude of organizations that are associated with the Internet Society (see Table 11.1) complicates governance. The second issue is who should be responsible for rule governance? Given the global nature of the Internet, every government has a responsibility to consider the following: regulation of business transactions and securities trading; consumer protection (including the protection of minors); fairness in advertising; the

Governance	Organization Responsibilities
Internet Architecture Board – IAB	The Internet Architecture Board (IAB) is responsible for defining the overall architecture of the Internet, providing guidance and broad direction to the IETF. The IAB also serves as the technology advisory group to the Internet Society, and oversees a number of critical activities in support of the Internet
Internet Society – ISOC	The Internet Society (ISOC) is a nonprofit, non-governmental, international, professional membership organization that focuses on standards, education, and policy issues
Internet Research Task Force – IRTF	The purpose of the Internet Research Task Force (IRTF) is to promote research of importance to the evolution of the future Internet by creating focused, long-term and small Research Groups working on topics related to Internet protocols, applications, architecture and technology
World Wide Web Consortium – W3C	The World Wide Web Consortium (W3C) was created in 1994 to develop common protocols that promote the Web's evolution and ensure its interoperability. W3C is composed of hundreds of member organizations from around the world
Task Force – IETF	The Internet Engineering Task Force (IETF) is the protocol engineering and development arm of the Internet formally established by the IAB in 1986
Internet Engineering Steering Group – IESG	The Internet Engineering Steering Group (IESG) is responsible for technical management of IETF activities and the Internet standards process. As part of the ISOC, it administers the process according to the rules and procedures that have been ratified by the ISOC Trustees. The IESG is directly responsible for the actions associated with entry into and movement along the Internet 'standards track', including final approval of specifications as Internet Standards
Internet Corporation for Assigned Names and Numbers – ICANN	The Internet Corporation for Assigned Names and Numbers (ICANN) is the non-profit corporation that was formed to assume responsibility for the IP address space allocation, protocol parameter assignment, domain name system management and root server system management functions now performed under US Government contract by ICANN and other entities
Internet Societal Task Force – ISTF	The Internet Societal Task Force (ISTF) is an open organization of people who are committed to furthering the mission of the ISOC. Its mission is 'To assure the open development, evolution and use of the Internet for the benefit of all people throughout the world'

(Source: Rappa, 2002 – taken from: IETF, ICANN, ISOC, W3C)

Table 11.1 A list of Internet governance bodies

protection of intellectual property; various forms of taxation on the sale of goods and services; prohibitions on gambling, the trafficking of alcohol and other controlled substances across borders; regulations on the safety of food and prescription drugs; the protection of free speech; and controls on the distribution of indecent materials (Rappa, 2002).

Another thought has been suggested by Brady (2000), who asserts that Internet stakeholders have conflicting interests. For example,

- Commercial firms would be looking to constrain rivals.
- Bureaucrats and politicians are looking to expand the influence of government.
- Legal practitioners are involved in redistribution through lawsuits.
- Non-governmental organizations (e.g. advocacy groups favouring free Internet access) would benefit from a redistribution of income through taxes and expenditures.

Shinohara (2001) views governance from four perspectives:

- *Self-regulation, government regulation and the technological approach* – some individuals are of the opinion that the industry should be left to self-regulation.
- *The role of the private sector, government and international organizations* – public and private groups throughout the world have formed partnerships that seek to maintain and uphold environmental protection and security.
- *Regional models of governance in the USA, Europe and Japan* – it is desirable to ensure that regulations reflect national and regional cultures (see Table 11.2)
- *Convergence to a single-rule model* – global cyber rules can either converge as a single-rule model or interact as a multiple-rule model.

ONLINE VIOLATIONS, CRIME, FRAUD AND DECEITFUL ACTS

Throughout this book, the Internet has predominantly been shown to be a positive event. However, given the increasing levels of Internet fraud and crime, these latter perspectives should be examined. Nevertheless, at the moment there would appear to be more questions than answers to cyber torts and crimes, so it is imperative that Internet law produces new procedures and rules, in order that the decisions adequately address the salient issues involved.

The question of whether such cyber torts and crime constitute a new type of social behaviour, or are classic forms of capitalistic excess appearing in a new medium, has been raised by Baker (2002). Areas investigated by Baker (2002) were

- Security law violations using the Internet
- Crime and fraud in e-commerce
- Deceitful acts by Internet companies

Security law violations
Email spam
Email spam is a virtual form of junk email, which is cheap and easy to create. It can be distributed widely using a bulk email program, where personalized messages can be sent to thousands of Internet users at a time. Email spam provides perpetuators with a technique to find unsuspecting investors for bogus investment schemes or to spread false information about a company. There are a number of laws against spamming, but it remains a problem.

Principle	Action
US model	Industry-led Tendency to accept government regulation in areas such as protection of privacy
European/EU model	Rapid developments towards regional integration by EU directives Assertion of distinctive regional values such as privacy and security
Japanese model	Government-led (less responsibility, slower pace of change) IT Strategy Council, new developments such as discussions over a comprehensive bill to amend the existing onerous documentation requirements for all private sector transactions
(Source: Shinohara, 2001)	

Table 11.2 Regional rule governance models

Online investment letters

Numerous online investment newsletters have appeared on the Internet. At first glance, investors are provided with sources of unbiased information about 'share picks' of the month. However, those operating the newsletters stand to profit handsomely, as recommended organizations have paid for the endorsement. Despite not being illegal, the US security laws require online investment newsletters to disclose who paid them, the amount and the type of payment.

Pump and dump

The pump and dump violation occurs when a small group of informed people buy a stock before they recommend it to thousands of online investors. The result is a quick spike in the price (the pump), at which time the people who have bought the stock early sell (the dump). Investors lose money when they are left with shares as the price collapses.

Bogus securities offerings

The trade-off between risk and reward can sometimes appear more alluring on the Internet, which makes some investors keener to invest in shares in companies promoted on the Internet. While the rewards can be great when it works, sometimes the cash raised from the offering is used for individual fraudulent use rather for legitimate corporate purposes.

The risk-free offer

Internet users sometimes receive messages such as 'superb, low-risk, high-return opportunity' inviting participation in a broad range of projects such as wireless cable projects or financial services. These hyped projects usually do not exist.

Crime and fraud in e-commerce

Carding cash

The offence of carding cash or ringing up fraudulent charges to a credit card has become easier through the Internet. The emerging black market for stolen credit cards provides a lucrative opportunity for those individuals who are able to satisfy demand. Users (carders) can use false merchant accounts and stolen credit cards to convert goods into cash.

Website capture

This can occur when a website is hijacked and visitors are held captive. Schemes can involve cloning of legitimate Web pages; when users try to escape the website by clicking on their browser's 'back' or 'home' buttons, they are directed to other websites, which may be of a pornographic nature.

Online auctions

This is one of the largest areas of online fraud and can involve: late arrivals; the arrival of the wrong item; the arrival of damaged items; or a complete lack of arrival of any kind – be it late, damaged or mistaken. The use of escrow services, where a third party holds the buyers' money and only forwards it to the seller when the buyer has received and accepted the goods, has proved useful, but has remained low profile, as buyers are reluctant to pay the commission.

Piracy

According to Microsoft (www.microsoft.com) the use of the Internet to distribute illegally copied or unauthorized software is Internet piracy. Offenders may use the Internet for all or some of their operations, including the advertising, offering, acquiring or distribution of pirated software. Internet piracy has kept pace with the rise in popularity of the Internet, as it is simple for a seemingly legitimate business to create a website and sell pirated software.

Online piracy is a growing problem for a movie industry that continues to splash out more than £100m on each big release. The quality of pirated footage has kept paced with technological advancements and becoming increasingly like the real thing, using the latest digital techniques to enhance sound and vision where necessary. Matters are not expected to get better with the increasing number of broadband Internet connections that allow users faster access to download memory-intensive files to their computers.

Deceitful acts by Internet companies

Misleading advertising revenues

As previously discussed in Chapter 8, Internet commentators spoke of a new bubble (e.g. Perkins and Perkins, 1999), where sales and earnings growth rates implied by 1999 prices were 'unparalleled in financial history'. However, Internet firms were valued not on the actual sale of goods and/or services but on projected revenues. Therefore, by citing misleading figures relating to the number of visitors to a website, it is possible to inflate advertising revenue and ultimately valuation without any uplift in cash flow.

Undisclosed kick-backs and payments

A good example of this is where comparison shopping sites do not disclose the methods by which listings are determined. Keywords may be paid for by advertisers. For example, in a search for a French dictionary the following might be returned: a (paid) banner for French dictionaries; a (paid) link to an online bookstore offering books on France; the (unpaid) search results links.

The ability to collect information on customers is one of the greatest benefits of e-business technology. However, it must be borne in mind that consumers should have some control over how much information should be divulged over the Internet. In an attempt to enhance marketing effectiveness, some websites frequently use cookies to solve problems relating to customer order information, user names and passwords by writing data to the user's hard drive. This eliminates the customer needing to log on to a website with a user name and password. Unfortunately, the collection of abundant personal data, together with data files, can lead to a violation of privacy rights and deceptive business practices.

Other problems can be created by hackers, malicious or otherwise and can involve a variety of techniques (Grippo, Siegel, Warner and Smith, 2001):

- *Spoofing* – this attempts to mislead others by pretending to be another person, computer terminal or business entity.
- *Sniffing* – this is used by hackers to intercept unencrypted data (such as passwords or a user ID) that passes over the Internet. Also called a man-in-the middle attack, this passive technique involves tapping or tracing communications.
- *Denial-of-service attacks* – these are used by unscrupulous individuals to try to shut down a website or disrupt its services through overwhelming its capacity or memory. Though such attacks can sometimes occur accidentally, denial-of-service breaches can nonetheless be debilitating and result in lost data and business.

OTHER CYBER RULES

Additional areas highlighted by Shinohara (2001) for cyber rules include:

- Contract validity and digital certification
- Taxes and custom duties
- Intellectual property rights
- Business model patents
- Internet domain names

Contract validity and digital certification

Two parties can sign a paper contract in which they agree to be bound in the future by any contracts digitally signed by them with a given signature method and minimum key size. In addition, digital signatures now have the potential to possess greater legal authority than handwritten signatures. For example, if a contract is signed by hand on the last page, it is possible to alter some of the previous pages. However, if the contract was signed with digital signatures, a third party can authenticate that the contract has not been altered.

From a consumer perspective, virtual malls, electronic financial services and other electronic services are becoming more commonplace, offering the convenience and flexibility of 24/7 service direct from home. Nevertheless, concerns about privacy and security have restricted the growth of online transactions.

Encryption alone is not enough, as it provides no assurance of the identity of the sender of the encrypted information. Without using special safeguards, such as Digital IDs, it is possible to be impersonated online. Digital IDs use public key encryption techniques that use two related keys, a public key and a private key. The private key is kept secret and the public key is disseminated to anyone who wants to correspond with the owner of the key pair. The public key can be used to verify a message signed with the private key or encrypt messages that can only be decrypted using the private key. The public key cryptography technique was invented by Whitfield Diffie and Martin Hellman in 1976. The technique solves the problem of exchanging keys by using two mathematically related digital keys. A one-way irreversible mathematical function is performed between the private and public key, but once the algorithm is applied, the input cannot be used to unencrypt the message.

Used together with encryption, Digital IDs provide an electronic means of verifying someone's identity and a more complete security solution. It is necessary for a server to have its own Digital ID to assure users that the server is authentic and is affiliated to the designated organization and that the content provided is legitimate.

New software and standards are being developed all the time to improve online transaction security. Three standards that are used at present are:

- Secure Sockets Layer (SSL)
- Secure HTTP (S-HTTP)
- Secure Electronic Transactions (SET)

SSL

The SSL security protocol provides data encryption, server authentication, message integrity and optional client authentication for a TCP/IP connection. SSL is built into the majority of browsers and Web servers, so the installation of a digital certificate turns on SSL capabilities. Websites can use the protocol to obtain confidential user information, such as credit card numbers. It is normal practice for URLs that require an SSL connection to start with https: instead of http:.

S-HTTP

Another protocol for transmitting online data securely is S-HTTP. While SSL creates a secure connection between a client and a server, over which any amount of data can be sent securely, S-HTTP cannot be used to secure non-HTTP messages and is designed to only transmit individual messages securely. SSL and S-HTTP, therefore, can be seen as complementary rather than competing technologies.

SET

SET is an open standard, developed and offered by Visa and Mastercard, that addresses the weaknesses of ordinary online credit card transactions on the Internet. Digital signatures are utilized by SET and enable merchants to verify that buyers are who they claim to be. The system is based on the customer and vendor each obtaining a digital wallet and digital certificate. Buyers are also protected by the opportunity for the credit card number to be transferred directly to the credit card issuer for verification and billing without the merchant being able to see the number.

Taxes and custom duties

In the USA online businesses are liable to several types of taxes including income taxes, transaction taxes and property taxes (Schneider, 2002). Income taxes are levied by national, state and local governments on surplus income generated by business activity. Transaction taxes, which include sales tax, use taxes and excise taxes, are levied on the products or services provided by the company. Customs duties and property taxes are levied on imports and personal property and real estate. The two taxes that pose the biggest problems are income and sales taxes.

Physical retailers have a problem with mail order and now Internet businesses, as it is felt that both retailers are siphoning business from brick-and-mortar retailers. Catalogue shoppers have taken advantage of the fact that they can avoid state and local taxes by purchasing from a catalogue company that is located in another state and has no branch outlets or sales force in the customer's state. For example, a Michigan retailer must collect a 6 per cent sales tax on purchases, but mail-order and now Internet businesses do not have to collect Michigan's 6 per cent use tax or similar taxes in other states, although purchasers legally owe the taxes.

The 1992 Supreme Court decision Quill Corp. v. North Dakota prohibits states from forcing retailers to collect sales taxes unless purchasers live in states where the company has a physical presence, such as a store. However, while Congress can authorize participating states to collect a single tax from 'remote sellers', this is felt to be too loose to be effective.

The sales tax issue has become intertwined with the moratorium as hard-up states have looked hopefully at cyberspace as a source of revenue. Conversely, others believe that, given the number of jobs created by the Internet, it should remain unshackled from burdensome taxes and regulation. This would enable the continued growth and development of online organizations. This has been supported by legislation; the high-tech industry won a difficult victory in November 2001, when the Senate agreed with the House to reinstate a moratorium on Internet-only taxes through 1 November 2003. The vote was a welcomed relief to the technology organizations that had suffered from the burst of the Internet bubble, as it was argued that a failure to extend the moratorium would lead to new taxes that could squash the Internet economy during the economic slowdown.

In Organization for Economic Cooperation and Development (OECD) countries, the profits of any business are taxed wherever it has a 'permanent establishment'. Interestingly, there has been some ambiguity about the taxation of online businesses. The OECD, which includes representatives from 30 industrialized nations, has agreed that the location of a server in another country does constitute a 'permanent establishment', but a number of countries, in particular the United Kingdom, disagree.

Intellectual property rights

The intangible properties created by organizations and individuals can be marketed online through the Internet. As explained in Chapter 1, during the early days of the Internet, infrastructure and software were developed under the sponsorship of public-sector scientific and military organizations in the USA and Europe. This early spirit of collaboration without consideration of personal wealth was replaced with the commercialization of the World Wide Web. Consequently e-business activity has directly increased the importance of software, networks, designs, chips, routers and switches, user interface, etc., which are all forms of intellectual property and are often protected by **intellectual property rights**.

The World Intellectual Property Organization (WIPO – www.wipo.org) refers to intellectual property as the creations of the mind: inventions; literary and artistic works; and symbols, names, images and designs used in business. WIPO then categorizes intellectual property into two categories: industrial property, which includes inventions (patents), trademarks, industrial designs and geographic indications of source; and copyright, which includes literary and artistic works such as novels, poems and plays, films, musical works, artistic works such as drawings, paintings, photographs and sculptures, and architectural designs. Intellectual property rights related to copyright include those of performing artists in their performances, those of producers of phonograms in their recordings and those of broadcasters in their radio and television programmes.

In today's buoyant service-sector economy, the ownership rights of intangible intellectual property are becoming increasingly more important than the ownership of tangible assets. In addition, the advent of e-commerce has enhanced the value of intellectual property assets relative to physical assets as a result of the explosion of creative works in the modern economy. A useful guide has been outlined by WIPO, using a ten-point check for e-commerce issues related to intellectual property (see Table 11.3).

Key Term...

Intellectual property rights

Refers to intellectual property as the creations of the mind: inventions; literary and artistic works; and symbols, names, images and designs used in business that are often protected by intellectual property rights

ILLUSTRATIVE EXAMPLE I
Ruling Issued In Bid to Enforce Internet Patent, by B. Sandburg, New York Law Journal, 15 March 2002
Reprinted with permission from the March 1st 2002 edition of New York Law Journal, © NLPIP Company. All rights reserved. Further publication without permission is prohibited

RULING ISSUED IN BID TO ENFORCE INTERNET PATENT

In a case closely watched by intellectual property lawyers, a New York federal judge has issued an initial ruling that may undermine British Telecommunications Inc.'s claims that it owns rights to the use of Internet hyperlinking, the technology that allows users to go from one Web site or page to another.

Though the order focuses solely on the meaning of specific terms in British Telecom's patent and does not address issues of invalidity and infringement, the judge's analysis may serve as the basis to have British Telecom's patent infringement suit against Prodigy Communications Corp. thrown out.

U.S. District Judge Colleen McMahon's Wednesday ruling – which is dense with computer jargon – attempts to unravel the terminology in British Telecom's patent and determine how closely related to the Internet it is. Judge McMahon appears to disagree with claims made by British Telecom that its patent closely mirrors methods common to the Internet.

Willem Schuurman, a partner in Houston-based Vinson & Elkins who represents Prodigy, touted Judge McMahon's order as giving "four or five independent reasons why there should be no infringement. She's laid out a pretty clear road map of the basis for a summary judgment motion of non-infringement."

However, other lawyers say it is too soon to decide how the suit will play out. "You can't really tell who 'won' a claim construction hearing until you do an analysis of how that is likely to affect the ability of the patentee to make those definitions read on the accused's products," said James Pooley, a partner at Milbank, Tweed, Hadley & McCloy's Palo Alto, Calif., office. British Telecom's suit against Prodigy is a test case, and if the company prevails it is expected to seek royalty payments from other Internet service providers for their use of hyperlinks. That could be a costly prospect for a host of companies.

British Telecom's attorneys at New York's Kenyon & Kenyon did not return calls seeking comment.

The case, British Telecommunications Inc. v. Prodigy Communications Corp., 00–9451, has been closely watched by industry, academia and intellectual property lawyers because it will help establish whether patents filed prior to the emergence of the Internet can be broadly interpreted to cover Internet-related technology. "Should the court rule in Prodigy's favor it will quell concerns within the high-tech sector about significant exposure relating to very basic features of the Internet's functionality," said Professor Peter Menell of the University of California, Berkeley's School of Law, Boalt Hall.

PRE-INTERNET PATENT

British Telecom's original patent application, filed in 1977, covers a system to allow users to access text-based information via a telephone network. The company submitted several successor applications before the patent issued in 1989. The issued patent describes an improved way for multiple users, each located at a remote terminal, to access data stored on a central computer. Communication between the terminals takes place over a telephone network.

Judge McMahon said in her ruling that the information accessed by the remote terminals is stored on the central computer in the form of blocks, each block identified by an address.

"In this patent, the computer is a single device, in one location," Judge McMahon wrote. "It is referred to as 'central' because it is connected to numerous physically separate stations, called 'remote terminals,' by the telephone lines of a telephone network."

This analysis "indicates their patent does not cover the Internet," Mr. Schuurman contends. "The way the Internet operates there is no single central computer. The Internet has hundreds of millions of computers."

While Professor Menell had not yet read the order, he said that if British Telecom's patent claim is limited to a central computer it "makes for a plausible argument that hyperlinking does not read on this claim."

How broadly the patent claims can be interpreted is a separate issue from whether the patent is valid. That question is to be addressed at a trial set to begin Sept. 9.

If the case continues to trial, Prodigy's attorneys plan to present prior art, including a demonstration by a Stanford Research Institute researcher in the 1960s of a system for linking files.

Internet-related businesses are normally based on some form of product or patent licensing. The increasing variety of different technologies required to create a product or service leads companies to outsource the development of some components, or share technologies through some form of licensing arrangement. The inherent high risk in e-business strategy makes it extremely dangerous for every company to develop and produce all technological aspects of every product independently. As explained in Chapter 2, the economics of e-business depends on companies collaborating through relationships. Working together to share, through licensing, makes e-business opportunities particularly attractive to SMEs.

Business model patents

There has been some controversy over patents for business processes. In particular, patents have become troublesome with respect to Internet-related activities. Traditionally patents were granted to 'new and useful processes, machines, manufacturers, or compositions of matter, or any new and useful improvement thereof' (Miller and Jentz, 2002). The US Patent and Trademark Office traditionally rejected computer systems and software

1. Understanding how intellectual property (IP) relates to e-commerce
2. Taking stock of your IP assets relevant to e-commerce
3. IP issues when you design and build your website
4. IP issues related to Internet domain names
5. How your e-commerce business is affected by patents
6. IP issues in the distribution of content on the Internet
7. Using care in disclosures on the Internet
8. Important contracts and IP
9. Partnerships with government and educational institutions
10. IP concerns about international transactions in e-commerce
(Source: World Intellectual Property Organization – www.wipo.org/about-ip/en/)

Table 11.3 The ten points used for checking intellectual property issues in e-commerce

applications because they were deemed not to be useful processes, machines, articles of manufacture or compositions of matter. They were reckoned to be simply mathematical algorithms, abstract ideas or methods of doing business.

However, in the 1998 landmark case of State Street Bank & Trust Co. v. Signature Financial Group Inc., the US Court of Appeal for the Federal Circuit ruled that only three classes of subject matter will remain unpatentable:

- The laws of nature
- Natural phenomena
- Abstract ideas

This created the opportunity for business process to be patented, but many commentators have declared that patent law entered territory that it was neither intended to, nor should, cover. Internet companies were well placed to take advantage of the landmark 1998 State Street Bank & Trust Co. v. Signature Financial Group Inc. ruling.

The famous Amazon.com's '1-click' patent, U.S. Patent No. 5,960,411, issued on 28 September 1999, was a watershed for Internet organizations, with more than 2500 applications being made and approximately 500 granted. Illustrative Example II shows the abstract of the Amazon.com's '1-click' patent application. The patented business model is a system and method for placing an order to purchase an item via the Internet. The patent relates to a methodology whereby information associated with a user is pre-stored by a website, and the user may thereafter order items from the website with only one click of the mouse (clicking on a link associated with the item).

The patent is more complicated that just a single click. The claim (which defines what is protected by the patent) goes into detail as to: (i) what is displayed to the user; (ii) what actions are taken by the user of a client computer; and (iii) what actions are taken by the server, and the results of all those actions. The Amazon.com 1-click patent is now frequently often cited as a classic example of a 'business-method patent'.

Some examples of other business method patents include:

- DoubleClick Banner Ad (U.S. No. 5,948,061), for a 'method of delivery, targeting, and measuring advertising over networks'
- Cyber GoldPatent (U.S. No. 5,855,008) for a ' "method of immediate payment for paying attention to banner ads'
- Priceline 'Reverse Auction' (U.S. No. 5,794,207), for a 'method and apparatus for a cryptographically assisted commercial network system designed to facilitate buyer-driven conditional purchase offers'

Despite the feeling among some commentators that business process patents will have a chilling affect on Internet business, the Amazon '1-click' patent can be classified as a business-method patent because it includes concepts for conducting an online business transaction. Nevertheless, there are still critics who believe that business process patents are harmful to the future of e-commerce. For example, Chiappetta (2001) states that the Patent Office has been too lenient, since in most instances, the supposed invention does not constitute a new invention. Others believe that licence fees will have to be paid in order to use patented business processes. These patented processes, being the building blocks of any online business, will lead to additional costs that ultimately have to be passed on to the consumer.

Amazon.com

United States Patent 5960411 (www.uspto.gov/patft/index.html)

Inventors:	**Hartman; Peri,** (Seattle, WA); **Bezos; Jeffrey P.** (Seattle, WA); **Kaphan; Shel** (Seattle, WA); **Spiegel; Joel** (Seattle, WA)
Assignee:	**Amazon.com, Inc.** (Seattle, WA)
Appl. No.:	**928951**
Filed:	**September 12, 1997**

Method and system for placing a purchase order via a communications network

ABSTRACT

A method and system for placing an order to purchase an item via the Internet. The order is placed by a purchaser at a client system and received by a server system. The server system receives purchaser information including identification of the purchaser, payment information, and shipment information from the client system. The server system then assigns a client identifier to the client system and associates the assigned client identifier with the received purchaser information. The server system sends to the client system the assigned client identifier and an HTML document identifying the item and including an order button. The client system receives and stores the assigned client identifier and receives and displays the HTML document. In response to the selection of the order button, the client system sends to the server system a request to purchase the identified item. The server system receives the request and combines the purchaser information associated with the client identifier of the client system to generate an order to purchase the item in accordance with the billing and shipment information whereby the purchaser effects the ordering of the product by selection of the order button.

SightSound.com

United States Patent 5966440 (www.uspto.gov/patft/index.html)

Inventors:	**Hair; Arthur R.** (Upper St. Clair, PA)
Assignee:	**Parsec Sight/Sound, Inc.** (Mt. Lebanon, PA)
Appl. No.:	**811266**
Filed:	**March 4, 1997**

Method and system for manipulation of audio or video signals

ABSTRACT

The present invention is a method and system to compress and/or convert audio and video signals into a static audio file format and/or a static video file format, respectively, in which a playing device can be instructed to commence playing specific sounds through an audio output device and/or commence displaying specific images composed of specific colors displayed, and/or replicated, within a plurality of discrete pixels on a video output device; continue to play, and/or replicate, such sounds or display, and/or replicate, such colors within such pixels without further input from the static audio and/or static video file; then cease playing the specific sounds and/or commence displaying, and/or replicated different colors within such pixels upon receipt of instruction from the static audio file and/or static video file.

Internet domain names

As more organizations place information, products and/or services onto the Internet, the disputes over Internet domain names have also increased. In an attempt to augment revenue, some firms seek to derive benefit from the intangible assets of a competitor. In a traditional environment, distance between organizations creates a form of barrier; however, in cyberspace there is one global market. The international aspect of cyberspace and its relative nascent period of existence can make litigation complex and costly.

A domain name is a part of an Internet address, which is divided into hierarchies with the top level domain (TLD) on the right of the first dot ('.') and represents the type of entity that operates the website, for example 'co' (gTLD – being the generic) and 'uk' (ccTLD – being the country). The second level, which is to the left of the first dot ('.') is chosen by the business or individual registering the domain name. Litigation normally involves 'second-level' domain names. The second-level name is the name directly to the left of the top-level domain name in an Internet address. For instance, in the address 'www.phillipspa.com', the second level domain name is phillipspa.

The .com name is the most common top-level domain name and is used to indicate that the domain name is owned by a commercial enterprise. Other common top-level domain names include: .ac (for academic colleges and universities), .org (for non-profit organizations), .net (for network and Internet-related organizations) and .gov (for government entities). Each country has its own unique top-level domain name. For instance, .bb indicates a domain in Barbados and .uk indicates a domain in the United Kingdom. Interestingly many US Internet firms outside of state and local government do not use the .us top-level domain name, but opt for one of the generic names (i.e. .com, .org, .net), which are available to Internet firms in any country.

A popular method for online arbitration of Internet disputes is by using the services of the Internet Corporation for Assigned Names and Numbers (ICANN – www.icann.com). ICANN provides a Uniform Dispute Resolution Policy for domain names. ICANN was created in 1998 and is a non-profit-making corporation that was formed to assume responsibility for the IP address space allocation, protocol parameter assignment, domain name system management and root server system management functions. If a party wishes to obtain relief from a trademark infringement, it is now possible to seek redress online. From 1 January 2000, ICANN began operating an online arbitration system to resolve domain name disputes. To initiate an administrative proceeding, the complainant selects one of service providers that ICANN has approved. As of April 2002, the following organizations were listed as approved dispute-resolution service providers:

- Asia Domain Name Dispute Resolution Centre (www.adndrc.org/adndrc/index.html)
- CPR Institute for Dispute Resolution (www.cpradr.org/)
- eResolution (www.eresolution.ca), who are not accepting proceedings after 30 November 2001
- National Arbitration Forum (www.arbforum.com/)
- World Intellectual Property Organisation (arbiter.wipo.int/)

INTERNET JURISDICTION

The lure of conducting business over the Internet is compelling, with a Web page being able to reach increasing numbers of users (www.drescherlaw.com/bullet01.htm). Ironically, the ubiquitous nature of the Internet presents a problem when a person claims an injury due to the use of the internet; they may sue in the place where the site is downloaded or they must travel to the site where the page is uploaded.

The ruling of the 9th Circuit in Cybersell, Inc. v. Cybersell, Inc., 1997 U.S. App. LEXIS 33871 (9th Cir., December 2, 1997) is particular relevant to the law of **Internet jurisdiction**. Cybersell, Inc. (Cybersell AZ) was an Arizona corporation formed in 1994 to provide Internet and Web advertising, marketing and consulting. In October, 1995, Cybersell AZ obtained approval to register the name 'Cybersell' as a federal service mark.

Cybersell, Inc. is also the name of a Florida corporation (Cybersell FL) with its principal place of business in Orlando, Florida, which was formed in 1995 to provide business consulting services for management and marketing on the Web. Cybersell FL maintained a Web page at the time Cybersell AZ obtained its federal service mark approval. After Cybersell FL failed to satisfactorily change its Web page following demand from Cybersell AZ, Cybersell AZ commenced an infringement lawsuit in the District of Arizona. The District Court granted Cybersell FL's motion to dismiss for lack of personal jurisdiction, and Cybersell AZ appealed.

In affirming, the 9th Circuit focused on traditional analysis established by the Supreme Court concerning the due process aspects of personal jurisdiction: 'it is essential in each case that there be some act by which the defendant purposefully avails itself of the privilege of conducting activities within the forum State, thus invoking the benefits and protections of its laws,' 1997 U.S. App. LEXIS 33871, p. 8, citing Hanson v. Denckla, 357 U.S. 235, 253, 2 L.Ed. 2d 1283, 78 S.Ct. 1228 (1958).

To apply this fundamental principle to the facts, the court examined the growing body of case law surrounding the issue of Internet jurisdiction; both the Second and Sixth Circuits and a number of District Courts have examined the issue with varying results. These decisions have involved the interplay between contractual relationships, tortuous effects and the Internet, as well as the nature of the defendant's use of the World Wide Web.

Key Term...

Internet jurisdiction

Internet jurisdiction is a legal term for the limitation on the ability of a court to determine disputes over the Internet. Given the dispersed nature of online transactions, there may be the necessity to draft new laws similar to the separate international conventions governing the Law of the Sea and Admiralty Law

SUMMARY

Data flowing through the Internet is now far more vulnerable to intrusion, theft and sabotage than in the traditional business environment. Rappa (2002) has postulated that there are two major issues relating to how the Internet itself, a technologically complex global communication network, can be managed so it can continue to grow. First, the multitude of organizations that are associated with the Internet society complicates governance. The second issue is who should be responsible for rule governance?

Online violations, crime, fraud and deceitful acts

The Internet has created a gateway for new online opportunities, but once a computer is attached to the Internet, the risks of subterfuge increase because of the bewildering number of new entry points into business networks and technological changes. Areas investigated by Baker (2002) were: security law violations using the Internet; crime and fraud in e-commerce; and deceitful acts by Internet companies.

Other cyber rules

Additional areas highlighted by Shinohara (2001) for cyber rules include: contract validity and digital certification; taxes and custom duties; intellectual property rights; business model patents; and Internet domain names.

Internet jurisdiction

The lure of conducting business over the Internet is compelling, with a Web page being able to reach increasing numbers of users. However, the ubiquitous nature of the Internet presents a problem when a person claims an injury due to the use of the Internet; they may sue in the place where the site is downloaded, or they must travel to the site where the page is uploaded.

USEFUL WEBSITES

Given the fluid nature of cyber rules it maybe useful to keep abreast of developments at the following websites:

- Internet Fraud Statistics from Internet Fraud Watch: www.fraud.org/internet/lt00totstats.htm; http://www.cybersource.com/fraud_resource_center/stats.xml
- eMarketer: www.emarketer.com
- The National Consumer League and The National Fraud Information Center – www.natlconsumersleague.org; www.fraud.com
- Hoovers: hoovnews.hoovers.com/fp.asp&layout=ticker_news&which=news&symbol=JMXI
- National Retail Federation (NRF): www.nrf.com
- Shop.org: www.shop.org
- CommerceNet: www.commercenet.com
- Nielsen/NetRatings: www.nielsen-netratings.com
- Statistics.com: www.statistics.com
- Nua Internet Surveys: www.nua.ie/surveys/
- The Internet Law Journal: www.tilj.com/content/ecommerce.htm
- The Cyberspace Law Journal: www.ku.edu/~cybermom/CLJ/clj.html
- Digital divide: www.digitaldivide.gov
- Findlaw: www.findlaw.com
- Gigalaw.com: www.gigalaw.com

For an international flavour look at:

- WIPO: www.wipo.int/about-ip/
- WIPO's Primer on Electronic Commerce and Intellectual Property Issues: ecommerce.wipo.int/primer/index.html
- Australia – IPAustralia: www.ipaustralia.gov.au
- Canada – Canadian IP Office: http://cipo.gc.ca
- Japan – Japan IP Resources: www.okuyama.com
- United Kingdom – UK Patent Office: www.intellectual-property.gov.uk
- USA: www.uspto.gov
- American Intellectual Property Law Association Web Site: www.aipla.org
- Intellectual Property Law: www.intelproplaw.com

DISCUSSION QUESTIONS

1. Why is Internet governance a significant issue in e-business? What are the biggest governance issues that need to be surmounted?

2. Do you believe that current cyber torts and crimes constitute a new type of social behaviour, or are they classical forms of capitalist excess appearing in a new medium?

3. Why is it difficult to enforce intellectual property rights on the Internet?

ASSESSMENT QUESTIONS

1. Why were cookies developed in the first place? What do you believe poses the biggest threat to privacy, cookies or website registrations? You are required to support your views with relevant examples.

2. Do you believe that it is controversial to allow Internet companies to obtain business process patents? Explain the justification for your views. You may find it useful to visit the US patent and Trademark Office website (www.usto.gov) to look at the actual business processes that are patented and also the stages involved in obtaining a patent.

3. Miller and Jentz (2002) use the anology 'had a business process patent been applied to the granting of frequent flyer miles, then all airlines would have to pay a licence fee for such programs'. If this had actually occurred, what would been the implication for consumers and customers who collect frequent flyer miles?

GROUP ASSIGNMENT QUESTIONS

1. In your opinion, who should be responsible for Internet governance? You are required to outline the advantages and disadvantages of self-regulation, non-commercial regulation and commercial regulation.

2. The OECD, which includes representatives from 30 industrialized nations, has agreed that the location of a server in another country does constitute a 'permanent establishment', but a number of countries, in particular the United Kingdom, disagree. What are your views regarding this apparent dichotomy?

3. Using any example of your choice, you are required to write a short report that outlines the salient issues of a domain name dispute case. What were the lessons learned? Did you agree with the verdict?

MAIN CASE STUDY
The Internet's new borders, The Economist, 9 August 2001
© *The Economist Newspaper Limited, London*

Long, long ago in the history of the Internet—way back in February 1996—John Perry Barlow, an Internet activist, published a "Declaration of the Independence of Cyberspace". It was a well-meaning stunt that captured the spirit of the time, when great hopes were pinned on the emerging medium as a force that would encourage freedom and democracy. "Governments of the industrial world," Mr Barlow declared, "on behalf of the future, I ask you of the past to leave us alone. You are not welcome among us. You have no sovereignty where we gather. You have no moral right to rule us nor do you possess any methods of enforcement we have true reason to fear. Cyberspace does not lie within your borders."

Those were the days. At the time, it was widely believed that the Internet would help undermine authoritarian regimes, reduce governments' abilities to levy taxes, and circumvent all kinds of local regulation. The Internet was a parallel universe of pure data, an exciting new frontier where a lawless freedom prevailed. But it now seems that this was simply a glorious illusion. For it turns out that governments do, in fact, have a great deal of sovereignty over cyberspace. The Internet is often perceived as being everywhere yet nowhere, as free-floating as a cloud—but in fact it is subject to geography after all, and therefore to law.

The idea that the Internet was impossible to regulate dates back to when its architecture was far simpler than now. All sorts of new technologies have since been bolted on to the network, to speed up the delivery of content, protect networks from intruders, or target advertising depending on a user's country or city of origin. All of these technologies have mundane commercial uses. But in some cases they have also provided governments with ways to start bringing the Internet under the rule of local laws.

The same firewall and filtering technology that is used to protect corporate networks from intrusion is also, for example, used to isolate Internet users in China from the rest of the network. A recent report on the Internet's impact in China by the Carnegie Endowment for International Peace (CEIP), a private think-tank based in Washington, DC, found that the government has been able to limit political discourse online. Chinese citizens are encouraged to get on the Internet, but access to overseas sites is strictly controlled, and what users post online is closely monitored. The banned Falun Gong movement has had its website shut down altogether. By firewalling the whole country, China has been able to stifle the Internet's supposedly democratising influence. "The diffusion of the Internet does not necessarily spell the demise of authoritarian rule," the CEIP report glumly concluded. Similarly, Singapore and Saudi Arabia filter and censor Internet content, and South Korea has banned access to gambling websites. In Iran, it is illegal for children to use the Internet, and access-providers are required to prevent access to immoral or anti-Iranian material. In these countries, local standards apply, even on the Internet.

To American cyber-libertarians, who had hoped that the Internet would spread their free-speech gospel around the world, this is horrifying. In May 2000, Jean Jacques Gomez, the judge in a case, ruled that Yahoo! had to make it impossible for French Web surfers to reach auctions of illegal memorabilia; see Vive la Liberté, *The Economist*, 23 November 2000, for background information. Yahoo! is appealing against the French decision, because it sets a precedent that would require websites to filter their content to avoid breaking country-specific laws. It would also have a chilling effect on free speech, since a page posted online in one country might break the laws of another. Enforcing a judgment against the original publisher might not be possible, but EU countries have already agreed to enforce each other's laws under the Brussels Convention, and there are moves afoot to extend this scheme to other countries too, at least in the areas of civil and commercial law, under the auspices of the Hague Convention.

It is true that filtering and geolocation are not watertight, and can be circumvented by skilled users. Filters and firewalls can be defeated by dialling out to an overseas Internet access-provider; geolocation can be fooled by accessing sites via another computer in another country. E-mail can be encrypted. But while dedicated dissidents will be prepared to go to all this trouble, many Internet users are unable to change their browsers' home pages, let alone resort to these sorts of measures. So it seems unlikely that the libertarian ethos of the Internet will trickle very far down in countries with authoritarian regimes. The upshot is that local laws are already being applied on the Internet. Old-style geographical borders are proving surprisingly resilient.

Getting real

In some ways this is a shame, in others not. It is certainly a pity that the Internet has not turned out to be quite the force for freedom that it once promised to be. But in many ways, the imposition of local rules may be better than the alternatives: no regulation at all, or a single set of rules for the whole world. A complete lack of regulation gives a free hand to cheats and criminals, and expecting countries with different cultural values to agree upon even a set of lowest-common-denominator rules is unrealistic. In some areas, maybe, such as extradition and consumer protection, some countries or groups of countries may be able to agree on common rules. But more controversial matters such as free speech, pornography and gambling are best regulated locally, even if that means some countries imposing laws that cyber-libertarians object to.

Figuring out whose laws apply will not always be easy, and thrashing all of this out will take years. But it will be reassuring for consumers and businesses alike to know that online transactions are governed and protected by laws. The likely outcome is that, like shipping and aviation, the Internet will be subject to a patchwork of overlapping regulations, with local laws that respect local sensibilities, supplemented by higher-level rules governing cross-border transactions and international standards. In that respect, the rules governing the Internet will end up like those governing the physical world. That was only to be expected. Though it is inspiring to think of the Internet as a placeless datasphere, the Internet is part of the real world. Like all frontiers, it was wild for a while, but policemen always show up eventually.

CASE QUESTIONS

Question 1 Geographical lines and locations are increasingly being imposed on the Internet. Do you feel that this good or bad?

Question 2 What actions are governments around the world taking to restrict Internet access and content?

Question 3 The Internet is often perceived as being everywhere yet nowhere, as free-floating as a cloud – but in fact it is subject to geography after all, and therefore to law. You are required to critique this statement, using any relevant examples to support your arguments.

MINI CASE STUDY 1
Napster, by Sarah Left, www.guardian.co.uk, 6 June 2001

Napster seems to be back on the road to success after signing a deal to distribute music online, at a cost. Sarah Left explains the issues

Why all the fuss about Napster?

Napster was an internet sensation, attracting millions of computer users to a popular, albeit potentially illegal, online music service that thrived as dotcoms all around it shrivelled and died. The company's founder, Shawn Fanning, was only 19 when he set out to do what the major music labels have still failed to match: making online music distribution as widespread and popular as high street stores. And thanks to a deal the company signed this week, it looks like it may be back on the road to success.

What is Napster?

Napster is known less for what it is now than for what it was before the recording industry sued the guts out of it. It used to be an innovative song-swap service that allowed its millions of members to exchange high-quality MP3 music files online. Members were able to search through each other's extensive music libraries to find the exact tracks they wanted. And best of all, there was no charge for the service.

So why isn't it as good as it used to be?

The world's five biggest music labels – AOL Time Warner, Bertelsmann, EMI, Sony and Vivendi Universal – did not take kindly to Napster's free distribution of music on which they would very much like to make a profit. The Recording Industry Association of America sued Napster for copyright infringement in December 1999. In March this year a California judge ordered Napster to stop distributing copyrighted material until the matter had been decided at trial. That injunction effectively shut down Napster.

Was Napster actually cutting into CD sales?

The music companies say yes, but at least one study of more than 2,000 online song-swappers found them 45% more likely to buy music than other fans.

So what is this new deal?

Three of the record companies – AOL Time Warner, Bertelsmann, and EMI – have agreed to licence their material to Napster, which means the company can set up a legally-sanctioned service. Now Napster just needs to find a way to make money from its catalogue, a problem it never had to face when it was a not-for-profit internet shareware organisation. The company has publicly discussed setting up a subscription service, but not everyone is convinced that its members will be willing to pay for music.

What is the alternative?

The software that fuelled the song-swap revolution is still in widespread use on other, Napster-like sites. Some of those sites, such as Scour.com, have already come under legal scrutiny themselves. But the record companies fear that users who want free music downloads will always be able to find an alternative source. There are also legal alternative digital music sites now from the likes of Yahoo! and MTV, and they have taken advantage of Napster's legal difficulties to court its users. The music companies themselves have also launched rival music download services. Last month, Sony and Vivendi Univeral launched Duet, a subscription service that uses RealNetworks MusicNet, the same platform that the new Napster service will use.

CASE QUESTIONS

Question 1 Why was Napster initially successful? What led to its demise? What are the lessons learned?

Question 2 Bearing in mind that other organizations have created alternative digital music websites, what do you think the future holds for Napster?

MINI CASE STUDY II
CBI study on Internet security and Internet fraud, Confederation of British Industry, www.cbi.org.uk, 29 August 2001

A Confederation of British Industry (CBI) (www.cbi.org.uk) study produced in collaboration with the Fraud Advisory Panel, PricewaterhouseCoopers, ArmorGroup and The Nottingham Trent University International Fraud Prevention Research Centre reported some interesting findings.

- Organisations are more confident about security procedures for conducting Business to Business (B2B) over the internet than they are about Business to Consumer (B2C) transactions. Around 53 per cent of respondents regard the internet as a safe place to do B2B but only 32 per cent regard it as safe to do B2C.
- Small and medium-sized firms (SMEs) are more willing to adopt B2C than B2B initiatives but are inhibited by lack of resources and a fear of cybercrime. Seventy per cent of firms with more than 10,000 employees have the facility to sell over the internet, compared with 32 per cent of SMEs (firms with fewer than 500 employees).
- Hackers and viruses now pose the main threat to organisations. Other surveys have previously identified that the greatest threat comes from within an organisation. Today's figures show the main perpetrators are hackers (45 per cent), former employees (13 per cent), organised crime (13 per cent) and current employees (11 per cent).
- The source of threats varies between sectors. Terrorists are viewed as an important source of threats by some parts of manufacturing but of minor importance to retailing and services. Threats from current and former employees are a higher priority in telecommunications and technology and the professional/consultancy sectors than in the financial services and manufacturing sectors. However, the threat of hackers is particularly high in the financial services industry.
- Loss of reputation, through adverse publicity and loss of trust is a greater fear than financial loss for most organisations. Sixty-nine per cent of respondents consider their e-business financial loss to be negligible and credit card fraud represents a mere four per cent of the most serious incidents over the past year.
- Companies need to review their security controls and ensure that they are given

high priority within the organisation. Seventy-two per cent of companies with a director responsible for risk management as well as 55 per cent of those without, report cases of serious attacks in the past year.

The survey concludes that there is a need for a co-ordinated approach to understanding and minimising the risks of cybercrime. The key recommendations include:

For Firms
- Regularly evaluate all e-business risks, including cybercrime risks.
- Review internet strategy and related risk management at board level, along the lines of the Turnbull Report's guidance on internal controls for directors of listed companies.
- Emphasise training and awareness for employees.

For Government
- Contribute to tackling and prosecution of cross-border cybercrime.
- Create a UK Centre for Cybercrime Complaints – similar to the Internet Fraud Complaint Centre in the US. A database of internet fraud from where complaints can be channelled to the relevant investigating bodies.
- Extend the Computer Misuse Act 1990 to attacks that cause IT systems to fail.

For Business Organisations and Advisory Bodies
- Work with Government in promoting awareness, preventative measures and best practice.

CASE QUESTIONS

Question 1 In your opinion, why are organizations more confident about security procedures for conducting Business to Business (B2B) transactions over the Internet than they are about Business to Consumer (B2C) transactions?

Question 2 Small and medium-sized firms (SMEs) are more willing to adopt B2C than B2B initiatives but are inhibited by lack of resources and a fear of cybercrime. What can be done by the Government to address this situation?

REFERENCES

Baker, R.C. (2002) Crime, fraud and deceit on the Internet: Is there hyperreality in cyberspace?, *Critical Perspectives on Accounting*, vol. 13, no. 1, pp. 1–15.

Brady, G.L. (2000) The Internet, economic growth and governance, *Economic Affairs*, vol. 20, no. 1, pp. 13–20.

Chiappetta, V. (2001) Defining the proper scope of Internet patents: If we don't know where we want to go, we're unlikely to get there, *Michigan Telecommunications Technology Law Review*, May, www.mttlr.org/volseven/Chiapetta_art.html.

Grippo, F.J., J.G. Siegel, P.D. Warner and L.M. Smith (2001) Security issues on the Internet, *CPA Journal*, vol. 71, no. 10, pp. 64–67.

Lemmey, T. (2001) Untethered data, *Harvard Business Review*, vol. 79, no. 7, pp. 21–22.

Miller, R.L. and G.A. Jentz (2002) *Law for E-Commerce*, West Legal Studies in Business, Thomson Learning, Cincinatti, OH.

Perkins M. and A. Perkins (1999) *The Internet Bubble*, HarperCollins, New York.

Rappa, M. (2002) *Managing the Digital Enterprise*, http://digitalenterprise.org/governance/gov.html.

Schneider, G.P. (2002) *Electronic Commerce*, 3rd Annual edn., Thomson, Boston, MA.

Shinohara, T. (2001) *Cyber Rules: The Rules Governing E-commerce and the Challenges Facing Japan*, Nomura Research Institute, Papers No. 22.

CHAPTER 12
E-BUSINESS STRATEGY: LESSONS LEARNED

LEARNING OUTCOMES

When you have read and worked through this chapter, you will be able to:

- Draw together the salient themes from this book
- Appreciate the e-business strategy lessons learned
- Understand how to turn e-business into a successful reality
- Appreciate the salient issues of future European e-commerce

INTRODUCTION

This book has examined the rollercoaster nature of the Internet from its inception, when in 1962 J.R. Licklider envisioned a globally interconnected set of computers through which users could quickly access data and programs remotely. While institutions of higher education and the military were among the first to adopt Internet technology, it is the private sector that appears to be most actively exploring and exploiting its potential. Since the early 1990s, commercial organizations such as Amazon, Yahoo!, eBay and Cisco Systems have been at the forefront of Internet developments.

Many organizations ventured into e-business with the view that the short-term profit potential was too great to ignore. This 'goldrush' mentality, unsupported by a clear business proposition, led in the first instance to a meteoric rise in 'dot.coms'. This period of euphoria lasted from 1998 to April 2000, when the NASDAQ fell by 25 per cent. This sudden decline in share values and job losses in the high-technology sector led to the dot.com failures dominating the business press. At the time, the general impression was that the e-business revolution had not only failed but would play a major part in causing a slow down in the global economic economy. Then, as the world markets were reacting nervously to the threat of a global economic recession, the events of 11 September 2001 added to the uncertainty and worry.

Many of the initial strategic concepts of the Internet era proposed by various authors during the first phase of the Internet have been largely debunked and there is now a focus on traditional strategic notions and the value creation process. Academics, consultants and e-business practitioners alike are now in the process of determining the best way to integrate Internet technology with core business processes.

There is still some debate about the merits of the Internet. For example, in contrast to Porter (2001), Tapscott (2001) is of the opinion that the networking effects produced by the Internet have vastly changed the competitive dynamics of different industries, facilitating a shift from vertically integrated companies to virtually integrated companies. Thus, 'this deep, rich, publicly available communications technology is enabling a new business architecture that challenges the industrial-age corporate structure as the basis for competitive strategy'. Tapscott defines the new Internet-enabled business architecture, which comprises suppliers, distributors, service providers and customers, as a 'business web'. Tapscott refutes the 'new fundamentalism' of strategy experts such as Michael Porter, who discounts the value of the Internet, and proposes six reasons why the 'New Economy' exists:

- New infrastructure for wealth creation
- New business models
- New sources of value
- New ownership of wealth
- New educational models and institutions
- New governance

New infrastructure for wealth creation

Networks, specifically the Internet, are becoming the basis of economic activity and progress. This is not unlike how railroads, roads, the power grid, and the telephone supported the vertically integrated corporation.

New business models

Instead of thinking of New Economy companies as Internet companies or dot.coms, think about them as companies that use the Internet infrastructure to create effective Web-based business models. In this sense, the New Economy can include steel companies, banks, gas distribution companies and furniture manufacturers, just as the old economy can include high-technology firms.

New sources of value

In today's economy, value is created by brain, not brawn, and most labour is knowledge work. Knowledge infuses itself throughout products and services. Porter (2001) and Tapscott (2001) are in agreement that intellectual capital has no intrinsic value. However, recent experiments in measuring knowledge-based assets suggest that wealth contained in such assets can outstrip the wealth contained in physical assets and even bank accounts.

New ownership of wealth

The silk-hatted tycoons owned the most wealth in industrial capitalism. Today 60 per cent of Americans own shares and the biggest shareholders are labour pension funds. Most economic growth comes from small companies; entrepreneurialism is everywhere.

New educational models and institutions

As lifelong learning becomes the norm, the services of private companies, not public institutions, are proliferating to meet growing demand. The model of pedagogy is also changing with the growth of interactive, self-paced, student-focused learning. Colleges are becoming nodes on communications networks, not just places where people go to study.

New governance

Industrial-age bureaucracies rose simultaneously with the vertically integrated corporation and mimicked its structure. New Net-driven governance structures, such as the Knowledge Network of Los Angeles, enable Internet-based co-operation between public and private organizations to deliver services for citizens. Expect to see similar changes in the democratic procedure (e.g. the voting processes) and the relationship between citizens and the state.

LESSONS LEARNED

The statistics cited in Chapter 1 suggest that there still remains a strong underlying commitment to e-commerce. According to a study by the Government (National Telecommunications and Information Administration and the Economics and Statistics Administration, 2002), Internet use in the USA is growing at a rate of two million new Internet users each month. etforecasts (www.etforecasts.com) reported that, at the year end of 2001, countries such as Sweden (546.31), Iceland (546.10), Canada (544.54), Denmark (540.32) and Norway (532.01), had more users per 1000 people than the USA (520.52).

As organizations rushed towards transforming their businesses, many discovered that this was not straightforward. Chapter 2 sought to go back to basics and consider in-depth how the Internet is changing business processes in three areas:

- Relationships between organizations and their suppliers
- Relationships between organizations and their customers
- Relationships within the organization

Chapter 3 takes the view that risk management is an important managerial concern for financial, non-financial and dot.com organizations. Therefore, the collapse in dot.coms was hardly surprising, given that venture capitalists were frequently prepared to invest in businesses that had no risk management controls, no strategy, no special competence or even no customers.

E-business provides a variety of benefits to organizations: improving the time to market; interaction with a broader base of customers and suppliers; improving efficiency; and reducing costs. To achieve these benefits and to help evaluate the business proposition thoroughly, the concept of strategic planning was proffered as an approach in Chapter 4. Twenty-eight European dot.coms, as listed by the Leaders Index in October 2000, were analysed for the period 2000 to 2001. The European dot.coms were drawn from the UK, Germany, France, Italy, Holland, Sweden and Norway. The fortunes of these organizations have been mixed, with some successes and some failures.

One of the buzz words in the early days of the Internet was 'business model'. A plethora of e-business models have been proposed and were reviewed in Chapter 5. Looking back, organizations were looking for the best 'business model'. It was felt that 'being online' was a sure route to instant riches; unfortunately many investors, entrepreneurs and executives got burned. However, with hindsight, it is obvious that even a good e-business model will fail if it does not cope with organization and industry dynamics. As eloquently put by Magretta (2002), a business model is not the same thing as strategy, even though many people use the terms synonymously. It must be borne in mind that business models describe, as a system, how the pieces of a business fit together. They ignore two important dimensions. Competition is one dimension, which is usually faced sooner or later. The other dimension ignored by business models is organizational dynamics and this was the focus of Chapter 6.

There is a paucity of systematic studies of the e-business and even fewer that explore the impact of e-commerce on organizational structure and processes. This book takes the view that the organization itself is the final piece in the e-business model jigsaw puzzle. The structure and culture of the organization may need reshaping as the firm migrates from a traditional to an e-business form. While an e-business infrastructure can quite significantly enhance internal communication between different functional areas, marketing, finance and human resources, with IT as the enabling process, it is pointless trying to integrate across organizational boundaries if there are ineffective internal processes and systems. The seven e-organizational dimensions proposed by Neilson, Pasternack and Viscio (2000), which view the e-business organization as an extended network consisting of a streamlined global core, market-focused business units and shared support services, is a good foundation for getting to grips with the challenge.

If organizations want to exploit online opportunities, then it is imperative that they use the Internet as a marketing tool. In Chapter 7, Wilson and Abell's (2002) five types of strategies for using the Internet as a marketing tool were presented. They were categorized as business enhancement (communication, market research and brand building) and revenue enhancement (e-commerce and e-organization). The promotion of e-business ventures for click-and-mortar organizations has led to a variety of approaches. For example, in the early days of the Internet, organizations piled money into advertising the website, as a way of obtaining web traffic. At the height of the bull market, valuations were based on the number of visitors drawn to a website. Dot.coms were purchased for significant sums of cash without any revenue. Chapter 8 used the example of Excite@Home, when it purchased BlueMountain.com for $780m in 1999 without revenues or profits. The business case apparently was in the acquisition of the 9.2m monthly visitors to the site and therefore the 'value' lay in prospects for the future. There is obviously the need to refine the approach to valuing e-business organization, but this book believes that psychological factors should not be ignored. The editorial of the *Journal of Psychology & Financial Market* (2000) – the old psychology behind 'new metrics' – suggested that what we have experienced in recent years is not just a financial phenomenon, but also a psychological one. This observation has significant implications for those shareholders who continue to research and invest in high-risk technology shares.

While the Internet provides a medium to perform online research for investing, the abundance of available information presents problems of where to look. Chapter 9 sought to address this problem by providing the reader with some tips on how to perform systematic searches on the Internet. Unfortunately, the Internet is not indexed like a library and, with more than three billion documents, quickly finding specific information is a priority for users – at home, school, college and work. If users are familiar with meta-search engines and subject directories, and can incorporate Boolean logic into their search strategies, then users can attain their objectives quicker. However, it must be borne in mind that the Invisible Web (sometimes called Deep Web) is 400 to 500 times larger than the World Wide Web. Chapter 10 suggests that the phenomenon of the virtual marketspace is here to stay. This is evidenced by the fact that analysts project that by 2005 the number of worldwide Internet users will double to 1.12bn with increasing numbers of Internet users using wireless devices such as Web-enabled cell phones and PDAs to go online. As organizations migrate towards e-business, the concept of virtual organizations become important if managers want to enhance the efficiency and effectiveness of systems (Khalil and Wang, 2002). Concepts such as virtual teams and trust can be used to enhance the co-operation among physically dispersed members. The ability to interact globally has been cited as one of the benefits of the Internet. Chapter 11 highlights the fact that interacting globally presents a significant governance issue. Problems relating to online violations, crime, fraud and deceitful acts have been highlighted by Baker (2002). Additional areas that remain unresolved are highlighted by Shinohara (2001). They include: contract validity and digital certification; taxes and custom duties; intellectual property rights; business model patents; and Internet domain names.

Looking back, it is important to realize that the rapid growth of the Internet, together with the changes that have occurred in businesses processes, has led to some hard lessons being learned. This chapter brings together the key themes throughout this book.

ILLUSTRATIVE EXAMPLE I
Universities learn the lexicon of business, by Phil Sommerich in Lisbon, The Guardian, http://education.guardian.co.uk, 3 June 2002

New global demands could mean a big harvest in the groves of academe

The talk in the common rooms and quads of British universities is of cross-border alliances, mergers, new global brands and public private partnerships [PPP]. The lexicon of the business world has well and truly entered academe, and it is likely fundamentally to change the way knowledge is delivered.

Local and global trends are behind these changes. In Britain, the £1bn funding gap which the Guardian reported last month is facing universities, and the government's ambitious aim of 50% higher education participation among under-30s by 2010 – meaning a 25% increase in provision – has created financial strains. In contrast the advent of e-learning across the internet, the growth in workplace learning and exploding demand for higher education in developing countries offer financial incentives.

At last month's World Education Market in Lisbon, which attracted nearly 1,000 organisations from 82 countries, British universities were relatively thin on the ground, but few experts doubt they will be part of the change. "It is not a question of if but when," said Ron Perkinson, senior education specialist at the World Bank's International Finance Corporation. "What is happening around the globe is that the larger traditional markets are being challenged through the globalisation of education. Britain and its fantastic tradition has so much to offer. It is certain politicians and government officials are going to look for better use of their education pounds."

In London, Colin Biggs, higher education analyst at PricewaterhouseCoopers, said some British universities are more suspicious of PPP than US or Australia counterparts, but things are changing. For a start, e-learning means universities are starting to talk of mergers. "The sort of market needed for e-learning means that a lot of institutions are going to look at whether they are the right size and have the critical mass. I expect to see at least a 10% reduction in the number of universities over this decade."

He thinks it unlikely that private funding will be kept out of this new academic landscape. "E-learning requires considerable levels of investment. Not only that but it requires the joined-up approach that universities need to act in consortiums, which they are not necessarily used to. A private sector partner can bring not only money but also provide a way of managing the relationships between the consortiums." He once regarded the tech sector as most likely to blaze the university PPP trail but suspects the dotcom implosion has quelled enthusiasm. Mr Perkinson is less sure. "[The] private education sector is one of the few sectors to have held firm since September 11 and, in the first quarter of this year, US post-secondary private education showed 15% growth."

Universitas 21, a consortium of 18 universities in 10 countries – including those in Birmingham, Edinburgh, Glasgow and Nottingham – has already formed a $50m alliance with Thomson Corporation, aiming "to take a substantial share of the global e-education market".

Sir Graeme Davies, vice-chancellor of Glasgow University, is cautious about the PPP potential. He points to the Unext consortium which he says has fallen to bits because it concentrated on the US market which "many would argue is already the best provided market in the world."

"We thought long and hard about the U21 partnership but e-learning is an arena into which no university can afford to go it alone. It is not a cheap business and if it is going to be done it has to be done well and professionally. This is why we are in such a focused arena. What has tended to happen is that people in the main focus on niche elements of the market. We are interested in medical ethics, travel medicine, things like that."

Does this mean esoteric subjects could be extinguished as PPPs pump funds into ones with global potential? Dr Biggs, a former lecturer in theoretical linguistics, smiles: "I remember speculation during the 1970s and 1980s that there would no longer be professors of Sanskrit about because it would no longer be sustainable. We still have professors of Sanskrit."

He denies e-learning replaces academic diversity and human contact with a homogenised, cheaply delivered curriculum. "The possibility exists that private sector money and expertise can go into producing content – collaboration with HE institutions – and those institutions will then work with and deliver those materials." For the foreseeable future, partnerships would be built around specific projects rather than entire courses.

Dr Barry McGaw, deputy director for education at the Organisation for Economic Co-operation and Development, told a Lisbon seminar: "Education has been largely absent from the debate about globalisation because it was thought to be essentially a non-trade service." Yet there are 1.5m post-secondary students attending colleges and universities abroad in OECD countries. Their grants and fees amounted to £2bn, equivalent to 3% of total services trade between OECD members.

While Britain has about 200,000 such students, second only to the 450,000 in the US, it is Australia which has shown by far the fastest growth. It earns £80 per capita of its population from exports of educational services, compared with £27 for the US and about £40 for Britain, according to Dr McGaw.

As the World Trade Organisation prepares to include education in its next general agreement on trade in services, it will also have to take account of three other fast-growing areas of global trade in education, he added: provision of services across borders through internet-delivered and other forms of distance learning; universities establishing "offshore campuses" abroad; and secondment of academic staff to foreign countries.

The downside, nobody denies, is a widening of the gap between the technological have and have-not nations. "It is one of the sad possibilities." Dr Biggs says. "It is clearly a challenge for the World Bank, the Asian Development Bank and other internationally focused bodies."

Bringing business practices into education is causing other worries. Philip Altbach, professor of higher education at Boston College in the US, said: "I have a deep concern about the public interest as we rush into new issues which are dominated by other considerations."

MAKING IT HAPPEN

E-business has gone through a number of phases during the last decade. In the period between 1995 and 1997, most of what happened was existing businesses taking over existing business models and putting them online. For example, banks were taking exactly the same cheque accounts and saving accounts products with the same rates and putting them online. So the Internet was initially viewed as another channel. Customers were offered the same products if they physically went into the bank or went online. Mail order companies placed their mail order catalogues online with the same selection and product set as their offline product. Since 1997, most of what has happened relates to businesses thinking about how they can develop a new business model, taking advantage of the Internet. The success of Amazon and eBay relates to the fact that their business model could only work on the Internet.

According to Magretta (2002), when business models do not work, it is because they fail either the narrative test (the story does not make sense) or the numbers test (the profit and loss account does not add up). An innovative business model that possesses the elements of a good story, precisely delineated characters, plausible motivations and a plot that turns on an insight about value makes a compelling business proposition. E-business strategy implementation has proved as difficult as offline strategy implementation. Methodologies are required that help e-business strategists evaluate the attractiveness of the e-business proposition. This is illustrated in an IBM study measuring e-business success (Howard, Hamilton and Polinsky, 2001), which involved analysing 300 e-business engagements conducted between April 2000 and February 2001. IBM noted that a vast majority of companies felt that they needed structural guidelines for making viable investments and implementation decisions. Surprisingly, only one in ten companies had taken concrete actions to update their management systems to meet the demands of e-business initiatives.

IBM's paragon test, which is based on a set of predictive variables, can be used by management to assess the readiness and quality of an e-business initiative. Figure 12.1

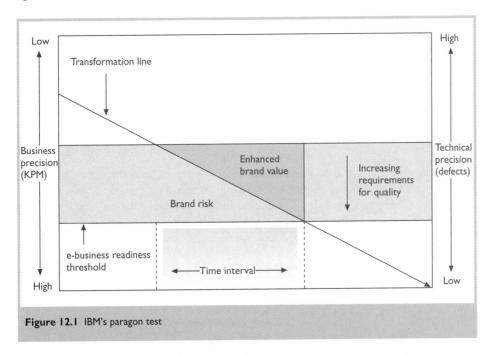

Figure 12.1 IBM's paragon test

Company	Business activities	Achievements
www.ebookers.com	Online travel agency	Expects sales of £300m and to reach profitability
www.lastminute.com	E-commerce lifestyle player	Achieved operational profitability in France and the UK during Quarter 2 of 2002
www.sportingbet.com	Stock market quoted online betting and casino business	Annual turnover of £991.5m and profits of £5m
www.datingdirect.com	Dating agency	Claims a membership of 260,000 worth up to £20m on paper.
www.friendsreunited.co.uk	Linking up legions of former school chums	Claiming six million members after two years

Table 12.1 Some profitable e-business organizations

illustrates the dynamic paragon test and the 'e-business readiness threshold' marks a minimum standard for a solution's usability, quality, security and performance. The vertical axis focuses on the 'precision' of a solution, which can be either in terms of key performance measures (KPM) attained or number of 'defects' detected. The horizontal axis measures investment in terms of time and effort and the slope of the transformation line conveys how quickly the e-business initiative is approaching a satisfactory level of performance. It is suggested that the application of the paragon test will help executives address five recurring questions:

- How will we know when we are done?
- Can we really finish the job?
- Is our brand adequately protected?
- Can we accelerate the project?
- Who is in charge?

There have been notable success stories in the UK and, according to David Pannell of Durlacher, travel, adult entertainment and betting are the three fastest-growing and most lucrative areas of e-commerce (Wall, 2002). Table 12.1 illustrates some organizations that have produced profitable online businesses.

EUROPEAN E-COMMERCE

Organizations are learning that cross-national differences in infrastructure, regulation, language, buyer demographics and behaviour, payments methods and currencies pose daunting challenges to the basic global model of international operations (Guillen, 2002). Guillen postulated the the overall Internet strategy needs to take into account the main differences across national Internet markets (see Table 12.2).

Those organizations that have global aspirations must keep in mind that being successful goes beyond the mere 'Let's go global' call to arms (Guillen, 2002).

Dimension	Examples	Relevant for ...
Infrastructure	International bandwidth Dominant visual interface: PC, TV set, mobile phone Cost of Internet use	Browsing speed, website design Overall strategy, website design Market potential and segmentation, website design
Geographic distance	Distribution and restocking logistics	Fulfilling international orders accurately and in time
Language	Search engines and directories are local and language specific Marketing always takes place in the buyer's language Contractual minutiae	Making buyers aware of your existence Encouraging buyers to like you Keep buyers happy
Buyer behaviour	Differences in tastes and preferences Lack of a culture of catalogue sales Differences in holiday dates Price elasticity of demand	Merchandise selection and stocking B2C of durables and non-durables Occasion-based B2C sales Market segmentation in B2C
User demographics	Proportion of women users Proportion of urban users	B2C of healthcare goods Distribution logistics
Payment systems	Means: credit cards, COD, bank transfers Legal and cultural norms regarding credit Security	Making sure that you get paid Making sure your buyers get what is customary in their countries B2C
Currency	Quoting prices Order payment lag	B2C, auctions Exchange rate risk exposure
Reputation	Location of website Origin of products or services being sold	B2C, B2B, infomediaries, auction sites B2C of branded goods and services; B2B of key suppliers

(Source: Guillen, 2002)`

Table 12.2 Main differences across national Internet markets

ILLUSTRATIVE EXAMPLE II
Prudential rolls out Internet strategy to build its business outside the U.S., by Ara C.
Tembly, Life & Health Financial Services, vol. 105, issue 42, 15 October 2001
© The National Underwriter Company

Prudential Financial has announced a new International Internet strategy designed to aggressively build business outside the United States and promote cross-selling among the company's product groups

According to Irene Dec, vice president, international investments, for Newark, N.J.-based Prudential, the company has created a team "to represent our business outside the U.S." and to set a direction that would take advantage of Prudential's brand implementation, user experiences, technology infrastructure and other factors. One of Dec's many responsibilities is to develop project management and implementation processes for the company's International Investments operation.

Addressing the brand component of the company's *strategy*, Dec states that "Prudential needs to have a common look and feel worldwide." Once an executive decision had been made to develop that "look," Prudential's marketing people identified graphic standards for the company's Web pages worldwide.

"Within our international sites, we set standards," Dec explains. "One of them is that if we have more than one business in a country, we create a country home page." All of the country home pages, she adds, link back to the company's primary site at www.prudential.com.

Each country home page will sport design elements that are specific to that country, but each will also have the company's common look and feel, says Dee. The country sites will be in the language of that country, she adds, while the primary site will contain a listing of "all the countries where we have business as well as all the business we have globally. The *Internet* is a key part of [our] marketing."

All country sites, says Dec, will utilize the company's "Growing and Protecting Your Wealth" tagline.

Dec notes that Prudential's experience with customers and potential customers dictated that standards for interaction with them are "mandatory." In order to make its international sites more "customer-centric," she says, Prudential has done analysis and market research within some foreign countries to understand their cultures. "The use of certain colors will have meaning in that country.

"As you implement in different countries, you must understand the culture," she continues. "It's not appropriate to assume that it should be presented [everywhere] in the same fashion."

Dec adds that while the European, Asian, Central American and South American regions Web sites will have common components, local compliance review regarding regulations will also be part of the sites. "This becomes a technology challenge," she notes.

The new *strategy* also extends to selecting and managing vendors related to the Web sites, says Dec. Beyond choosing the most efficient vendors, Prudential also seeks to find "local vendors who have an understanding of the culture and language," she explains. "Direct translations [of English Web sites] are not enough."

Dec notes that all the country home pages will reside on the company's servers in Roseland, N.J. Having them there means "it's easier to administer projects and it allows Prudential security standards to be implemented as well." While Prudential's standards could potentially clash with country-specific standards, Dec says there have been no conflicts to date.

"Having standards helps us leverage time, and this can impact delivery of the project," she observes. "We're looking to implement a process that reduces hovering—taking extra time to research" the process prior to implementation.

Dec is also helping to develop best practices for *Internet* development within Prudential. Building on the experience of its extensive Y2K preparation projects, Prudential is putting together a schedule and methodology that includes specific steps, she says. The results show in the international sites.

"In Japan, for example, the sites are very lively looking and much brighter than you would see [in the U.S.], due to cultural differences. Yet the standard look and feel of Prudential is still there," Dec states. Dec says the Prudential country sites in Brazil, Japan and Taiwan will be completed by the end of November. Specific business unit home pages (in countries where there is only one business) are expected to be up and running in Poland, Mexico, Ireland, Korea, China and Italy by the end of October.

"Where we're heading to is the cross-sell opportunity," says Dec. Before this initiat-

> ive, she notes, business units had "very separate sites" that "didn't look and feel like each other and had no links back to corporate. Now we have that."
>
> Dec adds that in the U.S., the same direction has been set for Prudential's Web sites and implemented. "By the end of this year, we'll have a common look and feel for all of our sites," she states. "It strengthens the brand and tells the customer in a local country that we are a much bigger company than [is shown in] the country site."

Accenture (www.accenture.com) reported in a 2001 study that e-business firms in Europe, the USA and Japan were fully committed to e-business. The overall results of the study were encouraging:

- In 2001, 50 per cent more European executives than in 2000 stated that their e-commerce activities had been successful and that on average they expected to increase their e-commerce spending by 15 per cent over the next year.
- Notwithstanding the problems of mobile commerce, 49 per cent expect to be pursuing significant opportunities in mobile commerce within three years.

These observations are encouraging and there is now growing sophistication and realism amongst executives about e-business. The impact of e-business is now a fact, and there is no longer the expectation that it will automatically transform organizations. E-business enables a significant array of business opportunities and activities and the time will soon come when it becomes truly embedded in all aspects of companies' operations. One leading technology analyst reported that more information can now be dispatched over a single cable of the Internet backbone in one second than was sent over the entire Internet in one month in 1997 (Gilder, 2000). It is now truly possible that e-business will revert back to business and successful organizations will take advantage of the opportunities provided by information and communications technology.

According to Accenture, successful companies:

- Take full advantage of the new opportunities of ubiquitous commerce (u-commerce), which will strengthen customer relationships.
- Use a variety of data warehousing and analysis tools to turn customer information into meaningful insight for new strategies and improved products and services.
- Deliver consistent service across a range of electronic channels, making the best possible use of the complementary capabilities of each channel.
- Make philosophical changes in systems and radical moves to focus culture, training and rewards on excellent customer service.
- Collaborate across the supply chain to improve effectiveness in areas of product design, forecasting, scheduling, inventory management and purchasing.
- Take broad advantage of u-commerce to improve safety and security, co-ordinate staff more efficiently, improve the management of physical assets and support outsourcing of some functions to other companies.
- Face the opportunities and threats of the new business world with resourcefulness and imagination.

SUMMARY

This book suggests that e-business is alive and well, with some organizations generating greater benefits that expected. The concept of e-business is becoming more commonplace, with successful organizations focusing on e-business solutions. However, whether the focus is on IT-based systems, the e-organization and/or the markets that they serve, there still remains a paucity of empirical evidence of what constitutes best practice across different industrial markets.

Adoption of a strategic perspective with an appreciation of both theory and practice will enable e-business students and practitioners to understand the bigger picture. This will hopefully enable them to learn from the past mistakes that have been made during the first wave of e-business. Matters are not helped by the fact that the term e-business suggests different thing to different people. This book provides a context, so that those who are faced with having to understand e-business strategy in an academic context or who are faced with making practical decisions in an e-business environment will be able to make better informed decisions. There is still an opportunity to be successful in an e-business environment and this should be seen as an opportunity to prosper.

DISCUSSION QUESTIONS

1. Summarize the salient lessons learned from the collapse of the first wave of Internet firms?

2. What do you believe will be the major forces of the future developments of e-business? What are the implications for B2B, B2C and C2C marketplaces?

3. Do you believe that there is any real long-term value in promoting or conducting e-business?

ASSESSMENT QUESTIONS

1. Magretta (2002) is of the opinion that an e-business model is not the same thing as strategy, even though many people use the terms synonymously. What do you understand by the term e-business model and how does this differ from strategy?

2. In contrast to Porter (2001), Tapscott (2001) is of the opinion that the networking effects produced by the Internet have vastly changed the competitive dynamics of different industries, facilitating a shift from vertically integrated companies to virtually integrated companies. You are required to critique both Porter's and Tapscott's views with appropriate examples to support your thoughts.

3. According to Guillen (2002), those organizations that have global aspirations must keep in mind that being successful goes beyond the mere 'Let's go global' call to arms. Using relevant examples to support your discussion, you are required to critically evaluate how successful e-business organizations have expanded globally.

GROUP ASSIGNMENT QUESTIONS

1. What do you believe will be the main drivers for gaining competitive advantage in the European e-commerce industry in the next five years? You should use any organization of your choice to illustrate your answer.

2. In your opinion what does the future hold for designing and implementing a global e-business strategy? Using any organization of your choice you are required to illustrate your views with appropriate examples of the salient decisions that need to be made.

3. You are required to perform a strategic analysis of any organization cited in Table 12.1. You should identify the critical success factors that have made the business profitable. In your opinion what have been the lessons learned and do you feel that the business model is sustainable?

MAIN CASE STUDY
MBA programmes refine e-business courses, by Adrian Barrett,
http://education.guardian.co.uk, 20 September 2001

The internet gold rush is over, and the new challenge is to balance entrepreneurial zeal and innovation with operational excellence and financial discipline, says Adrian Barrett

Two years ago the business school community around the world was in a quiet panic. Applications for MBA programmes were down for the first time since the second world war. The reason? The internet gold rush.

Faced with the prospect of making a fortune in a marketplace that was creating new millionaires on a daily basis, the bright young sparks who usually made up business school intake balked at the idea of devoting time to further education. Presented with this challenge, the business education sector welcomed the web revolution with open arms. E-business courses in MBA programmes became the norm, while many schools established funds to help students set up their own dot.com enterprises.

Get rich quick schemes are as old as civilisation – tulips in 17th century Holland, south seas trading in 18th century England, stocks and shares in the USA in the 1920s. And last year the internet went the same way as the rest of them – massive profits for a few and egg-on-the-face for the majority.

On campus in 2001, the panic is well and truly over with applications back to pre-boom levels. As Richard Crawley of the MBA programme at Lancaster University Management School in the north of England says, "Lancaster, like many other leading business schools, felt the effect last year of the dot.com phenomenon, and recruitment to the full-time MBA was hard work. This year we have had dramatically increased demand for the programme, which is full for the first time since its launch in 1989. We are handling phone calls every day now from applicants desperate to join the programme, but we are turning them away."

So in today's sober environment, with internet bankruptcy more common than internet millionaires, how are business schools teaching and dealing with the phenomenon of the web?

The business school community seems to be firmly behind the medium as a major commercial tool. For example INSEAD, one of the world's top schools, has established "elab@insead". This umbrella structure aims to unite the school's campuses in France and Singapore and link alumni and corporate partners in an attempt to make the web deliver the profits it has so long promised. Despite specialising in the area, INSEAD has not made e-business part of its core MBA curriculum, nor is it heavily marketing the subject as an elective course.

Wharton, at the University of Pennsylvania in the USA offers an MBA major called "Managing electronic commerce" which provides an in-depth foundation for students interested in pursuing internet-based ventures, such as electronic retailing, as well as serving traditional product or service firms attempting to define an appropriate role for electronic commerce. According to Wharton's dean, Patrick Harker, "The e-business initiative will soon be infused throughout the Wharton MBA program – yesterday's initiative is today's core component."

This commitment to the concept of e-business is mirrored around the world. The Michael Smurfit Graduate School of Business at University College Dublin, for example, has a dedicated chair in e-commerce. ESADE in Barcelona has formed a consortium with companies such as Microsoft and Telefonica to promote e-business in small and medium-sized companies. On the other side of the world, Nanyang in Singapore offers a specialisation in e-commerce, while the University of Technology in Sydney has launched a complete Master of Business in e-business, which covers the commercial and technical aspects of the industry.

However, what has changed in many cases is the business school sector's attitude to "pure" internet businesses. Veterans of the classes of 1999 and 2000 speak of faculties seduced by the possibilities of the new medium. As one alumnus puts it, "During my time, you couldn't so much as propose an entrepreneurship project that wasn't an e-business without being ridiculed by the professors, who would tell us that we were missing the biggest opportunity of the last 100 years."

Now the business school mission seems to be more about the application of sound commercial principles – good old-fashioned stuff like planning, costing and projecting – to an industry that believed it could operate on a whole new basis. According to John Arnold, dean of Manchester Business School, "Students on our full-time MBA and part-time executive MBA are increasingly learning about e-business through our project-based approach. For example, the entrepreneurship project provides the opportunity to study an e-commerce entrepreneurial idea and explore its commercial viability. The project is assessed on the basis of a full business plan and presentation of the new venture proposal to commercial clients and faculty."

Professor Chan Kim and Professor Renße Mauborgne at INSEAD best sum up the business school position in 2001. According to them, the battle of "clicks versus bricks" – old versus new economy – is now over. The future lies in a synthesis of the two and the challenge, for business schools and companies alike, is to balance the entrepreneurial zeal and innovation with time-tested concepts of operational excellence and financial discipline.

CASE QUESTIONS

Question 1 What has been the impact of the Internet on traditional MBA programmes? How have business schools responded to the challenge?

Question 2 According to Professor Chan Kim and Professor Renße Mauborgne at INSEAD, the battle of "clicks versus bricks" – old versus new economy – is now over. The future lies in a synthesis of the two and the challenge, for business schools and companies alike, is to balance the entrepreneurial zeal and innovation with time-tested concepts of operational excellence and financial discipline. You are required to critique this statement, using any appropriate examples to support your arguments.

Question 3 Do you believe that e-business should be taught as a separate topic or should it be infused into the traditional business modules? You are required to outline the implications of your views.

MINI CASE STUDY I
E-management: Older, wiser, webbier, The Economist, www.economist.com, 28 June 2000
© *The Economist Newspaper Limited, London*

The greatest impact of the Internet looks like being found in old firms, not new ones

The spectacular bursting of the Internet bubble has led some to question the very importance of the net. Eighteen months ago, it was said that this was the greatest change since the Industrial Revolution two centuries ago, and thus that it would have a greater effect on productivity and management than did electricity and the telephone in the first quarter of the 20th century. Executives queued up to attend e-business conferences in order to learn how to bring the magic of the web to their companies, and speakers vied to produce the best soundbites. "E-business or out of business" was one of the favourites. And now? "Delete or, insert and" would seem the right adjustment to that slogan.

Not so fast. Just as the hype in 1999 and early 2000 was hugely exaggerated, so is the gloom of today, with its increasingly common, peremptory dismissal of the Internet. The lesson of the boom and bust is that the Internet and associated new technologies do not magically bring eternal and rapid productivity growth. Nor was the sheer weight of venture capital and equity investment sufficient to change the behaviour of customers overnight, either in retail ("B2C" in the ghastly shorthand) or in wholesale (B2B) markets. People change rather more slowly than computers and telecoms might like them to; and they are less good at dreaming up new business models than venture capitalists might wish them to be.

But the lesson does not stop there. Where e-business has had a genuine and sometimes powerful effect is in the transformation of established companies. Even as the headlines have blared about the bust of first B2C and then B2B firms, these older giants have been quietly taking to new technology and the Internet with a new purpose.

Cut costs, demolish barriers

Over the past few weeks, we have been running a series of e-strategy briefs or case-studies that have examined how several large, older companies have responded. The spread has been broad: from America (GE) to Japan (Seven-Eleven), from manufacturing (Valeo) to financial services (Merrill Lynch), from emerging markets (Cemex) to rich ones (Siemens). Lessons from these companies' use of the net have been equally varied: squeezing suppliers at GE, knowledge-sharing across a big conglomerate at Siemens, going international at Cemex, responding to an outside threat at Merrill Lynch, building your own electronic network at Seven-Eleven and reaching a wider group of customers at Valeo.

Yet there are also some common threads that can be picked out from the experience of these companies. The most immediately important—and relevant, in these increasingly stringent economic times—is the huge scope for cost-cutting that the Internet offers. GE now does more business on its own private online marketplace than do all the public B2B exchanges put together. Siemens hopes to cut its annual costs in the medium term by 3–5%. The room for more is evident. One estimate suggests that, for routine office purchases, e-procurement costs only a tenth as much per order as does physical procurement. Low-cost airlines such as Ryanair have chopped their costs hugely by using the Internet to cut out travel agents and dispense with ticketing. And many companies have barely scratched the surface. A survey earlier this year by the National Association of Manufacturers found that only one-third of American manufacturers were using the Internet to sell or to procure products or services.

A second point is that, contrary to one of its early myths, the Internet does not seem to offer huge "first-mover" advantages. Most of the companies that we have studied took to the Internet relatively late and with some caution. Yet they do not seem to have suffered; indeed they may have gained from being able to avoid both the mistakes and the huge spending of the pioneers. The sad fate of many "pure-play" Internet retailers confirms that established companies seem able to catch up relatively easily: and it also suggests that the Internet may be lowering not raising barriers to entry. The contrast between this week's news that Britain's biggest supermarket chain, Tesco, is selling its e-buying system to America's Safeway and the troubles of the most ambitious and best-capitalised online grocery chain, Webvan, is telling. Third is the more intensified competition that the Internet is everywhere bringing. GE's Jack Welch famously took to the Internet after seeing his family do the Christmas shopping online in 1999; he then coined the address "destroyyourbusiness.com" as a graphic instruction to his divisions to embrace the Internet or risk being eaten up by competitors. That may have reflected some of the hype of the time, but there can be no doubt that in the coming months the pressure on costs, margins and prices will be intense in many markets. Valeo and Cemex illustrate well the effect of being able to extend a company's competitive reach globally thanks to the Internet, spreading their costs over a widening market.

The winning consumer

Does all this mean that business will, after all, be the main beneficiary of both the Internet and new technology more broadly? Maybe not. For although there seems to be plenty of scope for cost-cutting and even for productivity improvements, neither may end up feeding through into greater profits. Rather, greater competition, more transparency and lower barriers to entry suggest that the biggest beneficiaries may ultimately be consumers.

In this, as in so many other ways, the Internet may indeed resemble such earlier revolutions as electricity, the car and the telephone. It took companies some time to work out how best to use these new technologies; when they did so, the transformation of work habits and business structures was profound, especially in old companies; but the biggest winners were surely consumers, whose standard of living was hugely increased. That remains the promise that new technology and the Internet hold out today. It is a promise that it is well worth striving to deliver.

CASE QUESTIONS

Question 1 It is thought that 'people change rather more slowly than computers and telecoms might like them to; and they are less good at dreaming up new business models than venture capitalists might wish them to be'. Do you agree with this statement? You are required to use examples to support your views.

Question 2 Using one of the organizations mentioned in the case study, you are required to outline how the organization has responded to the Internet. You may find it useful to visit the organization's website and use some of the resources discussed in Chapter 9.

MINI CASE STUDY II
Extracted from Tale of a Bubble, by Stephen Baker, Business Week, 3 June 2002

How the 3G fiasco came close to wrecking Europe

Martin Bouygues thought he was the only sane man left in Europe. The cautious Frenchman ran Bouygues Telecom, France's No. 3 cell-phone network, and in the spring of 2000 he was under intense pressure to bid billions of euros for licenses to operate the so-called Third Generation (3G) of mobile networks. The technology behind 3G was certainly intriguing: It would turn a cell phone into the ultimate portable computer, the key to the mobile Internet. But shelling out billions just for a license in an unproven technology? To Bouygues, the scion of a French construction empire, this was sheer madness, a tulipmania that would bankrupt the entire European telecom industry.

So on May 6, he sat down to write a letter, a warning to the entire Continent. Three days later, it appeared on the front page of *Le Monde*. Many operators faced a grim choice, wrote Bouygues, between quitting the business—the price of not bidding for a license—or drowning in debt. "What should I tell my employees?" wrote Bouygues. "That we have a choice between a sudden death and a slow one?"

Few heeded Bouygues' warning. But sure enough, in the two years since he wrote that letter, the easy money has dried up. Europe's phone giants—after spending half a trillion dollars on licenses, acquisitions, and networks—are treading madly to stay afloat in a sea of debt. Chairman Ron Sommer of Deutsche Telekom is sitting on $60 billion in liabilities and casting about frantically for assets to sell. Onetime golden boys, such as Vivendi Universal's Jean-Marie Messier and France Télécom's Michel Bon, are struggling to hang on to their jobs. Handset manufacturers, such as Alcatel, Royal Philips Electronics, and even Ericsson are hurrying out of the business, and Nokia Chairman Jorma Ollila has seen his high-flying stock fall by 75%. Even Vodafone Group PLC's Chris Gent, 3G's biggest cheerleader, has fallen hard. In early 2000, he barely broke a sweat putting together $163 billion for his stock-and-cash takeover of Germany's Mannesmann. Now, Vodafone directors are debating whether to take a write-down on $25 billion to $50 billion of acquisitions purchased at the top of the bubble—a bubble Gent helped inflate to unheard-of proportions.

CASE QUESTIONS

Question 1 Why were Europe's phone giants willing to pay such a premium for 3G licences?

Question 2 Bearing in mind the problems of third-generation (3G) mobile networks, what do you believe will be the future of the European mobile phone industry? You may find it useful to look at some of the following websites: Nokia (www.nokia.com), Vodafone (www.vodafone.com), Deutsche Telekom (telekom.de) and France Telecom (www.francetelecom.com).

REFERENCES

Accenture (2001) The unexpected eEurope, 4th Annual eEurope Study, October.

Baker, R.C. (2002) Crime, fraud and deceit on the Internet: is there hyperreality in cyberspace, *Critical Perspectives on Accounting*, vol. 13, no. 1, pp. 1–15.

Gilder, G. (2000) *Telecosm: How Infinite Bandwidth will Revolutionize Our World*, Free Press, New York.

Guillen, M.F. (2002) What is the best global strategy for the Internet? *Business Horizons*, May–June, pp. 39–46.

Howard, P., D. Hamilton and M. Polinsky (2001) *The Paragon Test: Measuring e-business Success*, www-1.ibm.com/services/insights/paragon.html.

Journal of Psychology & Financial Market (2000). Editorial: The old psychology behind the 'new metrics', vol. 1, no. 3/4, pp. 888–960.

Khalil, O. and S. Wang (2002) Information technology enabled meta-management for virtual organisations, *International Journal of Production Economics*, vol. 75, pp. 127–134.

Magretta, J. (2002) Why business models matter, *Harvard Business Review*, May, pp. 86–92.

National Telecommunications and Information Administration and the Economics and Statistics Administration (2002) *A Nation Online: How Americans Are Expanding Their Use of the Internet*, February, www.ntia.doc.gov/ntiahome/dn/html/anationonline2.htm.

Neilson, G.L., B.A. Pasternack and A.J. Viscio (2000) Up the (E)organisation! A seven-dimensional model for the centerless enterprise, *Strategy and Business*, Booz Allen & Hamilton, First Quarter.

Porter, M.E. (2001) Strategy and the Internet, *Havard Business Review*, March, pp. 63–77.

Shinohara, T. (2001) *Cyber Rules: The Rules Governing E-commerce and the Challenges Facing Japan*, Nomura Research Institute, Papers No. 22.

Tapscott, D. (2001) Rethinking the Internet Rethinking Strategy in a Networked World (or Why Michael Porter is Wrong about the Internet), *Strategy and Business*, Booz Allen & Hamilton, Third Quarter, www.strategyobusiness.com.

Wall, M. (2002) The secret of dotcoms success, *Doors, Sunday Times*, 21 July.

Wilson, S.G. and I. Abell (2002) So you want to get involved in e-commerce, *Industrial Marketing Management*, vol. 31, pp. 85–94.

GLOSSARY

Auction

An e-business model that consists of an intermediary interacting with buyers and sellers

B2B

Business transactions between an organization and other organizations

B2C

Business transactions between an organization and consumers

Balanced scorecard

A performance measurement tool that adopts a balanced perspective of the organization, by considering financial, marketing, operations and organizational learning perspectives

Bandwidth

Relates to the volume of data that can be transmitted over the Internet in a fixed period of time. For Internet devices, which are digital, the bandwidth is usually expressed in bits per second (bps) or bytes per second. Conversely, the bandwidth for analogue devices is expressed in cycles per second, or Hertz (Hz)

Bear stock market

This occurs when stock markets such as the FTSE100 are falling

Boolean logic

Boolean logic consists of three logical operators – OR, AND, NOT

Bull stock market

This occurs when stock markets such as the FTSE100 are rising

C2B

Consumer-to-business transactions between a consumer and business

C2C

Consumer-to-consumer transactions between a consumer and other consumers

Capital asset price model (CAPM)

CAPM looks at risk and rates of return and compares them to the overall stock market. The basic premise is that most investors want to avoid risk but those who do take risks expect to be rewarded

Coherence design

The coherence design approach focuses on the alignment of the strategy, task, structure, reward systems and people processes

Collaboration, planning, forecasting and replenishment (CPFR)

A business model that takes a holistic approach to supply chain management

Content management

In the broadest terms, content management is a systems-based approach to indexing content, ensuring that it can be accessed through all platforms and providing direct publishing mechanisms

Cost of capital
This depends on the capital components of: ordinary shares, preference shares, bonds and retained earnings

Customer centric
This approach can be used as method of increasing the formalization of customer analysis processes and agreements

Customization
Customization allows website visitors to specifiy their own preferences

Cyber rules
Rules governing e-commerce

Deliberate e-business strategy
A deliberate e-business strategy is one that has been conceived by the top management team as a planned systematic response to the turbulent environment facing the e-business organization

Digital representation
Denotes the absence of physical contact in a virtual market, which can be a barrier to purchasing

Direct marketing
Relates to the advertisements of products and services directly to consumers by mail, telephone, magazine, Internet, radio or television

Disruptive technology
This is a term used to describe the innovations that create a new market through the creation of a new product or service

Domain name service (DNS)
Service that translates domain names into IP addresses. However, because domain names are alphabetic, they are easier to remember, but the Internet is based on IP addresses. Therefore, when the user uses a domain name, a DNS service must translate the name into the corresponding IP address

E-business
E-business encompasses e-commerce but goes far beyond it to include the application of information technologies for internal business processes as well for the activities in which a company engages during commercial activity. These activities can include functional activities such as finance, marketing, human resources management and operations

E-business model
An e-business model describes, as a system, how the pieces of a business fit together with emphasis on competition and organizational dynamics

E-business risk management

E-business risk management incorporates risk management and adopts a broader perspective by focusing on technology risk

E-business strategy

The online strategy used to connect with customers, partners and suppliers and the transformation of existing business processes to enhance shareholder value

E-cash

E-cash can be broadly defined as tokens of value and digital coins or other digital tokens of value

E-commerce

Relates to the buying and selling of goods and services online and concentrates on external relationships

E-services

A business concept developed by Hewlett Packard, e-services is the idea that the World Wide Web is moving beyond e-business and e-commerce. Instead of solely focusing on the issue of completing sales on the Web, organizations are now providing services for businesses or consumers using the Web

E-tailing

An e-business model that retail organizations use to transact online

EBITDA (earnings before tax, depreciation and amortization)

A good metric to evaluate profitability being Revenue less Expenses (excluding tax, interest, depreciation and amortization)

Electronic data interchange (EDI)

The electronic exchange of business documents between organizations in a standard format

Email

Short for electronic mail, which enables users to send messages over communications networks. Emails are now extensively used as they are fast, flexible, and reliable

Emergent e-business strategy

An emergent e-business strategy is one that evolves from lower down the organization without team management intervention

Enterprise Resource Planning

A term used for a broad range of activities supported by multi-module application software that assists organizations to manage salient business processes

File transfer protocol (FTP)

The standard protocol used on the Internet for moving files across the Internet

Fit

Measures the degree to which an investment complements existing processes, capabilities and culture

Five-track approach

The five-track organization design model is based on the premise that each organization has five leverage points: firm's culture, the managers' skills for problem solving, team-building approaches, strategy analysis and the reward system

Gordon's growth model

This dividend valuation model is equal to the dividend yield plus the expected growth rate in dividends

HTML

Short for HyperText Markup Language, the original coding scheme used for documents on the World Wide Web. HTML defines the structure and layout of a Web document by using a variety of tags and attributes. For example, the correct structure for an HTML document starts with <HTML><HEAD>(enter here what document is about)</HEAD><BODY> and ends with </BODY></HTML>

ICDT model

The ICDT model (see Figure 10.1) is a systematic approach to the analysis and classification of salient business-related Internet strategies

Individualism

How people define themselves and their relationships with others

Infrastructure Resource Management (IRM)

IRM has emerged to address the increasing need to manage effectively enterprise-wide changes while maintaining control over the total cost of ownership

Initial public offering (IPO)

IPO relates to when a security starts publicly trading

Intellectual property rights

Refers to intellectual property as the creations of the mind: inventions; literary and artistic works; and symbols, names, images and designs used in business that are often protected by intellectual property rights

Internet

The Internet is a global physical network of computers that is decentralized in design. Each Internet computer, called a host, is independent. Users can choose which Internet services to use and which local services to make available to the global Internet community

Internet Governance

Rules created that affect the growth and development of the Internet, including the creation and activities of organizations that develop technical standards, set policies, and otherwise influence the future of the Net

Internet jurisdiction

Internet jurisdiction is a legal term for the limitation on the ability of a court to determine disputes over the Internet. Given the dispersed nature of online transactions, there maybe the necessity to draft new laws similar to the separate international conventions governing the Law of the Sea and Admiralty Law

Internet portfolio analysis

A bundle of Internet projects that are selected systematically with the aim of maximizing investment return

Internet protocol (IP)

This specifies the format of packets, also called datagrams. Most networks combine IP with a higher-level protocol called Transmission Control Protocol (TCP), which establishes a virtual connection between applications

Internet service provider (ISP)

An organization that has a permanent connection to the Internet and sells temporary connections to subscribers

Invisible Web

Web pages that are excluded because search engine spiders cannot access them

Knowledge management (KM)

Knowledge management embodies organizational processes that seek synergistic combination of data and the information processing capacity of information technologies, which can be enhanced through creative strategies

Listservs

An automatic mailing list server that sends messages via email to all individuals on a specific list

M-commerce

Relates to online commerce performed from mobile phones or hand-held computers

Masculinity/femininity

How society is characterized by assertiveness (masculinity) versus nurturance (femininity)

Meta-search engines

These enable users to search simultaneously to several individual search engines and their Web pages

Middleware

Middleware, or 'glue', is a layer of software between the network and the applications. This software provides services such as identification, authentication, authorization, directories and security

NASDAQ (www.nasdaq.com)

The acronym original stood for National Association of Securities Dealers Automated Quotations. NASDAQ has quickly matured far beyond its original quote-service roots, evolving into what it is today – a major world stock market

Netoffer model

The NetOffer model developed through case study analysis has made a worthy contribution to the development of Internet offerings. The NetOffer model consists of two elements: customer participation and communication

Online fulfilment
Relates to the ability to promptly deliver what the online customer has requested

Personal digital assistant (PDAs)
PDAs are hand-held devices that combine computing, telephone/fax and networking features. A typical PDA can function as a cellular phone, fax sender and personal organizer

Personalization
Personalization does not rely on explicit user instructions, but uses artificial intelligence to identify patterns in customers' choices or demographics and to extrapolate projections from them

Portable Document Format (pdf)
This has become a popular method for electronic document distribution worldwide, as it enables files to be shared, viewed, navigated and printed exactly as intended

Portal
An e-business model that people use as a launching pad to enter the Web

Power distance
How society and its individual members tolerate an unequal distribution of power in organizations and in society as a whole

Price earnings P/E ratio
P/E ratio is a valuation ratio of a company's current share price to its earnings per share

Process approach
The process approach provides a mechanism for ongoing adaptation of the organization to the changing environment by defining and tracking the changes

Reach and richness
The new economics of information has altered the trade-off between reach and richness. Traditionally business strategy either could focus on 'rich' information, customized products and services tailored to a niche audience, or could reach out to a larger market, but with watered-down information that sacrificed richness in favour of a broad, general appeal. Now organizations can obtain high levels of reach and richness

Real options
Real-options analysis can be used to improve traditional multi-period investment decisions. Real-options analysis is superior to the ubiquitous net present value (NPV) approach

Relationship marketing
A philosophy that seeks to ensure a favourable balance among the organization, quality and customer service

Risk management
A method that adopts an enterprise approach to monitoring and managing risks, associated with competition, the organization, suppliers and customers

Self-design
The theory asserts that managers have an ongoing capability to conduct redesign activities, and that the organization can make a teacher out of the learner

Shopping agents
Sometimes called bots (short for robot), these are software programs given a specific task to locate and compare products

Sociotechnical system
The three determinants of organizations according to sociotechnical system theory are the social system, technical system and climate

Strategic planning
Strategic planning involves the entire process of defining the future direction and character of the organization, and of attempting over an adopted timetable to attain the desired state to accomplish related goals and outcomes

Strategic planning effectiveness
Planning; formality, participation, sophistication and thoroughness are important attributes of strategic planning effectiveness

Streaming audio and video
This is a technique for transferring data so that data can be processed as a steady and continuous stream. Streaming means that the client browser or plug-in can start displaying the data before the entire file has been transmitted

Subject directories
These types of directories are particularly useful for specifying websites on a variety of topics

Supply chain management (SCM)
In its simplest form SCM relates to the management of the product, information and finances flows within an organization

Techmark UK (www.londonstockexchange.com/techmark/)
This is an international market for innovative technology companies and has established itself as a leading global market for shares in businesses at the cutting edge of technological innovation

Telnet
The Internet protocol that allows users of one host to log into a remote host, so that they are seen as local users of that host

Third generation (3G)
3G promised increased bandwidth (analogue phones formed the first generation and digital phones the second) for mobile communications technology. 3G systems can handle data quickly and efficiently alongside voice calls and was initially placed to be used as one of the key technologies that will underpin m-commerce

Trust
Trust is most important in new and temporary organizations, as it acts as a substitute for the traditional mechanisms of control and co-ordination

Uncertainty avoidance

How people in a culture are made nervous by situations they perceive as being unstructured, unclear, or unpredictable

Universal Product Codes (UPC)

Universal Product Codes were the first bar code widely adopted and can be found on items purchased from retail organizations such as supermarkets

Value added network (VAN)

Value added network is a private network provider that is used by a company to facilitate EDI

Value cluster

The value cluster approach suggests that as a result of the customization capabilities available to e-commerce firms, multiple segments of customers can be addressed with a variety or combination of benefits offered

Value proposition

The value proposition requires management to consider three items: (i) choice of target segment; (ii) choice of focal support; and (iii) explanation why the firm's offering is better than competitors

Venture capitalists (VC)

Venture capitalists provide investment expertise with entrepreneurial skills to deliver funding to organizations well positioned for fast growth that have the potential to deliver outstanding returns to investors.

Viability

A proxy for the quantitative data on investment pay-off

Virtual organization

A virtual organization is primarily characterized as being a network of independent, geographical dispersed organizations with a partial mission overlap

Virtual team

A temporary, culturally diverse, geographically dispersed, electronically communicating work group

Web usability

The degree to which websites have been designed with the needs of users in mind

Web-enabled courses

The provision of education courses over the Internet, which can mean that business schools can expand distance learning and at the same time maintain healthy margins, due to low distribution costs

Weighted average cost of capital (WACC)

WACC is dependent upon the capital structure. By taking a weighted average, the cost that the company has to pay for every pound it borrows can be determined

World Wide Web

A popular method that supports specially formatted documents through web browsers. The documents are formatted in a script called HTML (HyperText Markup Language)/XML (Extensible Markup Language) that supports links to other documents, as well as graphics, audio, and video files

XML

The acronym XML is short for eXtensible Markup Language, which was created by the W3C. It allows users to produce enhanced documents, because XML provides users with the opportunity to create their own customized tags, enabling the definition, transmission, validation and interpretation of data between applications and between organizations

INDEX

development of strategy 97–107, 118
diagnosis 107
European main players 111, 118
first-mover advantage 104
formality in 96
initiation 107
Internet portfolio analysis 101
Internet portfolio mapping 103–4
investment spread 102
key terms 93
Leaders Index 111–14
levels of e-business 106
manufacturing sector 115–16, 118–19
measurement of effectiveness 96–7, 118
methodology for 105–7
mistakes (common) 102
network effects 105
objective data, lack of 95
participation in 97
performance, best practice and 95
planning matrices, traditional 103
portfolio planning 101–3
problems with traditional systems 94–6, 118
public sector 116–17, 119
rationale for 93–4, 118
reaction option 101
sophistication in 97
strategic options 100–1
substitution threat 99
suppliers, bargaining of 99
switching costs 104–5
thoroughness in 97
transition 107
trend-surfing 102
value creation 108
viability, fit and 103–4
strategic planning effectiveness 93, 365
strategic risk 71–2
strategy revolution, ten principles for 33–4
streaming audio and video 8, 365
Stride Rite 198
structural capital 50
structure, organizational 182–3, 192
student resources xxii
subject directories 270–2, 280, 365
subscription business model 145–6
substitution threat 99
Sun, Elizabeth 126–8
Sun Microsystems 101
SunSITE (Digital Library) 270
Superdrug Stores 88

suppliers
    bargaining of 99
    and organizations 35–41, 50
supply chain
    financial metrics 38–9
    management 38
    opportunities 38
    performance 37–9, 41
    value 36
    see also marketing
Supply Chain 40
Suzuki, Toshifumi 167
Swette, Brian 195
switching costs 104–5
synergistic search systems 268

T

task/structure fit, virtual teams 304
tax returns, filing of 151–2
TCP (Transmission Control Protocol) 3, 4
TechMark UK 66, 231, 365
Technological Revolutions and Financial Capital
        (Perez, C.) 23
technology
    adaptation of 24
    effective use of 55–6
    marketing and 209–11
    proliferation of 99
    S-curve 134–5
    technological risk 73
technophobia 16
Telecom France 356
Telefonica 352
Telnet 3, 6, 365
Tembly, Ara C. 347–9
Tennant, Roy 270
Teoma 285
terminal value 248
terms see key terms
Terra Networks 114
terrorist threat 336
Tesco Stores 106, 146, 355
Tesco.com 156, 221–5
text messaging 28
Thinknatural.com 88
Third generation (3G) 11, 356, 365
Thompson Corporation 343
thoroughness in strategic planning 97
Three Mile Island 21
3G Business Consulting 28
Thus Internet Services 15

387